MW01120647

UNDERSTANDING THE CISG
IN THE USA

Understanding the CISG
in the USA

A Compact Guide to the 1980 United Nations Convention
on Contracts for the International Sale of Goods

Second Edition

JOSEPH LOOKOFSKY

KLUWER LAW INTERNATIONAL
THE HAGUE / LONDON / NEW YORK

Published by:
Kluwer Law International,
P.O. Box 85889, 2508 CN The Hague, The Netherlands
sales@kluwerlaw.com
http://www.kluwerlaw.com

Sold and distributed in North, Central and South America by:
Aspen Publishers, Inc.
7201 McKinney Circle, Frederick, MD 21704, USA

Sold and distributed in all other countries by:
Turpin Distribution Services Limited
Blackhorse Road, Letchworth, Herts.,
SG6 1HN, United Kingdom

A C.I.P Catalogue record for this book is available from the Library of Congress.

Printed on acid-free paper.

ISBN 90-411-0956-0 (hb)
ISBN 90-411-2277-X (pb)
Printed in The Netherlands.

TABLE OF CONTENTS

PREFACE

Like the first (1995) edition of *Understanding the CISG in the USA,* this completely revised and updated edition is designed to meet the special needs of American jurists. For example, special emphasis is placed on the significance of the declaration (reservation) made by the United States pursuant to Article 95 of the treaty, just as particular attention is placed on the increasing number of CISG decisions rendered by American State and Federal courts. Such a custom-tailored edition also permits helpful comparisons with the American reader's domestic law, including the rules in UCC Article 2, currently applicable in most American States, as well as the the (2002) *NCCUSL Draft Revision* of Article 2.

Hopefully, such explanations and comparisons will make the CISG somewhat easier to "understand." As noted in the Preface to the First Edition, however, American lawyers should *not* view the CISG as if it were the "UCC in a new suit of clothes." On the contrary, the Convention represents a very different, international regulatory regime which demands an "autonomous" *international* interpretation, and in this respect the international – though not always uniform – CISG case law remains a key source for proper understanding of the treaty. Since the publication of the first edition, upwards of a thousand new CISG decisions have been reported worldwide, and this volume includes references to many of them, just as it also includes many new references to the increasingly abundant CISG literature (for a *Table of Authorities* cited in abbreviated form see Appendix IV).

My dear friend and colleague, Professor Herbert Bernstein – who helped me with the first edition of the present work and later co-authored *Understanding the CISG in Europe* – passed away on April 20, 2001, but his imprint remains. Once again, Albert Kritzer of the Pace University Institute of International Commercial Law was on-line to help provide me with a wealth of CISGW3-data, just as Morten Fogt of the EuroFaculty, Vilnius University, helped me check German language authorities. I also wish to extend my sincere thanks to Professor Harry Flechtner of the University of Pittsburgh for his valuable assistence and inspiration during the preparation of this edition of the *Understanding* series.

As for those errors and ambiguities which inevitably remain, I hope that readers who find them will be kind enough to let me know.

Joseph.Lookofsky@jur.ku.dk
Copenhagen and Espergœrde
Denmark, Fall 2003

CHAPTER ONE

INTRODUCTION & OVERVIEW

The "CISG" is shorthand for the United Nations Convention on Contracts for the International Sale of Goods.[1] The CISG (which is also sometimes referred to as the "Vienna Convention")[2] contains rules which regulate the rights of buyers and sellers in connection with contracts for the international sale of goods.

The CISG, which took effect in the United States (one of the first 11 States to ratify) in 1988,[3] is the first sales law treaty to win acceptance on a worldwide scale.[4] As of this writing, the more than 60 CISG Contracting States account for more than two-thirds of all world trade. Given the large and growing number of Contracting States, the CISG is fast becoming the international sales law of the world.[5]

The main purpose of this Chapter is to briefly introduce the CISG to American jurists: to sketch out its main field of application – in the United States and elsewhere – as well as the key features of its substantive rules. The Chapter also aims to place the Convention within its larger international context: to relate the Convention's own content to principles of jurisdiction and conflict of laws (private international law), since these related topics are also central to the resolution of international sales disputes.

§ 1.1 When Does the CISG Apply?

Each of the many States which has ratified the CISG Convention now has *two*, essentially distinct sets of sales law rules.[6] This is, for example, the situation in the United States, where the *domestic* sales law rules in Article 2 of the Uniform Commercial Code continue to apply to most sales between parties residing in the United States,[7] whereas the CISG applies to *international* sales, i.e., (primarily) to sales between parties residing in different CISG Contracting States.

---

[1] Some say the 4 letters individually; some say the acronym as one word (with a "soft" C).
[2] The Convention was finalized and approved at a diplomatic conference in Vienna in 1980.
[3] This group included the China, France and Italy: *see infra*, Appendix I.
[4] Regarding the ULIS and ULF Conventions, which preceded the CISG, *see* § 1.2 *infra.*
[5] As of 1 June 2003, 62 States had adopted the CISG. *See infra* Appendix I.
[6] Even the *Norwegian* SGA, which represents an attempt to "integrate" domestic and international sales law into a single statute, nonetheless contains a number of rules which apply exclusively to domestic sales or (as the case may be) to international sales. Regarding the special situation in Norway *see Lookofsky, CISG/Scandinavia,* § 2-2.
[7] It seems preferable in this context to refer to "domestic" rather than "national" sales law. Use of the term "national" tends to obscure the fact that, by the act of ratification and implementation (note 25 *infra*) in any given country, the *CISG* sales lawbecomes a *part* of that country's *own* legal system. *Accord* Herber in *Schlechtriem, Commentary,* Introduction to Articles 1–6, Rd.Nr. 4.

[handwritten margin note: use CISG! to assess if contract made, establish obligations. US - does not use CISG if dispute arises w/ non-Contracting Country... Some countries do.]

The Convention took effect in the USA on January 1 1988.[8] On that date, the CISG treaty became part of the "law of the [American] land,"[9] just as it simultaneously became a part of (e.g.) French law. For this reason, a sales contract made after that date between a US-based party and a party whose business is in another CISG Contracting State, like France, "automatically" (without resort to conflict-of-laws rules) becomes subject to the treaty's gap-filling (default) rules.[10]

> *Illustration 1a.* Merchant-buyer (B) in California sends an order for 10 dozen designer dresses to seller-manufacturer (S) in Paris, France. S purports to accept the order by faxing a brief confirmation to B. Later, B refuses to accept the goods, and S demands to be paid.

Since this international sale of goods becomes subject to the Convention, by default, an American or French court would apply the rules in CISG Part II as regards the contract formation process, deciding whether or not an agreement has been reached. If, on this basis, the court determines that a contract has been made, CISG Part III will then be used to fill in contractual gaps as regards the obligations of the parties,[11] their rights and remedies for breach,[12] etc.[13]

CISG application is not always limited to sales between parties located in (different) Contracting States. Rather, by virtue of Article 1(1)(b), the courts in *most* CISG States – though not American courts – will apply the CISG rules "when the rules of private international law [conflict-of-laws] lead to the application of the law of a Contracting State."[14] Consider the following example:

> *Illustration 1b.* Merchant-buyer B in England orders 10 dozen down-insulated coats from seller-manufacturer S in Canada. S accepts the order and ships the goods to B. Later, claiming the goods do not conform to the contract, B refuses to pay for them.

A Canadian court asked to decide this dispute might well apply the CISG, even though the United Kingdom is not (as of 2003) a CISG Contracting State.[15]

---

8   *See infra* Appendix I.
9   By virtue of the Supremacy Clause in the U.S. Federal Constitution, the treaty has the status of Federal legislation, thus preëmpting the application of State law (such as the rules in UCC Article 2) which might otherwise conflict. According to the proposed Comment 2 to the new UCC § 2-108(1), as set forth in the *NCCUSL Draft Revision* (2002), "it is assumed that Article 2 is subject to any applicable federal law, such as the United Nations Convention on Contracts for the International Sale of Goods (CISG) or the Magnuson-Moss Warranty Act." The new (and in this respect somewhat ambiguously drafted) conflict-of-laws rule set forth in the Draft Revision should not be applied to contracts falling within the CISG: *see infra* § 1.2.
10 This result follows from Article 1(1)(a), since the parties have not agreed to opt out of the Convention regime (Article 6). *See* previous note and *infra* §§ 2.1, 2.1, 2.3, 2.4 and 2.7.
11 *Infra* Chapter 4.
12 *Infra* Chapter 6.
13 The Convention also regulates (e.g.) the passing of risk: *see infra* Chapter 5.
14 Provided the two parties to the transaction have their places of business in different States. Regarding the Article 95 declaration made by the United States, which precludes CISG application by virtue of Article 1(1)(b), *see* §§ 2.4 and 8.7 *infra*.
15 For a more detailed discussion of this situation *see infra* § 2.4.

CISG replaced conflict-of-laws analysis for Contracting
Countries (for commercial disputes)

In view of the Convention's broad acceptance and wide range of application, lawyers, judges, and arbitrators engaged in international sales transactions need to familiarize themselves with the CISG rules. Given the growing body of CISG case law,[16] we now have the means to give this most significant piece of uniform legislation the international interpretation which it requires and deserves.[17]

§ 1.2   BRIEF HISTORICAL PERSPECTIVE; CISG RATIFICATION & IMPLEMENTATION

The CISG is not the first uniform sales law: the ULIS/ULF treaties date back to 1964.[18] But these pre-CISG efforts met with only limited success,[19] so most national courts, when confronted with an international sales dispute (involving questions of contract formation, parties' obligations, remedies for breach etc.), were obliged to make a choice-of-law determination, i.e., to decide which domestic sales law to apply. Consider this example:

> *Illustration 1c.*[20] In 1987, prior to the entry into effect of the CISG, a contract for the sale of a thoroughbred racehorse is made between seller (S) in France and buyer (B) in Virginia. Claiming that the horse subsequently delivered by S (in Virginia) was lame, B refuses to pay. S, however, claims conforming delivery and sues for the price in a Virginia court.

In this pre-CISG situation, a competent (State or Federal) court in Virginia would first have applied Virginian conflict-of-laws (private international law) rules in order to determine whether to apply Virginian or German sales law in order to resolve the merits of the case.[21] And in this particular situation, a competent Virginia court, applying its own conflicts rules, including the then applicable version of UCC § 1-105,[22] would probably have found

---

[16]   Made increasingly accessible worldwide by the UNCITRAL reporting system (CLOUT), the CISGW3 data base (*see infra* Appendix IV for the full Internet address), UNILEX (*see id.*) and other excellent electronic data services. As to these sources *see generally infra* § 2.9.

[17]   Re. CISG Article 7(1) *see infra* § 2.8.

[18]   The Uniform Law for the International Sale of Goods (ULIS) and the Uniform Law on the Formation of Contracts for the International Sale of Goods (ULF) were both signed at the Hague in 1964. The texts of these treaties are available at CISGW3 (*see supra* note 16).

[19]   Though somewhat similar in content and scope to the CISG, the ULIS and ULF were considered deficient in certain respects and were ultimately ratified only by nine States: Belgium, Gambia, (West) Germany, Israel (ULIS only), Italy, Luxembourg, the Netherlands, San Marino, and the United Kingdom. In places where the CISG has displaced ULIS and ULF (*see* re. CISG Article 99 *infra* § 8.2), comparisons will be inevitable, since many ULIS and ULF provisions bear a distinct resemblance to corresponding CISG rules. But treating the ULIS and ULF as a "secondary" source of CISG law may lead to questionable results, especially from the viewpoint of *non*-ULIS/ULF States (like the United States): *see, e.g., infra* § 2.5 with note 65 and § 2.9 with note 144.

[20]   Inspired by an American Federal Court case: *Madaus v. November Hill Farm, Inc.*, 630 F.Supp. 1246 (W.D. Va. 1986). For a discussion of this case *see* Lookofsky & Hertz, *Transnational Litigation*, Ch. 3.3.2.

[21]   Re. international competency (juridical jurisdiction) *see infra* § 1.4.

[22]   The original (and as of 2003 still applicable) Virginia version of UCC § 1-105 provides (*inter alia*): "(1) ... when a transaction bears a reasonable relation to this state and also to another state or nation the parties may agree that the law either of this state or such other state or nation shall govern their rights and duties. Failing such agreement this Act applies to transactions bearing an appropriate relation to this

an "appropriate relation" to Virginia, thus leading to the application of Virginian (UCC) sales law to decide the merits of this case.[23]

Confronted with the same (pre-CISG) situation, a competent court in France would almost surely have reached the opposite result. Like several other European countries, France has long been a party to the 1955 Hague Convention on the Law Applicable to International Sales of Goods. Since the main default rule under this Convention is that the "seller's law" applies,[24] the French court would probably have applied French domestic sales law to decide the merits of the case.

So, in the pre-CISG world, international sales disputes remained vulnerable to the dictates of differing domestic conflicts and sales law rules. Now that we have the Convention, however, we have a completely new situation: all CISG Contracting States are now obligated and enforce the same set of substantive rules for international sales.

By ratifying the CISG treaty, the United States became a party to a "contract among nations," and all CISG Contracting States and their courts are bound (by public international law) to uphold that contract, i.e., to implement and apply the rules laid down in the treaty text.[25] In the following sections, our main concern will be the proper understanding and application – in the United States and elsewhere – of the CISG treaty text.

§ 1.3 CISG PARTS I–IV: *A NUTSHELL OVERVIEW*

The CISG contains a total of 101 articles, and these rules are organized in four main Parts (I–IV). The substantive core of the Convention is located in Part II on Formation of the Contract and in Part III on the Sale of Goods. Part I of the Convention contains important provisions which tell us when and how to use the substantive rules in Parts II and III. The final provisions in Part IV regulate, among other things, the making of "reservations" to various CISG rules.[26]

CISG Part I defines the Convention Sphere of Application, including (e.g.) the "internationality" requirement and limitations regarding the sale of certain "goods."[27] CISG Part I

---

state. . . ." Re. the proposed revision of this "conflicts" rule *see* the (2002) *NCCUSL Draft Revision* of UCC § 1-301 (approved by the ABA in 2003).

[23] The fact that the horse in *Illustration 1c* was delivered in Virginia would have been a key factor for the (pre-CISG) choice of (UCC) law by a Virginia court. *See* the *Madaus* case, *supra* note 20 (where delivery took place in Germany) and Lookofsky & Hertz at *id.*

[24] *See* (e.g.) Lookofsky & Hertz, *id.*, Ch. 3.2.2(B).

[25] *See also supra* § 1.2 with note 9. Since the treaty is not "self-executing," each Contacting State must also pass domestic legislation to *implement* the Convention, so as to make the (private law) rules in the treaty part of that State's own *national law*. In this connection *nearly all* Contracting States have chosen to implement their CISG treaty obligation by *incorporation* of the authentic treaty text; as a result, the domestic and international sales laws of these States are now located in separate and distinct statutes. Significantly, *Norway* chose a different – and highly controversial – route. Alone among the more than 60 CISG Contracting States, Norway elected to *transform* ("re-write") the authentic Convention text, thus creating an unofficial and distinctly "Norwegian" version of the CISG. *See generally* Lookofsky, *CISG/Scandinavia,* § 1-2.

[26] *Infra* § 8.3.

[27] *See generally infra* Chapter 2A.

4   I. Internationality requirement, limitations on sale of certain goods

also contains General Provisions, and among these are important rules for the interpretation of the Convention text as well as for the interpretation of contracts which are subject to the Convention regime.[28] Part II of the Convention regulates the formation of international sales contracts. CISG offers are generally revocable until an acceptance is dispatched, unless the offeror indicates that the offer is irrevocable or the offeree has had reason to rely thereon.[29] To a large extent the CISG clings to the traditional "mirror image" rule which holds that a contract is formed only if the offer and acceptance match in every respect; this feature is particularly significant as regards the "battle of forms."[30] Although CISG Part II regulates the contract formation process, the Convention does not generally regulate contract validity. Therefore, to determine whether a party to a CISG contract has a "defense" to enforcement such as fraud or mistake, we need to look outside the CISG.[31]

Part III of the CISG, entitled "Sale of Goods," contains the substantive rules of greatest practical significance for international export and import transactions. This Part of the Convention defines the parties' obligations, rights and remedies for breach. The key to the seller's performance is that the right goods must be delivered at the right time and place, as required by the contract and the CISG supplementary rules. Unless otherwise agreed, the goods do not conform with the contract unless they are both fit for ordinary purposes and for any particular purpose made known to the seller at the time of contracting.[32] The buyer's obligations relate not only to timely payment, but also to timely acceptance of the goods.[33]

The Convention ties the passing of risk to the last significant act by which the seller completes delivery. In general, accidental loss of the goods after the risk has passed to the buyer does not discharge the buyer's obligation to pay the price. Although the CISG does not make a formal distinction between specific and generic sales (as do some – e.g., European – domestic sales laws), the risk will not pass to the buyer unless the goods have been identified to the contract.[34]

Every breach of a CISG obligation gives rise to one or more CISG remedies for breach. The three main remedial categories are specific performance, avoidance of the contract, and damages. In accordance with (e.g.) Scandinavian and Civil law traditions, the CISG provides for specific performance on a generous scale. However, no court is bound to enter a judgment for specific performance unless that court would do so under its own law applicable to similar contracts of sale not governed by the Convention.[35]

Under the Convention, the right to avoid (in UCC parlance: "cancel") the contract is generally conditioned upon a showing of a fundamental ("material") breach. However, the

---

[28]   The terms of the contract and international custom and usage take precedence over the CISG gap-filling rules: *see infra* Chapter 2B.
[29]   For details *see infra* § 3.6.
[30]   *See infra* § 3.8.
[31]   For details *see infra* § 3.10. *See also* § 2.6 and Chapter 7.
[32]   Chapter 4B *infra*.
[33]   Chapter 4C *infra*.
[34]   Chapter 5 *infra*.
[35]   *See* Article 28. For details *see infra* § 6.5.

no-fault

CISG also permits an injured party to avoid upon failure to perform after an additional time (a so-called *Nachfrist*) of reasonable length has been set for performance. The CISG rules which regulate the subject of anticipatory breach are in some respects closely related to the right of an injured party to avoid for fundamental breach.

As regards damages for breach, the CISG deals both with the basis and the measure of liability. In contrast with the fault (*culpa*) principle which often prevails in Civil law jurisdictions, the Convention provides an injured party with protection of its expectation-interest on a no-fault basis. But the Convention rules regarding liability "exemptions" modify the no-fault principle to a certain, albeit limited extent.[36] Under certain circumstances the Convention, in accordance with Scandinavian and Civil law tradition, permits a buyer to make use of the monetary remedy known as the proportionate reduction in *remedy* price.[37]

Because of the practical significance of contractually "agreed" remedies, as well as the validity-concerns associated with significant departures from the CISG default scheme, liability limitations and similar clauses are also deserving of special attention.[38] Finally, consideration will be given to the LPISG Convention, ratified by the USA in 1994, which lays down a uniform 4-year statute of limitations for the commencement of legal actions involving international sales.[39]

§ 1.4 THE CISG IN TRANSNATIONAL PERSPECTIVE: SUBSTANCE, PROCEDURE AND CONFLICT OF LAWS

The CISG fits the description of substantive (as opposed to procedural) law. So, as with domestic sales statutes – such as UCC Article 2 – the Convention provides the means whereby courts actually decide the merits of sales contract disputes. If, for example, the seller commits a breach, and the buyer brings suit, the CISG provides the buyer with remedies to help right the wrong and thus determine the outcome of the case.

In contrast with rules of substance, rules of procedure determine how the dispute resolution game is played. Within the international commercial arena, procedural rules which define the jurisdiction of national courts often assume special significance. If, for example, the buyer cannot bring an action in her own State, because the courts of that State lack jurisdiction to adjudicate, the buyer may decide to simply relinquish her claim rather than undertake the expense, inconvenience and uncertainty of a trip and trial abroad.

Without attempting here to catalog all relevant jurisdictional rules, it may be noted that a (State or Federal) court in a given American State will usually have jurisdiction in an international sales case (1) if the "long arm" statute of the State concerned provides an

---

36 *See infra* §§ 6.19, 6.32.
37 *See infra* § 6.13.
38 *Infra* Chapter 7.
39 The significance and key provisions of this UN Convention on the Limitation Period in the International Sale of Goods are set forth in Chapter 9 *infra*.

applicable rule,[40] and (2) if there are sufficient "minimum contacts" to satisfy the constitutional requirements of "due process of law." These conditions would typically be met (e.g.) if the contract contains an express clause conferring jurisdiction on the forum court, if the defendant (buyer or seller) is domiciled in the forum State, if the defendant generally "does business" in that State, or if the parties' obligations under the contract were to be performed in the forum State (etc.).[41]

As regards actions brought in European courts, it may be noted that courts in European Union Member States *often* determine their own jurisdiction in civil and commercial cases in accordance with the Brussels (I) Regulation,[42] whereas the jurisdictional rules of States in the *EFTA* group are often determined by the Lugano Convention rules.[43] Under the Brussels Regulation, as well as under the Lugano regime, a court in a Brussels/Lugano Contracting State will, for example, have jurisdiction to decide a sale-of-goods case if the contract contains a jurisdiction-conferring forum clause.[44] In other cases, the courts at the "place of performance of the obligation in question" may have jurisdiction under Article 5(1)(b) of the Brussels Regulation (Article 5(1) of the Brussels and Lugano Conventions),[45] and – as a preliminary matter – the CISG may even be relied upon to determine that place.[46] In some European States, so-called exorbitant bases of jurisdiction,

---

[40]   In a diversity case – (e.g.) involving a dispute between a New York buyer and a Japanese seller – a U.S. Federal court will determine its jurisdiction by applying the jurisdictional rules (long-arm statute) of the State in which it sits. See Lookofsky & Hertz, *Transnational Litigation*, Ch. 2.5.1.

[41]   *See generally id.*

[42]   *See* the Brussels Regulation on Jurisdiction and the Enforcement of Judgments in Civil and Commercial Matters which – as of March 1, 2002 – replaces the Brussels Convention of 1968 in all EU Member States (except Denmark, which is currently (2003) seeking to implement the Regulation by means of bilateral treaties with other EU Member States). Note, however, that *many* of the jurisdictional rules in the Brussels regime will *not* apply in actions brought against *non*-EU domiciliaries, such as US-based defendants, in EU Member State courts (*see also* note 44 *infra*). *See generally* Lookofsky & Hertz, *id.*, Ch. 2.2.

[43]   The Lugano Convention enables litigants in the EFTA States to take advantage of virtually all the benefits of the Brussels Convention/Regulation available in EU countries. *See generally* Lookofsky & Hertz, *id.*, Ch. 2.3.

[44]   In this case, Article 23 of the Brussels Regulation on Jurisdiction and Judgments will apply if *one* of the parties to the sales contract is *domiciled* in an EU Member State. *See* Lookofsky & Hertz, *id.*, Chapter 2.2.2(B). *See also* the corresponding provision in Art.17 of the Lugano Convention.

[45]   As indicated (*supra* with note 42) the Brussels *Regulation* supplants the Brussels Convention in all EU Member States – except Denmark – as of 1 March 2002. The Regulation maintains the same "place of performance" rule established in Article 5(1) of the 1968 Brussels Convention, but the Regulation also contains new "special" rules for jurisdiction, *inter alia*, in *sales contracts* cases; see Lookofsky & Hertz, *id.*, Chapter 2.2.2(A) re. Art. 5(1)(b) of the Regulation which *defines* the "place of performance of the obligation in question" as the place where the *goods* were (or should have been) *delivered*. In many situations, however, the application of the new Art. 5(1)(b) in sales cases will lead to the same results reached under the Art. 5(1) rule previously applied under the Convention: *see, e.g.,* the decision of Cour de Cassation, France, 16 July 1998, CLOUT Case 242, also in CISGW3, holding that since the goods were delivered in Germany, French courts did not have jurisdiction under Art. 5(1) of the Brussels Convention.

[46]   This remains true even after the adoption Brussels *Regulation*, notwithstanding the fact that the new "special" rule for jurisdiction in *sales contracts* in Article 5(1)(b) *defines* the "place of performance" as (always being) the place of (seller's) *delivery* – i.e., even in cases where the obligation in question is the (buyer's) obligation to *pay*: see Lookofsky & Hertz, *id.* For French cases illustrating the application of CISG

such as the plaintiff's nationality or the presence of defendant's property, might be applied to gain jurisdiction over a defendant not domiciled in an EU or EFTA State.[47]

Not uncommonly, an international sales contract will contain an arbitration clause purporting to give one or more arbitrators exclusive jurisdiction to decide disputes which arise; conversely, such a clause will purport to exclude the jurisdiction of American (and/or other) national courts. Absent special circumstances making such a clause unenforceable, American and other national courts will usually regard themselves as bound to give effect to an arbitration clause.[48]

Once an American (State or Federal) court determines that it has juridical jurisdiction to decide a case involving an international sale, that court must then – before ruling on the merits – determine the applicable substantive law. In a sales case where both parties have their places of business in different CISG Contracting States, American courts are "automatically" bound by the default rule in Article 1(1)(a) to apply the CISG as the applicable substantive law.[49] In other international sales cases, (e.g.) where one party's business is in a non-CISG State, an American court must look to its conflict-of-laws rules to select the applicable sales law.[50] Similar considerations apply in the case of arbitrations conducted on American soil.[51]

As indicated previously, courts (and arbitral tribunals) in *most* Contracting States – thought not United States courts – *also* apply the Convention by virtue of Article 1(1)(b),[52] i.e., when only one party has its business in a Contracting State, provided the conflicts (private international law) rules of the forum State lead to the application of the law of a CISG State.[53] If, on the other hand, the conflicts rules of the forum lead to the application of the sales law of a non-CISG State, that State's domestic sales law will be applied. Courts in non-CISG States must decide which sales law applies by using traditional choice-of-law rules which may also lead to the application of the CISG.[54]

Article 57 to determine the place of payment within the Brussels *Convention* context, thus helping to resolve the jurisdictional issue, *see* Grenoble, Chambre des Urgences, 16 June 1993, 29 March 1995, and Paris, 10 November 1993, both reported in UNILEX. For a German case using CISG Article 31 (place of delivery by seller in Italy) to deny jurisdiction in Germany under Article 5(1) of the Brussels Convention, *see* OLG Koblenz, 23 February 1990, also in UNILEX and analyzed by Witz, *Premières Applications*, no. 54.

47 *See also* notes 42 and 44 *supra*. *See generally* Lookofsky & Hertz, *id*. Chapter 2.1.2.
48 *See generally id., *Ch. 6. Regarding the enforcement of agreements to arbitrate under the 1958 New York Convention *see id.*, Ch. 6.3.
49 Regarding the preëmption of UCC choice-of-law rules in this situation *see infra* § 2.3. Re. situations where the parties (purport to) opt-out under Article 6 *see* § 2.7 *infra*.
50 *See supra* § 1.2.
51 Apart from situations where the CISG would apply or where the parties expressly choose another substantive law, the *lex loci arbitri* will generally give the arbitrators considerable latitude in determining which law to apply. *See generally* Lookofsky & Hertz, *Transnational Litigation*, Ch. 6.2.3.
52 *See* (e.g.) ICC Case 6653/1993 and ICC Case 7660/JK, 23-8-94, both reported in UNILEX. *See generally* (as re. arbitrators' choice of applicable law) Lookofsky & Hertz, *id.*, Ch. 6.2.3.
53 *See supra* with note 14. *See also* §§ 2.4 and 8.7 *infra*.
54 If (e.g.) a Portugese buyer sues an English seller in an English court, and the contract provides for the application of Swiss law, then – in the *absence* of a *clear* indication that the parties meant to refer to Swiss *domestic* sales law – the CISG would presumably be applied, since Switzerland (unlike Portugal and the U.K.) is a CISG State (as of July 2003). *See also infra* § 2.4 with note 26.

At some point, if the case is not settled, a judgment or arbitral award will be rendered by the competent court or tribunal, and – depending on the outcome – the key question may then become one of enforcement of the judgment or award abroad. While most American States will enforce a money judgment rendered by a European court,[55] not all European States are equally hospitable to judgments rendered by American courts.[56] So, although judgments rendered by courts in EU and EFTA States are readily enforceable elsewhere in the EU/EFTA region,[57] the same cannot be said of judgments rendered by non-EU courts, i.e., in situations where the Brussels and Lugano enforcement rules do not apply.[58] The awards rendered by arbitral tribunals, however, are usually afforded a high degree of respect in the courts of most major trading nations.[59]

As indicated, the procedural issues outlined in the foregoing – questions relating to international jurisdiction and choice of law – usually arise in the early stages of dispute resolution. At some point, the focus necessarily shifts to substance. When it comes to the rules which govern sales contract formation, the parties obligations, and their remedies for breach, the (substantive) CISG rules discussed in the following chapters will, of course, be our primary concern.

---

[55] Assuming an American court could have assumed jurisdiction (in accordance within the dictates of Due Process) if the tables were turned: *see* Lookofsky & Hertz, *Transnational Litigation*, Chapter 5.3.

[56] *Id.*, Chapter 5.2.1.

[57] The Brussels Regulation (in Denmark: Convention) and the Lugano Convention apply.

[58] *See* Lookofsky & Hertz, *id.*, Chapter 5.2.1.

[59] *See id.*, Chapter 6.4.

CHAPTER TWO

FIELD OF APPLICATION AND GENERAL PROVISIONS

Part I of the Convention contains the rules we use to determine whether or not the CISG applies. It also contains important general provisions regarding (e.g.) the proper interpretation of both the Convention (treaty) text and of individual sales contracts which are deemed subject to the Convention regime.

A good understanding of the Convention requires a certain familiarity with the "letter" of the law. Therefore – as regards the various subjects covered in this and subsequent chapters – readers are encouraged to make frequent reference to the treaty text itself (in Appendix II).

2A FIELD OF APPLICATION

§ 2.1 DETERMINING WHETHER THE CISG APPLIES

To determine whether the CISG applies in a given situation – i.e., whether we are within or without the CISG "field" – we ask the following questions (and provide some basic answers in the sections below):

– Is the sale "international"? Does the CISG apply under Article 1(1)(a)-(b)?
– Does the transaction qualify as a "sale of goods" under Articles 1–3?
– Is the matter in question "governed by" the Convention (Articles 4–5)?
– Or is the matter perhaps "governed-but-not-settled" under Article 7(2)?
– Have the parties exercised their freedom to "contract out" under Article 6?

§ 2.2 ARTICLE 1(1): INTERNATIONALITY

According to CISG Article 1(1), the Convention applies to sales of goods between parties whose places of business are in different States. "Internationality" is the label sometimes used to refer to the requirement that the relevant places of business of the parties be in different States, and this requirement is common to both subsections (a) and (b) of Article 1(1).[1] However, the Convention will not apply (under subsection a or b) if the fact that the parties' respective places of business are in different States is not "apparent" to the parties at the time of contracting.[2]

---

[1]   Article 10 defines the relevant place in the situation where a party has more than one place of business. For a discussion of this rule *see infra* § 2.3.
[2]   *See* paragraph 2 of Article 1 which applies to both subparagraphs (a) and (b). The situation contemplated by Article 1(2) is, of course, an unusual one.

Assuming a given sale is "international" in this sense,[3] the courts of most CISG Contracting State are obliged to apply the Convention when the requirements set forth in either subparagraph *(a) or (b)* of Article 1(1) are met. However – due to the Article declaration (reservation) made by the United States pursuant to Article 95 – American courts are not bound by the rule in subparagraph (b) of Article 1(1). These various points are discussed further in the sections below.[4]

§ 2.3 ARTICLE 1(1)(A): PARTIES IN DIFFERENT CONTRACTING STATES

Of the two Article 1(1) rules, subparagraph (a) is, by far, the easiest to apply. Whenever one party whose business in located a given Contracting State[5] (e.g., State X) sells goods to another party having its relevant place of business in another such State (Y), the Convention "automatically" applies, simply because the sale concerned involves a contract between parties whose places of business are in different (CISG) "Contracting States."[6]

Illustration 2a.[7] Merchant (S) in Italy sells machinery to merchant (B) in New York. Later, claiming the goods which S has delivered do not conform to the contract, B brings an action for damages in a New York (Federal) court.

Because this sale is between parties whose places of business are in different Contracting States, where the treaty has entered into force,[8] and because this case has been brought before a (competent) court in a Contracting State which is bound (by public international law) to apply the CISG treaty rules, the court must – by virtue of the rule in Article 1(1)(a) – apply the CISG to resolve the dispute.

Note that in a situation like this, the Convention applies solely by virtue of the Article 1(1)(a) rule.[9] American (Federal and State) courts need not – and indeed should not – use "conflict of laws" rules as the "vehicle" by which they ultimately arrive at Article 1(1)(a). In other words, no choice of law is called for or required with respect to Convention

---

3   I.e., that the parties have their places of business in different States and that the "exception" in Article 1(2) does not apply. *See* text with preceding note.

4   Regarding the special situation with respect to *inter-Scandinavian* sales resulting from the Article 94 declarations *see* Lookofsky, *CISG/Scandinavia,* § 8-6. Note also in this context that the situation in *Norway* with respect to the CISG field of application is unique, in that § 8.7 of the Norwegian SGA (1988) defines an "international sale" (simply) as a sale where the parties have their places of business in *different States. See* Lookofsky, *id.,* § 2.2.

5   A "Contracting State" is a State which has ratified the Convention, assuming the Convention has entered into effect in that State. Note that the Convention enters into force 12 months after ratification by the State concerned: *see* Article 99(1) and Appendix I *infra.*

6   Other factors, such as the nationality of the parties and the (civil or commercial) character of the sale are not relevant: *see* Article 1(3). Re. "consumer sales," however, *see* § 2.5 *infra.* Under ULIS (*see supra* § 1.2) "internationality" was determined on the basis of the parties' places of business coupled with other factors.

7   This illustration is based on *Delchi Carrier, SpA v. Rotorex Corp.,* discussed *infra* in § 6.15 with note 176 *et seq.*

8   *See infra* Appendix 1.

9   *Accord* Honnold, *Uniform Law* at 81 ("applicability based on Sub1(1)(a) . . . is not subject to the uncertainties inherent in general rules of conflicts (PIL)").

Some contracts only adopt certain parts
∵

application under Article 1(1)(a),[10] not only because the treaty "trumps" State (UCC) law by virtue of the Supremacy Clause of the Federal Constitution,[11] but also because the international sales law of all Contracting States is the *same*. In other words, in the Article 1(1)(a) situation, there is simply nothing to "choose" between,[12] at least not as regards the numerous sales law issues which are both "governed and settled" by the Convention.[13]

> *Illustration 2b.* Seller S, whose business is in Denmark, offers a large quantity of Danish bacon (at a substantial discount) to Arkansas merchant-buyer B. Before B can post his acceptance, S revokes his offer. Claiming that S remains bound by the offer, B demands damages for breach.

As regards the special situation exemplified by this illustration, it is significant that Denmark (like the other Scandinavian countries)[14] ratified the Convention subject to an Article 92 declaration, with the result that Denmark is not a Contracting State with respect to CISG Part II (Formation of Contract).[15] Since this renders Articles 14–24 of the Convention inapplicable to this contract,[16] the issue of whether S is bound by the offer can only be resolved by rules of domestic law. Note, however, that if an American or Danish court, applying (Danish or American) domestic contract formation rules,[17] finds that a contract has indeed been made, then Parts I and III of the Convention will regulate the

---

[10]   *See* para. 6 of *Secretariat Commentary* (Article 1(1)(a) applies "even if the rules of private international law of the forum would normally designate the law of a third country"). *See also* Winship, *Private International Law*, pp. 519–20.

[11]   *See Asante Technologies v. PMC-Sierra*, 164 F.Supp.2d 1142 (N.D. California 2001), also available in CISW3 and UNILEX (buyer's choice of applicable law adopted the "laws of" the State of California, and California is bound by the Supremacy Clause – U.S. Const. art. VI, cl. 2 – to the treaties of the United States: "This Constitution, and the laws of the United States which shall be made in pursuance thereof; and all treaties made, or which shall be made, under the authority of the United States, shall be the supreme law of the land.").

[12]   The decision of the U. S. Court of Appeals (5th Circuit, 2003) in *BP Oil International v. Empresa Estatal Petroleos de Ecuador* (http://cisgw3.law.pace.edu/cases/030611u1.html) is in *accord* with this analysis: "Given that the CISG *is* Ecuadorian law, a choice of law provision designating Ecuadorian law merely confirms that the treaty governs the transaction."

[13]   When it comes to "validity" questions and other matters neither "governed" nor "settled" by the Convention, however, it will be necessary to determine the *lex contractus* (applicable domestic law) by applying the choice-of-law rules which apply in the forum court's jurisdiction. *See supra* §§ 1.2 and 1.4 and *infra* § 2.6.

[14]   Finland, Norway and Sweden.

[15]   *See infra* §§ 3.1 and 8.4.

[16]   By virtue of the rule in Article 1(1)(a). Since the *non*-Scandinavian party in this *Illustration* has its relevant place of business in the United States, which has made an Article 95 declaration (*infra* § 8.7), we need not consider the possible applicability of CISG Part II by virtue of the application of Article 1(1)(b); regarding the complexities sometimes generated by the Article 92 declarations in contracts involving Scandinavian merchants *see infra* § 8.4.

[17]   In this situation the conflict of laws rules (private international law) applicable in a Danish court would surely lead to the application of the Danish seller's (domestic) law, i.e., the Danish Contracts Act (*Aftaleloven*). An American court might well reach the same result; *see supra*, §§ 1.2 and 1.4.

question of the contract's proper interpretation and enforcement,[18] including B's possible right to claim damages for breach.[19]

If a party to a CISG sales contract has more than one "place of business,"[20] Article 10(a) requires the court to determine which of the various places has the "closest relationship" to the contract and its performance.[21] Applying this rule in a complex case where a buyer in Austria (a CISG State) purchased goods from the Swiss branch of a company with head-quarters in Liechtenstein (notably: a *non*-CISG Contracting State), a Swiss court held that the contract was governed by the CISG, since it was the branch in Switzerland (a CISG State) which had the closest relationship to the contract and its performance.[22]

§ 2.4 ARTICLE 1(1)(B) AND ARTICLE 95 DECLARATIONS

In most – but not all! – CISG States, subsection (b) of Article 1(1) becomes relevant when the criterion in subsection (a) is not met, i.e., in cases where only party has its place of business in a CISG Contracting State.[23] As more fully explained below, the fact that the United States has made an Article 95 declaration (reservation) means that *American* courts are *not* bound by the rule in subsection (b). But since the 1(1)(b) rule is regularly applied by foreign courts and arbitral tribunals,[24] American lawyers should at least have some understanding of how this part of Article 1 works in most CISG States.

> *Illustration 2c:*[25] Merchant-buyer B in England orders 10 dozen down-insulated coats from seller-manufacturer S in Canada. S accepts the order and ships the goods to B. Later, claiming the goods do not conform to the contract, B refuses to pay for them.

A Canadian court asked to decide the dispute between S and B could not apply the CISG by virtue of Article 1(1)(a), simply because the United Kingdom is not (as of 2003) a CISG Contracting State. But the Canadian court would be bound by the 1(1)(b) rule to apply the CISG, provided the relevant Canadian conflict-of-laws rules (private international

---

18   Since Parts I and III apply in this situation by virtue of Article 1(1)(a).
19   Re. contract interpretation *see infra* § 2.12; re. damages as a remedy for breach *see infra* § 6.14.
20   In Europe corporate entities are generally understood to have their *main* place of business (e.g., *siège* in France, *Sitz* in Germany) at the actual center of their business activities (their "headquarters").
21   *See Asante Technologies, Inc. v. PMC-Sierra, Inc.*, 164 F.Supp.2d 1142 (N.D. California 2001), where the sales contract was between a California corporation and a corporation incorporated in Delaware. The court found, however, that the defendant's place of business that had the closest relationship to the contract and its performance was in British Columbia, Canada. This made the contract an (international) CISG contract.
22   *See* the decision of Bezirksgericht der Saane (Switzerland), 20 February 1997, reported as CLOUT Case 261. *See* also the *Asante* decision (preceding note).
23   Assuming both parties concerned have their places of business in *different* States: as to this "internationality" requirement *see* § 2.3 *supra*.
24   At least in cases involving non-American-based merchants. Regarding the American (Article 95) declaration and Article 1(1)(b) vis-a-vis American merchants *see* text *infra* with note 30 *et seq*.
25   Corresponding to *Illustration 1b* in § 1.1 *supra*.

law) – i.e., the rules to which Article 1(1)(b) refers – call for the application of the (Canadian) seller's law.[26]

Should the result in *Illustration 2c* be different if the contract itself expressly designates "Canadian law" as the applicable law? According to the prevailing doctrine and judicial practice, the answer is no![27] In such a situation, since the CISG is part of "Canadian law," applicable principles of contract interpretation should point to the CISG.[28] An alternative, more technical explanation is as follows: when the parties choose "Canadian law," CISG Article 1(1)(b) leads to the application of the Convention, because "the rules of the private international law [which recognize party autonomy] lead to the application of the law of [Canada, i.e.] a Contacting State."[29]

As already emphasized, a few Contracting States – including the United States and China – ratified the CISG subject to an Article 95 declaration (reservation),[30] with the result is that these States are not bound by subparagraph (1)(b) of Article 1. Now that we have seen how the rule in 1(1)(b) works in those places where it applies, we are in a better position to understand the non-application of the CISG in cases involving one party whose relevant place of business is in the United States and one party who business is not in a CISG State. Since, for example, a court in Texas asked to decide a sales dispute between a seller in Texas and a buyer in England would – by virtue of the Article 95 declaration – have no obligation to apply the subparagraph (1)(b) of Article 1, and since the Convention clearly would not apply by virtue of subparagraph (1)(a) either,[31] the only remaining "choice" of applicable law open to the Texas court in that situation would be to choose between domestic laws, i.e., the domestic sales law of Texas (that State's version of UCC Article 2)[32] or the English Sale of Goods Act (SGA).[33]

This brings us to a final example, involving the rather technical and complex question of whether a court in a CISG State which has not made an Article 95 declaration might itself apply the rule in Article 1(1)(b), with the possible result that the Convention could

---

[26] In all likelihood, the result would be the same if the dispute were brought before an *English* court, in that the private international law (PIL) of England would probably point to "Canadian law" (re. the EU "Rome" Convention on the Law Applicable to Contractual Obligations *see* Lookofsky & Hertz, *Transnational Litigation*, Ch. 3.2.1).When a court in a *non*-Contracting state applies the rule in CISG Article 1(1)(b), it is obviously not acting in performance of a (public international law) obligation based on the CISG treaty; it applies Art. 1(1)(b) because the PIL rules of the forum point to the "internal" law of a Contracting State, and this internal law includes CISG Art. 1(1)(b).

[27] *See* (e.g.) the decision of Cour de Cassation (France), 17 December 1996, reported in UNILEX.

[28] *See also infra* § 2.7.

[29] *See* (e.g.) OLG Düsseldorf, 8 January 1993, reported in UNILEX. *Accord* Ferrari, *Specific Topics* at 144 ff.

[30] As of June 2003, the list of countries which have made Article 95 reservations includes China, the Czech Republic, the United States, Singapore and Slovakia. Initially, Canada made an Article 95 Declaration (with effect only for the Province of British Columbia), but that reservation was subsequently withdrawn.

[31] As of 2003 the U.K. not a CISG State: *see* Appendix I *infra*.

[32] More precisely, the sales law rules in the Texas version of Article 2 of the Uniform Commercial Code.

[33] In certain circumstances a forum State which has made an Article 95 Declaration might still apply the CISG, e.g., if the forum's choice-of-law rules call for the application of the law of a CISG Contracting State which has not made an Article 95 declaration: *see generally* Winship, *Scope* at 1–32 and Heuzé, *Vente internationale*, no. 118.

Chapter Two – Field of Application and General Provisions

be applied to a contract involving a merchant whose business is in a CISG Contracting State (like the United States) which has made such a declaration.

Illustration 2d. Merchant-buyer B in England mails an order for 10 dozen down-insulated coats to seller-manufacturer S in Connecticut. S accepts the order by posting a brief confirmation letter to B. Later, claiming the goods do not conform to the contract, B refuses to accept them; S, however, disagrees and demands to be paid. To back up his demand, S sues B in a German court (which accepts jurisdiction because B has substantial assets in Germany).[34]

In a situation like this – involving a "conflict" of (contractual) laws in a dispute between a seller in State X and a buyer in State Y – a German court would ordinarily be expected to apply the "seller's law," i.e., the sales law applicable in the seller's State.[35] And since the CISG is an integral part of the law of CISG Contracting States, this German conflict-of-laws (PIL) rule – when read together with CISG Article 1(1)(b) – might lead us to expect the application of the CISG.[36] When Germany ratified the CISG, however, it "declared" (unofficially) that German courts would interpret the Convention so as *not* to apply the rule in Article 1(1)(b) in cases involving a party whose business is located in an Article 95-declaring State, i.e., presumably precluding the possibility that German PIL rules (which ordinarily lead to the "seller's law") could lead to CISG application in a situation like the one in *Illustration 2d.*[37] It remains to be seen whether other CISG States will adopt a similar interpretation of the Article 1(1)(b) rule.

§ 2.5 ARTICLES 1, 2 AND 3: SALE OF GOODS

The determination that the Convention applies by virtue of Article 1[38] presupposes that the transaction in question can be classified as a "sale" of "goods,"[39] but neither of these key Convention concepts is defined in the treaty text.

Here as elsewhere, an autonomous (international) interpretation of the treaty is our ultimate goal, but since this need not preclude consideration of comparable, non-Convention

---

34 Re. assets-based jurisdiction (e.g.) in Denmark and Germany *see* Lookofsky and Hertz, *Transnational Litigation*, Ch. 2.1.2.
35 I.e. the place of business of the party who is to perform the "characteristic [sales contract] obligation." Regarding this "presumption" in Article 4 of the 1980 (Rome) Convention (applicable when the parties have not themselves designated the applicable law under Article 3), *see id.*, Ch. 3.2.1(B).
36 Indeed, a German court would ordinarily reach this result, on the basis of Art. 1(1)(b), even if the contract itself called for the application of "German law." *See supra*, text with note 27 *et seq.*
37 Though the result would probably be different if the parties expressly choose "German law," since German courts should recognize the parties' freedom to opt into the CISG (part of "German law") under Article 3 of the Rome Convention (*see also* Lookofsky & Hertz, *supra* note 35 at *id.*). *See* Magnus in Staudinger, *Kommentar*, art. 6 Rn. 27. Re. the German declaration *see also* Ferrari, F., "Cross Reference and Editorial Analysis of Article 1," available at <http://cisgw3.law.pace.edu/cisg/text/cross/cross-1.html>. *See also* § 8.4 *infra.*
38 I.e., by virtue of the rule in subsection (a) or subsection (b). *See* discussion *supra* in § 2.4.
39 In the official French version of the CISG text: *vente de merchandises.*

conceptions,[40] we might start by noting that a sale of goods has traditionally, at the domestic sales law level, been understood as a transaction involving the transfer of a property right in a "moveable" (as opposed to an immovable) "thing."[41]

On the other hand, Articles 2 and 3 of the Convention expressly exclude *certain* specified types of transactions which might otherwise have qualified as CISG "sales of goods." For one thing, Article 2(a) provides that the CISG does not apply to sales of goods bought for "personal, family or household use," unless the seller neither knew nor ought to have known of the intended (consumer) use;[42] this exception does not, however, extend to all non-commercial transactions or to all transactions by a non-merchant.[43]

Other transactions specifically excluded from the scope of the CISG by virtue of Article 2 are sales by auction, forced sales, and sales of negotiable instruments, ships,[44] aircraft,[45] and electricity.[46] Of course, as regards sales of items specifically excluded by default, it will usually be possible for the parties to "contract in."[47] Moreover, the fact that sales of electricity, as well as shares of stock (and other securities),[48] are specifically excluded from

---

[40] As more fully developed *infra* (§ 2.9) CISG Article 7(1) requires that we "have regard" to the treaty's international character and the need to promote uniformity in its application (i.e., "autonomous" interpretation of its provisions), but this provision ought not be read to mean judges and arbitrators must work in a vacuum. *See, e.g., id.* note 141 re. the approach used by the European Court of Justice when interpreting EU law: searching for a "common core/denominator" among the laws and jurisprudence of the individual EU Member States.

[41] *Accord:* CISG Art. 30 ff. Whether that thing also need by *tangible* (to qualify as a "good") is a separate, more controversial question: *see* text *infra* with note 56 *et seq.* The original version of UCC § 2-105(1), still applicable in all American States as of 2003, defines goods as "all things . . . which are movable at the time of identification to the contract. . . ." *Accord* (re. goods/*løsøre* under Danish domestic law) Lookofsky, *Køb*, Ch. 2.3.a. According to the revised version of UCC § 2-102(4) set forth in the (2002) *NCCUSL Draft Proposal* (approved by the ABA at its annual meeting in 2003), however, a transaction in a product consisting of "computer information and goods that are solely the medium containing the computer information" is *not* a "transaction in goods"; also the – highly controversial – UCITA (note 61 *infra*) excludes "information" (data, programs) from its definition of goods (§ 102, subsecs. 33 and 35).

[42] *See, e.g.*, the decision of Oberster Gerichtshof, Austria, 11 February 1997, CLOUT Case 190, also reported in UNILEX, holding that the CISG was not applicable to the sale of Lamborghini automobile purchased for buyer's personal use.

[43] For example, the sale of an encyclopedia to a professional writer could qualify as a CISG sale: *see* Ferrari in Schlechtriem, *Kommentar*, Art. 2, Rd.Nr.9 (with more examples). Note also that according to Article 1(3) the "civil" or "commercial" character of the parties or transaction is, in and of itself, *irrelevant* in determining the applicability of the Convention.

[44] This exception, it seems, should have been applied in the case of OLG Koblenz, 16 January 1992, reported in UNILEX; *see* Witz, *Premières Applications*, no. 18.

[45] Although the CISG does not apply to sales of (whole) aircraft, it does apply to the sale of aircraft components. *See* Heuzé, *id.* and the decision of the Supreme Court of Hungary, 25 Sept. 1992, translation in 13 *J.L. & Com.* 31 (1993), also reported in UNILEX and CISGW3. For criticism of the exclusion of ships and aircraft *see* Heuzé, *Vente internationale*, no. 91.

[46] This exception cannot be extended, by analogy or otherwise, to sales of gas or oil. *Accord* Herber in Schlechtriem, *Commentary*, Rd.Nr. 37.

[47] Assuming that such an agreement would be valid under the applicable domestic law: *see infra* § 2.6. Re. Article 6 and "contracting in" to the CISG *see generally infra* § 2.7.

[48] Article 2(d).

the CISG scope ought not lead to the conclusion that the CISG "goods" concept is limited to "tangible" things.[49]

The CISG case law tells us that neither franchising contracts nor distribution contracts can be classified as "contracts of sale" under Article 1, but an individual sales contract which falls within such a "framework" agreement can qualify as a CISG sale.[50]

Since the CISG applies only to contracts rightly characterized as "sales," it does not apply to contracts for the provision of "services." The rules in CISG Article 3 are designed to draw the line in cases where the contract in question contains both a sales and a service element. For example, the Convention can apply to "mixed" transaction involving both the supply of goods (e.g., machinery) and services (installation and maintainence of machinery), but not if the service-element constitutes the "preponderant part."[51] Similarly, a contract for the supply of goods "to be manufactured" qualifies as a CISG sale of goods[52] (and this is true even if the value of the labor and services rendered in connection with the manufacturing process exceeds the value of the raw materials); on the other hand, the Convention will not apply to a contract for the supply of goods to be manufactured if the person who orders the goods (the "buyer") herself supplies a "substantial part"[53] of the necessary materials.[54] In cases where the CISG does not apply – e.g. in the case of a contract (mainly) for the supply of services – recourse must be made to the domestic rules applicable to transactions of the kind concerned.[55]

Since "goods" are usually equated with "moveable" things,[56] it seems clear that sales of (immovable) buildings and land (real property) fall outside the Convention scope. A more

---

49 *But* for a contrary view *see* Gillette & Walt, *Sales Law* at 42–43. Re. gas *see supra* note 46. Re. computer software *see infra*, text with note 56 *et seq.*

50 Re. distribution contracts *see* OLG Koblenz (Germany), 17 Sept. 1993, CLOUT Case 281, also reported in CISGW3 and UNILEX, holding that the CISG applies to individual sales within the *framework* of an exclusive *distribution* contract, but not to the distribution contract itself. *See also* the similar decision of the ICC Court of Arbitration, Case no. 8611/HV/JK 1997, reported UNILEX, and the decision of Bundesgerichtshof (Germany), 23 July 1997 ("Benetton II"), reported in UNILEX and translated in CISGW3. *Accord*: Schlechtriem, *Bundesgerichtshof* at 5 with note 37, also citing *Medical Marketing Int.l Inc. v. Internazionale Medico Scientifica, Sr.l.*, 1999 WL 311945 (E.D.La. 1999).

51 *See, e.g.,* the decision of Handelsgericht Zürich (Switzerland), 26 April 1995, reported in UNILEX (contract for sale and installation of a fitness device was essentially "sales contract" governed by the CISG). *See also* the decision of Cour d'Appel de Grenoble, Chambre Commerciale, 26 April 1995, Clout Case 152, also reported in CISGW3 and UNILEX.

52 *See* Article 3(1).

53 The "substantial part" referred to in para. (1) of Article 3 is surely less that the "predominant part" referred to in para. (2).

54 *See* Article 3(1). Relying on this provision, a French court held (incorrectly) that the CISG did not apply to a sales contract under which the buyer was obligated to provide a design for the manufacture of the goods: *see* Chambéry, 25 May 1993, reported in UNILEX. As noted by Witz (*Premières Applications* no. 16) the court overlooked Art. 42 (2)(b) of the Convention. In a similar German case the CISG was (rightly) applied, since a design does *not* constitute "materials" for manufacture: *see* OLG Frankfurt, 17 September 1991, RIW 1991, 950.

55 I.e., the contract law rules applicable by virtue of the forum court's private international law. Re. CISG Article 7(2) *see infra* § 2.11.

56 I.e., things which can be moved from one place to another by a ship, a postal carrier, the Internet or other some other "medium." This accords, *inter alia*, with the current (2003) definition under American domestic law: *see supra* text with note 41.

difficult problem is the proper classification of ideas, plans, concepts, know-how, research results, etc. – i.e., intangibles which fall within the purview of at least some domestic sales laws.[57] In one much-discussed decision, a German court refused to characterize an obligation to provide a "scholarly market analysis" as a contract for the provision of CISG "goods."[58] This holding – to limit the scope of the Convention, so as to exclude contracts concerning the right to use "ideas" (in this case: a market analysis) – might seem reasonable, but we should not then jump to the unwarranted conclusion that the CISG can only govern sales of tangible things.[59]

This brings us to the cutting edge of the much-debated, but hardly yet settled issue of computer software (programs).[60] Suppose, for example, that a merchant buys a standard word-processing program on the Internet, and that the buyer and seller have their places of business in different CISG States. If the program performs badly, can the buyer rightly claim that this sale falls within the CISG gap-filling regime?

Although the domestic (e.g. UCC/UCITA) version of this question remains highly controversial,[61] there is nonetheless good reason to suggest a clear and affirmative answer in

---

[57]   Sales of goodwill and other intangibles are, for example, covered by the Danish Sales Act (*Købeloven*): *see* Lookofsky, *Købeloven*, Ch. 2.3.a.

[58]   *See* the decision of OLG Köln, 26 August 1994, CLOUT Case 122, also reported in CISGW3 and UNILEX, holding that a contract for a "scholarly analysis" of a segment of the German market did not constitute a contract for the "sale of goods." In this connection, the court noted that a sale of goods is characterized by the transfer of property in an "object"; though the analysis results were embodied in a written report, the main concern of the parties was the *right to use the ideas* therein. *See also* Witz, *Premières Applications* at 32–33. As with the software issue (text *infra* with notes 66 ff.), however, the question of whether *know-how* is CISG goods should *not* depend on its "incorporation in a physical medium"; *accord* Magnus in Staudinger, *Kommentar*, Art. 1, Rd.Nr. 46; *but see* Ferrari in Schlechtriem, *Kommentar*, Art. 1, Rd.Nr. 38; *compare* Herber in Schlechtriem, *Commentary*, Art. 1, Rd.Nr. 21a.

[59]   I.e., notwithstanding the fact that *some* national legislators and courts might elect to limit their own domestic "goods" concept to tangible (touchy-feely) kinds of things. In this respect, the reasoning of OLG Köln, 26 August 1994 (preceding note), though supported by Herber's view (in *Schlechtreim,Commentary*, Art. 1, Rd.Nr. 20), remains unpursuasive. *Compare* the arguably better view expressed by OLG Koblenz, 17 September 1993, CLOUT Case 281, also reported in CISGW3 and UNILEX (CISG "goods" includes *all tangibles and intangibles*, such as computer chips or computer software, which might otherwise be the subject of an international sales contract); *but see* Ferrari in Schlechtriem, *Kommentar*, Art. 1, Rd.Nr. 38 and *compare supra* note 41 re. the NCCUSL proposal to limit the American UCC's current (2003) and elastic definition of "goods."

[60]   Re. the complex comparative and international issues involved *see generally* Diedrich, *Maintaining Uniformity*. *See also* Lookofsky, *International Sales Contracts*, pp. 37–38.

[61]   At least as of this writing (2003). For examples from case-law under Article 2 of the original UCC (still applicable to domestic sales in all Americn States as of August 2003) *see* notes 64 and 71 *infra*. Re. the limitation of the UCC "goods" definition (to exclude computer software and other "information") proposed by the NCCUSL in 2002 (and approved by the ABA in 2003) *see* note 41. Although the NCCUSL originally had intended that the UCITA would take up the resulting "slack" (i.e., if and when software were excluded from the UCC "goods" concept: *see* Gillette & Walt, Sales Law, pp. 24–26), the NCCUSL nonetheless felt compelled, on August 1, 2003, to officially *abandon its efforts* to promote the highly controversial UCITA model law – a decision which might also spell doom for the *NCCUSL Draft Proposal* to narrow the UCC definition of "goods." *See also supra* note 41 and *infra* note 67.

Computer programs should be under CISG

the international context.[62] In other words, an international sale of a computer program – i.e., software designed to provide machine-readable instructions to a computer-processor[63] – *should be* regarded as a CISG "sale of goods."[64] The main reasons why courts and international arbitral tribunals should adopt that classification may be summarized as follows: (1) the language of the Convention does not limit the concept of goods to tangible matter;[65] (2) the essential nature of a computer program designed and built to process words, bill customers or play games is that of a "machine," that is to say a very real and functional thing (neither "virtual reality" nor raw "information");[66] (3) the CISG provides a balanced regime which seems well-suited to regulate sales of such functional things;[67]

---

[62] *See generally* Lookofsky, *In Dubio Pro Conventione* at 268 ff.

[63] The definition of a computer program in sec. 102(a)(12) of the UCITA is in *accord*: "a set of statements or instructions to be used directly in a computer to bring about a cerain result." These *instructions*, which constitute the program's *input*, should be distinguished from the program's *output* (the information provided as a result of the processor's calculations). *See* Frost, *Informationsydelsen* at 117 f. and 220 ff. and the UCITA (*id.*): "The term [computer program] does not include separately identifiable informational content." *See also supra*, text with note 61.

[64] *Accord* as re. American domestic/UCC sales law (e.g.) *Advent Systems Ltd. v. Unisys Corp.*, 925 F.2d 670 (3rd Cir. 1991). For a critique of the reasoning in *Advent see* Gillette & Walt, *Sales Law*, 23–25. Regarding the revised (and more limited) UCC definition of "goods" proposed by the NCCUSL in August 2002 and approved by the ABA in 2003 *see* notes 41 and 61 *supra*.

[65] *See* OLG Koblenz (Germany), *supra* note 59. *Accord*: Herber in Schlechtriem, *Commentary*, Art.1 Rd.Nr. 21 with n. 37a. For a contrary view *see* Gillette & Walt, *Sales Law* at 43 (arguing that use of term "goods," when combined with express exclusions in Article 2, suggests CISG intended only to cover movable and tangible property); note in this connection that most Convention commentators rightly reject the analogous application of Article 2(f) re. sale of electricity to sale of gas (*see supra* with note 46). *Compare* Ferrari, *Specific Topics* with note 430, combining *obiter dictum* in OLG Köln, 26 August 1994 (CLOUT Case 122) with ULIS terminology and concluding that only "corporeal moveable goods" (*objets mobiliers corporels*) – e.g., a program embodied on disk – qualify as CISG "goods."

[66] Although "software" in the 21st century (*supra* note 63) "looks and feels" different than the tangible punched card programs of the 1970's (punched by hand on a key punch machine and read into a card reader: *see* <http://www.columbia.edu/acis/history/cards.html>), the nature and function of intangible software remains the same. To describe intangible or invisible goods as "virtual" goods wrongly implies they are "not real"; on the contrary, an intangible/invisible computer program is every bit as "real" as a typewriter, tractor or other tangible thing. It is therefore unfortunate that the misnomer "virtual good" seems to be gaining currency: *see, e.g.*, United Nations document A/CN.9/WG.IV/WP.95 (re. legal aspects of electronic commerce). Also regrettable is the tendency of some IT-buffs to regard "information" as the key characteristic of a program: lumping programs together with other kinds of electronic "information" (e.g. raw data in a database) ignores the nature of a program as a functional "machine" with a complex set of invisible parts (codes etc.) that help make it "work."

[67] The word "balanced" in this context means not unduly favoring the obligations and rights of one party vis-a-vis the other. This is not the place to debate the kinds of malfunction which might or might not constitute "non-conformity" in computer software under a CISG sale, but it seems clear that a CISG seller's (implied-by-default) obligation to deliver goods fit for "ordinary" purposes (*infra* § 4.7) does *not* mean that software buyers have a reasonable expectation of "perfect" (glitch-free) products (*accord*: Andersen & Lookofsky, *Obligationsret* at 69 f.). Perhaps overly fearful of the consequences of sales-statute regulation of software, the IT manufacturing-lobby has crusaded to transform the sales transactions under consideration here into (reduced warranty) "licenses." The political nature of the whole sale-vs-licence issue is well-illustrated by

and (4) the fact that the program may be protected by copyright does not change the nature of this intangible beast.[68]

So, assuming the parties have not otherwise (validly) agreed,[69] the CISG *should be* applied to international sales of computer software (and this includes at least some of the transactions which program-sellers choose to dub "licenses").[70] The CISG should apply not only to sales of software on disk, but also to sales of purely intangible software delivered/downloaded over the Internet.[71]

---

the "bombshelter" laws enacted in some American states which would *invalidate* contract clauses purporting to "opt in" to the Uniform Computer Information Transactions Act (UCITA)*: see, e.g.,* 70 *United States Law Week* 2439 (2001); *see also* <http://www.nccusl.org/nccusl/meetings/ucita_1101materials.htm>. On August 1, 2003, the NCCUSL Executive Committee, acknowledging massive UCIA opposition, announced it would "not expend any additional Conference energy or resources in having UCITA adopted": *see* <http://www.nccusl.org/nccusl/ucita/KKB_UCITA_Letter_8103.pdf>. Re. the UCITA *see also* Cox, *Chaos,* Part IV. *See also supra,* notes 41 and 61.

68   The fact that the purchaser of a single copy of an intangible program which is *protected by* (an intangible) copyright cannot copy (mass-reproduce and re-sell) the program without the copyright-holder's permission does *not* logically lead one to conclude that the subject matter of the sale (the program-copy) is not "goods." If the particular (intangible) program-copy sold is "packaged" in/on a (tangible) floppy disk or CD, then, I would submit, that hybrid thing is (all) goods. In other words, the fact that the program is protected by copyright means "only" that the buyer cannot legally copy (his copy of) the program without the copyright-holder's permission, whereas the main subject matter of the transaction – the individual *program-copy* purchased (on disk or not) – is CISG "goods." *But compare* Gillette & Walt, *Sales Law* at 24 (software as "intellectual property").

69   *See infra* § 2.7. This is, of course, an extremely important consideration, especially when it comes to the right of software sellers to limit their liability for software not fit for ordinary or special purposes under Article 35. Re. disclaimers and liability limitations and the right of buyers to "minimum adequate remedies" *see generally* Chapter 7 *infra.* Re. software "licences" *see* following note.

70   Though the IT-manufacturing lobby might continue to crusade in favor of legislation which would transform sales of goods into (reduced warranty) "licenses" (*supra* note 67), it remains up to the court or arbitral tribunal to determine whether the transaction in question qualifies as a "sale" or something else, e.g., a lease or "license"; *accord* Gillette & Walt, *Sales Law* at 27. If B in State X orders, receives and pays for a disk containing a word-processing program from S in State Y, that particular transaction might best be viewed as an (international) sale – not a "license" – of goods, and this is true even if S supplies fine-print, shrink-wrapped/click-wrapped terms which dub the transaction a "license." Copyright protection is one thing, but the fact that B can only (legally) use the goods purchased in ways which respect S's intellectual property rights does not somehow turn a transaction with the earmarks of sale into a license, and if S supplies terms which attempt to escape the reality of the situation, those terms ought not bind B (*see generally* Ch. 7 *infra*); instead, both the disk and the program-copy on it should become B's property, and B's rights as a buyer (with respect to *both*) should be governed by the CISG rules. *Accord: Softman Products Co., LLC v. Adobe Systems Inc.*, decided Oct. 19 2001, 2001 WL 1343955.

71   *Accord* Herber in Schlechtriem, *Commentary*, Art.1 Rd.Nr. 21 with n. 37a, with reference Diedrich, RIW 1993, 441. *Compare* (re. American domestic sales law) the decision by the U.S. District Court in *Specht v. Netscape Communications Corp.*, 150 F.Supp. 2d 585 (D.C.N.Y. 2001) ("parties' relationship essentially . . . that of a seller and a purchaser of goods . . . Plaintiff requested Defendant's product by clicking on an icon marked "Download," and Defendant then tendered the product"). Those who maintain that the CISG only applies to software contained in a "tangible medium" seem to be confusing the intangible good (the software) with the (tangible or intangible) medium which "carries" and/or "contains" that good. If B buys a program on a disk, she has really bought two "things": a program and a disk. Both are goods and either can be sold

tailor-made programs - if labor costs outweigh "tangible"
costs, then it should be excluded

Although the logic set forth here is especially relevant as regards the sale of "standard" programs,[72] it is submitted that less-common transactions providing for the (development and) sale of specialized programs might also be held to fall within the Convention ambit.[73] The "tailor-made" software discussion should not, however, be confused with the separate (and not necessarily IT-connected) question of mixed transactions involving both the sale of goods and the supply of services: if the service element in such a mixed transaction (e.g., a supplier's post-delivery obligation to service and maintain computer hardware and/or software) predominates – such that the value of the service and maintenance is greater than the value of the goods (the hardware and/or software) – then Article 3(2) will remove the entire transaction from the CISG scope.[74]

§ 2.6 ISSUES NOT GOVERNED, DOMESTIC LAW & CONCURRENT REMEDIES

The Convention has 101 Articles, but it was not designed to deal with all of the substantive problems which might arise in connection with an international sale. So, even assuming that the transaction concerned qualifies as an international "sale of goods" (within the scope of CISG Articles 1 to 3), one still needs to ask whether the particular issue concerned is actually governed by the rules in CISG Parts II and III. The answer to this question is likely to be found in Articles 4 and 5 and (in certain borderline cases) in Article 7(2).

---

separately. If S sells a program to B and then "delivers" that program to B by making it downloadable over the Internet, the cyberspace "delivery" might be seen as a service (like the delivery of a package by post), but the software delivered remains a (real) good. *Accord* Frost, *Informationsydelsen* at 123 (see also the English abstract of Frost's thesis, *id*. at 291). *But see* Cox, T., *Chaos*, text with note 17 (arguing that software is a good because it is "incorporated" into a tangible good) and Ferrari in Schlechtriem, *Kommentar, supra* note 13, Art. 1, Rd.Nr. 38 (corporeal/*körperlichen* medium "necessary"). *See also supra*, note 59. Article 2 of the European E-Commerce Directive (2000/31/EC) defines – *for the purpose of this Directive* (only) – "information society services" as services provided at a distance by electronic means at the individual recipient's request: *see* Art. 1(2), Technical Standards Directive (98/34/EC, 998/48/EC), and Annex V of this directive specifically excludes "Off-line services: distribution of CD-ROMs or software on diskettes." Neither the definition nor the exclusion justify the conclusion by Cox (*id.*, Part III) that "[c]ourts and commentators will logically be forced to conclude that a transaction for electronic software is a service contract." Obviously, the E-Commerce Directive is "more focused on protecting and providing information than establishing rules for contract law" (Cox at *id.*), and if a given transaction – (e.g.) an on-line sale of software – qualifies as a CISG sale of goods, the definitions and exclusions in the European E-Commerce Directive do not compel anyone (anywhere) to conclude otherwise.

72 A German court has held that a contract for the sale of (standard) software is governed by the CISG: *see* the decision of LG München, 8 February 1995, CLOUT Case 131, also reported in UNILEX.

73 *See also supra,* text with note 51, *but see* Ferrari, *Specific Topics*, text with note 439. These days, a "tailor made" software transaction is likely to involve the adaptation af standard software to individual needs, but the value of the (intangible) creativity, technology, information and/or man-hours needed to produce a thing is irrelevant when considering whether or not that "thing" is (CISG) "goods." *et seq.* For an arguably contradictory line of reasoning by a Danish court *compare infra* note 74.

74 *Compare* (re. the application of the Lugano Convention, noted *supra* § 1.4) the decision of the Eastern High Court of Denmark, 7 March 2002, reported in *UfR* 2002.1370 ∅ (development of web-site characterized as "service," even though the contract's "characteristic obligation" was described as development of web-site software).

According to Article 4 the Convention regulates sales contract formation (in CISG Part II) and the rights and obligations of the parties to the sale (in Part III). Conversely, the CISG is generally "not concerned" with such subjects as sales contract validity or with the effect which the contract may have on the property in the goods sold.[75]

In most cases, questions of "validity" arise when national courts or arbitrators are asked to "police" (sales and other) agreements against unfairness by placing limits on their enforceability.[76] Since the CISG is generally not concerned with validity, most problems which fall under this heading – such as fraud, duress, mistake or the unreasonableness (unconscionability) of contract terms – must be resolved in accordance with domestic (non-CISG)[77] rules of law.[78]

There are, however, some exceptions, as indicated by the so-called "except clause" in CISG Article 4;[79] in other words, the Convention deals with a few "validity" matters. One such matter – the lack of formal requirements – is expressly dealt with in CISG Article 11.[80] Another such provision is Article 29 which provides that a CISG contract can be modified by mere "agreement"; for this reason, a CISG party's commitment to modify a contract – e.g., a seller's promise to accept a price lower than the price originally agreed – is valid and binding even in the absence of what American lawyers call "consideration."[81] Article 29 does not, however, (itself) resolve the more general question of whether a CISG contract not supported by consideration (or a consideration substitute) is valid and binding when the applicable PIL (choice of law) rules point to American law.[82]

---

[75]   Re. exceptions *see infra* with note 79 *et seq.* The words "in particular" should indicate that validity and property are not the only subjects not covered by the CISG: *see* Herber in Schlechtriem, *Commentary*, Art. 4 Rd.Nr. 19–24; Ferrari in Schlechtriem, *Kommentar*, Art. 4, Rd.Nr. 12, 32–41.

[76]   *Accord*, as regards American domestic law, Farnsworth, *Contracts*, Ch. 4.

[77]   *See* (e.g.) *infra* § 7.4.

[78]   The private international law (choice-of-law rules) of the forum court determines which State's domestic validity rules to apply. If a clause in a CISG contract is held invalid by virtue of these domestic rules, the CISG (and not domestic sales law) should be used to fill the gap.

[79]   I.e., the phrase ". . . except as otherwise expressly provided in this Convention. . . ."

[80]   *See infra* § 2.14.

[81]   I.e., even if such a promise might not be binding under the otherwise applicable domestic rules. *Compare* the seller's unilateral attempt to modify the agreement in *Chateau des Charmes Wines Ltd. v. Sabate USA, Sabate S.A.*, 5 May 2003 (9th Cir. 2003) discussed *infra* in § 3.8, text with note 93 *et seq.* For a German case arguably involving a modification agreement *see* LG Aachen, 14 May 1993, reported in UNILEX and analyzed by Witz, *Premières Applications*, nos. 21, 87.

[82]   One might, however, argue that "no consideration necessary" is a CISG "general principle," reflected in Articles 29 and 16(2)(a) and thus capable of "settling" the "matter" (whether CISG contracts are binding without consideration). Regarding the resolution of matters "governed-but-not-settled" by the application of CISG Article 7(2) *see* § 2.11 *infra*. For arguments and counter-arguments concering the larger consideration issue *see generally* Flechtner, *More U.S. Decisions*, at 166–69. *Compare* (as regards Articles 16 and 29) Schlechtriem, *Commentary*, Article 16, Rd.nr. 2; Article 29, Rd.nr. 2; *see also infra* § 3.10. For a case suggesting that the Convention does not settle the consideration matter (thus requiring resort to PIL and domestic validity rules) *see Geneva Pharmaceuticals Technology Corp. v. Barr Laboratories, Inc.*, U.S. District Court (New York), 10 May 2002; the *Geneva* case is discussed *infra* (see note 107 *et seq.* and accompanying text).

[Handwritten margin notes at top: "Many aspects of validity not covered, mutual mistake, negligent/fraudulent misrepresentation" and "CISG does not determine validity of "substantive" provisions"]

In most cases, the validity of the parties' contract (and its individual terms) cannot be resolved on the basis of the CISG, simply because the CISG was not designed to "police" sales agreements.[83] The CISG drafters made no attempt whatsoever to prescribe the legal effect of (e.g.) a mutual mistake as to the existence of the subject matter of the contract,[84] a seller's negligent or fraudulent misrepresentation as to the quality of the goods, a seller's threat of non-performance (economic duress), an unreasonable disclaimer or liability limitation, a "penalty" clause,[85] etc.

Suppose, for example, that a seller in Stockholm (Sweden) sells goods to a buyer in Boise (Idaho) on the basis of the seller's standard contract which purports to disclaim "all liability" in the event the goods do not conform. Since the CISG (default) starting point is full compensation for breach,[86] such a disclaimer – if measured by the Convention "yardstick" – might seem surprising and unreasonable; but since the validity of a liability disclaimer is a matter which lies outside the CISG scope, the question of whether the buyer is actually "bound" by the term must be resolved on the basis of domestic law.[87] Since the conflict-of-laws rules (private international law) applicable in this situation would probably point to Swedish domestic law (at least in a Swedish court),[88] the disclaimer would only be held effective (and displace the CISG remedies ordinarily available to the buyer) if it satisfies the "reasonableness" requirement set forth in the "General Clause" of the Swedish Contracts Act.[89]

Subsection (b) of Article 4 indicates another area where we sometimes need supplement the CISG with domestic law. Though a CISG seller is obligated to transfer the property in the goods to the buyer, as required by the contract and the Convention,[90] Article 4(b) shows the Convention is generally "not concerned" with the effect which the contract may have on the property in the goods sold. Therefore, the question (e.g.) of whether the buyer, acting in good faith, cuts off rights which creditors or other third parties might otherwise have in the goods is clearly not a CISG problem, but rather an issue to be decided under the

---

83 I.e., so as to preclude the enforcement of one-sided or otherwise unfair deals. The CISG remedial rules may, however, be relevant in assessing the reasonableness of agreed remedies, since the CISG gap-filling solution is recognized as a reasonable solution in the "average" case. *See generally infra* § 7.4.

84 *See* the decision of Handelsgericht St. Gallen (Switzerland), 24 August 1995 (UNILEX).

85 *See* the decision of Gerechtshof Arnhem (Netherlands), 24 August 1995 (UNILEX).

86 Re. the buyer's CISG remedies *see generally* Chapter 6B *infra.*

87 Though the CISG default solution may be relevant in this context (*see supra* note 83). Note also that an onerous contract term which contravenes *CISG* "fundamental principles" (*Grundwertungen*) might be denied effect for that reason alone, i.e. even if the term would be valid under domestic law. As to this possibility *see infra* § 7.4.

88 In this situation, Swedish courts would apply the 1955 Hague Convention to determine the law applicable to the validity question: *see supra* § 1.4. Regarding the more flexible (and to this extent less predictable) solutions of similar conflicts question in American courts, *see generally* Lookofsky and Hertz, *Transnational Litigation*, Ch. 3.3.

89 To be effective, such a clause must *also* pass the "incorporation" and "interpretation" tests (*see generally infra*, Ch. 7). For a comparison between Danish domestic validity rules and the (*lex mercatoria*) validity provisions of the UNIDRIOT Principles *see* Lookofsky, *Limits*.

90 Re. Article 30 *see infra* §§ 4.3 and 4.11.

otherwise applicable domestic law.[91] Similarly, the right of a seller to obtain restitution of goods sold under a reservation of title may well be restricted by local laws (*lex rei sitae*) protecting the rights of creditors.[92]

According to Article 5 the Convention does "not apply" to questions regarding the liability of the seller for death or personal injury caused by the goods. But this provision does not exclude all "product liability" issues from the Convention's scope; indeed, by clear implication (*argumentum e contrario*), Article 5 permits a CISG buyer to make a claim for compensation under the Convention regime in cases where the goods delivered do not conform and cause damage to the buyer's property.[93]

Illustration 2e:[94] Dentist (B) in CISG State X purchases a combined chair-and-drill unit from a supplier (S) in CISG State Y. Soon after delivery, a fire caused by defective wiring in the unit destroys the unit itself and also does damage to B's office. B brings an action (in X or Y) against S – not only to recover the purchase price of the unit, but also for consequential loss (damage to the office, loss of profit etc.).

Since this is a CISG "sale of goods" under the default rule in Article 1(1)(a), and since the goods delivered by the seller do not conform under Article 35,[95] B is likely to have a viable CISG (contractual) cause of action for damages, and the damages recoverably might well include compensation for the (foreseeable) losses in question.[96] In some domestic legal systems, however, a claim grounded in tort (*delict*) might co-exist (and thus "compete") with a contract-based claim;[97] in these jurisdictions a plaintiff seeking damages

---

[91]   *See* Herber in Schlechtriem, *Commentary*, Art. 4, Rd.Nr. 19.

[92]   Re. the difficult retention-of-title issues addressed by the German BGH in its decision of 15 February 1995 (the "key press machine case") *see* Schlechtriem, *Bundesgerichtshof* at 6 with note 40 and *compare* the decision of the Australian Federal Court, South District of Adelaide, 28 April 1995, 57 Fed. Ct. Reports (1995) (question of whether German seller validly retained title not governed by CISG). The Australian decision was later cited with approval in *Usinor Industeel v. Leeco Steel Products, Inc.*, U. S. District Court, N.D., Illinois, 28 March 2002. All these decisions are reported in CISGW3 andUNILEX. Re. restitution under Article 81(2) *see infra* § 6.25.

[93]   The decision of Handelsgericht Zürich, 26 April 1995 (UNILEX) is in *accord*. Nor would Article 5 seem to preclude an Article 74 indemnification claim by the buyer against the seller for sums payable to a third party (the buyer's buyer) who suffers personal injury as a result of defective goods: *see* OLG Düsseldorf, 2 July 1993, reported in UNILEX, and (approving that decision) Ferrari in Schlechtriem, *Kommentar*, Art. 5, Rd.Nr. 6–8; *but see* Witz, *Premières Applications*, no. 23, and Kritzer, *Manual*, Vol.2. Absent special agreement, however, a third party cannot assert a CISG-based (contract) claim against the (first) seller for losses due to a product defect: *see* Article 4 (CISG governs rights & obligations of seller & buyer).

[94]   Portions of the fact pattern in this illustration were inspired by an American case: *Lloyd F. Smith Co. v. Den-Tal-Ez*, 491 N.W. 2d 11 (Min. Sup. Ct. 1992).

[95]   *See infra* § 4.7.

[96]   *See* Article 74, discussed *infra* § 6.15.

[97]   This is, for example, the view in Denmark: *see* Andersen & Lookofsky, *Obligationsret*, Ch. 5.5.e. In France, however, the doctrine of *non-cumul* would seem to preclude a non-contractual theory of recovery. Regarding American law *see, e.g., Geneva Pharmaceuticals Technology Corp. v. Barr Laboratories, Inc., et al.*, U.S. District Court (New York), 10 May 2002, reported in UNLIEX and CISGW3 (in New Jersey, "purely" economic expectations protected by contract principles not entitled to supplemental protection by negligence

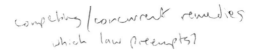

competing/concurrent remedies
which law preempts?

would be allowed to recover if he succeeds in proving the facts needed to support either claim.[98]

The possibility of concurrent – and thus potentially "competing" – remedies can also arise in other contexts. Assume, for example, that a CISG seller is guilty of a negligent or even fraudulent "misrepresentation" as to the quality of the goods and that – for that reason, under the otherwise applicable domestic law – the buyer would be entitled to rescind (i.e., declare invalid and terminate) the contract. In this situation the domestic rescission remedy might be seen to "overlap" with the CISG avoidance rules which allow the buyer to avoid ("cancel") in the case of a fundamental breach.[99] Similarly, a seller's delictual (tort) liability for the economic consequences of a negligent or fraudulent misrepresentation might – in some places and situations – also overlap with the Convention damages regime,[100] thus raising a question of Convention interpretation: should the applicable CISG remedy be held to displace – i.e., preëmpt – the otherwise applicable domestic remedy? Or should the domestic rule be allowed to compete with – i.e., serve concurrently, "side by side" – with the CISG rule?

There is no simple solution to this complex conundrum.[101] In some situations, courts and arbitrators will have good reason to exercise restraint before they permit domestic rules to compete with the uniform remedial solution provided by the CISG.[102] But the command in Article 7 – to have "regard" to the need to promote uniform Convention interpretation – does not force us to conclude that domestic remedies are preëmpted ("trumped") whenever the "operative facts" of a given case seem "covered" by a CISG remedial rule.[103] On the

---

    principles; judge-made exceptions for intentional fraudulent conduct, but rule still holds for negligence actions). *Compare* (as re. tortuous interference) *Viva Vino Import Corp. v. Farnese Vini S.r.l.*, U.S. District Court (E.D. Pa.), 29 August 2000 (in UNILEX): "The CISG does not apply to tort claims. Consequently, it is inapplicable to plaintiff's claim of tortious interference with business relations."

[98]   The situation is, however, different in an international context if the CISG (contract) rules are interpreted as precluding a plaintiff (like B in *Illustration 2e*) from asserting an alternative tort claim under domestic law. *See* discussion *infra* with note 108 and § 4.6.

[99]   Under American domestic law, avoidance might be allowed for a fraudulent misrepresentation without concern for its materiality (Farnsworth, *Contracts*, §§ 4.10 to 4.15), whereas under CISG Article 49(1)(a) a fundamental breach is the *condicio sine qua non* for avoidance (*see* Huber in Schlechtriem, *Commentary* at 416 and in Schlechtriem, *Kommentar* at 535).

[100] For a discussion of this question *see infra* § 4.6.

[101] *See generally* Lookofsky, *In Dubio Pro Conventione*.

[102] Since, for example, the exemption "safety valve" in Article 79(1) provides a flexible tool for reaching fair solutions in cases of *force majeure*-type "impediments" to performance, including certain situations which might (also) be subsumed under domestic headings of "impossibility" or "mistake," the argument for preëmption of domestic remedies in *force majeure* situations seems strong: *see* the decision of Corte di Appello di Milano (Italy), 11 December 1998, reported in UNILEX. But since Article 79 was hardly designed to cover *hardship*, courts and arbitrators should apply applicable *domestic* law (*accord* Southerington: <http://www.cisg.law.pace.edu/cisg/biblio/southerington.html>); since the *hardship* "rules" set forth in Ch. 6(2) of the UNIDROIT Principles do *not* "restate" generally applicable principles of international commercial law (*see* Lookofsky, *Limits*, pp. 500–501), Ch. 6(2) ought *not* be applied as a general/uniform "supplement" to the CISG.

[103] *But see* Schlechtriem *Borderland*, and Gillette & Walt, *Sales Law* (rev. ed. 2002) at 49 (concurring with Honnold) and *compare* Huber in Schlechtriem, *Commentary* at 370, also in Schlechtriem, *Kommentar*

contrary, a given State's accession to the Convention indicates its willingness to substitute its domestic sales law (as such) with the CISG; it does not necessarily indicate that State's intent to "merge" CISG (contract) law with domestic tort and/or validity-related regimes.[104] In one application of this important distinction, a U.S. Federal Court held that the provisions of the Illinois Beer Industry Fair Dealing Act (IBIFDA) – which limit the right of (e.g.) Polish brewers to terminate contracts with their American buyers (wholesalers)[105] – were *not* preëmpted (trumped) by the arguably "conflicting" (avoidance) provisions of the CISG.[106]

Other aspects of the preëmption conundrum were confronted by a U.S. District Court in *Geneva Pharmaceuticals,*[107] a case brought against the Canadian manufacturer (S) of a chemical ingredient used in the production of an anticoagulant (blood-thinning) medication. S supplied the American plaintiff (B) with samples of the ingredient and confirmed it would support B's application for approval by the Food and Drug Administration (FDA) as the supplier of the ingredient for the manufacture of the drug; S also issued a letter to the FDA confirming it would serve as supplier to B. Two years later, after B received FDA approval, S (having incurred conflicting commitments to third parties) refused to honor a

---

at 476 (rejecting rule-concurrence in the absence of three "preconditions") and the decision of LG Aachen (Germany), 14 May 1993, reported in UNILEX (application of CISG precluded recourse to domestic law regarding mistake as to the quality of the goods). Some commentators have argued that CISG *avoidance* rules displace (some) domestic rules permitting a "mistaken" buyer to rescind: *compare supra* note 99 and – for a comparison of the widely diverging views on this point – Hartnell, *Rousing the Sleeping Dog*, 72–78; *see also e.g.,* Schlechtriem, *Experience.* Regarding "hardship" and Article 79 *see* preceding note.

[104] Nor does the CISG legislative history indicate that the CISG drafters harbored "preëmptive" intent. As regards actions in respect of non-conforming goods, the CISG drafters themselves rejected a proposal to limit recourse to competing rules of domestic law. The ULIS Convention of 1964, which preceded the CISG, expressly excluded the buyer's right of recourse to domestic law in the case of non-conforming goods (ULIS Article 34), except in cases of fraud (ULIS Article 89), whereas the Vienna drafters – hoping it would be possible to create a separate, internationally uniform set of validity rules – intentionally refrained from including a similar provision in the CISG: *compare* Huber in Schlechtriem, *Commentary,* Art. 45, Rd.Nr. 46–48 with n. 86, also in Schlechtriem, *Kommentar,* Art. 45, Rd.Nr. 46–48 with n. 106.

[105] These restrictions are deemed incorporated into *every agreement* between an Illinois wholesaler and a brewer. 815 ILCS 720/2(b). Section 3 of the IBIFDA, for example, restricts a brewer from canceling or failing to renew an agreement without proper notice, which the Act defines as a notice of cancellation in writing, sent by certified mail and containing, *inter alia,* "a complete statement of the reasons therefore, including all data and documentation necessary to fully apprise the wholesaler of the reasons for the action."

[106] *See Stawski Distributing Co., Inc. v. Zywiec Breweries PLC,* U.S. District Court (N.D. Illinois), 6 October 2003, 2003 WL 22290412 (N.D.Ill.), also in CISGW3, holding that the CISG is to be given same weight as any other Federal statute in a case implicating issues regulated by State law in accordance with the Twenty-first Amendment to the U.S. Constitution. As an alternative and/or supportive *ratio* for the District Court's holding on this particular (CISG) point, one might argue that the IBIFDA constitutes a "validity"-related regime (designed to protect wholesalers with arguably inferior bargaining power) containing rules which, pursuant to Article 4 (*supra* § 2.6), lie outside the CISG's scope, and this logic hardly seems impaired by the Court of Appeal's decision in *Stawski,* 349 F.3d 1023 (7th Cir. 2003), reversing the District Court's order which had granted Stawski's motion to stay arbitration (*see* 2003 WL 21209860 & 22595266).

[107] *Geneva Pharmaceuticals Technology Corp. v. Barr Laboratories, Inc., et al.,* U.S. District Court (New York), 10 May 2002, reconsideration denied by the same court on 21 August 2002, both decisions reported in UNLIEX and CISGW3.

purchase order submitted by B. In considering B's various CISG and domestic law claims against S, the *Geneva* Court distinguished between intentional and negligent torts and held that (only) B's "business tort" claims (for tortuous interference with contract and business relations) were *not preempted* by the CISG.[108] Then, applying somewhat similar reasoning to resolve a related, equally complex problem, the *Geneva* court held that B should also be allowed to assert the (American) doctrine of promissory estoppel to support its "equitable" claim that the CISG sales contract in question – even if not supported by "consideration"[109] – was nonetheless valid and binding under the applicable domestic (New Jersey) law.[110]

The problems created by the juxtaposition of the contractual (CISG) and non-contractual (domestic) law will be reconsidered in a subsequent section.[111]

§ 2.7 CONTRACTUAL FREEDOM UNDER ARTICLE 6

The CISG is a "default" sales law regime.[112] As under Article 2 of the UCC (and other domestic sales laws), contractual freedom is also the international rule, and so CISG Article 6 provides direct authority for "contracting out" of the CISG – in whole or in part.

If, for example, a seller in Finland sells goods (mobile phones) to a buyer in California, the starting point for that contract is the CISG, so issues arising with respect to non-conformity will be regulated by the default rule in Article 35.[113] But if the seller's standard

---

108 In this connection the *Geneva* Court (*id.*) noted that under domestic (New Jersey) law economic expectations protected by contract principles are generally not entitled to supplemental protection by negligence principles, i.e., even when the application of such principles is not preempted by the Convention; in a related statement (*id.*, note 30), the *Geneva* Court opined that "a tort claim which is actually a contract claim, or that bridges the gap between contract and tort law," might be preempted by the CISG.

109 Regarding consideration in the Article 29 (contract modification) context *see supra*, note 81 and accompanying text; *see also infra* § 3.10.

110 I.e., as in the case of the business tort claim (*supra* note 108), B's "equitable" claim was held *not preempted* by the CISG (*see* part VI.B of the court's opinion), though the court described this preemption issue as "a closer question" (*id.*), noting that a party to a CISG contract would *not* be allowed to employ (U.S. domestic) promissory estoppel doctrine to deny the existence of a CISG "firm offer" (though Article 16(2)(b) does not match the UCC rule: *see infra*, § 3.6). Although the *Geneva* court first deals with consideration and its "substitutes" under the general heading of *validity* (outside the Convention under Article 4: *see* part IV.A.3.b of the opinion), it then proceeds to treat the plaintiff's promissory estoppel (detrimental reliance) claim as if it were an equitable cause of action separate from breach of contract (part VI.D of the opinion) – this notwithstanding the fact that promissory estoppel provides an alternative to "consideration," i.e., a sufficient reason for enforcing a promise under American law. While Article 29 makes clear that consideration is not required for modifications to a CISG contract for sale (*see* preceding note), that leaves open the question of whether an unmodified CISG contract (or the original of a modified contract) requires consideration (or a consideration substitute) if U.S. law is applicable under PIL rules, and the Geneva court's affirmative, but essentially undocumented answer ought not preclude further consideration of the question. For arguments and counter-arguments *see* Harry Flechtner, *More U.S. Decisions*, at 166–69. Professor Lookofsky extends his thanks to Professor Flechtner for reviewing a previous draft of this note and for helping shed light on the difficult consideration-related issues in *Geneva*.

111 *See infra* § 4.6.

112 *See supra* § 1.1 with note 10.

113 Unless the parties otherwise agree. *See generally infra* Ch. 4B.

Adopting domestic law of a certain Contracting Country =
Contracting under CISG

terms set forth remedies for breach, and if these remedies become an enforceable part of the contract, they displace the remedies set forth in the CISG. (Since "validity" questions remain outside the CISG scope,[114] the validity of "agreed remedies" must be determined by domestic law rules.[115])

As regards the parties' power to exclude Convention application entirely, we might consider a different example: Suppose a seller in New York and a buyer in Russia agree that their sales contract shall be governed by the "Swedish Sale of Goods Act of 1990." This term can only be interpreted to mean that Swedish domestic sales law should displace the CISG (entirely), i.e., even though American and Russian courts otherwise (without the clause) would have applied the Convention, simply because the parties reside in different Contracting States.[116]

On the other hand, numerous CISG precedents confirm that an express contractual choice of (e.g.) "Austrian law,"[117] "the laws of Switzerland,"[118] "the laws of the Province of Ontario, Canada,"[119] or "the law of the seller's country [e.g. Russia]"[120] should be understood/interpreted – not as a reference to domestic sales law, but rather – as the parties' reaffirmation of the applicability of the CISG (the rule-set which would apply without the choice-of-law clause).[121] In this connection it is significant that Article 6 represents

---

[114] *See supra* § 2.6.

[115] This subject is considered in Chapter 7 *infra*.

[116] Re. Article 1(1)(a) *see supra* § 2.3. Just as we should use Article 8 to interpret the choice-of-law clause (and thus whether it takes the contract out of the CISG) the formation rules in CISG Part II should be applied to determine whether the parties have concluded (formed) an agreement to contract out (*see* Bailey, *Facing the Truth* at 303), since the CISG applies by virtue of Article 1(1)(a) by default and without resort to PIL rules (*see supra* § 2.3). *Compare* (as re. situations where the parties expressly agree that CISG contract conclusion/ formation is to be determined by domestic law) Huber in Schlechtriem, *Commentary* at 56–57, and Ferrari in Schlechtriem, *Kommentar* at 118.

[117] *See* ICC Case 7660/JK of 23 August 1994, reported in UNILEX. *See also* ICC Case 6653/1993, reported in UNILEX (reference to "French law" in a sales contract between Turkish seller and Syrian buyer included CISG). *Accord* U.S. District Court, S.D., New York, 26 March 2002 (*St. Paul Guardian Insurance Co., et al. v. Neuromed Medical Systems & Support, et al.*), citing German authority in support of its holding that a choice of "German law" includes a reference to the CISG.

[118] *See* ICC Case 7565/1994, reported in UNILEX. *See also* Oberlandesgericht Frankfurt, decision of 30 August 2000, also reported in UNILEX (invoice stated "all transactions and sales are subject to Swiss law"; clause did not exclude application of CISG, since it did not refer to relevant provisions of Swiss *domestic* law).

[119] *Ajax Tool Works, Inc. v. Can-Eng Manufacturing Ltd*, U.S. District Court, Northern District of Illinois, Eastern Division, 29 January 2003, in CISGW3 and UNILEX.

[120] *See* International Court of Commercial Arbitration, Chamber of Commerce & Industry of the Russian Federation, decision of 24 January 2000, reported and translated in CISGW3.

[121] *Accord* Schlechtriem, *Bundesgerichtshof* at p. 2 with note 13. *See also supra* § 2.3. Nearly all reported CISG decisions support this view. *See, e.g.,* the decision of LG Düsseldorf (Germany), 11 October 1995, reported in UNILEX, applying the CISG on the basis of Art. 1(1)(a), though seller's standard terms provided for application of "German law" (express choice of German law could *not* in itself amount to implied exclusion of CISG, because CISG *is* "German law"). *See also Asante Technologies, Inc. v. PMC-Sierra, Inc.*, 164 F.Supp.2d 1142 (N.D. California 2001), CISW3 & UNILEX, and OLG Koblenz (Germany), decision of 17 September 1993, CLOUT Case 281 (parties' choice of "French law" and Art. 1(1)(b) led to CISG). In situations like these, where the *starting point* is that the CISG applies by virtue of Article 1(1)(a)-(b), the

in non Contracting countries, parties
can choose to contract under CISG

an exception to the rule in Article 1(1). Since Article 1 determines when the Convention applies *by default*, courts and arbitrators should presume CISG application as their point of departure whenever the Article 1(1) rule would lead to Convention application; a party who seeks to rebut this presumption should be required to present clear evidence of both parties' intent to contract out.[122]

In those cases where the Convention would not ordinarily apply by default,[123] the parties have the ability to contract into the CISG regime.[124] They have this power (not by virtue of Article 6,[125] but rather) because freedom of contract is the generally applicable rule, even in jurisdictions not bound by the CISG rules.[126] This freedom can be exercised in one of two ways. First, the contract can designate the law of a CISG State as the law applicable to the contract (*lex contractus*).

> *Illustration 2f*: Seller in Japan contracts to supply steel bars to buyer in England. According to the terms of the sales contract "this agreement shall be governed by the law of Switzerland" and "any disputes arising shall be submitted to ICC arbitration."

This is (as of 2003) not a sales contract between parties in CISG Contracting States.[127] However, since the arbitrators would almost surely consider themselves bound by the parties' express choice of Swiss law, and since the CISG has been an integral part of Swiss law since 1991, the parties should be held to have indirectly "contracted in" to the Convention regime.[128]

---

interpretation of "statements" (clauses) like "German law" or "French law" should be governed by Article 8 (discussed *infra* § 2.12), so the intention of the party who "made" the statement (drafted the clause) should not lead to domestic law, unless that interpretation was shared by the other party or a reasonable person in his or her shoes would so understand the statement: *see also* § 2.12 *infra* and (re. the interpretation of such clauses under ULIS) Schlechtriem, *Experience*, p. 7. Supplementing Article 8(2) with the *contra proferentem* principle (UNIDROIT Principles Art. 4.6) will lead to similar results; *compare* Junge in Schlechtriem, *Commentary* pp. 72–73 (*Kommentar*, p. 144).

[122] The decision by the U.S. District Court in *Asante* (preceding note) is in *accord* (under general California law, CISG is applicable to contracts where contracting parties are from different CISG States; given absence of *clear* language indicating that *both* contracting parties intended to opt out, Convention was held to apply). Re. the applicability of Article 8 in such a situation *see supra* note 116.

[123] Either because Article 1 does not lead to CISG application (*supra* §§ 2.2, 2.3, 2.4) or because the Convention does not automatically apply to that kind of sale (*supra* § 2.5).

[124] Such choice should also be possible after contract formation and even after an action has been brought in court; *see* OLG Düsseldorf, 8 January 1993, and OLG Köln, 22 February 1994, both cases reported in UNILEX.

[125] Since one must be "within" the Convention by virtue of the default rules in Article 1(1)(a)-(b) before Article 6 can apply.

[126] In certain fora the freedom to "contract in" might be restricted by a mandatory substantive rule made applicable by virtue of the applicable private international law rule. Re. (e.g.) the application of Articles 3 and 7 of the EU/Rome Convention on the Applicable Law to Contractual Obligations *see* Lookofsky and Hertz, *Transnational Litigation*, Ch. 3.2.1.

[127] *See* Appendix I *infra*.

[128] At least in the absence of clear evidence of contrary mutual intent. Regarding the law applicable in international commercial arbitration *see generally* Lookofsky & Hertz, *Transnational Litigation*, Ch. 6. The *Mitsubishi* case, decided by the U.S. Supreme Court in 1985 and famous for its holding on the arbitrability of an antitrust claim, involved an international commercial contract containing arbitration and choice-of-law clauses much like those in *Illustration* 2f: *see* Lookofsky & Hertz, *id.*, Ch. 6.3.1.

The parties to an international sales contract also enjoy the freedom to draft a clause which affirmativly states "this contract is governed by the CISG." The parties can also select in advance a set of domestic law rules as a supplement to the Convention rules; properly drafted,[129] such a clause can help reduce the uncertainty sometimes associated with the application of conflict-of-laws (private international law) rules.

Contract draftsmen should also note that there are six equally authentic versions of the CISG: the Arabic, Chinese, English, French, Russian and Spanish texts.[130] Unfortunately, the "plain meaning" of these authentic texts is not always exactly the same.[131] Just as parties can save time and money by including a contract term which designates the English language version of the Convention as the text applicable to their contract, parties who include an arbitration clause should also designate the language of dispute resolution.[132]

2B GENERAL PROVISIONS

§ 2.8 INTERPRETATION OF THE CISG TREATY TEXT

Article 7(1) deals with interpretation of the CISG treaty itself. When a dispute arises as to the meaning or application of a given Convention rule, the wording of the treaty – sometimes described as a "contract among nations" – is the most natural place to start. In many cases, however, no single "plain meaning" can be gleaned from the Convention text.[133]

For this reason courts and arbitrators often have good reason to consult secondary sources of CISG law.[134] Since the Convention is the creation of an international "legislator," we might, for example, look to the CISG "legislative history" (*travaux préparatoires*) for evidence of the legislator's intent.[135] Unfortunately, but not surprisingly, the (voluminous)[136]

---

[129] For example: "This contract shall be interpreted in accordance with and governed by the 1980 Convention on Contracts for the International Sale of Goods (CISG). Any and all disputes relating to, or arising in connection with, the contract which cannot be resolved in accordance with the contract or the CISG shall be resolved in accordance with the domestic law of State [X]."

[130] Article 101.

[131] For an example *see infra* § 3.6 with note 52.

[132] For example: "The language of the arbitration proceedings shall be English." *See generally* Lookofsky & Hertz, *Transnational Litigation*, Ch. 6.2.

[133] *See* Article 31 of the 1969 Vienna Convention on the Law of Treaties. Re. the 6 equally authentic versions of the treaty text *see supra* with note 130. Re. the arguably "plain meaning" of Article 55 *see infra* § 4.13 with note 195.

[134] *See* Article 32 of the 1969 Vienna Convention on the Law of Treaties.

[135] Professor Honnold has performed a helpful task by organizing the most relevant documents in his *Documentary History*. For examples of decisions which cite the Convention's legislative history (*travaux*) *see* the German case involving New Zealand mussels: OLG Frankfurt, 20 April 1994, and BGH, 8 March 1995, both decisions reported in UNILEX.

[136] Many commentators trace the CISG "history" back to the first uniform sales laws, ULIS and ULF (*supra* § 1.2), but those treaties were found unacceptable by most States who later became CISG States, and the application of ULIS/ULF interpretations and precedents will not always advance the goal of a uniform (autonomous) interpretation of the CISG; *but compare* Mann in 99 *L.Q. Rev.* 383 (1983). For examples of the use of ULIS as a CISG interpretative tool *see supra* § 2.5 note 65, § 2.6 note 104 and *infra* § 2.9 note 144.

legislative history is seldom conclusive:[137] we could hardly expect the proposals, counter-proposals and comments made by the many scores of national delegates during years of drafting and re-drafting to provide simple solutions to complex questions of Convention interpretation.[138] And while the *Secretariat Commentary* to the 1978 Draft CISG Convention[139] is, in some respects, a helpful tool, it does not provide binding authority as to what the (real) 1980 Convention means.[140]

§ 2.9 INTERNATIONAL INTERPRETATION; CLOUT, CISGW3 & UNILEX

CISG Article 7(1) provides: "In the interpretation of this [CISG] Convention, regard is to be had to its international character and to the need to promote uniformity in its application . . ." This amounts to a (public international law) command to all Contracting States and their courts: you *shall* "have regard" to the character of the treaty; you *shall* undertake an independent, essentially non-national (autonomous) interpretation. Although non-CISG sources may sometimes provide useful information,[141] domestic conceptions should not be permitted to subvert a uniform application of the CISG rules.[142] In the real CISG world, however, national courts sometimes slip into a parochial kind of interpretation, especially when the relevant Convention terminology is reminiscent of their own local law.[143] Worse yet, national courts sometimes overlook the new legislative message entirely, failing to recognize that the previously applicable local law has been replaced by a different CISG rule.[144]

---

[137] *Compare*, for example, the U.S. Supreme Court's interpretation of the Hague Service Convention in *Volkswagenwerk A.G. v. Schlunk*, 486 U.S. 694 (1988), where the majority and minority of the Court each found excerpts from the same legislative history to support their own results. *See also* Ferrari, *Uniform Interpretation* at 206–08.

[138] As regards the use of his *Documentary History* as an interpretative aid, even Professor Honnold (*Uniform Law* at 463) urges restraint: "Interpretation based on discussions by a large legislative body is more meaningful for decisions of broad issues of policy than for detailed applications."

[139] Document A/CONF.97/5, reprinted in Honnold, *Documentary History* at 404.

[140] An American proposal to draft an official Commentary to the 1980 Convention was rejected (*see* Winship, *Scope* at 1–27). The subsequent proposal by Bailey (*Facing the Truth* at 300) that the US adopt the (unofficial) Draft Convention Commentary as the "official American" CISG commentary seems highly ill-advised.

[141] Re. (e.g.) the "sale of goods" concept *see supra* § 2.5 with note 40. *Compare* the "common core" method employed by the Court of Justice to interpret the Brussels Convention: *see* re. Art. 5(3) Case 21/76 [1976] ECR 1735 (Handelskwekerij G.J. Bier B.V. v. Mines de Potasse D'Alsace S.A.). Emphasizing the flexible nature of the "regard is to be had" command in Article 7(1), Professor Flechtner (*Pitfalls*) has suggested the possibility of a *regional* CISG interpretation as a step towards increased uniformity: an essentially uniform interpretation of the CISG treaty within the NAFTA and/or European Union areas might represent a "critical first step in transcending familiar but parochial approaches . . . the initial stage [of courts] becoming accustomed to adopting an international perspective . . ." (*id.*).

[142] For instance, interpretation of the concept of "impediments" in Article 79 ought not be guided exclusively by (sometimes too narrow) notions of Anglo-American law. Re. Article 79 *see generally infra* §§ 6.19 and 6.32.

[143] For example, the "foreseeability" rule in Article 74 is clearly reminiscent of domestic analogues: *see generally infra* § 6.15.

[144] Witz, *Premières Applications*, no. 62 and Magnus in Staudinger, *Kommentar*, Art. 39, Rd.Nr. 36–41 fault the German judges for their seeming failure to recognize that the CISG Article 39 rule (*infra* § 4.9) is *not the*

When called upon to interpret domestic law, a given national court is likely to be bound – or at least influenced – by decisions previously rendered by the courts of that State. When it comes to application of the Convention, however, national courts cannot rely solely on local precedents: regard must also "be had" to the (emerging) international view. Recognizing the formidable problems connected with access to foreign case law, UNCITRAL took an important first step in 1993, establishing the CLOUT system for the collection and dissemination of court decisions and arbitral awards relating to the CISG (and other UNCITRAL texts).[145] Under this system, national correspondents collect and prepare abstracts of available court decisions and arbitral awards which are then published by the UNCITRAL Secretariat in English and the other official U.N. languages.[146]

The CLOUT system, though important, does not provide all the information CISG decision-makers need.[147] Considering the substantial number of CISG Contracting States,[148] and the very large number of CISG decisions already rendered by courts and arbitral tribunals all over the world,[149] we are now fortunate to have much more comprehensive access to CISG decisions worldwide. One prominent example is the CISGW3 website <http://cisgw3.pace.edu>. Developed and maintained by the Pace Institute of International Commercial Law in New York, CISGW3 makes a wealth of CISG information, including English translations of many foreign-language cases, easily available.[150] The UNILEX data base, developed and maintained by the Centre for Comparative and Foreign Law Studies in Rome, is another very convenient and useful CISG source.[151]

One significant barrier which still stands in the way of uniform interpretation is the hard fact that the CISG decisions rendered by the highest national courts cannot be appealed.[152] In other words, no international court has been placed at the top the CISG "pyramid"; no single court has authority to iron out differences in opinion among the many national

---

same as its "predecessor" in ULIS (*supra* § 1.2). Another example is the *Beijing Metals* case (*infra* § 4.5 with notes 49 & 55) which ignores the effect of Article 8 in relation to parol evidence. And then there are the not-so-few cases where neither the court nor the parties' lawyers even knew that the CISG applied (*see* Flechtner, *Pitfalls* re. *GPL Treatment, Ltd. v. Louisiana-Pacific Corp.*, decided by the Oregon Court of Appeals in 1996).

[145] CLOUT stands for Case Law on UNCITRAL Texts. In addition to CISG cases, the system reports on cases decided under statutes based on UNCITRAL model legislation such as the Model Law of International Commercial Arbitration (adopted in 1985).

[146] The decisions and awards themselves are also made available (in the language of origin) by the Secretariat.

[147] Not all CISG decisions are reported in CLOUT; moreover, the length and quality of the CLOUT case-reports (based on abstracts prepared by national reporters and then edited by UNCITRAL) varies considerably from case to case.

[148] *See infra*, Appendix I.

[149] As of this writing (2003) more than 1,000 CISG decisions have been reported. The total number of CISG cases is, however, much larger, in part because most arbitral awards are not reported, in part because many jurisdictions report only a fraction of cases decided by their courts.

[150] The list of local CISG websites includes the University of Freiburg, Germany site (http://www.jura. unifreiburg.de/ipri/cisg) and the University of Tromsø, Norway site (http://www.itl.irv.uit. no/trade_law).

[151] The UNILEX data base is available on-line at <www.unilex.info>.

[152] CISG decisions rendered by arbitral tribunals (in the form of awards) cannot be appealed either. Depending on the *lex arbitri* of the jurisdiction concerned, however, arbitral awards sometimes can be "set aside" (invalidated). *See generally* Lookofsky & Hertz, *Transnational Litigation*, Ch. 6.

instances below.[153] A related obstacle is the absence of any established system or scale which a given national court (or arbitrator) might use to evaluate the "weight" (precedential value) to be attributed to foreign precedents on point.[154] For these reasons, the national courts in the various Contracting States resemble (and sometimes act like) "members of an orchestra without a conductor";[155] and though we find many good examples of harmonious interpretation,[156] the numerous CISG musicians do not always play the same tune.[157] Indeed, differences in language and other domestic idiosyncracies may make it difficult for outsiders to even "hear" the message sounded by foreign precedent.[158]

All this is not intended to suggest that problems of interpretation are insurmountable (or that international merchants should opt out of the CISG),[159] but it does serve to remind us that the law of international commerce is still at a relatively early stage of development. The interpretation and application of CISG case law cannot be regarded as an exact (mathematical) science,[160] especially since foreign CISG "precedents" interpreting the Convention can *at most* provide a given court or arbitral tribunal with *persuasive* (as opposed to binding) authority as regards the particular rule or issue concerned.[161]

To be sure, the forthcoming UNCITRAL *Case Digests* will help "organize" the increasingly voluminous CISG case law (reported in the CLOUT system and elsewhere), thus helping make it more useful to practitioners. But since the narrow mandate which UNCITRAL has given the Digest authors permits neither "critique" of the cases nor citation of scholarly commentary,[162] the Digests will hardly provide decision-makers and practitioners with all the CISG information they need. This particular Digest-limitation ought not, however, suggest the need for a UNCITRAL panel of academics to iron out judicial differences and/or replace healthy academic debate with a "politically correct" (UNCITRAL) point of view.[163]

---

153 Contrast the authority granted to the European Court to answer questions submitted by the courts of EU Member States re. the proper interpretation of EU legislation.

154 For a full discussion of this problem – and a proposed method for determining the precedential authority of foreign decisions – *see* Flechtner, *Attorneys Fees & Foreign Case Law*. In any case, a given foreign CISG "precedent" can *at most* be said to constitute *persuasive* (as opposed to binding) authority; for a fuller discussion *see generally* Lookofsky, *CISG Foreign Case Law*.

155 Schlechtriem, *Bundesgerichtshof* at 2.

156 For an example of uniform interpretation under Article 6 *see supra* § 2.7 (given the parties' choice of the law of (CISG) "State X," nearly all courts and arbitrators have required clear evidence of the parties' mutual intent to "contract out" of the CISG).

157 Re. the varied interpretations of the notice provisions in Articles 39–39 *see infra* § 4.9.

158 Relying on debatable foreign "precedent" regarding the interpretation of the "full compensation" principle expressed in Article 74, a U.S. District Court awarded attorneys' fees to the prevailing party, but the decision was subseqently overturned on appeal: *see infra* § 6.15, text with note 181 *et seq.*

159 *Accord* Erauw & Flechtner, *Remedies* at 74.

160 *Accord* Lookofsky, *Loose Ends*.

161 Regarding the (Article 7) issue of "how much regard" courts in a given CISG jurisdiction should have to foreign CISG precedent *see generally* Lookofsky, *CISG Foreign Case Law*.

162 *See id.* (particularly note 29 and accompanying text).

163 *See generally* Lookofsky at *id.* Also noteworthy in this context is the *CISG Advisory Council* (CISG-AC), a *private* initiative which also aims at promoting a uniform interpretation of the CISG. The AC's members do not represent countries or legal cultures; rather they are scholars who profess to look beyond the "cooking

§ 2.10   GOOD FAITH

In the interpretation of the CISG treaty itself,[164] "regard is to be had" (*inter alia*) to the observance of good faith in international trade. This rule of interpretation was designed to allay some Convention drafters' fears that a rule which required good-faith conduct might lead to "uncertainty."[165] But though the letter of Article 7(1) falls short of domestic analogues which obligate contracting parties to act in good faith,[166] CISG case law is diminishing the distinction. Significantly, good faith under Article 7(1) has been linked to the pervasive Convention standard of "reasonableness"[167] – a CISG general principle capable of meeting a multitude of "good faith" needs.[168] In a related development, the good-faith rule in Article 7(1) has been cited in support of a decision which declares estoppel[169] to be a general Convention principle as well.[170] On this basis, the deduction of a CISG general principle requiring the parties to act in good-faith seems like a logical step,[171] even if that might seem to contradict the Convention's legislative history (*travaux préparatoires*).[172] Significantly, the UNIDROIT Principles of International Commercial Contracts reaffirm the existence of a broad (*lex mercatoria*) obligation to act good faith, and this UNIDRIOT standard can serve not only to supplement the Convention but also to encourage the discernment and further development of a corresponding principle under Article 7(2).[173]

§ 2.11   MATTERS GOVERNED BUT NOT SETTLED BY THE CISG

Article 7(2) is a significant, albeit elusive rule which provides a tool for plugging certain "gaps" in the CISG text. Using this tool, courts and arbitrators can sometimes adhere to

---

pot" for ideas, in search of a more "profound" understanding of CISG issues. Unlike the UNCITRAL Case Digesters (*compare* preceding note), the AC-group is afforded the luxury of being critical of judicial or arbitral decision and of addressing issues not dealt with previously by adjudicating bodies. The primary purpose of the CISG-AC is to issue opinions relating to the interpretation and application of the Convention, on request or on its own initiative. *See generally* <http://cisgw3.law.pace.edu/cisg/CISG-AC.html>. The CISG-AC issued its first opinion in 2003: *see infra* § 3.11, notes 131–32 and accompanying text.

[164]   Article 7(1). Re. the interpretation of CISG contracts – (i.e.) the "statements" of the parties – *see* Article 8, discussed *infra* in § 2.12.

[165]   *See* Honnold, *Uniform Law* at 99. *Compare* the *obligation* set forth in UCC § 1–203.

[166]   *See also infra* note 173.

[167]   *See* Schlechtriem, *Uniform Law* at 39, Audit, *Vente internationale* no. 55, and Honnold, *id.* at 101 noting a similar linkage in UCC § 2-103(1)(b).

[168]   Re. general principles under Article 7(2) *see infra* § 2.11.

[169]   I.e., the principle that no one may set himself in contradiction to his own previous conduct (*non concedit venire contra factum proprium*).

[170]   *See* arbitral award no. SCH-4318, decided on 15 June 1994 by Internationales Schiedsgericht der Bundeskammer der gewerblichen Wirtschaft Wien, reported in UNILEX, discussed *infra* in § 2.11; *accord* Ferrari in Schlechtriem, *Kommentar*, Art. 7, Rd.Nr. 50. *See also* <http://tldb.uni-koeln.de/TLDB.html> characterizing estoppel as *lex mercatoria*.

[171]   *But compare* Honnold, *Uniform Law* at 99. *See also* Kritzer, *Manual*, Suppl. 7 at 82 (Detailed Analysis of Article 7(1), with references to Bonell, Sevón, Ziegel and others).

[172]   *See* Honnold *id.*.

[173]   *UNIDROIT Principles* Article 1.7. As regards the use of the UNIDROIT Principles as a *supplement* to the CISG *see* <www.unilex.info> and Bonell, *Restatement*, Ch. 4.3(b).

the treaty regime as the "exclusive" source of applicable law, as opposed to the alternative of reverting to supplementary domestic rules. If, in a given case – and according to the Article 7(2) procedure described below – an (unwritten) CISG general principle is discerned and deemed capable of filling a gap in the Convention text, this principle may obviate the need to find and apply a corresponding, potentially "competing" domestic rule.[174] Among the numerous (unwritten) CISG general principles which have already been discerned and accepted by many CISG courts and commentators are the principles of good faith,[175] reasonableness,[176] and estoppel (*venire contra factum proprium*).[177]

Before we consider the application of these and other CISG general principles, it should be emphasized that paragraph (2) of Article 7 affects only matters which are "governed" by the Convention but not expressly "settled" in it. In other words, Article 7(2) has no application with respect to the very large group of CISG matters which are both governed by and expressly settled by the rules in the Convention text: as regards these matters, we simply rely on the rules laid down in the treaty text.[178]

Moving to the other extreme, we note that matters not governed by the Convention can only be settled by resorting to non-Convention rules and principles.[179] For example, since the Convention is generally "not concerned" with matters relating to the validity of the sales contract or obligations grounded in delict,[180] such matters can hardly be settled by CISG general principles. There may also be a grey area between matters that are governed by the Convention and those that are not.[181] For example, since CISG Article 38 does not specify the way in which goods delivered should be inspected (or how a given non-conformity should be "certified"), an Argentinian court has held that domestic law should be applied to settle this particular matter.[182] To take a different – and perhaps more persuasive – example, an arbitral tribunal might decide that the three sentences in Article 8 were not designed to regulate each and every aspect of the contract interpretation "matter," thus

---

[174] *See also* discussion *supra* § 2.6 and *infra* § 4.6.

[175] Re. good faith under Article 7(1) *see* the discussion *supra* in § 2.10.

[176] The adjective "reasonable" (or "unreasonable") appears 47 times in the CISG text: *see* Appendix II *infra*.

[177] Said to be reflected in Article 16(2)(b) (discussed *infra* in § 3.6) and in the second sentence of Article 29(2) noted *infra* in § 2.14. For other examples *see infra* with notes 184 *et seq.*

[178] For example, since the CISG contains rules which "govern" the passing of risk (Articles 66–70), and since these rules "settle" most risk-of-loss "matters," there is little if any need to seek solutions by the application of CISG general principles or domestic rules of law.

[179] *See* Lookofsky, *Loose Ends* at 407. *Accord* Ferrari in Schlechtriem, *Kommentar*, Art. 7, Rd.Nr. 42.

[180] According to the first sentence of Article 4: "This Convention governs only the formation of the contract of sale and the rights and obligations of the seller and buyer arising from such a contract."

[181] Since the CISG rule-set can hardly be said to be the exclusive source of law in respect of all matters which might relate to sales contract formation and the rights and obligations of the parties. *Id.*

[182] *See* the decision of Camara Nacional de Apelaciones en lo Comercial de Buenos Aires – Sala E, 24 April 2000, reported in UNILEX (according to the applicable Argentinian law, non-conformities could only be ascertained according to a specific procedure of arbitration and expertise; since such procedure had not been initiated by the buyer upon delivery of the goods – FOB Buenos Aires – its cross-action based on non-conformity was rejected). *Compare* the views expressed in § 4.9 *infra* with respect to the "intensity" of the buyer's examination under Article 38.

opening the door for the application of certain supplementary principles, especially those principles of interpretation reflected in the internationally accepted "common core."[183]

In an increasing number of instances, however, CISG decision makers have been able to locate CISG general principles capable of filling perceived gaps in the Convention text. The emerging general principle which requires the parties to act in good faith has already been discussed.[184] Another example: suppose we face the issue of whether a telefax or an e-mail should be treated as a "writing" under the CISG. Since the Convention defines the term "writing," but does so in terms which expressly include only telegram and telex,[185] we might conclude that the question of whether a telefax or e-mail is (also) a "writing" is a matter which is governed-but-not-settled by the CISG and then proceed to "settle" the matter by discerning, at a slightly higher level of abstraction, a (more) general CISG principle which defines the term "writing" to include other, more modern means of communication.[186] In this sense Article 7(2) authorizes not only decision-making by analogy with express written rules,[187] but also on the basis of a broader principle, and CISG courts, arbitrators and commentators have had numerous opportunities to take advantage of both techniques.[188]

In some instances, however, it may require considerable creativity to flesh out an (unarticulated) "general principle" with which to "settle" the given gap-filling problem at hand.[189] Suppose, for example, that a decision-maker needs to determine whether (under what circumstances) a CISG buyer's declaration of avoidance can be revoked.[190] Rather than seek to resolve this CISG question using domestic rules (obviously unrelated to the CISG regime), we might regard the unsettled matter in question as governed by the

---

[183] For this reason courts and arbitrators should feel free to *supplement* Article 8 with the *contra proferentem* principle, as that (non-CISG) "common core" principle is generally understood in both domestic and international commercial law. *See also infra* §§ 2.12 and 7.3.

[184] *See supra* § 2.10.

[185] Article 13.

[186] This would accord with the elastic definition of "writing" in Article 1.10 of the *UNIDROIT Principles*. *Accord* (re. e-mail) Magnus in Staudinger, *Kommentar*, Art. 13, Rd.Nr. 5, Art. 29, Rd.Nr. 13; *but see* Schlechtriem, *Int. UN-Kaufrecht* Rd.Nr. 68 (who would treat e-mail differently from other modes of visible communication).

[187] *See* sources cited in Kritzer, *Manual*, Suppl. 7, 80–81 (Detailed Analysis of Article 7(2)).

[188] *See* (e.g.) the decision of Oberster Gerichtshof (Austria), 29 June 1999, reported in CISGW3 and UNILEX (goods which buyer had right to return were destroyed during shipment to seller; matter settled by reference to general principles in CISG Art. 66 et. seq. governing loss during shipment to buyer).

[189] For suggestions of general principles to be found in the Convention *see* Magnus in Staudinger, *Kommentar*, Art.7, Rd.Nr. 41–57, Audit, *Vente internationale* no. 55, Ferrari, *Uniform Interpretation* at 225, Honnold, *Uniform Law* § 99, and Hyland, *Conformity of Goods* at 331–33. For another example regarding the possible application of the principle underlying Article 21(2) in connection with a breaching seller's duty to demand that the buyer provide a supplementary specification of (serious) defects *see infra* § 4.9, text with note 146.

[190] Because avoidance can have serious consequences for the party in breach, Article 26 provides that a declaration of avoidance of the contract, e.g. under Article 49, is effective only if made by notice to the other party; the contract is avoided as of the point in time when the notice is given. *See infra* § 6.8.

CISG,[191] and then seek to settle the problem by applying the general estoppel principle;[192] so if the seller refused to accept the buyer's rightful avoidance declaration, this could give the buyer good grounds to revoke.[193]

In a related application, an arbitral tribunal found that the estoppel principle could limit a German buyer's obligation to pay an Austrian seller for non-conforming rolled metal sheets.[194] Though the buyer had not provided the seller with timely notice in accordance with Articles 38 and 39,[195] the seller had previously led the buyer to believe that failure to notify would not be raised as a defense,[196] and the arbitrators held the seller estopped from now setting it up.[197]

A more surprising application of Article 7(2) by the same tribunal relates to a recurring CISG problem: whereas Article 78 provides for the payment of interest on the price and other sums in arrears, it does not set the rate.[198] Most courts and arbitrators have filled this gap by reference to the otherwise applicable domestic law, but the Austrian tribunal in the cases concerned elected to treat the interest rate as a matter governed-but-not-settled by the CISG and then settled the matter (the rate) by reference to the general CISG principle of full compensation for loss which flows from the breach.[199]

Indeed, the flexible Article 7(2) machine may lead to even bolder expeditions within the governed-but-not-settled realm. In one application, a German appellate court ruled that – for purposes of determining its juridical jurisdiction vis-a-vis an American (defendant) seller[200] – the place at which that seller was to pay damages was a matter governed-but-not-settled by the CISG.[201] Citing Article 57(1)(a) as evidence of a general principle that

---

[191] Since the narrow "matter" in question – whether a declaration of avoidance is binding upon the declaring party – was left untouched by the drafters, one might dispute whether that particular question is to be regarded as "governed" by the Convention text, but clearly the larger "matter" – i.e., avoidance of CISG contracts – is (generally) governed thereby.

[192] *See supra* § 2.10, text with note 169.

[193] *Accord* Schlechtriem, *Commentary* at 197 and *Kommentar* at 283. *Compare* the similar result reached by Huber, using different reasoning, *Commentary, id.* at 365.

[194] Arbitral awards no. SCH-4318 and SCH-4366, both decided on 15 June 1994 by Internationales Schiedsgericht der Bundeskammer der gewerblichen Wirtschaft – Wien, reported in UNILEX.

[195] This issue arose in Arbitral award no. SCH-4318, *id.* Re. the CISG notice provisions, which have been very strictly construed by Austrian and German courts, *see infra* § 4.9.

[196] After receiving late notice (6 months after delivery) from the buyer, the seller had, *inter alia*, requested information from the buyer regarding the status of the complaints and had pursued negotiations to reach a settlement agreement. *Query*: whether these acts should (reasonably) lead the buyer to believe that the defense would not be raised if the dispute were not settled by amicable means?

[197] As authority for this proposition (abstraction) the Austrian tribunal cites Bonell in Bianca-Bonell, *Commentary* at 81, and Herber & Czerwenka, *Internationales Kaufrecht* at 48 (1991); it could also have cited Honnold, *Uniform Law* (2d & 3rd ed.) § 99.

[198] *See infra* §§ 6.18 and 6.31.

[199] *Compare* the decision LG Aachen, 20 July 1995, reported in UNILEX, expressly rejecting the Article 7(2) approach taken by the Austrian tribunal. *See also infra* § 6.31.

[200] Re. the international jurisdiction of European courts in sales cases *see supra* § 1.4.

[201] OLG Düsseldorf, 2 July 1993, reported in UNILEX. In this case a German buyer purchased a machine from an American (Indiana) seller at a time when the CISG had been adopted by the U.S.A., but not by Germany.

"all payments" are to be made at the creditor's place of business, the court held it had jurisdiction to decide the case.[202] The decision has been criticized previously on various grounds,[203] and the court's overreaching application of Article 7(2) should be tacked onto the list.[204]

Convention "hard-liners" – who disfavor supplementing the Convention with domestic law – tend to be bold when applying the Article 7(2) rule;[205] they might even use it to "settle" matters deemed insoluble by those who drafted the treaty.[206] Others will prefer to take the more traditional "conflicts" (private international law) route.[207] Given a gap not readily amenable to settlement by a CISG general principle, Article 7(2) requires settlement "in conformity with the law applicable by virtue of the rules of private international law"; depending on the circumstances, this law may take the form of an international rule (*lex mercatoria*).[208]

The machine was delivered to, and installed in, a factory in Russia. In the course of its operation an accident occurred which killed one worker and injured several others. In the action brought by the buyer in Germany, relief was sought from the seller in the form of damages for repair costs incurred by the buyer, and in the form of a declaratory judgment finding the seller liable for all losses that the buyer might incur as a result of the Russian workers' death and personal injuries.

[202] Re. the place of performance (payment) *see* sources cited § 4.12 *infra*.

[203] *See* Schlechtriem, *EWiR* Art. 1 CISG 1/93, 1075–76; in English in Kritzer, *Manual*, Vol. 2, Suppl. 9, 1994.

[204] The relevant principal obligation is the seller's duty to deliver conforming goods (Article 35); *see* Huber in Schlechtriem, *Commentary*, Art. 45, Rd.Nr. 64; *see also* the decision OLG Koblenz, 23 February 1990; *but see* Herber *id.*, Art. 7, Rd.Nr. 41 and Schlechtriem, previous note at *id.* Even assuming, *arguendo*, that the payment of damages was the relevant obligation under the then-applicable rule in the Brussels Convention, the issue of *where* a judgment debtor has to perform (pay damages) is hardly a "matter . . . governed by" the CISG; *accord*: Oberster Gerichtshof (Austria), decision of 8 September 1997, reported in UNILEX. One could, however, apply Art. 57(1)(a) to determine the place of performance of the obligation to pay the price and then use this result to resolve the jurisdictional issue in an action for the price brought under Art. 5(1) of the Brussels Convention: *see infra* § 4.12 and Custom Made Commercial v. Stawa Metallbau, 29 June 1994, [1994] E.C.R. I-2913. Note that as of 1 March 2002, the Brussels Regulation (which replaces the Convention) expands the Art. 5(1) rule: *see supra* § 1.4.

[205] Honnold, *Uniform Law* at 108 ff. seems to end up opting for a "bold" Article 7(2) approach.

[206] As persuasive grounds for *rejecting* an Article 7(2) solution, the LG Aachen, 20 July 1995, *supra* note 199, found that the drafters tried but failed to solve the interest-rate problem. In contrast, the Vienna arbitrators in the awards cited *supra* (text with note 194 *et seq*.) "settled" the very same problem using Article 7(2).

[207] *See* (e.g.) Lookofsky, *Loose Ends*. For a comprehensive sampling of scholarly opinion on Article 7(2), *see* Kritzer, *Manual*, Suppl. 7, pp. 77 ff. (Detailed Analysis of Article 7(2)).

[208] *See generally* Lowenfeld, "*Lex Mercatoria*: an Arbitrator's View," 6 *Arbitration International* 133 (1990) and Lookofsky & Hertz, *Transnational Litigation*, Chapter 6.2.3. *Compare* Bonell, *UNIDROIT Principles*, with the somewhat controversial suggestion that the UNIDROIT Principles can provide the content of CISG "general principles" (*id.* at 36 with n. 35). Other commentators, taking the "reverse" route, see the *CISG* as a new source of lex mercatoria: *see* Audit, *Vente internationale* no. 203; the arbitration award rendered in ICC Case 9887 (August 1999), UNILEX, is in *accord* (under new ICC Rules tribunal was not bound to make use of domestic law, including conflict of law rules, but was free to apply "recognized international legal standards"; CISG applicable, considering its strong recognition in arbitration practice as rules reflecting evolution of international law in the field of international sale of goods).

§ 2.12 INTERPRETATION OF CISG CONTRACTS

Article 8 of the CISG is concerned – not with the interpretation of the Convention itself,[209] but rather – with the interpretation of "statements" made (and conduct exhibited) by the parties. In other words, Article 8 is a CISG *contract*-interpretation tool.[210]

CISG Article 8 provides a tool to help deal with the very common situation where the parties attach different meanings to the same contractual language. Depending on the circumstances, the statements of the parties are to be interpreted pursuant to either a subjective or an objective test. One party's statements and conduct are to be interpreted subjectively where the other party knew or could not have been unaware what that intent was. Where, however, such other party neither knew nor could have been so aware, the first party's statements are to be interpreted objectively, according to the understanding that a reasonable person in the same circumstances would have had.[211] This conforms generally with the process of contract interpretation as practiced under U.S. domestic law.[212]

In situations where the parties elect to derogate from or supplement the CISG default regime,[213] (e.g.) by incorporation of one party's standard form,[214] the interpreter is likely to attach an objective (reasonable) interpretation to the terms in that form.[215] Similar considerations apply in a "battle of forms." Suppose, for example, that the standard terms proffered by the parties include differing formulations as regards the applicable law: the buyer's form subjects the contract to the "laws of California," whereas the seller's form states that the "laws of Canada" apply. Interpreting these seemingly conflicting statements under Article 8(2), we are likely to conclude that a reasonable person would read both clauses as pointing to the CISG.[216]

Although Article 8 clearly "governs" certain key aspects of CISG contract interpretation, the provision can hardly be said to "cover" (and thus occupy) the entire interpretation field, so courts and arbitrators may sometimes have occasion to look for additional

---

[209] I.e., the problem addressed by Article 7(1): *see supra* §§ 2.8 and 2.9.

[210] The subject matter to be interpreted in accordance with Article 8 consists not only of the individual statements made by the offeror and offeree during the contract formation process, but also the language of the resulting contract between the parties (in its entirety). *See generally* Magnus in Staudinger, *Kommentar*, Art.8 Rd.Nr.7 (& authors cited there) and Lookofsky, *United Nations Convention*, No. 82.

[211] For a case involving an issue of party identity, decided alternatively under both standards, *see* LG Hamburg, 26 September 1990, reported in UNILEX, analyzed by Witz, *Premières Applications*, no. 32.

[212] Re. American law *see* Farnsworth, *Contracts*, § 7.10.

[213] *See supra* § 2.7.

[214] *See infra* § 3.8 re. the rule in Article 19.

[215] Provided that the other party neither knew nor "could not have been unaware" of the proferring party's actual intent: Art. 8(3). *See* Junge in Schlechtriem, *Commentary/Kommentar*, Art. 8, Rd.Nr. 8a; Magnus in Staudinger, *Kommentar*, Art. 8, Rd.Nr. 18.

[216] *See supra* § 2.7 and *Asante Technologies, Inc. v. PMC-Sierra, Inc.*, 164 F.Supp.2d 1142 (N.D. California 2001), where the District Court – without resort to Article 8 – correctly concluded that the parties did not "contract out" of the CISG (*see also supra* § 2.7). Since the starting point in an *Asante*-type situation is that the Convention applies by default, the *Asante* Court, interpreting the parties' statements, should have referred to Article 8.

principles to supplement the very general rules laid down in Article 8.[217] However, since subsection (3) of Article 8 clearly requires that due consideration be given to "all relevant circumstances of the case including the negotiations," the CISG prohibits (preëmpts) application of the "parol evidence rule" which, under American domestic law, might otherwise operate to exclude extrinsic evidence;[218] the consequences of this prohibition are discussed below.[219]

Where, by application of Article 8, the contract or a particular statement seems to assume a meaning that the party who made it did not intend, such a "unilateral mistake" may have different consequences under the domestic laws of different Contracting States.[220] Since this involves an issue of contract validity which the Convention does not address, Article 4 tells us to turn outside the CISG and determine the applicable law by virtue of private international law rules.[221]

§ 2.13 TRADE USAGE AND PARTY PRACTICES

Reading CISG Article 9 together with the freedom-of-contract rule in Article 6, we see that much international sales law is to be found – not in the CISG text, but rather – within the "consensus" reached by CISG merchants themselves, what American jurists might refer to as their "bargain in fact."[222] In other words, the CISG parties are not only bound by the express terms of their contract; they are also bound by their own established "practices" and the more widely observed "usages" of the relevant branch of international trade. Only after considering all these bargain-elements do we resort to the CISG gap-filling rules.

Although CISG parties will seldom "agree" to be bound by a given trade usage, parties who have dealt with each other previously may, by their conduct, have established a binding

---

[217] Re. (e.g.) the applicability of the *contra proferentem* maxim to standard form disclaimers and limitations of liability *see infra* § 7.3.

[218] *See* the decision of the U.S. Court of Appeals in *MCC Marble Ceramic Center Inc. v. Ceramica Nuova D'Agostino S.p.A.*, 144 F.3d 1384 (11th Cir. 1998), CLOUT Case 222, also reported in CISGW3, citing, *inter alia*, Bernstein & Lookofsky, *CISG/Europe* § 2-12; *accord* Honnold, *Uniform Law*, § 110. As to "merger clauses," which purport to deprive any prior or contemporaneous agreement effect, *see infra* § 7.3.

[219] *See infra* §§ 4.5 and 7.3.

[220] Suppose, for example, that buyer B (in State X) believes she has purchased frying chicken from seller S (in State Y), but the language used in the writings is not specific, so the agreement, if interpreted objectively, would allow any kind of chicken (including stewing chicken) to be delivered. In this situation some jurisdictions tend to deny the buyer any relief, whereas in others the mistaken party is permitted to avoid the contract, provided she compensates the seller for reliance damages. *See generally* Zweigert & Kötz, *Comparataive Law*, Ch. 31. For an American case involving facts like those in the example *compare Frigaliment Importing Co. v. B.N.S. International Sales Corp.*, 190 F. Supp. 116 (S.D.N.Y. 1960).

[221] *Accord* Magnus in Staudinger, *Kommentar*, Art. 8 Rd.Nr. 21, Herber & Czerwenka, *Internationales Kaufrecht*, Art. 8 Rd.Nr.7. For a case arguably involving such a situation *see* LG Memmingen, 1 December 1993, reported in UNILEX and analyzed by Witz, *Premières Applications*, no. 33.

[222] The American Uniform Commercial Code § 1-201(3) defines "agreement" to mean "the bargain of the parties in fact as found in their language or by implication from other circumstances including course of dealing or usage of trade or course of performance. . . ." The content of the rule in the (2002) *NCCUSL Draft Revision* is essentially the same.

"practice." This aspect of Article 9(1) clearly covers situations involving a sequence of con-duct established under prior contracts[223] (a "course of dealing");[224] presumably, it also applies in situations where a single contract involves repeated occasions for performance.[225]

By virtue of Article 9(2) the parties are also held to impliedly agree to the usages in the entire branch of international trade concerned. However, the "agreement" of parties is only implied if the usage is one which (1) both parties knew or ought to have known and (2) in international trade is widely known and regularly observed by parties to contracts of the type involved in the particular trade concerned.[226] These two limitations, designed to protect parties in less developed countries,[227] have not reduced the significance of Article 9(2) – a rule regularly cited in the CISG decisions of courts and arbitral tribunals worldwide.[228]

§ 2.14 FORMAL WRITING REQUIREMENT: DECLARATIONS UNDER ARTICLE 96

As a starting point, the Convention does not require the parties' agreement be expressed in a "writing."[229] In particular, Article 11 of the Convention dispenses with the formal writ-ing requirement as regards the sales contract itself, and Article 29(1) dispenses with the same requirement as regards contract modifications;[230] similarly, an oral offer or accept-ance is binding under CISG Part II.[231]

---

223 In a pre-CISG (ULIS) case, a seller had repeatedly cured defective deliveries upon buyer's demand, even though no timely notice was given, as then required by the ULIS Convention. Under such circumstances, the OLG Düsseldorf (12 Nov. 1982, *IPRax* 1984,185) held that this amounted to a practice between the parties by which they were bound in their subsequent contractual relationship. The result under CISG Article 9 would surely be the same.

224 This is the American (domestic) term: *see* UCC § 1-205. The similarity between the UCC and CISG con-cepts was highlighted by the U.S. District Court in *Calzaturificio Claudia s.n.c. v. Olivieri Footwear Ltd.*, WESTLAW 16482 (S.D.N.Y. 1998), also reported in CISGW3 and UNILEX. Citing CISG Article 9(1), the court held that delivery ex works did not amount to a "course of dealing," since seller failed to submit sufficient evidence with regard to similar terms in other transactions with buyer.

225 In American law a "course of dealing" (*see* text with previous note) is a sequence of conduct between the parties prior to entering into a particular agreement, whereas a "course of performance" arises subsequent to entry into the agreement and involves repeated occasions for performance thereunder. *See* UCC § 1-205(1) and § 2-208(1) and *compare* the slightly modified version set forth in § 1-303 of the (2002) *NCCUSL Draft Revision* of Article 1.

226 *Compare* UCC § 1-205(2) which defines usage of trade as "any practice or method of dealing having such regularity of observance . . . as to justify an expectation that it will be observed with respect to the transac-tion in question."

227 Since such parties might be unfamiliar with certain usages among more industrialized trading nations.

228 *See, e.g.*, the decision of Gerechtshof's Hertogenbosch (Netherlands), 24 April 1996, UNILEX (B, an experi-enced businessman in the trade, could not have been unaware of (i) widespread use of the standard terms referred in S's confirmation of B's order, nor (ii) specific provisions on interest, which were not of such a char-acter that B could not have expected them, especially since B had made such contracts with S in the past). *See also, e.g.*, LG Hamburg, 26 September 1990, UNILEX (bill of exchange effectively postponing payment date).

229 The CISG term "writing" is defined in Article 13: *see supra* § 2.11, text with notes 185–86.

230 If a given CISG sales contract stipulates that a modification of that contract must be in writing, this require-ment is binding on the parties under Article 29(2).

231 The rules in CISG Part II on sales contract formation are discussed in Chapter 3 *infra*.

However, as a concession to those States which maintain formal writing requirements under their own domestic law, such States are permitted to make a declaration (reservation) under Article 96.[232] The effect of such a reservation is that the relevant CISG provision (in Article 11, 29 or Part II) which would otherwise dispense with the writing requirement "does not apply." As a consequence, where one (but not both) of the parties to a CISG sales contract resides in a State which has made an Article 96 declaration, the question of whether the contract (or a contract modification, etc.) needs to be in writing must be resolved under the applicable domestic law designated by the private international law rules of the forum;[233] as discussed and illustrated in Chapter 8, the combined effect of an Article 96 reservation and the PIL (conflict-of-laws) procedure may sometimes lead to surprising results.[234]

---

[232] *See* Articles 12 and 29. The European countries which have made declarations under Article 96 include Belarus, Estonia, Hungary, Latvia, Lithuania, Russia, and Ukraine: *see* <http://cisgw3.law.pace.edu/cisg/countries/cntries.html>. If a contract itself requires that modifications have to be in writing, it cannot be modified by oral means, unless one party has been led by the other's conduct or verbal statements to believe otherwise and has acted in reliance on such belief; *see* Article 29(2) and (re. the principle prohibiting *venire contra factum proprium* in other CISG contexts) *supra* § 2.11.

[233] *See* Flechtner, *Several Texts. Accord* Schlechtriem, *Commentary,* Art. 12, Rd.Nr.2, and Herber in Schlechtriem, *Commentary,* Art. 96, Rd.Nr. 3. Like the author of the present work, Honnold (*Uniform Law* at 139) has modified his earlier opinion on the effect of an Article 96 reservation, so all sources cited here are now in accord.

[234] § 8.8 *infra.*

CHAPTER THREE

SALES CONTRACT FORMATION

§ 3.1 Two Substantive Treaties in One

CISG Parts II and III constitute the substantive core of the Convention. Part II deals with the "Formation of the Contract," i.e., the rules relating to offer, acceptance and the like, whereas Part III is about the "Sale of Goods," i.e., the rights and obligations of the parties to the sales contract duly formed. The present chapter is concerned mainly with the formation rules in CISG Part II, but it also contains some observations on the subject of sales contract validity – a matter with which the Convention is generally "not concerned."[1]

The Convention provisions on contract formation are based, in part, on 19th century contract conceptions, and some have been quite critical of the results achieved.[2] Indeed, the four Scandinavian countries,[3] which share rather different conceptions,[4] chose to ratify the CISG subject to Article 92 declarations, so that – in respect of matters governed by Part II – the Scandinavian countries are not Contracting States within the meaning of paragraph (1) of Article 1.[5] It is, however, important to recognize that the Article 92 declarations have not achieved the far-reaching results which the Scandinavian legislators once seemed to expect.[6] It should also be emphasized that the content of a CISG contract, if made,[7] will nearly always be determined on the basis of the Convention (Parts I and III)[8] and not on the basis of the otherwise applicable domestic law.[9]

The overall solution to the various contract formation issues provided by Part II of the Convention represents a necessary – and in some respects difficult – compromise

---

[1]   Re. Article 4 *see supra* § 2.6 and *infra* § 3.10.

[2]   *See generally* (e.g.) Schlechtriem, *Budesgerichtshof* at 6 with note 41. *Compare* Murray, *Formation* at 42–43 (describing the rule in Article 19(2) as "absurd").

[3]   Denmark, Finland, Norway, and Sweden. (Note that Iceland is *not* in this "Scandinavian" group: *see* note 5 *infra*).

[4]   *Inter alia*, as regards the *non*-binding nature of CISG offers: *see infra* § 3.6.

[5]   The CISG took effect in the *Scandinavian* countries (*supra* note 3) during the period 1989–1990. The CISG took effect in *Iceland* – which is a "Nordic," though not a "Scandinavian" country – in June 2002 (see *supra* § 1.1 and Appendix 1 *infra*); notably, Iceland did *not* make an Article 92 declaration.

[6]   In that these declarations do not preclude the application of Part II when the applicable PIL rules of the forum point to the law of a non-Scandinavian Contracting State. *See infra* § 8.4. For a commentary on a Danish case which illustrates how CISG Part II is to be given effect by Scandinavian courts *see* Lookofsky, *Alive & Well*.

[7]   On the basis of domestic law or CISG Part II, as the case may be: *see supra*, preceding note.

[8]   *All* CISG Contracting States, including the Scandinavian States, have ratified CISG Part I (containing, *inter alia*, the contract interpretation rule in Article 8: *infra* § 2.12) and Part III (containing, *inter alia*, the key rules on conformity in Article 35: *infra* § 4.4 ff.).

[9]   This distinction seems to have caused some confusion in a case decided by the Danish Maritime and Commercial Court on 31 January 2002: *see infra* § 4.4, text with note 37 *et seq.*

among diverging domestic views,[10] and we could hardly expect jurists with fundamentally different domestic backgrounds to praise all aspects of the result.[11] But now that national courts and arbitrators have had the opportunity to interpret and apply the Part II rules in practice, it seems that this part of the Convention provides adequate tools to deal with international needs, and it surely represents a significant improvement on the previously existing state of affairs – i.e., a global business environment with no uniform sales contract formation rules.[12]

§ 3.2 THE OFFER: MINIMUM REQUIREMENTS

Offer and acceptance are the two essential elements in the contract formation process. In order to constitute an offer to sell or buy goods in the international market, a given proposal must meet certain minimum Convention requirements.

According to the first sentence in Article 14(1), an offer must – as a general rule – be addressed to one or more specific persons;[13] the offer must also be sufficiently definite and indicate the intention of the offeror to be bound.[14] Some see the elements of specificity and definiteness as subsets of the more general requirement that the offer indicate an intention to be bound,[15] but there is good reason to consider each of these elements separately.[16]

The second sentence of Article 14(1) defines a proposal as "sufficiently definite" if it (a) "indicates the goods" and (b) "expressly or implicitly fixes the price."[17] A purchase order which identifies a given computer program (standard software) and the compensation to be paid for it will satisfy these requirements,[18] just as an order for chinchilla pelts of "middle or better quality" at a price "between 35 and 65 German marks" has been held sufficiently definite under the same rule.[19] To take another example, an American court has held that a contract for the future supply of "commercial quantities" of a chemical ingredient was sufficiently definite under Article 14.[20]

---

10   *See* (e.g.) text *infra* § 3.6.

11   *See, e.g.*, Schlechtriem, *Borderland.*

12   Re. the largely unsuccessful ULF and ULIS conventions *see supra* § 1.2.

13   Paragraph (2), discussed *infra* § 3.4, sets forth an exception to the rule.

14   In most cases, such an intention will depend upon the understanding that a reasonable person would have had. *See* Article 8 (*supra* § 2.12).

15   *See* (e.g.) Honnold, *Uniform Law*, § 134.

16   For one thing, a sufficiently specific and definite communication will not always reflect an offeror's intention to be bound: indeed, such non-binding communications are often exchanged to serve as (non-binding) memoranda of understanding on those particular points on which agreement has been reached. Apart from providing evidence of intention to be bound, the specificity/definiteness requirement ensures that an enforceable obligation has been incurred. Without some measure of specificity and definiteness, no court could determine whether a given promise has been performed, nor could a court, in the case of breach, order that the obligation be performed (re. specific performance *see infra* § 6.4).

17   The special problem raised by this requirement (b) is discussed immediately below.

18   *See* the decision of LG München, 8 February 1995, CLOUT Case 131, also reported in UNILEX.

19   *See* the decision of the Austrian Supreme Court (Oberster Gerichtshof) of 10 November 1994, CLOUT Case 106.

20   Decision of the U.S. District Court for the S.D. of New York, 21 August 2002, reconsidering and affirming its decision of 10 May 2002 in *Geneva Pharmaceuticals Technology Corp. v. Barr Laboratories, Inc.*, both decisions reported in UNILEX and CISGW3.

Conversely, a proposal which fails to satisfy the requirement of definiteness in Article 14(1) cannot qualify as a CISG offer, nor can it qualify as a counter-offer under Article 19(1). However, even if a given communication seems incomplete at first blush, custom and usage may serve to fill it out. In a Hungarian case, a seemingly nebulous oral communication by a German seller was held sufficiently definite under Article 14(1),[21] in that the quality, quantity and price of the goods were impliedly fixed by the parties' prior course of dealing in accordance with Article 9(2): on several previous occasions the seller had delivered goods ordered by the buyer who had regularly and without objection paid the price after delivery.[22]

Assuming a particular proposal is sufficiently definite, it will qualify as an offer if it is addressed to one or more specific persons; proposals not so addressed must be evaluated in accordance with Article 14, paragraph 2.[23]

§ 3.3   THE PROBLEM OF THE OPEN PRICE TERM

Domestic laws vary with respect to the question of whether parties can conclude a (binding) sales contract without finally settling or "fixing" the price.[24] According to the second sentence in CISG Article 14(1), a proposal for concluding a sales contract is sufficiently definite, thus constituting an offer, if it (indicates the goods[25] and) "expressly or implicitly fixes or makes provision for determining the quantity and price." A much-debated question concerns the *e contrario* implication which some Convention commentators have seen in this rule: that a proposal which does not fix or make provision for determining the price is not "sufficiently definite" and cannot constitute a (valid) offer which forms the basis for a binding CISG contract.[26]

Other commentators, rejecting such an *e contrario* implication, point out that Article 55 provides a gap-filling reference to the price generally charged in cases "[w]here a contract has been validly concluded but does not expressly or implicitly fix or make provision for determining the price";[27] since Article 55 provides a method of dealing with (and effectively "closing") price gaps in at least some CISG contracts, this provision would seem to negate the inference that a price gap is necessarily fatal under Article 14.[28]

---

[21]   *See infra* § 3.3.

[22]   *See* Metropolitan Court of Budapest, 24 March 1992, reported in UNILEX.

[23]   *See infra* § 3.4.

[24]   According to American sales law, for example, the parties can conclude a sales contract even though the price is not settled (re. UCC § 2-305 *see* Farnsworth, *Formation* at 3-8). According to the Swiss Code of Obligations Article 212(1), a buyer's firm order which does not state a price results in contract formation at the average price on the day and at the place of performance. On the other hand, French law is particularly strict in requiring a determined or determinable price; *see* Art.1591 of the French Civil Code. Re. differing national views *see* Honnold, *Uniform Law*, § 325.3, and Amato, *Open Price Term* 18–21.

[25]   *See supra* § 3.2.

[26]   *See* (e.g.) Witz, *Premières Applications*, no. 40 and authors cited *id.* in note 24. *See also* Farnsworth, *Formation* at 3–8, Murray, *Formation* at 13–17 and Schlechtriem, *Uniform Law* at 50–51. *But compare* Honnold, *Uniform Law* (2nd & 3rd ed.) § 137 (modifying the position taken in the 1st/1981 edition at 164).

[27]   *See generally infra* § 4.13.

[28]   Among French authors, Corbisier (*Rev. int. dr. comp. 1988*, 767) has argued in favor of treating open-price sales as valid on the basis of Article 55. *Contra* Heuzé, *Vente internationale*, nos. 168–174.

In one of the first reported cases to deal with the problem, the Supreme Court of Hungary held that an offer by an American manufacturer of aircraft engines to a Hungarian airline company which did not specify the price of all the engines offered was not sufficiently definite – and thus not binding – under Article 14(1);[29] unfortunately, the reasoning behind the decision and the court's view of the relationship between Articles 14 and 55 remain unclear.[30] Moving in a different direction, the Austrian Supreme Court has been quite liberal in a case involving an arguably insufficient price determination.[31]

To find a viable solution to the Article 14 conundrum, courts and arbitrators should first attempt to discern the true intention of the parties, not only because this is the overriding principle of Article 14,[32] but also because Article 6 lets the parties derogate from or vary the effect of any CISG provision pertaining to contract formation.[33] Party autonomy should therefore be the overriding consideration in connection with open-price terms.[34] To discern the parties' intentions we can interpret their "statements" in accordance with the principles set forth in Article 8.[35] If, on this basis, it appears that the parties concerned in fact intended to be bound without a "fixed" price clause, then the parties' intention should prevail.[36] Since Article 55 clearly accepts the possibility of contracts with price-gaps that bind, we should reject the contention that a price gap is necessarily fatal to an offer under Article 14.[37] After all, CISG Article 14 does not say that a proposal is invalid if it fails to fix the price, and a domestic law rule, such as Article 1591 of the French Civil Code, should not be allowed to govern the disposition of a CISG contract formation case.[38]

---

29 *See* Supreme Court of Hungary, 25 September 1992, in English in 13 J.L.&Com.31 (1993), overruling Metropolitan Court of Budapest (*id.* at 49), both decisions in UNILEX. *See also* Amato, *Open Price Term* at 11.

30 At least in the translation (*id.*). *Accord*: Amato, *id.* at 17.The case can also be read to hold that there was no effective acceptance since the offeree did not express a binding commitment. *See also* the detailed critical analysis by Witz, *Premières Applications*, no. 41–43.

31 Re. the decision of Oberster Gerichtshof of 10 November 1994 *see* Schlechtriem, *Bundesgerichtshof* at 7 with note 46.

32 *See* the second sentence of Article 14(1). *Accord* Honnold, *Uniform Law*, § 137.7.

33 Except for Article 12. Re. the parties' contractual freedom under Article 6 *see supra* § 2.7.

34 *See* (e.g.) the German authorities cited by Bernstein & Lookofsky, *CISG/Europe*, § 3-3.

35 *Accord* Murray, *Formation* at 17. Re. Article 8 *see supra* § 2.12.

36 *Accord* Schlechtriem, *Int. UN-Kaufrecht* Rd.Nr. 76, Witz, *Premières Applications* no. 44, Lookofsky, *United Nations Convention*, No. 102. The decision of the French Cour de Cassation of 4 January 1995 appears to accord with this view: *see* Schlechtriem, *Bundesgerichtshof* at 7 with note 47.

37 The legislative history of Article 55 hardly warrants the conclusion that the effect of an open price term depends on whether or not the parties reside in States which have ratified CISG Part II: all States which ratify CISG Part III must surely be bound by "the same" Article 55, whatever it means. *But see* Murray, *Formation* at 16 and *compare* Amato (*id.* at 9–10) defending the opposite view. *Compare* also the unofficial *Secretariat Commentary* cited *infra* in § 4.13 note 195.

38 *Accord* Witz, *Premières Applications* no. 44 at 70, Magnus in Staudinger, *Kommentar*, Art. 14, Rd.Nr. 34 and numerous authors cited there. *See also* Article 2.2 of the *UNIDROIT Principles* indicating that the position taken here is an internationally acceptable interpretation of the Article 14 rule; re. CISG Article 7(1) *see supra* § 2.9.

§ 3.4 Offer Invitations: Article 14(2)

Like most domestic contractual regimes, the Convention distinguishes between an offer, which binds the offeror, and an "invitation [that others] make offers" which has no such binding effect. Paragraph (2) of Article 14 reaffirms the starting point in paragraph (1): a proposal not addressed to one or more specific persons is, as a starting point (presumption), interpreted merely as an invitation to make offers.[39] However, one who clearly indicates an intention to be bound by such a proposal, (e.g.) by a statement in the text itself, will be treated as having made an offer, and the various rules pertaining to offers (and their acceptance) in CISG Part II (Articles 15 et seq.) will then apply.

§ 3.5 Offer Effective; Withdrawal (Article 15)

Assuming a proposal constitutes an offer under CISG Article 14, the next step is to determine when that offer takes effect. According to paragraph (1) of Article 15, an offer becomes effective when it "reaches" the offeree. An oral offer, which reaches the offeree instantaneously, is considered effective when made, whereas a written offer first reaches the offeree when delivered to his place of business.[40] Until that point in time, according to paragraph (2), the offer may be withdrawn; indeed, the same is true even if the offer is irrevocable, a term defined in Article 16 (discussed below).

Note that Article 15 concerns the offeror's right to withdraw an offer. Unlike the right to revoke in Article 16 (discussed in the following section), the right to withdraw deals with offers which have never taken effect.

§ 3.6 Revocation (Article 16) and Rejection (Article 17)

Once an offer – not effectively withdrawn in accordance with Article 15(2) – reaches the offeree (and takes effect), we need to consider the offeror's right to revoke. The Convention rules on this point (Article 16) may be viewed against the background of competing conceptions in domestic law. In Germanic and Scandinavian systems the default rule is that an offer, once communicated, remains binding and thus irrevocable, at least for a reasonable time.[41] In Common law systems, however, the traditional starting point is that

---

[39] The converse proposition – that a proposal addressed to one or more specific persons *is* considered to be an offer – does not necessarily follow from paragraph (2). *But see* Murray, *Formation* at 18.

[40] *See* Article 24. Note that the offeree may not be aware that a given offer has "reached" him. As regards certain orders placed through technological means Article 11(1) of the European E-Commerce Directive (2000/31/EC) provides that the "service provider" *has to acknowledge* the "service recipient's" order without delay and by electronic means, and that the order and the acknowledgment are *deemed to be received* when the addressee is able to *access* it. Re. the tenuous relationship between this EU-Directive and CISG sales of "goods" *see supra* § 2.5 with note 71.

[41] Re. (e.g.) Danish law *see* Andersen, *Aftaleret*, Ch. 3.2. Re. German law *see* (new) Civil Code § 145. Re. other systems *see* Zweigert & Kötz, *Comparative Law*, p. 356 ff.

a communicated (but still unaccepted) offer can be freely revoked.[42] Article 16 of the CISG represents a compromise between these two "extremes."

The starting point in the Convention is that offers are freely revocable:[43] according to Article 16(1) an offer may be revoked if the revocation reaches the offeree before he has dispatched an acceptance. The underlying logic here will be obvious to jurists trained in U.S. domestic law: the offeror, as "master of the offer," should remain free to revoke it (and take his business elsewhere) – at least until the offeree has accepted the offeror's terms, thus concluding the contract and binding both parties to the deal. Why should one party be bound when the other is not?

Although paragraph (1) would seem to accord with the traditional Common law view, it should be noted that (contrary to Common law precepts) the CISG revocability rule does not carry any implications as regards the point in time when a contract is deemed concluded.[44] More significantly, paragraph (1) of Article 16 represents but a starting point which must be read in conjunction with the two significant modifications contained in paragraph (2), both of which find analogues in American domestic law. As indicated below, these exceptions to the principle of revocability bring the net result under the CISG quite close to the position of Civil law systems which (as a starting point) embrace the opposite principle.

The first important modification to the CISG revocability rule is that an offer to enter an international contract of sale cannot be revoked (a) if it "indicates . . . that it is irrevocable."[45] The idea underlying subparagraph 2(a) is that a CISG offeror enjoys the freedom to limit her own future course of action; and if she indicates to the offeree that she will not revoke, then she is bound by her word. The offeror may make such an indication of irrevocability either by stating a fixed time for acceptance or otherwise. If, for example, the offeror states expressly that her offer "will be held open" until a given date, this represents a clear indication of irrevocability, and such an offer cannot be revoked during the time stated, even if the offeror should later change her mind.

One particular aspect of subparagraph (2)(a) has, however, provoked a good deal of doctrinal debate.[46] The issue is whether an offer which "fixes a time for acceptance" should – for that reason, i.e., without more – be read as irrevocable. Suppose, for example, that the offeror states merely that the offeree's "acceptance must be received before January 1st." Some

---

[42] This traditional Common law position is still the rule in England, in spite of much criticism; *see* Treitel, *Law of Contract*, Ch. 3, Sec. 8(4). Under American domestic law, numerous and significant exceptions apply.

[43] To the extent that a CISG offeror is at liberty to revoke under Article 16, some Convention commentators argue that this rule (or starting point) ought not be undercut by the imposition of non-contractual liability based (e.g.) on a domestic *culpa in contrahendo* rule (*see, e.g.,* Schlechtriem, *Int. UN-Kaufrecht* Rd.Nr. 81 and *Borderland* at 475). A counter-argument, however, is that the Part II rules on offer and acceptance were not designed to supplant bad-faith conduct regulation by domestic *culpa in contrahendo* rules: *see infra* § 4.6.

[44] As regards Article 23 *see* discussion *infra* § 3.9.

[45] *Compare* the American domestic sales rule in UCC § 2-205 (re. an offer "which by its terms gives assurance that it will be held open"); unlike this UCC analogue, CISG Article 16(2)(a) does not require a writing and does not set forth a 3-month maximum (*see also* Gillette & Walt, *Sales Law*, Ch. 3.II.B).The differences between the CISG rule and English domestic law are much more dramatic: *see* Nicholas, *Vienna Convention* at 215.

[46] Re. the controversy *see* (e.g.) Honnold, *Uniform Law*, § 143; Schlechtriem, *Uniform Sales Law* at 53 with note 173, and Schlechtriem in Schlechtriem, *Kommentar*, Art. 16, Rd.Nr. 9.

might read this statement as relating only to the time frame which the offeror has fixed for acceptance; others might say that this statement – by virtue of subparagraph (2)(a) – should also be construed (or at least presumed) to indicate irrevocability.[47] There is, however, no fixed solution to the problem. Since the offeror is generally treated as the "master" of a given CISG offer, each such offer should be interpreted on its own terms. Depending on the words used by the offeror, the individual circumstances and the larger contractual context, the fact that an offer contains a statement relating to the time for acceptance may – but does not necessarily – imply a (binding) indication of irrevocability by the offeror.[48]

Turning now to subparagraph (2)(b) of Article 16, we see an additional modification of the starting point set forth in paragraph (1): an offer may not be revoked if the offeree acts in reasonable reliance on the offer.

> *Illustration 3a*: S (in CISG State X) makes an offer to supply certain cloth at a given price to a potential buyer B-1 (in CISG State Y). Having received – but not yet replied to – that offer, B-1, who has often bought cloth from S in the past, uses the offer to calculate and make a bid to supply finished goods (women's dresses) to B-2: a bid which B-2 promptly accepts. B-1 then prepares to accept the original offer by S, but before B-1 puts her acceptance into the fax-machine, she receives a statement of revocation from S. In the meantime, the market price of the cloth has risen significantly (this is, incidentally, the reason S chose to revoke). Assuming the agreement between B-1 and B-2 is binding, can B-1 hold S to his original word?

Since the offer by S in this case does not "fix a time for acceptance" (by B-1), S remains free to revoke at any time prior to B-1's acceptance, unless the "reliance-exception" in subparagraph (2)(b) applies. According to the first part of this exception to the revocability rule, it must be *reasonable* for the offeree (in our illustration: B-1) to have *relied* on the offer "as being irrevocable."[49] This CISG provision might well be understood as posing a requirement that the offeree (B-1) had reason to anticipate that the offeror (S) would not revoke (i.e., even though S, as a starting point, was free to do so).[50] If S knows or should

---

[47] The prevailing opinion among German and French commentators appears to be that the statement of a fixed time for acceptance raises (at most) a rebuttable presumption of irrevocability; *see* (e.g.) Schlechtriem at *id*. This interpretation would help to overcome concerns that "the unwary common lawyer" might be trapped by Art. 16(2)(a): *compare* Nicholas, *Vienna Convention* at 215.

[48] Article 8. *See* Audit, *Vente internationale* no. 64, Schlechtriem, *Int. UN-Kaufrecht* Rd.Nr. 80. *See also* Murray, *Formation* at 25 (advising that offerors who seek to retain the right to revoke expressly so state).

[49] *Compare* the deceptively similar, but different – and arguably better – rule in American domestic law (§ 87 of the *Restatement Second of Contracts*) which requires that the offeree's act of reliance be *foreseeable* by the *offeror*. A U.S. District Court has noted that the American doctrine of promissory estoppel differs from Art. 16 (2)(b) of CISG, "in so far that the latter provision did not expressly require that the offeree's reliance must have been foreseeable to the offeror and does not expressly require that the offeree's reliance be detrimental." *See Geneva Pharmaceuticals Technology Corp. v. Barr Laboratories, Inc., et al.*, discussed *supra* in § 2.6, text with notes 107 *et seq.*

[50] I.e., even thought the CISG provision – unlike the similar American domestic rule (preceding note) – does not mention "foreseeabilty" as such. *Compare* Schlechtriem, *Commentary/Kommentar*, Art. 16, Rd.Nr. 11, who would require that the offer indicate the offeror's intention to be bound. Since CISG offers are, as a

know that B-1 intends to submit such a bid to B-2, that fact might give B-1 good reason to expect S not to revoke.[51]

In addition, the rule in subparagraph (2)(b) requires that the offeree (B-1) must actually have acted in reliance on the offer. Although the rule does not expressly require that the act of reliance itself be of a reasonable nature,[52] (only) reasonable acts in reliance are likely to deserve protection. For this reason, it might be difficult to characterize an offeree's "extensive investigation" concerning the advisability of acceptance as an act of reasonable reliance under Article 16(2)(b), unless the offer itself was of such a special nature that the offeror would not expect the offeree's acceptance before such an extensive investigation had been made.[53]

Assuming an offer is irrevocable under Article 16(2), the offeree can – by definition – accept it even after learning of the offeror's subsequent attempt to revoke. On the other hand, according to Article 17, an offer is terminated when the offeror receives a rejection from his offeree, and this is true even if the offer was "irrevocable" under the rule in Article 16. Therefore, upon receipt of such a rejection,[54] the offeror is free to take his business elsewhere.

§ 3.7 Acceptance

Articles 18–22 deal with the subject of acceptance, and Article 18(1) defines the essential elements. An acceptance may consist of a statement or of other conduct. As an example of the latter, an offeree who enters into a contract with a carrier for shipment of the goods offered would seem to have indicated his acceptance by conduct.[55] In any case, the key to an acceptance is the offeree's indication of assent.[56]

Since the CISG does not charge the offeree with a general duty to reply, silence or inactivity does not – in itself – amount to an acceptance,[57] and the offeror cannot circumvent this rule by stating in the offer that silence by the offeree will be taken to indicate the offeree's assent. If, however, the offeree initiates a transaction by soliciting an offer, she (the offeree) may choose to bind herself in advance by indicating that an offer, if made,

---

starting point, *revocable*, and since we are not here in the situation contemplated by subsection (2)(a), Professor Schlechtriem's interpretation seems difficult to square with the (2)(b) rule.

[51] *Accord* Honnold, *Uniform Law* at 164.

[52] The official French version of the CISG text, which is slightly different and somewhat more appropriate, demands: "*et s'il a agi en conséquence*" (of reasonably considering the offer as irrevocable).

[53] Where the offeree "would *have to* engage" in such an investigation (emphasis added), the U.N. *Secretariat Commentary* would make the offer irrevocable for the period of time necessary for the offeree to make his determination: *see id.*, Comment 8 to Article 14 of the 1978 Draft.

[54] As regards a purported acceptance which varies from the content of the original offer *see* Article 19 and § 3.8 *infra*.

[55] For other examples, *see* Schlechtriem in Schlechtriem, *Commentary/Kommentar*, Art. 18, Rd.Nr. 7. Re. the related rule in Article 18(3) *see* text *infra* with notes 64 *et seq.*

[56] *See* LG Krefeld, 24 November 1992, reported in UNILEX, analyzed by Witz, *Premières Applications* no. 35.

[57] Article 18(1) second sentence.

will be deemed accepted (e.g., absent contrary indication by the offeree within a specified period of time).[58]

Under Article 18(2) an acceptance becomes effective when the offeree's indication of assent reaches the offeror,[59] assuming the indication reaches the offeror "in time."[60] A significant consequence of this receipt theory of acceptance is that the sender-offeree bears the risk of transmission, i.e., the risk that the acceptance may be delayed or never arrive. On the other hand, actual notice is not required: it is sufficient that the acceptance "reach" the offeror's sphere of business, so she at least has an opportunity to take notice of it.[61] Note also that the offeror loses her right to revoke once the acceptance has been dispatched.[62]

In accordance with the principle that the offeror is the master of the offer, the acceptance must reach the offeror within the time which the offeror has fixed.[63] If no time is fixed, the CISG default rule is that the acceptance must reach its destination within a reasonable time, taking due account of all the circumstances. To take one example, an offer sent by telefax will usually imply the need for a more prompt reply than an offer sent by post. Absent contrary indication, an oral offer requires an immediate acceptance.

As regards the time at which acceptance takes effect, Article 18(3) provides for the special case where the offeree indicates assent by performing an act. Sometimes, the offeror will request (or at least impliedly condone) that the offeree accept by merely performing an act, (e.g.) to ship goods ordered by the offeror. In one such situation, a U.S. District Court has held that the provision of a reference letter to the Food and Drug Administration could qualify as an act indicating assent to a contract.[64] Such an understanding may also follow from an established practice between the parties,[65] or from a broader usage within the trade. In such cases, assuming the act is performed in timely fashion, the acceptance becomes effective at the moment the act is performed (or performance is commenced). The logical consequence of this is that the offeror cannot revoke even a revocable offer if the purported revocation reaches the offeree after the act requested has been performed.[66]

---

[58] *See* the decision of Cour de Cassation (France) of 27 January 1998, UNILEX (applying the *principle* in Article 18(1) in a case where a buyer had requested goods purchased be modified and had accepted them without reservation). *See also* the decision of OLG Köln (Germany), 22 February 1994, UNILEX (silence, linked to other circumstances, constituted an acceptance). In a judgment rendered on 23 April 1998 (reported in CLOUT and UNILEX) the Danish Eastern High Court, citing Article 18, held that silence on the part of an offeree doing business in France did *not* constitute an acceptance of a Danish seller's offer: for further details *see* Lookofsky, *Alive and Well*.

[59] As to when such a communication "reaches" the offeror *see* Article 24. Once the acceptance becomes effective a contract is formed: *see* Article 23.

[60] *See infra*, text with note 63.

[61] *See* Article 24 and Magnus in Staudinger, *Kommentar*, Art. 24, Rd.Nr. 15.

[62] *See* Article 16(1), *supra* § 3.6, and *infra* § 3.9.

[63] Re. the time at which such a period begins to run *see* Article 20 and § 3.9 *infra*.

[64] *See* the U.S. District Court decision in *Geneva Chemicals*, cited *supra* § 3.6 note 49. According to the court, whether the defendant-seller's acts actually indicated assent to a contract under the circumstances would be analyzed at trial on the basis of industry custom.

[65] Re. this concept *see* Article 9(1) discussed *supra* § 2.13.

[66] Or performance of the act commenced. This accords with the principle laid down in Article 16(1): *see supra* § 3.6.

§ 3.8 Acceptance, Counter-Offer and the Battle of Forms

The starting point of Article 19 is that an acceptance, to be effective, must correspond to the offer which it purports to accept. In other words, Article 19(1) conforms with the traditional idea that an acceptance must match the offer – be its "mirror image," so to speak.[67] Conversely, a reply which purports to be an acceptance, but which does not actually reflect the terms of the offer, constitutes (not an acceptance, but) a rejection and counter-offer instead.

> *Illustration 3b*: S offers to sell goods to buyer B at a stated price X, and B "accepts" by agreeing to buy the same goods at price Y (which is lower than X).

In this illustration there is obviously no "meeting of minds," since B's purported "acceptance" does not mirror the offer made by S. For this reason, B's reply serves as a rejection which effectively kills the offer originally made. Note, however, that the rejection here also serves as a counter-offer, (i.e.) a new offer, capable of being accepted on its own terms; so, if S replies by agreeing to sell at price Y, these parties' minds will then have met.[68]

It should also be noted that not every reply/response to a CISG offer will "purport to be an acceptance" of the offer received. A reply might, for example, make inquiries or suggest the possibility of different or additional terms, thus exploring the willingness of the offeror to bargain (accept terms more favorable to the offeree), while leaving open the possibility that the offeree might still be willing to accept the offeror's original terms.[69]

> *Illustration 3c*: S offers to sell goods to buyer B at a stated price X. B replies: "I am certainly interested, but would you consider selling the same goods for price Y?"

The effect of an "independent communication" like this is not set forth in the Convention text, but there can be little doubt that a such communication – which does *not* "purport to be an acceptance"[70] – should not be interpreted as a rejection (coupled with a counter-offer).

The foregoing examples (3b and 3c) involve relatively clear cut indications of the parties' intent. But parties who negotiate an international sales contract do not always reach an express agreement on all relevant points. A sales contract might, for example, come to consist of the seller's standard invoice sent as a "positive" reply to the (very differently formulated) purchase order which initiated the transaction in question. In another group of common cases, the parties first exchange brief telex, telefax or e-mail communications which cement the key contract terms (goods, price, delivery date); only later do the parties provide, exchange – or perhaps even engage in a "battle" of – (standard business) forms.[71]

---

67 The underlying idea is, of course, that contractual obligations arise out of expressions of mutual agreement.
68 *See, e.g.,* OLG Hamm (Germany), 22 September 1992, UNILEX (buyer requested wrapped bacon; seller's reply to deliver unwrapped bacon was rejection and counter offer). *See also,* the decision of OLG Frankfurt (Germany), 23 May 1995, UNILEX (delivery by seller of quantity less than that ordered by buyer constituted rejection and counter offer).
69 *See Secretariat Commentary,* Comment 4 to Article 17(1) of the 1978 Draft.
70 Since that would not be a reasonable interpretation of the offeree's intent: *see* Article 8.
71 *See also* Witz, *Premières Applications* no. 36 (*la bataille des formulaires*).

In situations such as these, where one party supplies (additional) terms not expressly agreed to by the other, or where the terms set forth by the parties do not match, the judge or arbitrator needs first to ask whether a binding contract has been formed; if the contract "exists," the decision-maker then needs to determine the terms of the deal. As domestic legislative experierience (e.g.) with UCC § 2–207 indicates, these are difficult questions.[72]

According to the international compromise reflected in Article 19(2) of the CISG treaty, an acceptance must – as a starting point – correspond to the offer it purports to accept. Non-material modifications, however, need not break the deal; in other words, a purported acceptance containing additional or different terms which do not materially alter the offer constitutes a true acceptance. Only if the offeror, without undue delay, objects to the immaterial discrepancy will the offeree's otherwise conforming reply be deemed a rejection;[73] if the offeror does not "so object" to the non-material modifications, these become part of the CISG deal.

When compared with the UCC domestic approach, and even with other international solutions, Article 19 seems to represent a conservatively formulated exception to the mirror-image rule,[74] especially since paragraph (3) lays down a long and non-exhaustive ("among other things") list of provisions considered to be "material" in the Article 19(2) sense. Indeed, based on this list, some CISG commentators have even found it difficult to imagine modifications that would not be "material."[75] Other scholars, inspired by more progressive transnational paradigms,[76] have advocated a flexible application of Article 19(3),[77] with some even suggesting that the rule merely establishes a rebuttable presumption of materiality.[78]

Since clauses relating to the "settlement of disputes" are among the items listed in Article 19(3), the highest court in France (Cour de Cassation) has characterized a jurisdiction clause in one party's form as a material term.[79] This does not, of course, suggest that the

---

[72] Regarding the controversial rule in UCC § 2-207 *see, e.g.,* Gillette & Walt, *Sales Law*, pp. 69–77, also discussing (*id*. at 76) the simplified *NCCUSL Draft Revision* of the rule.

[73] Because this might permit speculation at the expense of the offeree, Murray (*Formation* at 42–43) calls this part of Article 19 an "objectively absurd" rule.

[74] *Compare* the subsequent, more progressive solution provided in the *UNIDROIT Principles*, Articles 2.19– 2.22. Article 19(1) and (2) correspond with Articles 7(1) and (2) of ULF (*supra* § 1.2). Numerous ULF cases involved the distinction between material and immaterial modifications; paragraph 3 of Article 19 now attempts to provide some guidance.

[75] *See* Heuzé, *Vente internationale* no.186 and authors cited there; *see also* Farnsworth, *Formation* at 3–16.

[76] E.g., in the *UNIDROIT Principles, supra* note 74..

[77] *See* (e.g.) Audit, *Vente internationale*, no. 70, and Schlechtriem in Schlechtriem, *Commentary/Kommentar*, Art. 19, Rd.Nr. 8.

[78] These scholars emphasize that terms relating to the subjects listed in Article 19(3) "are considered" (*sont considérés*) material; the provision does *not* say they *must* be so considered: *see* Magnus in Staudinger, *Kommentar*, Art.19, Rd.Nr.16 and authors cited there. *Compare* Herber & Czerwenka, *Internationales Kaufrecht*, Art.19, Rd.Nr.11and *id.* Rd.Nr. 12 (advocating the relevance of trade usages). *Generally opposed*: Heuzé, *Vente internationale* no. 186 (insisting that the text of Article 19(3) *"malheureusement"* does not permit flexibility).

[79] *See* Cour de Cassation, 16 July 1998, UNILEX (clause conferring jurisdiction on French court, contrary to rule in Art. 5(1) of Brussels Convention, was material alteration). *See also Filanto S.p.a. v. Chilewich Internat'l Corp.*, 984 F.2d 58 (2d Cir. 1993) which involved an arbitration clause in one party's standard form.

same court (or other courts) would consider *any* reply containing an additional term or alteration to be material.[80] Indeed, a German court has held that a clause requiring notice of defects within 30 days after the date of the invoice is non-material under Article 19(2), notwithstanding the fact that the buyer's failure to notify within the stated time period effectively insulated the seller from all liability claims based on non-conforming goods.[81]

Whichever approach a given court prefers, Article 19 should not be read in isolation from other Convention provisions. To take one important example, a reply containing an additional term (as opposed to a modification) which conforms to international trade usage should not be held to constitute a material addition, even if it deals with an otherwise "material" topic listed in paragraph (3).[82] Nor can Article 19 be said to provide the only solution – let alone an effective solution – to all problems relating to standard business terms and/or the "battle of forms."[83] This inadequacy is especially prominent in cases where the provisions of the documents exchanged at the contract formation stage do not match (e.g. where only one party's form limits liability for breach), but where the parties proceed nonetheless to perform their main obligations (to deliver and pay) without regard to the contractual discrepancy and its potential consequences. In such cases – since neither the parties nor the court can "go back in time" – some sort of CISG contract must be said to exist,[84] i.e., even though the (material) terms of that contract are now in dispute.[85]

In some of these situations, Article 19 might lend itself to the "formalistic" approach – first established in domestic battle-of-forms cases – which looks to the standard terms of the party who, by putting forth the last (standard) document, got in the "last (unobjected to) shot;"[86] similarly, a buyer's acceptance of goods shipped and delivered might (also) be held to imply an acceptance of the seller's standard terms.[87]

---

80 *See* the decision of Cour de Cassation (France), 4 January 1995, UNILEX and CISGW3 (buyer's order specified that seller's price indication would be revised taking into account possible market decrease; S replied price would have to be revised according to both increase and decrease in market prices: held not a material alteration).

81 *See* LG Baden-Baden, 14 August 1991, UNILEX.

82 *See* Honnold, *Uniform Law* at 187. Re. party practices and trade usage *see* Article 9: *supra* § 2.13. *Accord*: Schlechtriem, *Commentary*, Art. 19, Rd.Nr. 20 with note 63; *Kommentar* at *id*. with note 81 (who sees party practices as the essence of the decision in *Filanto*, cited *supra* note 79). Even those who interpret Art. 19 (3) strictly must recognize the relevance of trade usage.

83 *But see* Schlechtriem, *Commentary*, Art. 19, Rd.Nr. 20 with note 52; *Kommentar* at *id*. with note 61.

84 Re. an acceptance by conduct *see* Article 18(1), *supra* § 3.7.

85 By its own terms, the first sentence in Article 19(2) applies *only* to a purported acceptance containing *non*-material (additional or different) terms. Under the "last shot" rule in the second sentence, these (non-material) "modifications" become part of the contract when the offeror does not "*so object*" (i.e., to the non-material modifications).

86 *Compare* Schlechtriem, *Commentary/Kommentar*, Art. 19, Rd.Nr. 20 (problem of conflicting business forms *must* be solved using the mechanism of Article 19).

87 Or we might (conversely) characterize the seller's shipment as an acceptance of buyer's terms. *See* (e.g.) the decision of Tribunal Commercial de Nivelles (Belgium), 19 September 1995, in CISGW3 and UNILEX (Belgian buyer accepted Swiss seller's offer containing express, bold-type *reference* to Swiss Machinery Manufacturers' standard terms which, in turn, contained Swiss forum selection clause; buyer held to have accepted offer without modification, so Belgian court was without jurisdiction).

A different – often less arbitrary, and therefore often more fair – method is the "knock-out" approach which cancels out the conflicting terms in the forms submitted by the parties and looks instead to the CISG to supply the gap-filling rule.[88] The language of Article 19 does not preclude a solution based on this approach,[89] thus leading to solutions more in line with the progressive *UNIDROIT Principles*.[90]

To round out the present discussion, it should be noted that – once a CISG contract has been validly *concluded* (on the basis of the Formation rules in Part II)[91] – a *subsequent* "unilateral" communication (from one contracting party to the other) does not "automatically" become part of (or otherwise serve to modify) the original/bilateral deal.[92] This point was made clear in a case decided in 2003 by a U.S. Court of Appeals.[93] A Canadian winery (B) had agreed by telephone to buy 1.2 million corks from (S), the U.S. subsidiary of a French manufacturer.[94] Together with each of the 11 shipments which ensued, S sent an invoice,[95] stating (in French) that "Any dispute arising under the present contract is under the sole jurisdiction of the Court of Commerce of the City of Perpignan [France]."[96] B took delivery and paid for each shipment, but made no objection (or other comment) in relation to the clause. Later, claiming that wine bottled with the S-corks was tainted by cork flavors, B filed suit in Federal Court against S (and its French parent). Holding the forum selection clauses to be valid and enforceable, the District Court granted a motion by S to dismiss, but the Court of Appeals for the 9th Circuit reversed: the forum clauses proffered by S had *not* (by virtue of CISG Article 19 or otherwise) become part of the oral agreement between the parties.[97]

---

[88]   *See* Cour de Cassation (France), 16 July 1998, UNILEX and CISGW3 (neither of 2 conflicting jurisdiction clauses held effective; court applied supplementary rule in Art. 5(1) of the Brussels Convention). *See also* Amtsgericht Kiel, 6 October 1995, in UNILEX and CISGW3 (rule in Art. 19(1) not applied, as parties commenced performance despite conflicting standard terms; court applied consistent terms, whereas conflicting terms were "knocked out," leaving the rules which applied by default). Similarly, if the seller's form disclaims liability for indirect loss, and the buyer's form would hold the seller liable, the conflicting terms could be held to knock each other out, with the result that the CISG gap-filling rule would allow the injured party full expectation damages for breach (under Article 74: *see infra* § 6.15). This accords with the *UNIDROIT Principles*: *see* Article 2.22.

[89]   *Accord*: Magnus in Staudinger, *Kommentar*, Art. 19, Rd.Nr. 25. *Compare* Schlechtriem, *Commentary*, Art. 19, Rd.Nr. 20 with note 55 (*Kommentar* at *id.* with note 74).

[90]   *UNIDROIT Principles* Article 2.22.

[91]   Or (in some CISG cases involving a Scandinavian-based party) on the basis of domestic law. Regarding the Article 92 declarations made by the Scandinavian States *see infra* § 8.4.

[92]   Regarding the rule on contract modification in CISG Article 29 *see supra* §§ 2.6 and 2.14.

[93]   *Chateau des Charmes Wines Ltd. v. Sabate USA, Sabate S.A.*, 5 May 2003 (9th Cir. 2003), available at CISGW3 and UNILEX.

[94]   The parties had agreed on payment and shipping terms, but no other terms were discussed, nor did the parties have any history of prior dealings.

[95]   Some arrived before the shipments, some with the shipments, and some after the shipments.

[96]   On the back of each invoice a number of provisions were printed in French, including a clause specifying that disputes arising out of the agreement should be brought before a court in the judicial district where Seller's office was located.

[97]   *See Chateau des Charmes*, note 93 *supra*: "The oral agreements between [S] and [B] as to the kind of cork, the quantity, and the price were sufficient to create complete and binding contracts. The terms of those agreements

§ 3.9 Time for Acceptance

As noted previously, a CISG acceptance must reach the offeror within the period of time which the offeror has fixed or within a reasonable time.[98] In either case, Article 20(1) helps to fix the point in time at which that period begins in the concrete case.[99] As regards periods fixed by "instantaneous" means of communication (telephone, telefax, e-mail),[100] the time begins to run from the moment that the offer "reaches" the offeree. As regards non-instantaneous means of communication (telegram or letter), however, the CISG default rule is that the period begins to run from the moment the communication is handed in for dispatch or from the date shown on the letter.[101] To this extent Article 20(1) stands in contrast to the CISG rule that an acceptance first becomes effective when it "reaches" the offeree,[102] and the combined operation of the two rules may not always lead to reasonable results.[103]

According to the general Article 18(2) rule, an acceptance is not effective if the indication of assent does not reach the offeror within the time he has fixed or within a reasonable time. Article 21 of the CISG provides two exceptions to the rule. The first of these relates to Article 18(2) whereby a late acceptance is of no effect. Under the exception set forth in Article 21(1), a late acceptance is nevertheless effective as such if the offeror promptly notifies the offeree to that effect. In such event, the acceptance becomes effective upon its receipt (and before the subsequent notice by the offeror).[104]

Article 21(2) deals with a somewhat more complex situation: the late acceptance shows that it has been sent in such circumstances that, if its transmission had been normal, it would have reached the offeror in time. In this case the CISG adopts the German and

---

did not include any forum selection clause. . . . Under the Convention [Art. 29], a "contract may be modified or terminated by the mere agreement of the parties." . However, the Convention clearly states that "[a]dditional or different terms relating, among other things, to . . . the settlement of disputes are considered to alter the terms of the offer materially." [Art. 19(3)]. There is no indication that [B] conducted itself in a manner that evidenced any affirmative assent to the forum selection clauses in the invoices. Rather, [B] merely performed its obligations under the oral contract. Nothing in the Convention suggests that the failure to object to a party's unilateral attempt to alter materially the terms of an otherwise valid agreement is an "agreement" within the terms of Article 29. *Cf.* [Art. 8(3)]."

98   *See* Article 18(2), discussed *supra* § 3.7.
99   A companion rule regarding the effect of official holidays or non-business days on the period of acceptance is set forth in Article 20(2).
100   The English House of Lords has held (in a non-CISG jurisdictional context) that telex belongs to the "instantaneous communication" category: *see Brinkibon Ltd. v. Stahag Stahl Etc.*, 2 AC 34 [1983], discussed in Lookofsky & Hertz, *Transnational Litigation*, Ch. 2.4. Assuming that judgment to be sound, telefax and e-mail communications must surely qualify as "instantaneous" CISG communications; *see also supra* § 2.11, text with notes 185–86.
101   As always, the offeror – who remains the master of the terms of the offer – can set forth another solution in the offer itself.
102   *See* Article 15(1), discussed in § 3.5 *supra*. Article 24 defines the point in time when a declaration of intention (offer, acceptance, etc.) is considered to "reach" the addressee.
103   For a fuller analysis *see* Murray, *Formation* at 20–23.
104   The *Secretariat Commentary*, Comment 3 to Article 19(1) of the 1978 Draft is in *accord*.

Scandinavian rule: the late acceptance is effective as such, unless the offeror promptly informs the offeree that he considers his offer as having lapsed.[105]

The CISG rule regarding withdrawal of an offer (made, but not yet received) has been previously discussed.[106] It follows from Article 22 that an acceptance may not be withdrawn after it has become effective. Once the acceptance is effective, however, a binding contract is made,[107] so "withdrawal" after this point will constitute an unjustifiable revocation and thus a breach by the offeree.

As stated in Article 23 of the CISG: "A contract is concluded at the moment when an acceptance of an offer becomes effective in accordance with the provisions of this Convention." According to the main rule in Article 18(2), an acceptance becomes effective at the moment the indication of assent reaches the offeror.[108]

§ 3.10 SALES CONTRACT VALIDITY AND DEFENSES TO CONTRACT ENFORCEMENT

The content of the rules just discussed reaffirms a key message set forth in Article 4: Part II of the Convention deals with contract formation, but *not* with contract validity – this latter subject being left mainly for determination by (domestic) rules outside the CISG.[109] In other words, Part II of the Convention is designed to govern the mechanics of consent (offer, acceptance etc.), but not "defenses" to enforcement of the agreement so made. Although a CISG contract is "formed" upon timely receipt of the offeree's acceptance,[110] there is no real consent – and thus no binding contract – if the offeree sets forth a viable defense, such as fraud, duress, misrepresentation, etc.

The Convention drafters had no choice but to draw the line,[111] but the distinction between formation and validity sometimes seems difficult to maintain, since both these (allegedly separable) subjects deal with the overall "process" by which a contract comes to be.[112] And although the Convention is "not [generally] concerned" with validity, it does in fact address a few matters which clearly impact upon that very subject.[113] One controversial validity-related question (already discussed) is whether an "offer" which contains an open price term is "sufficiently definite" to bind the parties to a contract under

---

[105] *Compare* (e.g.) § 149 of the new German Civil Code and § 4 of the Scandinavian Contracts Act.

[106] *Supra* § 3.5.

[107] *See* Article 23.

[108] Assuming the acceptance reaches the offeror within the time fixed, etc. *See* Article 18; *see also* Article 24 which defines the point in time when a declaration of intention (offer, acceptance, etc.) is considered to "reach" the addressee.

[109] As noted previously in § 2.6, and again in the text *infra*, there are some exceptions.

[110] Article 18(2) and 23.

[111] The legislative history makes it clear that the same delegates who were able to reach the compromises necessary for the Formation rules in CISG Part II were not nearly ready to make the concessions necessary to iron out differing domestic conceptions as regards sales contract validity.

[112] *See* Lookofsky, *Loose Ends* at 405 (noting the Scandinavian objections to CISG Part II).

[113] Article 4 itself holds the validity door open a crack: "except as otherwise expressly provided in this Convention."

Article 14.[114] Another CISG provision relating to the subject of sales contract validity is Article 29. According to this rule, a sales contract may be modified or terminated by the "mere agreement" of the parties. Therefore, a sales contract modification – (e.g.) whereby the seller agrees to deliver the goods for a price lower than originally agreed – is generally binding and cannot be attacked for lack of (what American and other Common lawyers call) "consideration."[115] Article 29 does not, however, address duress or other validity issues, so CISG lawyers still need to draw the line between agreements made under the influence of threats and extortion ("economic duress") and agreements which satisfy the (Article 7) requirement of "good faith in international trade."[116] It remains to be seen whether courts and arbitrators will seek the solution to such problems within the Convention itself or whether they will turn to sources outside of the CISG.[117]

Also likely to generate problems of validity are contractual disclaimers or limitations of liability (and similarly clauses likely to be contained in a CISG seller' standard terms). Here as elsewhere, the CISG leaves the parties "free" to contract out of its default-rule regime, but in most instances the applicable domestic rules of validity delimit the boundaries for the acceptable exercise of the freedom which CISG parties enjoy.[118]

§ 3.11 FORMATION OF E-COMMERCE CONTRACTS

Commercial legislation cannot always keep up with the fast pace of commercial trade, and this is especially true when it comes to international commercial legislation. Of course, since the Convention was negotiated in the 1970's and not even opened for signature until 1980, one can hardly blame the Convention drafters for not taking the special problems of modern electronic commerce – including "e-contract" formation – into account.

Now, in the first years of the 21st century, we see the beginnings of "special" (or revised) legislation designed to regulate e-commerce at the local and regional levels, both in the United States and elsewhere.[119] But just as jurists dealing with domestic transactions still need to look to traditional rules of law to regulate e-contract formation,[120] the contracts

---

[114] *See supra* § 3.3 and *infra* § 4.13.

[115] For a comparative perspective *see* Lookofsky, *Consequential Damages*, Ch. 2.1. For a case upholding the validity of an allegedly "one-sided" CISG sales contract (as opposed to a sales contract modification) on the basis of domestic law *see* the U.S. District Court decision in *Geneva Pharmaceuticals Technology Corp. v. Barr Laboratories, Inc.*, 10 May 2002 (S.D. of New York), reconsidered as re. other issues on 21 August 2002, both decisions in UNILEX and CISGW3.

[116] On this standard *see supra* § 2.10.

[117] The non-CISG sources need not necessarily be domestic; they could be *lex mercatoria* rules. *See supra* § 2.11. *See also* (re. threats/duress) Article 3.9 of the *UNIDROIT Principles*.

[118] Re. limits to the freedom-of-contract rule in Article 6 *see* Chapter 7 *infra*.

[119] *See* (e.g.) re. American domestic law the (August 2002) *NCCUSL Draft Revision* of UCC § 2-204 which comprises contracts concluded by the "interaction of electronic agents." Re. the Uniform Electronic Transaction Act *see* Maggs, G., "The Waning Importance of UCC Article 2," 78 *Notre Dame L. Rev.* 595 (2003). Re. EU-legislation *see infra* note 128.

[120] The original UCC rules must, for example, still be applied to electronic contract formation situations until a newer set of UCC rules becomes applicable (*see* preceding note).

made by international e-traders must, for the time being, look to the formation rules in CISG Part II.

Although the amenability of CISG Part II to e-trade has not yet been tested in the courts,[121] some Convention commentators have nonetheless been willing to provide some predications, and the forecast seems quite positive.[122]

In much the same way that Part III of the Convention seems well-suited to the regulation of contracts for the sale of computer software,[123] we can also expect the CISG Part II rules to deal adequately with the process of e-contract formation by modern communications techniques.[124] Electronic communications occupy a functional position somewhere between traditional letter and telephone communications, and there should be no great difficulty "pressing" EDI and e-mail into the Convention's traditional offer and acceptance grid.[125] Nor should the new technology of electronic signatures raise "special" concerns as regards those exceptional CISG sales contracts which need to be evidenced by a (signed) writing.[126]

Indeed, "electronic contracts" are not fundamentally different from paper-based contracts.[127] And while there may be a need to *supplement* CISG Part II (and other contract formation) rules to achieve greater "certainty" in electronic contracting,[128] the "areas where the approach or solution followed in the CISG has been shown to be problematic stem not from the use of more modern forms of communication, but rather are structural or conceptual deficiencies that existed from the outset and are applicable to all forms of communication."[129] CISG courts and arbitrators do not seem to have been unduly hampered by these deficiencies,[130] so – both as regards e-commerce and otherwise – we can surely make do with Part II of the Convention for a good time to come.

---

[121]   As of this writing (2003), the reported decisions do not seem to have addressed these issues, *inter alia,* the effectiveness of legally relevant statements in Articles 24, 26 and 27. *See also* Schlechtriem, *Bundesgerichtshof* at 6.

[122]   *See* Eiselen, *Electronic Commerce.*

[123]   *See generally supra* § 2.5.

[124]   *Accord*: Eiselen, *Electronic Commerce.*

[125]   *See generally* Eiselen, *id.* In the case of an EDI message, the offer, acceptance, order or notice will be legally effective once it has been received by the third party network operator and placed in the recipient's electronic mailbox, when store and retrieve communication is used, or where it has been received by the recipient's computer system; in the case of an e-mail, the offer, acceptance, order or notice will be legally effective once it has been deposited in the recipient's electronic post box. *Id.*

[126]   Re. Articles 11 and 96 *see supra* § 2.14 and *infra* § 8.8.

[127]   *See* the note re. "Legal aspects of electronic commerce" by the United Nations Secretariat A/CN.9/WG.IVWP.95 (20 Sept. 2001) p. 5, citing Pompian, S., in 85 *Virginia Law Review* 1479.

[128]   Re. this argument in support of the proposed draft convention on electronic contracting *see* United Nations Secretariat, *id.* at 13. *See also* Article 11(1) of the European E-Commerce Directive (2000/31/EC) which, as regards certain orders placed through technological means, provides that the "service provider" *has to acknowledge* the "service recipient's" order without delay and by electronic means, and that the order and the acknowledgment are *deemed to be received* when the addressee is able to *access* it. Re. the relationship between this Directive and CISG sales of "goods" *see supra* § 2.5 with note 71.

[129]   Eiselen, *Electronic Commerce.*

[130]   *See, e.g.,* cases cited *supra* in the present Chapter.

These preliminary views have been confirmed by an opinion, promulgated by the CISG-AC[131] in response to a recuest by the International Chamber of Commerce asking the CISG-AC to reflect on the issue of electronic communications and the ability of the CISG to respond to such challenges. The CISG-AC shares the opinion that the Convention can accommodate electronic communications as well as it does traditional communications.[132]

---

[131] Regarding the CISG-AC *see supra* § 2.9 with note 163.

[132] *See* CISG-AC Opinion no 1, Electronic Communications under CISG, 15 August 2003. The opinion is available at <http://cisgw3.law.pace.edu/cisg/CISG-AC-op1.html>.

CHAPTER FOUR

OBLIGATIONS OF THE PARTIES

§ 4.1 INTRODUCTION: OBLIGATION, RISK & REMEDY

It is of utmost importance to determine the obligations of the CISG contracting parties, in other words: what the seller and buyer have each (expressly or impliedly) promised to do. Nearly all sales disputes, both domestic and international, involve a claim by one (allegedly injured) party that the other (allegedly breaching) party failed to perform an obligation incurred: (e.g.) that the seller did not deliver the goods, or that the goods delivered did not "conform" to the contract, or that the buyer did not pay at the contractually agreed time, etc. Some of these cases focus on the question of performance and risk; others focus on the relationship between performance and breach.[1]

If, for example, the seller can establish that her obligation (under the contract and the Convention) was simply to "hand over" the goods to the first carrier (for subsequent shipment to the buyer), and that this delivery promise was kept, then the fact that the goods never actually arrived at their ultimate destination will not constitute a contractual breach. If, on the other hand, the buyer can establish a breach – some failure by the seller to perform as promised[2] – then that injured buyer will surely qualify for some remedy to set things right.

In the present chapter we concentrate on those CISG Part III rules which define the parties' obligations. In this way, we set the stage for the related discussion of risk of loss,[3] as well as for the all-important subject of remedial relief.[4] The rest of this chapter is divided into three main parts, covering considerations which relate to (A) CISG obligations generally, (B) the CISG seller's obligations, and (C) the CISG buyer's obligations.

---

[1]   As indicated, this text employs the familiar Common law term "breach" – a term found in Article 25, but not in Articles 45 or 61 – to indicate a CISG party's "failure to perform." Although a Common lawyer would not equate the 2 concepts (because not every failure to perform qualifies as a breach: Lookofsky, *Consequential Damages*, Ch. 4.4.1.1), it would be artificial to avoid using the term breach in an English language presentation of the CISG rules. Regarding the strict "basis" of CISG liability and "exemptions" for failure to perform *see infra* §§ 6.3, 6.14, 6.19, 6.27 and 6.32.

[2]   I.e., a failure to make conforming delivery at the time and place (expressly or impliedly) agreed: *see* preceding note.

[3]   The passing of risk is discussed *infra* in Chapter 5.

[4]   The gap-filling remedies provided by the CISG are discussed *infra* in Chapter 6. Contractually agreed remedies are discussed in Chapter 7.

4A CISG OBLIGATIONS IN GENERAL

§ 4.2 THE CONVENTION HIERARCHY: CONTRACT, CUSTOM, CISG

As under the UCC and other domestic sales law, the obligations of the parties under a CISG contract are established at three levels: (1) obligations based upon (express) consent to terms set forth in the sales contract concerned, (2) obligations based upon (usually implied) consent to usages of trade; and (3) obligations based upon the gap-filling application of CISG rules.

This three-tiered structure indicates the subordinate, though significant role of the CISG. As a gap-filling regime, the Convention must defer to the first two tiers on the scale. To the extent the parties do not take active steps to "deactivate" automatic CISG application (Article 1) by "opting out" (Article 6),[5] the Convention applies "by default" – but only to that extent. Since the parties to an interational sale often "derogate from or vary the effect of" *some* CISG provisions,[6] i.e., as opposed to discarding the entire Convention regime, numerous CISG cases involve a considerable mixture and interplay between what UCC lawyers refer to as the "bargain-in-fact" (the parties' express agreement as supplemented by applicable trade usages)[7] and the default rules of the Convention which serve to fill in the remaining bargain-gaps.

So, assuming the CISG is our starting point,[8] and assuming the parties have not clearly indicated their intention to contract out of the entire Convention regime,[9] we must determine the concrete "mix" between express promise, implied custom, and CISG rule. Since express promise takes precedence over implied custom,[10] and since the parties are free to derogate from nearly any CISG rule,[11] we look first to the parties' own "private law," i.e., the performance-obligations expressly required by the contract concerned.[12]

Suppose a seller in Italy agrees to deliver special pipes for the production of natural gas "in Denmark" on "February 1st." If a court or arbitral tribunal later determines that the pipes were actually delivered in a different place or at a different time, the seller's failure to perform as expressly promised would constitute a breach of the contract concerned; and since the parties' express agreement clearly "covers the case," there would be no reason to consult the applicable CISG gap-filling rules which require delivery "to the first carrier . . . within a reasonable time . . . ."[13]

---

5   *See supra* Chapter 2A.
6   *Id.*
7   *See supra* § 2.13.
8   I.e., because the parties reside or have their places of business in "different Contracting States" (*see supra* § 2.3).
9   As indicated *supra* in § 2.7 courts and arbitrators should always presume CISG application as their point of departure in cases where the Article 1(1) rule itself would lead to Convention application; a party who seeks to rebut this presumption should be required to present clear evidence of both parties' intent to contract out (under Article 6).
10   *See* Article 9(2) discussed *supra* in § 2.13.
11   At least within the range permitted by the validity limitations of the applicable non-CISG rules. Re. Article 4(a) *see supra* § 2.6 and *infra* § 7.4.
12   *See* (e.g.) Articles 30 and 53 (seller and buyer must deliver and pay as "required by the contract").
13   Re. the time and place of delivery under CISG Articles 31(a) and 33(c) *see infra* § 4.3.

Similar considerations apply with respect to the quality of the goods to be delivered. If, for example, an American buyer contracts with an Italian seller for the purchase of "type 4436 rust-free and acid-resistant" pipe,[14] the seller must deliver that kind of pipe, i.e., pipe of the "quality and description required by the contract." And if a different type pipe is delivered, or if it rusts, the seller will have failed to perform his obligations regarding the "conformity of the goods,"[15] just as that failure will automatically trigger CISG remedies for breach.[16]

Even if the contract drafted by the parties contains no express provision which defines the seller's obligation to deliver goods of a given quality at a particular time and place, there may still be an implied "bargain" on one or more of these points, since the practices which the parties have established between themselves, as well as usages more widely observed in the trade concerned, automatically become part of the CISG deal.[17] In the *BP Oil* case,[18] for example, the U.S. Court of Appeals for the 5th Circuit held that the delivery term "CFR" is a widely used "Incoterm" which the CISG effectively "incorporates" by means of Article 9(2); so, simply by virtue of the reference to "CFR" in the contract, the seller was held to fulfill its contractual obligations if the gasoline met the contract's qualitative specifications at the point in time when the goods passed the ship's rail.[19]

It is against the background of this broader, 3-tiered picture that we now proceed to take a closer look at the supplementary Convention rules, the rules which help us determine the obligations of the parties, the seller and the buyer, in a given international sale.

4B OBLIGATIONS OF THE SELLER

§ 4.3 TIME AND PLACE OF DELIVERY

The various obligations of the seller are summarized in Article 30. In essence, the seller must deliver the right goods and documents at the right time and place, i.e., as required by the contract (and custom) and the CISG rules. By providing that the seller must deliver the goods "as required by the contract" Article 30 restates the primary importance of terms to which the parties have actually agreed; only absent agreement (or applicable custom) do we need the CISG to fill in the resulting gaps.

The obligations to deliver the goods and hand over documents at the right time and place are more fully explained in Articles 31–34. As regards the time of delivery an international sales contract will usually require that delivery take place on a particular date or (at least) within a given time-period, and in these kinds of cases paragraphs (a)–(b) of Article 33

---

[14] This was the contractual description of the goods in a CISG case (involving a Danish buyer and an Italian seller) decided by the Supreme Court of Denmark on 15 February 2001, reported in *UfR* 2001.1039 H, also reported in CISGW3.

[15] Re. Article 35(1) *see infra* § 4.4.

[16] Re. Buyer's Remedies *see infra* § 6.3 *et seq.*

[17] *See supra* § 2.13.

[18] *BP Oil International v. Empresa Estatal Petroleos de Ecuador*, U. S. Court of Appeals (5th Circuit, 11 June 2003), available at <http://cisgw3.law.pace.edu/cases/030611u1.html>, also available in UNILEX.

[19] *Id.*, citing Article 36 (discussed *infra* § 5.2). *See also* text *infra* with notes 21–22.

clearly bind the seller to deliver at the time (or within the period) agreed. Absent such specific agreement, the seller must deliver within a "reasonable time."[20]

The CISG also provides default rules as regards the place of delivery in an international sale, but here again the contract is likely to preëmpt the default regime by specifying the place concerned, perhaps in conjunction with a shorthand delivery symbol such as CFR, CIF or FOB. Indeed, since the precise demarcation of the place of delivery is a key function of the well-known and widely used Incoterms regime,[21] there will often be little use for the CISG rules on this point.[22]

If the particular contract and the relevant usages do not fix the place of delivery, Article 31 can fill in the gap. Paragraph (a) deals with the most common kind of international sales case, i.e., where performance of the contract involves "carriage" of the goods.[23] In such cases, the seller's default delivery obligation consists in handing over the goods to the "first carrier"– this being a reference to the first independent carrier, i.e., a third party not under seller's or buyer's direct control.[24] So, in this (very common) situation, the place of delivery is the place where the "handing over" should take occur. In other (far less common) cases, where an international sales contract does not contemplate carriage by an independent carrier, paragraphs (b) and (c) of Article 31 lay down the rules which then apply by default.[25]

In the most typical situation just described (i.e., where the contract involves carriage), the seller will sometimes dispatch the goods on terms whereby documents controlling their disposition (e.g., a negotiable bill of lading) are not to be handed over to the buyer except as "against" (in exchange for) payment of the price. If, in such case, the documents do not conform to the contract, the CISG rules may give the seller the right to "cure" the defect;[26] the same is true with respect to defects in the goods themselves.[27]

---

[20] This period begins to run after the "conclusion of the contract": *see* Article 33(c).

[21] As promulgated by the International Chamber of Commerce (ICC), headquartered in Paris, France. *See* <www.iccwbo.org>. *See also infra* § 5.2.

[22] A given Incoterm can become operative by virtue of an express contractual provision providing (e.g.) for delivery "FOB Le Havre (Incoterms)." In the *BP Oil* case (discussed in the text *supra* with notes 18–19) the contract simply set forth the trade term "CFR," but the Incoterm definition of that term was held to have been "incorporated" into the contract as an international trade usage (re. Article 9 *see supra* § 2.13; re. the use of trade terms *see also infra* § 5.2); this was, moreover, a *reasonable* interpretation under Article 8 (*supra* § 2.12).

[23] Even if the contract does not expressly refer to the use of a carrier, the distance which separates the parties and/or their practices may carry the necessary implication. *See* Huber in Schlechtriem, *Kommentar/Commentary,* Art. 31, Rd.Nr. 20.

[24] *Accord* Huber *id.,* Rd.Nr. 24–25.

[25] In the case of specific goods in a specific place, such as a particular painting currently on exhibit in a given gallery, the default rule in paragraph (b) requires the seller to place the goods at the buyer's disposal at that specific place. In other (paragraph c) cases – (i.e.) cases contemplating neither carriage nor specific goods in a specific place – the seller's default obligation is to place the goods at the buyer's disposal at the seller's place of business. Since, by virtue of the language and the policy of Article 31(a), it is irrelevant who pays for the carriage, Article 31(a) should also apply when the buyer is the one who makes the technical arrangements (typically involving the making of a contract with the carrier): *accord* Magnus in Staudinger, *Kommentar,* Art. 31, Rd.Nr. 14–17.

[26] *See* Article 34.

[27] Re. the seller's right to cure defects in the goods themselves *see infra* § 6.9.

As discussed more fully in subsequent sections, the place of delivery is of particular significance as regards the issue of the passing of risk,[28] and since the evaluation of whether the goods which the seller has delivered conform to the contract is made as of the passing of risk,[29] the time and place of delivery also affect that key (conformity) determination. In addition, the place of delivery (as determined by the contract or, by default, the CISG) may ultimately determine the outcome of a fundamental procedural question: whether a given court enjoys juridical jurisdiction to decide the merits of a CISG case.[30]

§ 4.4   CONFORMITY (QUANTITY AND QUALITY) OF THE GOODS: INTRODUCTION & EXPRESS OBLIGATIONS

A substantial portion of all sales litigation (both domestic and international) relates to claims that the goods delivered "do not conform with the contract" – a fact which hundreds of reported CISG cases confirm.

In this section, we focus on the basic – yet very important – rule in Article 35(1) – a rule designed to regulate the relatively straightforward situations where the buyer claims that the goods do not conform to the quantity, quality and description required by the express terms of the individual contract concerned. In subsequent sections, we shall consider related, but often more complex claims based on the implied quality-standards defined by the supplementary rules in Article 35(2).[31] We shall also have occasion to consider additional rules which can affect any CISG non-conformity claim. One of these additional provisions (Article 36) establishes the relevant point in time for the non-conformity determination. Two other – extremely important – rules concern the buyer's duty to examine the goods under Article 38 and the buyer's obligation to provide the seller with timely notice of a given non-conformity claim (Article 39).[32]

Article 35(1) confirms that which any commercial lawyer should expect: the CISG conformity determination begins with the terms of the contract,[33] including the obligations

---

[28]   *See generally infra* Chapter 5.

[29]   Re. Article 36 *see generally infra* § 4.9.

[30]   *See supra* § 1.4. In one of many cases applying the CISG place-of-delivery rule to resolve this jurisdictional issue under the (EU) Brussels Convention, an Italian seller and a Danish buyer concluded a CISG contract for the sale of iron pipes; the buyer alleged that the seller delivered non-conforming pipe and brought suit seeking damages in a Danish court. According to the relevant rule in Article 5(1) of the Convention, the seller could bring suit at "the place of performance of the obligation in question," and since, by virtue of the gap-filling rule in CISG Article 31(a), the place of performance of the seller's obligation to deliver conforming goods was Italy, the Supreme Court of Denmark rightly held that Danish courts did *not* have jurisdiction to decide the merits of the case. *See* the decision of Højesteret (Supreme Court of Denmark) of 15 February 2001 reported in *UfR* 2001.1039 H. According to some CISG commentators, the parties' agreement as to a delivery term should not be interpreted as affecting jurisdiction, but this view, which runs counter to the logic of the Danish decision just cited, also conflicts with the European Court's interpretation of the Brussels Convention. *See generally,* Lookofsky & Hertz, *Transnational Litigation,* Ch. 2.2.

[31]   *See infra* §§ 4.7 and 4.8.

[32]   *See generally infra* § 4.9.

[33]   *See also supra* § 4.2.

expressly undertaken by the seller as regards the quantity and quality of the goods. In one simple yet illustrative case,[34] a Turkish company promised to deliver 1,000 tons of fresh cucumbers (suitable for pickling) to a buyer doing business in Germany, but the seller allegedly delivered less than that amount. Since the CISG was held to apply,[35] the seller was obligated to deliver goods of the quantity, quality and description required by the contract, so delivery of less than 1,000 tons was a non-conforming delivery, a contractual breach.[36]

A case decided in 2002 by the Danish Maritime and Commercial Court involved 80 tons of frozen fish,[37] with middleman/seller (S) in Denmark having first offered "Whole Round" mackerel to middleman/buyer (B) in Germany. In subsequent telefax communications, S specified the goods as "Trachurus Symmetricus Murphyi." On the basis of these precise descriptions, and given the fact that these particular parties – in accordance with the custom of fish merchants generally – had previously traded fish using Latin designations, the Court held that B could not deny that the subject matter of the contract was mackerel of the kind specified, notwithstanding the fact the subsequent order confirmation and invoice sent by S described the goods as "Whole Round mackerel" – i.e., without the Latin or German specifications (which B during the trial claimed not to understand).[38]

Another illustrative dispute involved a German seller's obligation to sell steel bars in lots to a Syrian buyer.[39] The contract, expressly made subject to French law (and thus, by implication, the CISG),[40] permitted a weight variation of 5%, and since some of the bars delivered fell outside this range, the seller had clearly breached its obligation under Article 35(1) to deliver steel bars of the "quality and description required by the contract."

In some domestic systems, including Article 2 of the American UCC, the kind of obligation breached by the German seller in the steel bars case is referred to as an (express) "warranty".[41] According to CISG terminology and conceptions, however, the seller's delivery *obligation* (not a "warranty") was breached. Since Article 35(1) requires that the seller deliver goods of the quality and description required by the contact, and since the Convention starting point is that any breach of obligation (failure to perform) entitles

---

34   *See* OLG Düsseldorf, 8 January 1993, UNILEX.
35   Because the parties agreed (while the case was being litigated) that the contract was to be governed by "German law." Re. "contracting in" to the Convention (which usually occurs at the time of contract formation) *see supra* § 2.7.
36   Since timely notice of non-conformity was not given pursuant to Articles 38(1) and 39(1), however, the buyer lost the right to rely on the alleged breach. This aspect of the case is considered *infra* § 4.9.
37   Case H-0126-98 decided by the Danish Maritime and Commercial Court on 31 January 2002.
38   Although the opinion of the Court does not provide any indication of which rules it used as the basis of its decision on this particular point, CISG Articles 8, 9 and 35(1) all clearly support the holding, whereas the allegation by S – that the conformity issue should be governed by (Danish) *domestic* law – seems wholly out of place.
39   ICC CASE No. 6653/1993, UNILEX. *See also* Witz, *Premières Applications*, no. 57.
40   *See supra* § 2.7.
41   *See* UCC § 2-313. *See also* the Comments to the *NCCUSL Revised Draft* (2002), confirming that UCC "express" warranties rest on "dickered" aspects of the individual bargain and go so clearly to the essence of that bargain that words of disclaimer (in a standard form) are repugnant to the basic dickered terms, and this is true even if the seller had no actual intent to "warrant."

the injured party to damages,[42] there may be little difference between the situation where a seller actually "guarantees" (e.g.) that a machine will run for a "minimum of 10,000 working hours" and the corresponding situation where the seller simply "describes" the minimum performance characteristics of the goods.[43] Similarities notwithstanding, it is submitted that (domestic) warranty terminology is best left to sales cases decided under domestic (e.g., UCC) law.[44]

It should also be noted in this (express obligations) context that a CISG agreement as to quality need not take the form of words. Suppose, for example, that prior to the conclusion of a contract for the sale of marble slabs, the buyer, seeking to demonstrate her expectations, provides the seller with a "model" slab. If the seller does not then indicate his unwillingness or inability to deliver goods of that kind, the characteristics of the slab automatically become part and parcel of parties' contract under Article 35(1).[45]

§ 4.5 ORAL AGREEMENTS, PAROL EVIDENCE

In a particular (sub)group of CISG cases it may be difficult to delimit the content of the "contract" referred to in Article 35(1). Suppose, for example, that the written sales contract does not include (or refer to) certain oral statements made – or at least allegedly made – by the seller prior to or during the contract negotiations. Should the CISG buyer be entitled to introduce "extraneous" evidence to prove that the seller made such oral statements and that these statements constitute an unwritten, but still significant "part" of the overall sales contract?

Illustration 4a:[46] German Buyer (B) buys 200 tons of bacon from Texas seller (S). According to the written agreement, the goods are to be delivered in 10 installments for a stated price. After B accepts 4 installments, German health authorities raise objections regarding the condition of the bacon, and B refuses to take or pay for more. B claims

---

[42] CISG liability is based on an essentially no-fault set of rules: *see generally infra* § 6.14. Under American domestic sales law, "warranty imposes liability regardless of negligence or fault" (Gillette & Walt, *Sales Law* at 282); the situation is *basically* same under the CISG, although a CISG seller's obligation to deliver conforming goods is not really "absolute," since the seller can seek shelter from liability under the "exemption" provision in Article 79. Actually *qualifying* for such an exemption in a non-conformity case, however, is a monumental task: *see infra* § 6.19 (*inter alia*, the important decision of the *Bundesgerichtshof* in the "Vine Wax" case).

[43] For this reason, it is difficult to see the need for the special guarantee rule set forth in paragraph (2) of Article 36: *see infra* § 4.9. However, an express guarantee with respect to durability (etc.) might be significant if interpreted as a contractual deviation from the usual 2-year period in paragraph (2) of Article 39: *see infra* § 4.10.

[44] *Accord* Witz, *Premières Applications*, nos. 55, 56 (Convention does not distinguish between *garantie des vices cachés* and *obligation de délivrance*); the irrelevance of *garantie des vices cachés* was confirmed by the Cour de Cassation (France) in its decision of 17 December 1996, UNILEX and CISGW3, reversing the decision by Cour d'Appel of 26 September 1995. *Compare* Gillette & Walt, *Sales Law*, Ch. 8-III (re. "Warranties Under the CISG").

[45] *See* the decision of OLG Graz (Austria), 9 November 1995, reported in UNILEX. As noted in the decision, the same result can be reached by analogy with Article 35(2)(c) – a rule directly applicable where the *seller* provides the sample or model: *see infra* § 4.8.

[46] This illustration is inspired by a German-Italian case: *see* OLG Hamm, 22 September 1992, reported in UNILEX.

69

that, during the negotiations, S *said* that B could cancel the contract at any time if such objections were raised. The written contract, however, contains no such term.

The sales contract in this Illustration is governed (not by domestic law, but) by the CISG.[47] For comparative purposes, however, we note that *if* the contract had been governed by the (domestic) law of Texas,[48] the American parol evidence rule would deny effect to the oral statement allegedly made by S, simply because that statement, if proved, would tend to vary (add to and/or contradict) the written contract of sale.[49] Indeed, since the parol evidence rule is actually a rule of substantive (as opposed to procedural) law, the rule would simply limit the content of the parties' contract to the "four corners" of the written document. For this reason, Texas domestic law would not permit B to even present evidence (witnesses etc.) that an oral statement was made.[50]

Returning to the *CISG* (the law which in fact applies to this Illustration), we note the rule in Article 8(3): to determine the intent of the parties to a CISG contract, "due consideration is be given to *all* relevant circumstances of the case including the negotiations" (etc.).[51] Furthermore, under Article 11, the content of a CISG contract "may be proved by *any means*, including witnesses."[52] Since the fact-finder (judge, jury or arbitrator)[53] in a CISG case can hear proof of – and must then give "due consideration" to – oral statements allegedly made during contract negations, the (domestic) parol evidence rule ought not be applied in a CISG contract case.[54] Fortunately, the most significant American precedents now provide clear support for this international interpretation of the relevant CISG rules.[55]

Then again, the fact that the parol evidence hurdle has been removed in CISG cases does not mean that a statement made by one party during the negotiations necessarily becomes part

---

47 An international sale of goods (bacon) under Article 1(1)(a): *see supra* §§ 2.2 and 2.3.

48 This would, for example, be the case if the parties had "opted out" of the CISG (re. Article 6 *see supra* § 2.7). The Texas "seller's law" would, in any case, be likely to govern "validity issues" (re. Article 4 *see supra* § 2.6).

49 In general, the "parol evidence rule" applies only in the case of a fully "integrated" written instrument, but under Texas law, written agreements are *presumed* to be fully integrated: *see Beijing Metals v. American Business Center*, 993 F.2d 1178 (5th Cir 1993). So as to meet the needs of electronic commerce, the (2002) *NCCUSL Draft Proposal* for revision of UCC Article 2–202 is headed "Final Expression in a *Record*: Parol or Extrinsic Evidence" (emphasis added), just as the currently (2003) applicable term "writing" would be replaced with the term "record" in the text of the rule.

50 This is true even under the relatively flexible UCC version of the parol evidence rule: *see generally* White & Summers, *Uniform Commercial Code* §§ 2-9, 2-10, 2-11 and 2-12.

51 Re. the rule in Article 8 *see also supra* § 2.12.

52 Emphasis added here. See Schlechtriem in Schlechtriem, *Commentary/Kommentar*, Art. 11, Rd.Nr. 13. Re. the rule in Article 11 *see also supra* § 2.14.

53 Re. the UCC version of the rule, applicable in the United States in domestic sales cases, *see* White & Summers, *Uniform Commercial Code* § 2-9. Re. the application of the parol evidence rule in England *see* Treitel, *Law of Contract*, Ch. 6, Section 1, point 1(2).

54 Even if the law of an American State would be the otherwise applicable law. Using Article 7(2) terminology, the "matter" of oral contract terms is expressly *governed and settled* by the CISG, thus leaving no room in a CISG case for the domestic substantive (parol evidence) rule. *Accord* Schlechtriem at *id.;* Witz, *Premières Applications* no. 47; Honnold, *Uniform Law* § 110; Lookofsky, *Loose Ends* at 407–09 and *1980 Convention*, No. 86.

55 *See MCC-Marble Ceramic Center Inc. v. Ceramica Nuova D'Agostino S.p.A.*, 144 F.3d 1384 (11th Cir. 1998), also reported as CLOUT Case 222, citing, *inter alia*, the views of Bernstein & Lookofsky,

of the CISG deal. In other words, Articles 8 and 11 do not determine when a given statement should be treated as part of the contract.[56] What these CISG provisions do require is that courts and arbitral tribunals allow proof of and consider the effect of statements allegedly (perhaps even incontrovertably) made.[57] For this reason, even courts and arbitrators in non-Common law jurisdictions may maintain a presumption in favour of the completeness and correctness of a written contract, and – after hearing witnesses – conclude that this presumption has not been overcome.[58]

§ 4.6   CONTRACTUAL AND NON-CONTRACTUAL CLAIMS

Before moving on to consider the nature of the seller's implied obligations under Article 35(2), it seems appropriate to mention another issue which – like the parol evidence question, just discussed – relates to the "borderland" between the seller's express obligations under CISG Article 35 and the possible applicability of related domestic law rules. If a CISG seller fails to perform the obligations set forth in Article 35 with respect to quality, the buyer can then demand CISG – contractual – remedies for breach.[59] To this extent, the CISG contractual regime supplants (replaces, preëmpts) corresponding domestic sales law remedies. But it does not necessarily follow that the CISG buyer should be denied access to other, non-contractual remedial rules.[60] Under the domestic law of some countries (including some CISG Contracting States), a given set of facts can sometimes give rise to both a contractually based claim and to a tort-based (delictual) liability claim as well.[61] Given this tradition, some CISG buyers might seek to supplement a Convention-based claim with a claim grounded in the domestic law of tort.[62] So far, only a few CISG decisions deal with such

---

Understanding the CISG in Europe (1997). *See also Mitchell Aircraft Spares Inc. v. European Aircraft Service AB,* 23 F.Supp. 2d 915 (N.D.Ill. 1998). *But see* the contrary *obiter dictum* in the *Beijing Metals* case (*supra* note 49, at 1183 with note 9); for a comment on that case *see* Flechtner, *Pitfalls.*

56   I.e., whether the statement-maker "intended" his pre-contractual statement to bind and/or whether it was reasonable for the other party to understand it as such. Re. interpretation of statements under Article 8 *see supra* § 2.12. *See also* Lookofsky, *Loose Ends,* pp. 407–10.

57   Note that the *contract* between the parties can contain an *express provision* providing that prior statements, representations and the like have no effect: *see infra* § 7.3 with *Illustration 7b.*

58   As did the German court in the case (cited *supra* in note 46) underlying *Illustration 4a.*

59   Chapter 6 *infra.*

60   *See generally supra* § 2.6.

61   In some of these systems the contractual and delictual bases of liability are seen as "competing" with each other, at least in certain situations, so that (e.g.) a seller who makes a negligent or fraudulent "misrepresentation" concerning the quality of his goods might conceivably be sued in *both* contract and tort: re. English law *see* Treitel, *Law of Contract,* Ch. 9, Sec. 3; re. German law *see* Schlechtriem, *Borderland* at 470. In other systems (e.g. in France) the doctrine of *non-cumul* may prevent a party bound by contract from bring a tort action in respect of acts involving that relationship; in most American jurisdictions, a similar view prevails as regards tort-based *product liablity* claims seeking compensation for "pure economic loss."

62   *See, e.g.,* Erauw & Flechtner, *Remedies* at 65 f. (overlap between claims and remedies in tort and in contract "unavoidable").

domestic-based claims,[63] but we can illustrate further by means of a hypothetical example or two.

> *Illustration 4b*: B in CISG State X asks S in CISG State Y for information regarding the performance of a given machine. S, who is anxious to generate income for his fledgling business, negligently provides information which applies to a more costly model with a higher maximum capacity. Acting in reliance on this information, B orders the machine. After delivery, B makes repeated, unsuccessful attempts to run the machine at the stated capacity. Three weeks after the final attempt, B gives notice of non-conformity to S.

Although the seller in this illustration has breached his obligation under Article 35(1) to supply conforming goods, B may have lost his right to any contractual (CISG) remedy, in that S (arguably) has not been notified of the non-conformity within a "reasonable time."[64] In this situation some commentators would argue that the Convention remedial rules should be interpreted as occupying the entire non-conformity "field," thus preventing B's access to alternative domestic law remedies for (e.g.) negligent misrepresentation.[65] Other commentators, arguing that remedies for misrepresentation lie outside the CISG scope, would allow B access to such a competing domestic law claim.[66]

A related problem arises if goods purchased in an international sale cause physical damage to the buyer's property. In such a situation, we have noted that the buyer may assert a CISG-based (contractual) claim;[67] but he might also be entitled to assert a domestic (tort-based, product liability) claim. Reconsider this example:

> *Illustration 4c*:[68] Dentist (B) in CISG State X purchases a combined chair-and-drill unit from a supplier (S) in CISG State Y. Soon after delivery of the unit, defective wiring in the unit causes a fire which destroys the unit and does damage to B's office. B brings an action (in X or Y) against S – not only to recover the purchase price of the unit itself, but also for consequential loss (damage to the office, loss of profit etc.).

---

[63]   *See*, e.g., *Geneva Pharmaceuticals*, discussed *supra* in § 2.6, note 107 and accompanying text. For a CISG case dealing with a related rule-concurrence problem (mistake) *see id.* with note 103; *see also* note 65 *infra*.

[64]   Re. the sometimes strict application of Article 39(1) *see infra* § 4.9.

[65]   *Compare* the decision of LG Aachen (Germany), 14 May 1993, UNILEX and Witz, *Premières Applications* nos. 21, 87. *Compare* Audit, *Vente internationale* no. 121 (somewhat undecided). *See also* (e.g.) Huber in Schlechtriem, *Commentary/Kommentar*, Art. 45, Rd.Nr. 53–43; Schlechtriem, *Borderland* at 469, 473. The same commentators might, however, allow competing domestic rules re. negligent misstatements relating to something *other than non-conformity*: (e.g.) incorrect information about buyer's chance to resell goods at profit, seller's production capability, buyer's financial statement; *see* Schechtriem, *Borderland* at 474 f.

[66]   *See* (e.g.) Lookofsky, *Consequential Damages* at 276 ff, *Loose Ends* at 409 and *United Nations Convention* No. 63. *Accord* Ramberg, *Köplagen* at 112–13.

[67]   If, however, the goods cause death or injury to any *person*, Article 5 declares the Convention inapplicable to the resulting liability. *See supra* § 2.6.

[68]   Identical to *Illustration 2e, supra* § 2.6.

Assuming the unit in this illustration does "not conform" to the contract,[69] B has the basis of a contractual (CISG) cause of action for breach, and the damages recoverable would include the particular loss in question.[70] B might, however, also seek to assert a supplementary delictual claim.[71] Depending on which tort law the forum court finds applicable,[72] an action based on domestic product liability rules might be allowed to compete with (i.e., supplement) B's CISG claim.[73]

Indeed, contractual and delictual remedies have coexisted in many jurisdictions for centuries.[74] Since there is "no difficulty in regarding the imposition of a duty of care in tort as independent of any contractual liability,"[75] a State's ratification of the sales Convention does not necessarily imply its intention to "merge" contract with tort, especially since the CISG was designed solely to deal with the contractual side.[76] So, although courts and arbitrators should exercise caution before allowing domestic rules to supplement (and to this extent disturb) the uniformity resulting from exclusive application of the Convention regime,[77] the delicate question of whether to permit "competition" – as opposed to "preemption" – in the concrete CISG context seems best left to the discretion of the decision-makers in the individual case and jurisdiction concerned.[78]

§ 4.7   IMPLIED OBLIGATIONS OF QUALITY: FITNESS FOR ORDINARY PURPOSES

We now return to the "mainstream" of practical problems which CISG Article 35 was designed to solve. As noted previously, the first paragraph (1) of this key provision concerns obligations expressly undertaken by the seller as regards the quantity and quality of the goods.[79] Paragraph (2) sets forth a series of implied Convention obligations in respect of quality which apply "[e]xcept where the parties have agreed otherwise."[80] The CISG

---

[69]   Either under Article 35(1), if the goods do not match to the quality and description set forth in the contract, and/or under Article 35(2), in that the unit is surely unfit for its purpose: *see infra* §§ 4.7 and 4.8.

[70]   Re. Article 74 *see infra* § 6.15.

[71]   E.g., because his notice (of seller's *breach*) might be held untimely under Article 39. *See infra* § 4.9.

[72]   Depending on the conflict-of-law rules of the forum in a tort case like this, courts might apply the product liability law of the place where the relevant injury-causing act occurred (presumably State Y) or the law of the place of injury (State X).

[73]   *See* (e.g.) Ferrari in Schlechtriem, *Kommentar*, Art. 5, Rd.Nr. 5; Schlechtriem, *Borderland* at 473 f. *But see* (e.g.) Honnold, *Uniform Law* § 73; Herber in Schlechtriem, *Commentary*, Art. 5, Rd.Nr. 10–13 (except as to EC/EU-based product liability laws).

[74]   *See, e.g.*, re. English law, Burrows, *Obligations* at 24 ff.

[75]   *Id.* at 28. Professor Burrows' logic (emphasizing, as regards misrepresentation, the presence or absence of reasonable *reliance*) seems more persuasive than that of Professor Honnold, *Uniform Law*, § 65 (arguing on the basis of "operative facts").

[76]   Indeed, the Convention drafters themselves *rejected* a proposal to limit recourse to competing rules of domestic law: *see supra* § 2.6, text with note 104.

[77]   *See id.* with note 102.

[78]   For a discussion of the opinion of the U.S. District Court decision in the *Geneva Pharmecueticals* case *see supra* § 2.6, notes 107–110 and accompanying text.

[79]   Article 35(1) is discussed *supra* in § 4.4.

[80]   *See also* Article 6 (*supra* § 2.7).

imposes these implied obligations because today's international buyer is entitled to expect the goods to possess certain basic qualities, even if the contract does not expressly so state,[81] and the obligations in Article 35(2) apply irrespective of the seller's good or bad faith.[82]

Among the seller's implied obligations as to quality in Article 35(2), subparagraph (a) is probably the most important. Goods "do not conform with the contract unless they are . . . fit for the purposes for which goods of the same description would ordinarily be used." This is the CISG version of a familiar concept under domestic (e.g., UCC) law.[83]

Goods are often ordered by general description, without any indication as to intended use. Still, goods are always purchased with some purpose in mind, and CISG merchant-buyers are entitled to expect reasonable use-value for their money. So, absent contrary intent, the buyer is entitled to expect at least fitness for ordinary purposes: bowling balls must be suitable for bowling, canned tomatoes must be suitable for consumption, etc.

Within the context of international trade, resale should also be considered an ordinary use, so a CISG buyer who purchases for resale is entitled to expect goods resalable in the ordinary course of business.[84] What constitutes "resalable" will depend upon the reasonable expectations of the ultimate purchasers. If a furniture merchant purchases sofas for resale to consumers, the goods are not fit if the cushions slide forward when the consumers sit down.[85]

Depending on the particular goods, "ordinary use" may mean different things in different jurisdictions, thus raising the question of *which market* should be considered as determinative. In one leading CISG decision, the Supreme Court of Germany held that New Zealand mussels sold by a Swiss seller to a German buyer were "fit" for ordinary purposes, notwithstanding the fact that the mussels delivered contained cadmium at a level higher than that recommended by the German Federal Department of Health. Significantly, the cadmium in the mussels delivered would have only put persons who consumed great quantities at risk; moreover, the maximum level fixed by the Department was the subject of a recommendation, as opposed to a binding ruling.[86] In a somewhat similar American case, however, the local

---

[81]   *See Secretariat Commentary*, Comment 13 at 94 (re. Article 33 of the 1978 Draft).

[82]   Although the Convention does *not* obligate the buyer to undertake a *pre*-contractual inspection of the goods, a limited *caveat emptor* exception under Article 35(3) renders the seller "not liable" for breach of an implied Article 35(2) obligation if the buyer "knew or could not have been unaware" of such breach: *see infra* § 4.8, notes 96–99 and accompanying text.

[83]   Regarding an American seller's implied warranty of merchantability under UCC § 2-314, *see* Gillette & Walt, *Sales Law*, pp. 295–302. As noted previously (text *supra* § 4.4 with note 41 *et seq.*) the CISG speaks of *obligations*, not "warranties."

[84]   The *Secretariat Commentary*, Comment 5 to Article 33 of the 1978 Draft is in *accord*.

[85]   *See* the decision of the Pretura della giurisdizione di Locarno-Campagna, Switzerland, 27 April 1992, reported in UNILEX. In this case, however, the buyer lost the right to rely on the non-conformity because of failure to provide timely notification under Article 39: *see infra* § 4.9.

[86]   *See* BGH, 8 March 1995, affirming OLG Frankfurt, 20 April 1994, both in UNILEX. In its decision, the OLG noted that a Canadian proposal to amend the Article 35 conformity definition so as to require the delivery of "average quality" goods was rejected by the drafters of the CISG; the BGH, however, left open the question of whether the goods must be of "average quality" or merely "merchantable" under Article 35, since the buyer had not established (in the court below) that the mussels delivered contained more cadmium than New Zealand mussels in general.

(public-law) quality requirements in the buyer's country (the USA) were held determinative in the Article 35(2) context, since the seller in this case had "reason to know" of their existence.[87]

The kind of goods which are sometimes described as "durable" – washing machines, industrial machinery, automobiles etc. – are not fit for their "ordinary" purposes unless they remain durable (usable) for an "ordinary" period of time. Thus, a (new) industrial refrigeration unit with a life-span of only weeks or months would hardly be considered fit for the ordinary purposes (long-term use) to which such units are usually put. The precise period is, of course, a determination which will vary depending on the nature of the particular goods (and their price).

§ 4.8 PARTICULAR PURPOSE; SAMPLE, MODEL, PACKAGING; BUYER'S KNOWLEDGE OF NON-CONFORMITY

Sometimes, prior to the conclusion of a CISG contract, a given seller may be aware ("made known") of the particular use to which his goods, if purchased, would be put. In such cases, the seller may subsequently assume an implied obligation under Article 35(2)(b) that the goods will be fit for that particular purpose, but only if the buyer, at the time of contracting, reasonably relies on the seller's skill and judgment in this respect.[88] Once again, we see the CISG version of a concept familiar under domestic (e.g., UCC) law.[89]

As is sometimes the case under the corresponding domestic sales law, the CISG implied fitness obligations set forth in subparagraphs (2)(a) and (2)(b) often overlap: a given buyer's particular purpose – (e.g.) to use a generator to generate electricity – is likely to correspond to the purpose to which such goods are ordinarily put. This is not, however, always the case. In one relevant example, a French seller and a Portuguese buyer concluded a CISG contract for the sale and dismantlement of a second-hand aircraft hangar. In an ensuing litigation, a French court held the seller had breached the contract by delivering certain elements which were not fit for the buyer's particular (though not necessarily ordinary) purpose, which was to reassemble and make of use the hangar in the "original way."[90]

---

[87]   *See Medical Marketing International, Inc. v. Internazionale Medico Scientifica S.r.l.*, 1999 WL 311945 (E.D. La.), 1999 U.S. Dist. LEXIS 7380 (also in UNILEX and CISGW3), affirming arbitral award holding Italian seller of medical equipment liable since goods did not comply with American public law, citing – and distinguishing – the 1995 BGH decision (*see* preceding note); arbitrators found that, due to special circumstances, seller *knew or should have known* of the regulations at issue. *Accord* Oberster Gerichtshof (Austria), 13 April 2000, CISGW3 and UNILEX. *Accord* Schlechtriem, *Bundesgerichtshof* at 11 with notes 87–88. *See also* LG Ellwangen (Germany), 21 August 1995, UNILEX (paprika containing high concentration of chemical did not meet minimum standards of German food law; seller who had previously delivered to same buyer in Germany had agreed to certificates of conformity).

[88]   Conversely, if the buyer does not rely, or if reliance is held unreasonable, no obligation as to fitness for the purpose may be implied.

[89]   Regarding an American seller's Implied Warranty of Fitness for Particular Purpose under UCC § 2-315, *see* Gillette & Walt, *Sales Law*, 294–295. As noted previously (§ 4.4 *surpa* with note 41 *et seq.*), the CISG speaks of *obligations*, not "warranties."

[90]   *See* decision of Cour d'Appel de Grenoble, Chambre Commerciale, 26 April 1995, CLOUT Case 152, also reported in CISGW3 and UNILEX.

In a CISG case decided by a U.S. Federal Court of Appeal,[91] a German manufacturer (B) purchased fabric from an American seller (S). During their negotiations S stated that the fabric was particularly suited for transfer printing. After delivery and printing, however, certain problems with the fabric became apparent, but S urged B to continue printing the fabric. The American court held that S – by virtue of its statement as to suitability – gave B a "warranty" of fitness for a particular purpose (transfer printing) under Article 35(2)(b).[92]

Subparagraph (2)(c) of Article 35 imposes a further conformity obligation upon the seller with respect to the "qualities of goods which the seller has held out to the buyer as a sample or model."[93] So if a CISG seller provides the buyer with samples of cherry tomatoes or standard computer software, the seller is obligated to deliver tomatoes or software which conform to the samples.[94]

According to Article 35(2)(d), the buyer can also expect the goods to be packaged in the "usual" manner or in a manner "adequate to protect" the goods. In one application of this rule, a seller who was aware of his buyer's intention to resell the goods (foodstuffs) in France was obligated to deliver foodstuffs wrapped in the usual manner, which in this case meant as required by French (public) law.[95]

Paragraph (3) of Article 35 sets forth a certain narrow limitation of the CISG seller's quality obligations: the seller is "not liable" for any lack of conformity under paragraph (2), subparagraphs (a)–(d), if – at the time of the conclusion of the contract – the buyer knew or could not have been unaware of such lack of conformity. In other words, although the CISG does not require the buyer to undertake a pre-contractual inspection,[96] a buyer

---

91 7th Circuit U.S. Court of Appeals, 26 May 2002, UNILEX (*Schmitz-Werke GmbH & Co. v. Rockland Industries Inc.*).

92 In this connection the Court of Appeals upheld the findings of the court below: that the goods did not conform to the *warranty* S had given B (*compare supra* note 89), and that B had met its *burden of proving* that the defect existed at the time the fabric left S's plant (*see also infra* § 4.9). The Court of Appeals also held that B *need not prove* the "exact mechanism" of the defect, and that showing that the transfer printing process used on the fabric was ordinary and competent was enough to establish that the fabric was unfit for the purpose of transfer printing (*compare id.* re. the arguably stricter stance taken by German courts, *inter alia* in relation to Article 39). Since the fabric was held to have had *latent* defects which were not detectable before the fabric was transfer printed *(see also id.)*, B's continued printing of the fabric even after it began to discover problems was found reasonable, especially since it was at the express urging of S and was in any event the best way for B to *mitigate* its damages (*infra* § 6.17).

93 The corresponding UCC rule (§ 2-313: *supra* § 4.4 with note 41) puts such samples and models in the "express warranty" category.

94 *See* (re. sample software) LG München (Germany), 8 February 1995, CLOUT Case 131, also reported in CISGW3 and UNILEX. Some, including American jurists used to the UCC approach (preceding note), might prefer to reach the same result by the application of Article 35(1), in that the *sample* provided will usually serve to *specify the quality required by the contract*, i.e., without the need to resort to a gap-filling rule.

95 *See* Cour d'Appel de Grenoble (France), Chambre Commerciale, 13 September 1995, also reported in UNILEX. The logic here is clearly similar to the relevance of local requirements as regards fitness for ordinary purposes under subraragraph 35(2)(a), discussed *supra* § 4.7. *See also, e.g.,* the COMPRIMEX award of 29 April 1996 reported in UNILEX.

96 Re. *post*-contractual inspection under Article 38 *see infra* § 4.9.

who (having undertaken such an inspection) actually becomes aware that the goods are not fit (e.g.) for ordinary purposes cannot then purchase the goods and hold the seller "liable" for breach; the same rule applies to a buyer who, having undertaken an inspection, "could not have been unaware" of an (obvious) lack of conformity.[97] In these relatively clear-cut situations, when the buyer gets exactly what he sees and pays for, it seems eminently fair to allow the seller to seek refuge in the limited modification set forth in Article 35(3),[98] thus displacing the obligations otherwise ordinarily implied under paragraph (2).[99]

§ 4.9   TIME DETERMINATION; EXAMINATION OF GOODS; NOTICE OF NON-CONFORMITY

Although every CISG seller is bound to deliver conforming goods, the viability of a given non-conformity claim will depend – not only on Article 35, but also, in many cases – on other, related CISG (Part III) rules. One of these is the provision in Article 36 which sets forth the relevant point in time for the non-conformity determination. Even more important are the rules in Articles 38 and 39 regarding the buyer's duties to examine the goods and to provide the seller with timely notice of any non-conformity claim.[100]

First, as regards the point in time for the non-conformity determination, paragraph (1) of Article 36 renders the seller liable for any lack of conformity which exists at the time when the risk passes to the buyer, even if the non-conformity becomes "apparent" after that time. In other words, although the "risk" (of the goods' accidental loss or destruction) in an international sale often "passes" before the buyer takes possession,[101] the seller remains liable for any non-conformity which exists when the risk passes, and this is true even if the defect in question is first discovered at a later point in time.[102] If, for example, a seller delivers washing machines which – due to a latent (hidden) defect – are not capable of running more than a few weeks or months, the machines "do not conform" under Article 35,[103]

---

[97]   This test is arguably more buyer-friendly than the familiar "ought to know" standard. *Compare* the decision of Tribunal Cantonal Valais (Switzerland), 28 October 1997, CLOUT Case 219 (buyer who had *tested* tractor before purchase *must have been aware* of patent defects).

[98]   If, under domestic sales law conceptions, we say that the *caveat emptor* ("what you see is what you get") principle applies in a given situation, that is the functional equivalent of saying the goods *conform to the contract.*

[99]   Although paragraph (3) does not expressly apply to an Article 35(1) express promise of quality, the same principle can be applied by analogy. *See also* OLG Köln, 21 May 1996, CLOUT Case 168, where the documents incorrectly indicated that the car sold was first registered in 1992 and that the mileage was low; even if the buyer (a car dealer) "could not have been unaware" of the non-conformity, the seller – who, acting *fraudulently*, had breached his obligation under Article 35(1) – could not rely on Article 35(3). *But compare* Schwenzer in Schlechtriem, *Commentary/Kommentar*, Art. 35, citing sources that indicate disagreement on the relationship between Articles 35(1) and 35(3).

[100]   So as to provide seller with an opportunity to refute the claim, document his own position, cure, etc.

[101]   When the contract involves carriage, the risk will typically pass when the seller hands the goods over to an independent carrier (for transmission to the buyer). *See generally infra* Chapter 5.

[102]   Provided the buyer provides timely notice under Article 39 (discussed *infra*). *See e.g.,*the COMPRIMEX award of 29 April 1996 reported in UNILEX (seller liable for non-conformity – inadequate packaging – which existed when risk passed, even though nonconformity first became apparent later).

[103]   Re. the requirement that durable goods *remain* durable (fit) for a reasonable time *see supra* § 4.7.

because they are clearly unfit (not durable) as of the delivery date, i.e., although this kind of defect will probably first be discovered later, when the machines actually break down.

Paragraph (2) of Article 36 applies in the (much less common) situation where a given non-conformity – although "due to seller's breach" – first "occurs" after delivery. Although this rule might be relevant in a few atypical cases not already covered by paragraph (1),[104] its main thrust seems directed at a situation already covered by the main rule in paragraph (1), i.e., the breach of a guarantee that the goods will remain fit (or retain specified qualities). If, for example, a seller sells goods guaranteed to last for 3 years, a breach of that obligation clearly "occurs" at the moment he delivers goods not capable of lasting 3 years. In this respect, there was no need for the "clarification" in paragraph (2);[105] and the provision may even end up causing the kind of confusion it was designed to avoid.[106]

The CISG does not – at least not expressly – determine which party bears the burden of proof of an alleged non-conformity. Some courts and commentators categorize this "matter" as "governed, but not (expressly) settled" by the CISG,[107] whereas other tribunals and commentators defer to the applicable domestic law;[108] still others have adopted an intermediate position.[109] As a starting point, at least, the buyer should bear the burden of proving the goods were defective as of the passing of risk, but because this issue lies in the borderland between (CISG) substance and (domestic) procedural rules, we can hardly expect or demand a completely "uniform" (CISG) approach.

Before we turn our attention to the important CISG rules which require buyers to give sellers notice of defects, we should emphasize the significant distinction between notice rules (such as those in CISG Articles 38–40) and other, non-CISG rules which set time limits for bringing legal actions in respect of international sales contracts.[110] As emphasized in a subsequent chapter,[111] the latter topic is regulated by the "Limitation

---

[104] It would, for example, cover the situation where the seller – during the course of an attempt to cure a given non-conformity in goods previously delivered – bungles the job, thus giving rise to a second non-conformity which did not "exist" at the time of delivery.

[105] *See* A/CONF./97/5, *Secretariat's Commentary* to Article 34(2) of the 1978 Draft Convention, indicating that the drafters found it necessary to "clarify" the rule in Article 36(1).

[106] *Accord* Schwenzer in Schlechtriem, *Commentary/Kommentar*, Art. 36, Rd.Nr. 7.

[107] *See supra* § 2.11. *Compare* Herber in Schlechtriem, *Commentary*, Art. 4, Rd.Nr. 22 (arguing that the CISG contains "implicit rules" on this subject and that the application of domestic law would not be "practicable"); *see also* Ferrari in Schlechtriem, *Kommentar*, Art. 4, Rd.Nr. 49–50 (who sees this view as the "prevailing" one). The fact that one CISG rule (Art. 79) expressly regulates the burden of proof hardly provides conclusive evidence of a "general [Art. 7(2)] principle" which can be used to resolve burden-of-proof issues arising in other Convention contexts.

[108] *See* Herber, *id.* with note 39a and ICC award No. 6653/93 (26 March 1993), CLOUT Case 103, also reported in CISGW3 and UNILEX.

[109] *See* (e.g.) Tribunale di Appelo di Lugano (Switzerland), 15 January 1998, CLOUT Case 253, also in CISGW3 and UNILEX (concluding this allocation of the burden conforms with CISG general principles *and* with the otherwise applicable domestic law).

[110] *Accord*: Honnold, *Uniform Law* § 254.2(a). Note that, unlike the rules on notice of *defects*, the rules regarding the bringing of legal actions apply to *any* such actions.

[111] Chapter 9, *infra*.

Convention" (also know as the LPISG). Although the United States has ratififed this Convention, the limited number of LPISG Contracting States will often necessitate the application domestic limitation-of-actions rules.[112]

As regards notice of defects under the CISG, Article 39(1) lays down a straightforward – and very significant – rule: a buyer seeking to assert a non-conformity claim under Article 35 must provide the seller with proper (specific) notice of breach within a "reasonable" time.[113] American lawyers familiar with domestic sales law under UCC Article 2 will see significant similarities between the CISG notice rule and the one in UCC § 2-607(3)(a).[114] Under the CISG, as under the UCC, a buyer who fails to properly notify of a given non-conformity within a reasonable time after she has – or should have – discovered it simply loses the right to rely on the seller's alleged breach.[115] Of course, by losing this "right to rely," the CISG buyer completely loses her claim!

Obviously, a CISG buyer can first provide notice of non-conformity pursuant to Article 39 after she becomes "aware" that a non-conformity exists. In most situations, the buyer will acquire such knowledge at the time when she undertakes a post-delivery examination of the goods.[116] In fact, CISG Article 38(1) *requires* the buyer to undertake (or arrange for) such an examination "within as short a period as is practicable in the circumstances."[117] For this reason, most courts have required CISG buyers to move quickly,[118] but if the contract involves carriage of the goods, the examination may at least be deferred until after the goods have arrived at their destination.[119]

The timeliness of both the examination and the subsequent notice pursuant to the CISG rules will depend, *inter alia,* on the nature of the goods in question as well as the customs

---

[112]   As determined by the choice of law rules applied by the forum court or arbitral tribunal. Significantly, the U.S. has made a LPISG declaration limiting the application of that Convention (and corresponding to the Article 95 declaration made by the U.S. in respect of the CISG). *See generally infra.* §§ 9.1 and 9.2.

[113]   At least as against a seller who has delivered non-conforming goods in good faith. By virtue of Article 40 a seller who is or should be aware of a defect will not enjoy the protection which Articles 38 and 39 (discussed *infra*) would otherwise provide; for a case involving this issue, *see* Rb. Roermond, 19 December 1991, reported in UNILEX.

[114]   According to this UCC rule (which applies where "a tender has been accepted") "the buyer must within a reasonable time after he discovers or should have discovered any breach notify the seller of breach or be barred from any remedy."

[115]   Re. the UCC rule *see id.* Re. the CISG rule *see, e.g. La San Giuseppe v. Forti Moulding Ltd.,* Ontario Superior Court of Justice, 31 August 1999, reported in CISGW3 and UNILEX. Note that the corresponding rule in ULIS was stricter, requiring that notice be given "promptly" (*see also supra* § 2.9 note 144).

[116]   Re. *pre-contractual* inspection and non-conformity of which the buyer at the *conclusion of the contract* "knew or could not have been unaware" *see supra* § 4.8, notes 96–99.

[117]   Article 38. *Compare* UCC § 2-513(1) which gives the buyer "a right before payment or acceptance to inspect [the goods] at any reasonable place and time and in any reasonable manner."

[118]   *See* the discussion and cases cited *infra.*

[119]   Because inspection is presumed to first become "practicable" at that time: *see* Article 38(2). *See* (e.g.) International Court of Commercial Arbitration, Chamber of Commerce & Industry of the Russian Federation, decision of 24 January 2000, in CISGW3. *See also* Article 38(3) which deals with cases where the goods are redirected in transit or redispatched.

prevailing in the particular trade.[120] In the case of perishable goods, for example, courts are likely to require an "immediate" examination,[121] and though the time periods laid down in Articles 38(1) and 39(1) are different, a court which determines that an "immediate" examination is "practicable" in the circumstances might then find it "reasonable" to require "immediate" notice of the examination results.[122] In other circumstances, notice given several weeks – or even months – after delivery may suffice.[123]

Since the "timeliness" of a given inspection and subsequent notice ought to depend on the concrete circumstances, the Supreme Court of France has rightly decided to leave this (highly discretionary) determination in the hands of the individual French judges below.[124] American courts have taken a similarly flexible stance, with one District Court holding that the determination of what period of time is "practicable" is a factual one.[125] Seeking to determine what a practicable period of examination was for equipment designed to produce plastic gardening pots, the Court observed that "[t]he wording of the [CISG] reveals an intent that buyers examine goods promptly and give notice of defects to sellers promptly. However, it is also clear from the statute that on occasion it will not be practicable to require notification in a matter of a few weeks."[126]

Taking a different approach, the German Supreme Court (*Bundesgerichtshof*) has established *one month* as a "general" – i.e., standard or generally acceptable – notification

---

[120] *See* OGH (Austria), 15 October 1998, CLOUT Case No. 240, also in CISGW3; *see also* the OGH (Austria), 21 March 2000. Re. usages of trade under Article in 9(2) *see supra* § 2.13.

[121] *See, e.g.,* OLG Saarbrücken, 3 June 1998, UNILEX (in international flower trade reasonable for buyer to inspect on same day goods were received). Quite apart from the dictates of Article 38, when the goods deteriorate quickly, a prompt examination is required if the buyer is to establish non-conformity as of the passing of risk under Article 36 (*see supra*, text with notes 101–03).

[122] However, since the time frames for inspection and the subsequent giving of notice are based on independent criteria, same-day notice should only be required where also "practicable" under Article 39(1). *Compare* the decision of the Danish Western High Court of Appeal, 10 November 1999 (Christmas trees sold in December; notice of defects 2 days after delivery was timely, but avoidance declaration 7 days later was too late).

[123] *See, e.g.,* Cour de Cassation (France), 26 May 1999, CLOUT Case 315, also in CISGW3 (buyer of rolled metal sheets gave notice 5 weeks after deliveries commenced; timely under Articles 38(1) and 39(1)). *See also* Cour d'Appel de Versailles, 29 January 1998, CLOUT Case 225, also in UNILEX and CISGW3 (buyer sent notice of non-conformity *2 weeks* after provisional test of 2 high-tech machines at seller's premises; *1 month* after second test, buyer sent notice refusing to take delivery until certain modifications made; further letters specifying defects sent *6 months* after delivery of first machine and *11 months* after delivery of second. Held: *all* these notices satisfied requirements of Art. 39). *See also* Cour d'Appel de Colmar, 24 October 2000, CLOUT Case 400, CISG & UNILEX (notice of defects in glue given *2 months after discovery* held timely).

[124] *Id.*

[125] U.S. District Court for the Northern District of Illinois, 29 May 2003, available at http://cisgw3.law.pace.edu/cisg/wais/db/cases2/030529u1.html#cs (*Chicago Prime Packers, Inc. v. Northam Food Trading Co., et al.*).

[126] *Id.* For a similarly flexible holding *see* U.S. District Court, S.D., Michigan, 7 December 2001 (*Shuttle Packaging Systems, L.L.C. v. Jacob Tsonakis, INA S.A., et al.*), UNILEX; according to the Court in *Shuttle,* "[t]he international cases cited by Defendants are not apposite to this discussion, because they concern the inspection of simple goods and not complicated machinery like that involved in this case."

period,[127] and while this might represent an improvement upon earlier, very "seller-friendly" German decisions,[128] the concept of a "standard" notification period seems out of tune with the letter and spirit of the flexible Convention rules. The same may be said of the decision by the Austrian Supreme Court to set 14 days as a "regular" maximum period for the buyer's examination and subsequent notice combined.[129] Both the Austrian and the German approaches give cause for concern, especially in light of the flexible and arguably more balanced precedents established (e.g.) by courts in France and the United States.[130]

Under the UCC (domestic) regime, "the most important reason for requiring notice is to enable the seller to make adjustments or replacements or to suggest opportunites for cure to the end of minimizing the buyer's loss and reducing the seller's own liability to the buyer,"[131] and the fundamental soundness of this policy-consideration is underlined by the NCCUSL (2002) proposal to bend the letter of the original UCC rule in a more "buyer-friendly" direction, so as to guard against its misuse by sellers *not actually prejudiced* by their buyers' failure to provide prompt notice.[132] Hopefully, courts interpreting the timeliness of inspection and notices under Articles 38 and 39 will recognize this same policy consideration as legitimate within the CISG context as well, i.e., so as not deprive buyers of non-conforming goods of their rights in cases where (or to the extent that) the sellers concerned have not been prejudiced by defect-notification "delay."[133]

Article 38 defines the allowable time period, but it says nothing about the "intensity" of the examination. Still, a "reasonable" (reasonably intensive) examination should suffice,[134] i.e., as opposed to one which would reveal every conceivable defect.[135] If we cannot expect a given CISG buyer to possess technical expertise or special equipment, we ought not expect her to uncover defects discoverable only by experts,[136] at least not unless a more

---

[127] BGH, 3 November 1999, CLOUT Case 319, CISGW3 & UNILEX. *See also* OLG Oldenburg, 5 December 2000, UNILEX. A Swiss court has held notice of non-conformity to be timely if given within one month after delivery, describing this period as a good compromise between the (earlier) German and the (far more lenient) American views: *see* Obergericht Kanton Luzern, 8 January 1997, CLOUT Case 192, UNILEX.

[128] *Compare* (e.g.) cases discussed by Witz, *Premières Applications*, Nos. 60–63.

[129] Unless "special circumstances" indicate the reasonableness of a shorter or longer period. *See* OGH (Austria), 15 October 1998, CLOUT Case 240, also in CISGW3. *See also* OGH (Austria), 28 August 1999, UNILEX.

[130] *Accord* (as to the German decision) Schlechtriem, *Bundesgerichtshof* at 12 with note 112. For a more favorable view of the one-month standard *compare* Andersen, *Reasonable Time*.

[131] White & Summers, *Uniform Commercial Code*, § 10-11.

[132] *See* the *NCCUSL Draft Revision* (2002) of UCC § 2-607(3)(a): "failure to give timely notice bars the buyer from a remedy only to the extent that the seller is prejudiced by the failure."

[133] *Accord* Flechtner, *Buyer's Obligation*, arguing that Article 39 notice of lack of conformity given in time to prevent the seller from suffering prejudice should be deemed timely, and citing the similar rule in proposed revisions to UCC § 2-607 (*see* preceding note).

[134] Regarding "reasonableness" as a CISG *general principle* under Article 7(2) *see supra* § 2.11 with note 176.

[135] *Accord* Schwenzer in Schlechtriem, *Commentary/Kommentar*, Art. 38, Rd.Nr. 13–14. Examples include a German case involving discolored shoes (LG Stuttgart, 31 August 1989) and a Dutch case involving cheese with maggots (Rb. Roermund, 19 December 1991), both in UNILEX.

[136] *See Secretariat Commentary* at 99 (para. 3 of commentary on Article 36 of 1978 Draft).

demanding standard has been established by usages in the trade concerned.[137] Absent special considerations, we ought not expect a middleman who purchases goods in sealed containers (e.g. tomatoes in cans) to undertake or secure a laboratory analysis prior to resale;[138] in such instances the middleman should be able to rely on the seller's obligation to deliver conforming (re-saleable) goods, at least until buyer's own customers (the end-users) complain.[139] So, although CISG sellers also have legitimate interests worthy of protection,[140] some decisions which require prompt spot checks and laboratory test treatments to discover latent defects seem to overshoot the mark.[141] Conversely, there is good reason to applaud the more "buyer friendly" (and thus more balanced) precedents established (e.g.) by courts in Finland.[142]

Article 39(1) requires that the buyer "specify the nature of the lack of conformity." As regards this specificity requirement, German courts originally took a highly demanding (i.e. very seller-friendly) stance.[143] In one early case, a German buyer of wearing apparel was held to have lost all remedial rights, since the buyer's notifications of "poor workmanship and improper fitting" did not specify the defects with sufficient precision.[144] More recently, however, the *Bundesgerichtshof* has sent a signal which should help relax

---

[137] *See Secretariat Commentary* at 100 (para. 3 of commentary on Article 36 of 1978 Draft). *Accord* Oberster Gerichtshof (Austria), 28 August 1999 (large quantity shoes, defects difficult to discern; buyer should have called in experts skilled in shoe trade to conduct thorough, professional and appropriately diligent examination).

[138] On resale situations *see also* Article 38(3) and the Award of Int. Schiedsgericht der öst. Bundeskammer der gewerblichen Wirtschaft (Austria), 15 June 1994, UNILEX (Article 38 period did not begin before rolled-up metal sheets could be unrolled at the end-user's place).

[139] *See, e.g.,* LG Paderborn (Germany), 26 June 1996, UNILEX and CISGW3 (seller delivered PVC containing lower percentage of certain substance than agreed; defective composition could only be discovered by special chemical analysis; buyer who first examined upon receiving customers' complaints did *not* lose right to rely). *Accord* BGH (Germany), 25 June 1997, in UNILEX (defect first discoverable after processing).

[140] Sellers should be allowed to "see (and react to) the evidence" of an alleged non-conformity without undue delay, especially when it comes to perishable goods, just as time may also be important as regards the seller's right to cure (*infra* § 6.9).

[141] *See* Oberlandesgericht Karlsruhe, 25 June 1997, CLOUT Case 230, also CISGW3 (hidden defects in adhesive film could have been discovered by spot-checks and testing within 7 days after delivery; notice given 24 days after delivery barred buyer, who was end-user's business partner, from any remedy). This decision was reversed by the Bundesgerichtshof on 25 November 1998 (CLOUT Case 270, also in CISGW3), but on different grounds (seller impliedly waived right to timely inspection and notice under Articles 38 and 39), thus avoiding a reassessment of the OLG position on Article 38.

[142] Re. the extent of a CISG buyer's duty to test (and re-test) the chemical content of samples supplied by the seller *see* Helsinki Court of Appeals, decision of 30 June 1998, CISGW3 and UNILEX. As noted by Kuoppala, *Examination*, this Finnish decision represents a much more "buyer-friendly" approach than that previously taken in Germany.

[143] Even where this cuts against a German party: *see* the cases discussed by Witz, *Premières Applications*, nos. 60–63. The stance originally taken by German courts has been linked both to the strict notice requirements under German domestic law (Schwenzer in Schlechtriem, *Commentary/Kommentar*, Art. 39, Rd.Nr. 6), as well as to the inappropriate wording (*genau bezeichnen*) of the unofficial German version of the CISG text (Fogt, *Reklamation*).

[144] *See* LG München, 3 July 1989, UNILEX.

the substantiation requirements: in a case involving machine parts, it was held sufficient that the buyer passed on end-users' complaints indicating the general nature of the non-conformity in question.[145] In many cases where the buyer gives timely notice of a serious non-conformity, but does not, in the first instance, specify that defect with sufficient precision, it would seem fair – and in accord with the spirit of the Convention – to then require the seller to demand that the buyer provide a (prompt) supplementary specification,[146] i.e., instead of letting the seller (perhaps guilty of a fundamental breach) escape all liability on the basis of a "technicality."

A buyer who ought to – but does not – discover a defect (in time) is treated the same way as a buyer who does discover, but fails to notify in time. In one case, a German buyer of 48 pairs of shoes alleged improper sewing, measurement and poor color quality. Since these were not "latent" defects, the buyer's duty to inspect and discover had not been discharged by a superficial post-delivery examination of a few (conforming) pairs; therefore, notice given to the Italian seller 16 days after delivery was too late, and the buyer lost all her remedial rights.[147]

The situation just discussed must, however, be distinguished from cases involving the kind of latent or hidden non-conformity not revealed or discoverable by a reasonable (Article 38) inspection. For example, a German court has held that the purchaser of packaged tiles could not be expected to open and inspect for possible defects all packages upon their receipt.[148] If a buyer performs a reasonable (i.e., reasonably intensive) inspection upon delivery, but first discovers a latent defect at some later point, she must, of course, provide the seller with an Article 39 notice within a reasonable time after that.[149]

The Convention also contains a rule in Article 40 designed to guard against the possibility that the inspection and notice regime might otherwise lead to an unfair result: a seller who knew or could not have been unaware of a given non-conformity, but does not disclose that information, cannot hide behind the protection of Article 39.[150] And while Article 40 represents an essentially narrow "safety valve," designed for exceptional circumstances, it

---

[145]   BGH (Germany), 3 November 1999, CISGW3.

[146]   *Compare* the "duty to reply" imposed upon the offeree in CISG Article 21(2); re. the duty to act in good faith as a CISG "general principle" *see supra* § 2.11 with note 175.

[147]   *See* LG Stuttgart, 31 August 1989, UNILEX (seller "forewarned" by customer complaints concerning first lot of shoes had special reason to promptly and carefully examine *all* shoes delivered in the second lot).

[148]   *See* LG Baden-Baden, 14 August 1991, in UNILEX. *But compare* Oberlandesgericht Karlsruhe, 25 June 1997, CLOUT Case 230, CISGW3, *supra* note 141 (hidden defects in adhesive film could have been discovered by spot-checks and testing within 7 days after delivery).

[149]   *Accord* Hoge Raad (Netherlands), 20 February 1998, UNILEX (Dutch buyer of Italian floor tiles resold to customers; seven months after delivery buyer received customer complaints regarding quality of tiles allegedly worn down; held: buyer should have inspected immediately after receiving the customer's complaints, i.e. in July, instead of waiting until mid August, and given notice to seller shortly after that). *See also* of LG Düsseldorf, 23 June 1994, reported in UNILEX (buyer could not reasonably be expected to discover possible defects before he had installed aircraft engines and put them into operation).

[150]   Since the rule is designed to deal with near-fraudulent conduct, it would seem that the time of contracting would be the relevant point in time for such disclosure. *But see* Schwenzer in Schlechtriem, *Commentary/Kommentar*, Art. 40, Rd.Nr. 8.

nonetheless echoes the important general principle that CISG parties must always act in good faith.[151] The prime example of application so far is an arbitral award concerning the manufacture and delivery of a large press, guaranteed to be of "the best materials with first class workmanship."[152] During manufacture, the American seller substituted a key part, but did not advise the Chinese buyer of the substitution or of the need to properly install the part. So, although the part broke some 4 years after delivery of the machine, the tribunal held that the buyer could rely on the non-conformity (and claim damages), Article 39 notwithstanding, since the seller had "consciously disregarded facts which were of evident relevance" thereto.

As already indicated, a buyer who fails to comply with Articles 38 and 39 risks losing the right to assert any and all remedies for breach (the right to require performance, to avoid, to claim damages or a proportionate reduction, etc.). Quite apart from the safety valve in Article 40, however, a court or arbitral tribunal can award limited remedial relief to a buyer who – pursuant to Article 44 – is able to establish a "reasonable excuse" for failing to notify the seller in accordance with the general Article 39(1) rule.[153] Note, however, that the two-year cut-off rule in Article 39(2)[154] remains unaffected by Article 44.

§ 4.10 ABSOLUTE (2-YEAR) CUT-OFF RULE, ETC.

Paragraph (2) of Article 39 supplements the reasonable time standard in paragraph (1) with an absolute cut-off – a maximum time period after which a CISG buyer is barred from asserting a claim in respect of (any) non-conformity. In any event (though subject to the Article 40 safety-value just discussed), the buyer loses the right to rely on a lack of conformity of the goods if he does not give the seller notice within a period of two (2) years from the date on which the goods were actually handed over to the buyer, unless this time-limit is inconsistent with a contractual period of guarantee. Once the goods are actually handed over to the buyer,[155] the two-year period begins to run. A CISG buyer who fails to give notice of a given non-conformity before the expiration of the period loses the "right to rely" (and thus, any rights connected with a given non-conformity claim).[156]

---

[151] Re. interpretation of the Convention having "due regard" to good faith *see* Article 7(1) discussed in § 2.10 *supra*. Re. good faith as an emerging general principle pursuant to Article 7(2) *see supra* § 2.11.

[152] *See* award by Arbitration Institute of the Stockholm Chamber of Commerce, 5 June 1998, CLOUT Case 237, CISGW3 and UNILEX. *See also* Spanogle & Winship, *International Sales Law* at 299–300.

[153] For an example of the rule's application, *see* Gerechtshof's Hertogenbosch (Netherlands), 15 December 1997 (UNILEX) (considering that buyer could have appointed expert to take and examine sample of goods (furs) at time of delivery, and taking existing means of communication into account, failure to discover non-conformity before processing by third party was not "reasonable excuse"). Note that a buyer having a "reasonable excuse" under Article 44 retains the right to a proportionate reduction in price (re. Article 50 *see infra* § 6.13) as well as a limited right to claim damages (*see infra* § 6.14 *et seq.*).

[154] Discussed in § 4.10 *infra*.

[155] This act and not the "delivery" sets the two-year period in motion.

[156] *Compare* § 2-607(3) of the American Uniform Commercial Code which requires only that notice of defects be given within a "reasonable time." UCC § 2-725(1) – which provides for the commencement of actions within four years after accrual – is noted *infra* (§ 9.1, text with note 4) in connection with the corresponding limitation in the "LPISG."

Article 39(2) has particular significance for "latent" defects. Though the buyer retains the right to rely on defects not discoverable in connection with a reasonably intense inspection under Article 38, Article 39(2) helps protect the seller against "stale" claims which may be of doubtful validity.[157]

Since the contract between the parties always takes precedence over the Convention's supplementary rule,[158] the two-year limit will not apply if the contract expressly (and validly) sets forth a cut-off period of shorter or longer duration.[159] The special provision at the end of Article 39(2) relates (not to contractual cut-off clauses, but rather) to contractual periods of guarantee;[160] whether such a guarantee clause is inconsistent with (and thus overrides) the two-year cut-off period in Article 39(2) is a matter to be interpreted by the court or arbitral tribunal concerned.[161]

A buyer who gives notice within the time period defined in Article 39(2) may also be required to take additional steps to preserve his rights. Under Articles 8 and 10 of the Limitation Convention applicable to international sales, the buyer must commence judicial proceedings against the seller within four (4) years of the date the goods were actually handed over.[162] Nations not yet bound by the Limitation Convention will apply the limitation period dictated by the applicable rules of private international law.[163]

§ 4.11   OBLIGATION TO DELIVER FREE OF THIRD PARTY CLAIMS

The implied Convention obligation set forth in Article 30 requires the seller to transfer the property in the goods. Elaborating on this basic theme, Article 41 requires the seller to deliver goods free from any right or claim of a third party, unless the buyer agreed to take the goods subject to that right or claim.

A seller who, absent authority, sells goods owned by a third party commits a clear breach of the obligation laid down in Article 41; the same is true where the goods delivered are encumbered by a security interest held by a third party. In either case, the seller's knowledge regarding the third party claim at the time of contracting is irrelevant.[164] Beyond this, the Convention protects the buyer even against third party claims, in that the

---

[157] *See Secretariat Commentary* at 102 (para. 5–6).

[158] Re. Article 6 *see supra* § 2.7.

[159] An unreasonably short cut-off period would be subject to a validity-attack: *see generally infra* Chapter 7.

[160] E.g., where the seller "guarantees" conformity of the goods for a one-year or three-year period. Such guarantee-clauses will often also entitle or require the seller to repair or replace defective goods.

[161] According to most European commentators, both a shorter and a longer guarantee period will affect the Article 39(2) period: *see* (e.g.) Schwenzer in Schlechtriem, *Commentary/Kommentar,* Art. 39, Rd.Nr. 26. *Contra* Honnold, *Uniform Law* § 258 (guarantees can only extend).

[162] *See* Chapter 9 *infra.*

[163] *Compare, e.g.*, Cour de Justice Genève (Switzerland), 10 October 1997, CLOUT Case 249, also in CISGW3 and UNILEX.

[164] On the other hand, the *buyer's* knowledge of an existing right or claim does not necessarily amount to an *agreement* "to take the goods subject to that right or claim"; note in this connection that Article 41 does not include a clause corresponding to Article 42(2)(a).

mere assertion by a third party of such a claim constitutes a breach by the seller and entitles the buyer to exercise the remedies which the Convention provides.[165] In an interesting application of the Article 41 rule, an Austrian court held that a German seller of natural gas did not comply with its obligation to deliver goods free from any right or claim of third parties when, after the formation of the contract, delivery was made subject to export limitations originally imposed by the seller's supplier; under these circumstances, the buyer was held entitled to damages.[166]

Note that the Convention governs only the rights and obligations of the seller and buyer; it is "not concerned with the effect which the contract may have on the property in the goods sold."[167] In accordance with this principle, Article 41 makes the seller liable for claims which third parties may assert against the buyer,[168] but the question of whether a third party's rights are cut off by virtue of a buyer's good-faith purchase from a seller under a contract otherwise regulated by the CISG lies outside the Convention scope.

Where a given third party right or claim is based on industrial property or other intellectual property (patents, copyrights or trademarks), the seller's obligation is governed by Article 42. Here too, the mere assertion of such a claim constitutes a breach by the seller and entitles the buyer to exercise the remedies which the Convention provides.[169] Unlike the corresponding rule in Article 41, however, the seller's (lack of) knowledge regarding a third party right or claim at the time of contracting may be relevant when industrial or intellectual property rights are involved. In the international context, where an (alleged) infringement will usually take place outside the seller's territory, the Convention limits the implied obligation of the seller to deliver unencumbered goods.[170]

As in cases where an alleged breach relates to non-conforming goods (Article 35), a buyer alleging breach of an obligation under Articles 41–42 must give the seller timely and specific

---

[165] If the claim is frivolous (and/or quickly and effectively disposed of), the buyer suffers no substantial detriment and cannot avoid the contract by virtue of a fundamental breach; *compare* the "colorable" claim requirement set forth in the *NCCUSL Draft Revision* (2002) of UCC § 2-312(1)(a). In certain cases, the CISG buyer may be able to require specific performance, i.e., require that the seller supply unencumbered goods by taking appropriate legal action (instituting or defending a lawsuit). In any case, a buyer who suffers a monetary loss will be entitled to damages: *see infra* Chapter 6.

[166] *See* Oberster Gerichtshof, 6 February 1996, CLOUT Case 176, also in CISGW3 and UNILEX.

[167] Re. Article 4 *see supra* § 2.6.

[168] In addition to damages, the buyer has the remedies under Articles 46–52, including the right to specific performance under Article 46.

[169] Re. buyer's remedies under Articles 45–52 *see infra* Chapter 6B. As in the case of claims relating to non-conforming goods, Article 44 provides a limited exception to these rules: a buyer with a "reasonable excuse" for failure to notify does not lose all rights: *see supra* § 4.9.

[170] First, the seller's Article 42 obligation is limited to cases where, at the time of contracting, he "knew or could not have been unaware" of the right or claim concerned. Second, the obligation is limited by the specification of which State's industrial or intellectual property laws are relevant: (a) the State of resale or use, if contemplated by the parties at the conclusion of the contract; in other cases (b) the buyer's State of business. Article 42(2) places a further limit on the seller's obligation in two situations where the buyer clearly ought to bear the risk of a conflicting right or claim: (a) where buyer contracted with knowledge of the risk and (b) where buyer provided the specifications, etc., which created the conflict with the third-party right or claim concerned.

notice thereof. If the buyer becomes aware of a conflicting third-party right or claim, Article 43(1) requires notification within a reasonable time. If the buyer does not provide the seller with such timely and specific notice, he loses "the right to rely" on the provisions of Article 41 or 42.[171] Conversely, a seller who is aware of the right or claim concerned (and its nature) will not be permitted to enjoy the protection which Article 43(1) provides.[172]

4C OBLIGATIONS OF THE BUYER

§ 4.12 TIME AND PLACE OF PAYMENT

The main obligations of the CISG buyer are summarized in Article 53. The buyer must pay the price for the goods and take delivery as required by the contract and the CISG. Of paramount importance, of course, is the obligation to pay the price.

The requirement that the buyer pay "as required by the contract" restates the supremacy of the parties' consensus, their bargain in fact.[173] More often than not, an international sales contract will specify not only the precise amount to be paid,[174] but also the exact time and place of payment: (e.g.) a requirement that the buyer must make payment at the seller's place of business on or before a given date, or (e.g.) in a letter of credit transaction, upon the presentation of documents demonstrating that conforming goods have been shipped.[175]

If the contract itself is silent as to the proper payment place, Article 57(1) provides a starting point which differs from the corresponding UCC rule:[176] absent contrary agreement, the CISG buyer must pay at the seller's place of business,[177] though if payment is to be made against the handing over of the goods or of documents, as is often the case in an international sale, payment must be made where the handing over takes place.[178]

The place of payment – as determined by the contract or, by default, the CISG – is frequently used to resolve the preliminary, yet fundamental question of whether a given forum court enjoys international jurisdiction to decide disputes which relate to the buyer's performance of the obligation to pay.[179] The place of payment may also be significant in an international context (e.g.) if currency export restrictions are involved.

---

[171] As a starting point, the buyer loses the right to assert all remedies, but this starting point is modified in cases where buyer can provide a "reasonable excuse" (Article 44).

[172] *See* Article 43(2). In contrast with the slightly more buyer-friendly rule in Article 40, Article 43(2) precludes seller (S) from relying on buyer's failure to notify if S *actually knew* of the right or third party claim; "could not have been unaware" will not suffice.

[173] Re. custom and usages *see* Article 9 and *supra* § 2.13.

[174] Re. cases where the contract is silent on this fundamental point *see infra* § 4.13.

[175] Re. letters of credit *see* text *infra* with note 185.

[176] Re. UCC § 2-310(a) *see* White & Summers, *Uniform Commercial Code*, § 3-6.

[177] In this respect some European domestic sales laws are more debtor-friendly: *see, e.g.*, Article 1247 of the French Civil Code; the new German Civil Code maintains similar rules (§§ 269–270).

[178] *See generally* Sevón, *Obligations of Buyer* at 212.

[179] *See supra* §§ 1.4, 2.11 and 4.3. As of 1 March 2002 the jurisdiction of European (except Danish) courts in CISG cases will be determined by the special Brussels Regulation rule in Article 5(1), litre (b) which – as regards sales of goods cases – defines "the place of performance of the obligation in question" in a sales

For cases where the contract is silent as to the proper payment time, Article 58(1) restates a familiar principle applicable to bilateral contracts generally. Unless otherwise agreed, the parties are to exchange their performance obligations at the same point in time. So, absent special agreement, the CISG seller has no obligation to extend credit, and the buyer must pay when the seller places the goods (or the controlling documents) at the buyer's disposal; conversely, the CISG buyer need not pay before the seller performs. A Common lawyer might say that CISG "payment and delivery are constructive concurrent conditions"[180] (a concept similar to the Civil law *synallagma* between the parties' obligations).[181]

In an international sales context, the contract will ordinarily involve carriage of the goods by an independent carrier.[182] In this common situation, Article 58(2) provides that the seller may dispatch the goods on terms whereby the goods (or documents controlling their disposition) will not be handed over to the buyer except against payment of the price.[183] Since the seller may not wish to ship under such terms without some assurance that the ultimate exchange will proceed as planned,[184] the contract will often require the buyer to arrange for the issuance of a letter of credit in the seller's favor;[185] if so, payment will be made "in exchange for documents" in the seller's locale (by the local "confirming" bank concerned).

Before making payment, and before taking delivery,[186] the buyer is entitled (though not obligated) to examine the goods.[187] In the Article 58(2) situation, when the seller elects to ship under terms whereby the goods or documents are to be handed over to the buyer against payment, the seller must preserve the buyer's right to inspect (e.g.) by providing buyer with access to the goods at the point of destination.

The buyer's general obligation to pay the price includes an implied obligation to take such steps as may be required – by contract or by law – to enable payment to be made.[188] In a case arbitrated under the auspices of the ICC,[189] a Bulgarian buyer purchased goods

---

jurisdiction case as the place of delivery of the goods (*id.*). So if a seller brings an action against an EU-domiciliary in the seller's own jurisdiction, and the buyer's *payment*-obligation is the "obligation in question," the issue of whether that court has jurisdiction may be resolved on the basis of the (default) place-of-delivery rule in CISG Article 31: *see generally* Lookofsky & Hertz, *Transnational Litigation*, Ch. 2.2. Although U.S. courts have not yet faced such issues under the CISG, they have often assumed jurisdiction in domestic cases where the forum is the "place of performance" (payment). Re. (e.g.) the application of the Florida long-arm statute in *Burger King Corp. v. Rudzewicz*, 471 U.S. 462 (1985) *see* Lookofsky & Hertz, *id.*, Ch. 2.5.2(A).

180 *See* (e.g.) UCC § 2-310(a) and sec. 28 of the Sale of Goods Act (U.K.).
181 *See* (e.g.) Article 1651 of the French and § 320 of the new German Civil Code.
182 Re. seller's obligation to deliver under Article 31 *see supra* § 4.3.
183 In this situation payment will ordinarily be made where the handing over takes place: *see* Article 57(1)(b).
184 Article 58(2) protects the seller against having to deliver without receiving payment; it does not protect against the risk of buyer's insolvency which may first become apparent when the goods arrive in buyer's State.
185 *See generally* Gillette & Walt, *Sales Law*, Ch. 11.
186 *See infra* § 4.14.
187 Article 58(3). Contrast the "obligation" under Article 38(2) to inspect within as short a period as practicable *following* delivery: *see* § 4.9 *supra*.
188 Article 54.
189 ICC Case no. 7197/1992, CISGW3 and UNILEX.

from a seller in Austria. The contract provided for payment by documentary credit to be opened by a certain date. The credit was not opened on time, and the seller claimed (*inter alia*) damages for breach. The tribunal held for the seller, observing that the buyer had an obligation under Article 54 to take all measures and comply with all formalities required for payment of the price.

§ 4.13   Contract With "Open" Price Term

According to Article 53 the buyer must pay the price as required by the contract and the Convention. If the contract leaves a price gap, the question is how – and indeed whether – the gap should be filled.

Article 55 provides a gap-filling reference to the price "generally charged" in cases "[w]here a contract has been validly concluded but does not expressly or implicitly fix or make provision for determining the price." As we have seen, the relationship between this provision and Article 14 (which requires a "sufficiently definite" offer) is somewhat unclear.[190]

In one Hungarian CISG case,[191] it was held that an offer made by a German seller was sufficiently definite, even though no price was stated therein. In this case, the price of the goods was held to have been impliedly fixed by the practices established between the parties,[192] in that the seller had repeatedly delivered goods ordered by the buyer who had paid the price charged after delivery. So, in this situation, the price "gap" proved more apparent than real.

However, in another (previously discussed) CISG case, the Hungarian Supreme Court held that an offer by an American seller to supply aircraft parts was not sufficiently definite (and the contract between the parties therefore not validly concluded), in that the seller's offer did not specify the price.[193]

Although we can hardly declare all CISG open-price-term contracts valid on the basis of Article 55, we should not go the other extreme and declare every open price term invalid on the basis of Article 14. Rather, courts and arbitrators should try to discern the true intention of the parties in the concrete case: if they intended to be bound without a price clause, then their intention should prevail in accordance with Article 6 – a rule which allows the parties to derogate from or vary the effect of virtually any CISG provision, including those pertaining to contract formation.[194] If the open-price contract is upheld, because the parties intended to be bound, the price-gap can be filled by the price "generally charged" at the time of the conclusion of the contract.[195]

---

[190]   Under Article 14 a given proposal is sufficiently definite, *inter alia*, if it "expressly or implicitly fixes or makes provision for determining the . . . price." Re. the possible *e contrario* implication of this rule *see supra* § 3.3.

[191]   *See* Metropolitan Court of Budapest, 24 March 1992, UNILEX (cited *supra* § 3.2 note 22).

[192]   Pursuant to Article 9(1): *see supra* § 2.13.

[193]   *See supra* § 3.3, text with note 29.

[194]   *Id.*

[195]   As indicated previously (§ 3.3 with note 37) this solution should apply in all Contracting States, not just the Scandinavian States which have elected to opt out of CISG Part II (*supra* § 3.1 and *infra* § 8.4). According to the unofficial *Secretariat Commentary* to the 1978 Draft, Article 51 (corresponding to Article 55 of the

§ 4.14 BUYER'S OBLIGATION TO TAKE DELIVERY; SELLER'S OBLIGATION TO PRESERVE THE GOODS

According to Article 60: "The buyer's obligation to take delivery consists: (a) in doing all the acts which could reasonably be expected of him in order to enable the seller to make delivery; and (b) in taking over the goods."

In some situations, it will be up to the buyer to arrange for carriage; in other cases the buyer will need to designate the destination, so that the seller can arrange for timely shipment. The buyer's obligation to take over the goods in paragraph (b) is significant, *inter alia*, where the seller's delivery obligation involves placing the goods at buyer's disposal.[196] The buyer who fails to take over such goods on time not only breaches his CISG obligation to accept the seller's performance;[197] he will also bear the risk of accidental loss or damage after that time.[198] In cases involving carriage, the buyer's failure to take over the goods (from the carrier) is a remedy-provoking breach, and the buyer will be liable in damages for the seller's extra expenses vis-a-vis the carrier in this regard. If the buyer delays in taking delivery and the seller is either in possession of the goods or otherwise able to control their disposition, the seller must take such steps as are reasonable in the circumstances to preserve them; the same is true where the buyer fails to pay the price in a situation where payment and delivery are to take place concurrently. In either such case, the seller is entitled to retain the goods until he has been reimbursed for his reasonable expenses by the buyer.[199]

1980 Convention) has *effect only* if one of the parties has his place of business in a Contracting State which has ratified or accepted Part III but not Part II and if that State accepts open-price contracts as valid (*id.* at 136), but this view runs counter to the "plain meaning" of the text of Article 55.

[196] See Article 31, paragraphs (b) and (c).

[197] *See* Landgericht München, 8 February 1995, CLOUT Case 133, CISGW3 (buyer's failure to pick up cars was breach). Unlike some domestic systems which provide a separate *mora creditoris* category for such instances (*see* Treitel, *Remedies* pp. 39–41), a CISG buyer's failure to take a delivery is treated like any other "failure to perform" (breach).

[198] Re. Article 69 *see infra* § 5.5.

[199] Article 85.

CHAPTER FIVE

PASSING OF RISK

§ 5.1 Introduction

CISG Articles 66–70 regulate the Passing of Risk. As in the case of the corresponding UCC risk rules,[1] the ultimate issue to be resolved by these CISG provisions is which party (the seller or the buyer) should bear the economic consequences in the (unlikely) event that the goods are accidentally lost, damaged or destroyed. As in the case of most matters governed by the Convention, the CISG provides a set of supplementary, gap-filling rules designed for cases where the contract itself does not otherwise provide. And it must be emphasized that an international sales contract will often incorporate a simple trade term (such as CRF or FOB), with the effect that the Convention's own risk-regulating regime will be regarded as displaced.[2]

Articles 66–70 refer to – but do not actually define – "the risk." It is, however, a well-known fact of life that goods are sometimes damaged or destroyed by fire, storms, theft, vandalism, etc.[3] And the risk, even if "covered" by insurance, is real: the fact that one or both parties may carry insurance designed to protect against the economic consequences of such risks does not dispense with the need to determine which of the two parties actually carries the risk when the loss or damage occurs: the party who bears the risk must bear the burden of asserting a claim against the insurer, suffer depletion of current assets while waiting for settlement, etc.

Of course, before the seller even makes an agreement to sell certain goods which she owns, she (as the owner in possession) is the only logical candidate to bear "risks" such as these; so, if the goods are accidentally lost or damaged at or before the time of contracting, the risk of such loss is clearly hers. Nor will the mere fact that the seller enters an agreement to sell the goods ordinarily work to transfer the risk.[4] At some point in time, however, after the seller has done what the contract requires regarding the delivery of the goods, the buyer must accept the fact that the risk of loss has passed to him.

Chapter IV of CISG Part III contains rules which provide a gap-filling determination of the precise point in time at which the risk passes from the seller to the buyer. The simple message in Article 66 is that once the risk has in fact passed, in accordance with the

---

[1] UCC §§ 2-509 and 2-510. *See generally* Gillette & Walt, *Sales Law*, Ch. 7.
[2] *See infra* § 5.2.
[3] Note that certain acts of third parties are considered *accidental* events in this context. Whether certain governmental acts which prevent the use of the goods are to be included in the concept of "risk" under Articles 66–70 is a matter of controversy: *see* (e.g.) the discussion by Hager in Schlechtriem, *Commentary*, Rd.Nr. 4.
[4] For a limited exception *see* Article 68 (*infra* § 5.4).

contract and the Convention, the buyer must pay the price agreed, and the rule applies even though the goods which are delivered are damaged beyond repair – indeed, even if the goods never arrive. In other words, once the risk has passed to the buyer, the seller has done all she promised to do, and the buyer must proceed to perform his part of the deal.

If, on the other hand, the loss or damage suffered is due to an act or omission of the seller, the buyer need not pay, even if the risk has passed in the technical sense.[5] Another way of stating this is that the rules regarding the passing of risk apply only to "accidental" loss or damage: a figure of speech which covers both "acts of God" and the acts of mortal third parties (thieves, vandals, etc.), but which does not cover the acts or omissions of the seller herself. Similarly, if the loss or damage in question is attributable to the buyer's own act or omission, he should be the one to bear this "risk."

§ 5.2 USE OF TRADE TERMS (CIF, CFR, FOB, FAS, CPT, CIP, ETC.)

The most important risk-rules in the Convention are those which apply when the contract of sale involves carriage of the goods.[6] As a practical matter, however, even these gap-filling rules will often be displaced. So, before considering the workings of the Convention's gap-filling risk regime, some attention should be given to the realities of ordinary sales contract life.

According to the general freedom-of-contract rule, the parties may "derogate from or vary the effect of any [Convention] provision(s),"[7] including, *inter alia*, the CISG provisions regarding the passing of risk. And while perhaps only a minority of international sales contracts set forth rules which would displace the Convention regime regarding (e.g.) sales contract formation, a large percentage of such contracts contain trade terms clearly designed to regulate the passing of risk.

Under well-recognized trade "shipment" terms such as CIF, CFR, and FOB, the risk passes to the buyer when the goods are actually put on board the vessel;[8] under more modern shipment terms designed for containerized transport – such as CPT[9] and CIP[10] – the buyer bears all risks from the time the goods are delivered into the custody of the first carrier. The various shipment contracts should be distinguished from "destination" contracts where the risk remains with the seller until the goods arrive at the buyer's place of business or other specified destination.[11]

The International Chamber of Commerce, a federation composed of merchant organizations from around the world, has set forth a comprehensive set of definitions for

---

[5]   In a documentary sale the buyer must first pay against documents and then bring an action against the seller, but Article 66 is not concerned with documentary sales: *see* Berman and Ladd, *Risk* at 427.

[6]   Regarding Article 67 *see infra* this section.

[7]   Regarding Article 6 *see supra* § 2.7.

[8]   Or at least pass the ship's rail.

[9]   Carriage Paid to . . . (named place of destination).

[10] Carriage and Insurance paid to . . . (named place of destination).

[11] E.g., if the goods are to be "delivered ex ship" or "free carrier (point of destination)." For a French/German case involving the clause "frei Haus" ("franco domicile" of buyer) *see* OLG Karlsruhe, 20 November 1992, UNILEX.

the "Incoterms" now in use.[12] By including a shorthand reference to a particular ICC (shipment or destination) trade term in their contract, the parties effectively incorporate a detailed set of risk rules with respect to that term. Even if the contract itelf simply uses a shorhand version of a common trade term, like CIF or CFR, without specific reference to the Incoterms, that term will likely be well-known by virtue of widespread trade usage.[13] In the *BP Oil* case,[14] the U.S. Court of Appeals for the 5th Circuit held that "CFR" is a part of the Incoterms which the CISG "incorporates" through Article 9(2). As the Court put it: "Even if the usage of Incoterms is not global, the fact that they are well known in international trade means that they are incorporated through Article 9(2)."[15]

It should also be noted that most overseas sales and many other cross-border sales involving delivery by land or air are "documentary sales" where the seller hands the goods over to a carrier and receives, in exchange, a bill of lading or equivalent document. This bill, together with other relevant documents, is then tendered to the buyer (or to the buyer's bank) in return for payment of the price.[16] If the contract is a shipment contract, the holder of the bill of lading normally bears the risk of loss or damage from the time the goods are placed on board; in the case of a destination contract the risk remains with the seller until the carrier arrives at the designated destination.

Against the background of commercial practice, the Convention provides gap-filling rules on the passing of risk. If the international sale concerned involves "carriage of the goods," but the seller is not bound to hand over the goods at any particular place, Article 67(1) regulates the risk along lines familiar to American jurists: the risk passes to the buyer when the goods are "handed over" to the "first carrier." Thus, in a case where a German buyer purchased pizza cartons from an Italian seller, the risk passed to the buyer as soon as the cartons were handed over to the carrier (in Italy), so any damage allegedly occurring during shipment was of no consequence to the seller.[17] As in most carriage cases, the transit risks fell on the buyer, and both the general delivery principle as well as practical considerations accord with this rule:[18] the buyer will be in a better position to inspect goods allegedly damaged by transit-related risks and make claims against the carrier or insurer concerned.[19]

Goods are only "handed over to the first carrier" if the carrier is a third party. If the seller delivers using means of transportation and personnel under his own control, the goods are

---

[12]   Incoterms 2000 is the latest edition as of this writing (2003).

[13]   Regarding Article 9 *see supra* § 2.13. Re. Incoterms and the place of delivery *see supra* § 4.3. *Compare* Tribunale di Appelo di Lugano (Switzerland), 15 January 1998, also in CISGW3 and UNILEX (CIF contract, risk passed *under that contract term* when goods handed over to carrier).

[14]   *BP Oil International v. Empresa Estatal Petroleos de Ecuador*, U. S. Court of Appeals (5th Circuit, 11 June 2003), also discussed *supra* § 4.2, notes 18–19 and accompanying text.

[15]   *Id.*, citing *St. Paul Guardian Ins.*, 2002 U.S. Dist. LEXIS 5096 (stating that "INCOTERMS are incorporated into the CISG through Article 9(2)").

[16]   For example, in a transaction financed by a letter of credit. For a full description and explanation of this payment term *see* Spanogle & Winship, *International Sales Law*, pp. 28–40. *See also supra* § 4.12 text with note 185.

[17]   *See* Amtsgericht Duisberg (Germany), 13 April 2000, CLOUT Case 360, CISGW3.

[18]   *See* Article 31 for the *principle* that delivery occurs at the seller's place of business.

[19]   In documentary sales the buyer will normally be in possession of documents controlling and insuring the goods: *see generally* Honnold, *Uniform Law*, § 367.

not handed over to a carrier in the Article 67(1) sense,[20] and the risk does not pass until the buyer actually "takes over the goods."[21]

Article 67(1) concludes with the observation that the seller's retention of documents controlling the disposition of the goods does not affect the passage of the risk.[22]

§ 5.3 Goods Not Identified to the Contract

The buyer will sometimes need special assurance that goods purportedly damaged or lost in transit were indeed the very goods which the seller originally intended buyer to receive. Where the seller regularly ships large quantities of fungible goods to various purchasers, a given CISG buyer should only bear the risk if it is clear that the goods damaged in a given shipment were "his."[23] Therefore, Article 67(1) operates only with respect to identified goods; the risk does not pass to the buyer unless and until the goods are clearly identified to the contract: by markings on the goods, by shipping documents, by notice given to the buyer or otherwise.[24] In sales involving the carriage of "bulk" goods, a particular buyer only bears the risk as to his undivided share in the bulk if that share has somehow been identified to the contract in question. Notice to the buyer that a particular bulk contains "his/her" goods, is sufficient to transfer the risk; in case of a partial loss or partial damage, the various buyers should share the loss in proportion to the quantities owed each of them.[25]

§ 5.4 Goods Sold in Transit

Article 68 deals with the special problem of goods sold while in transit. As in other cases involving carriage of the goods, the contract will usually contain a trade term which allocates the risk of loss.[26] The general default rule set forth in the first sentence of Article 68, whereby the risk passes at the time of contracting, was intended by its proponents to protect buyers in developing countries,[27] but it has been criticized by Western experts as "unworkable" in most cases.[28] Particularly when damage during transport results from an

---

[20] *See* Hager in Schlechtriem, *Commentary/Kommentar*, Art. 67, Rd.Nr. 5.

[21] If the seller arranges for carriage by two successive (independent) carriers, the risk usually passes when the goods are handed over to the first of these; however, if the seller is contractually bound to hand the goods over at the transshipment point, the risk passes first at that "particular place." *See* Schlechtriem, *Int. UN-Kaufrecht* Rd.Nr. 225.

[22] *See* Honnold, *Uniform Law*, § 370 (citing policy behind UCC § 2-509(1)(a)); Berman & Ladd, *Risk* at 429 (noting that risk in documentary FOB sale does not pass until seller tenders bill of lading; then risk passes, by relation back, at the time goods loaded on board).

[23] Since, under the CISG, the risk issue is divorced from the question of who has title to the goods, the buyer need not have become the legal owner of the goods in order to bear the risk in this situation.

[24] Article 67(2). In the case of a notification sent to the buyer, Article 27 applies.

[25] *Accord* Magnus in Staudinger, *Kommentar*, Art. 67, Rd.Nr. 31 and authors cited there; *compare* Honnold, *Uniform Law* § 371.

[26] *See supra* § 5.2.

[27] *See* (e.g.) Honnold, *Uniform Law*, § 372.1.

[28] *See* Berman & Ladd, *Risk* at 430.

event difficult to pinpoint in time (water seepage, etc.), the principle set forth in the second sentence (which passes the risk, retroactively, at the time the goods were handed over to the carrier) seems preferable, but this exception applies only where "circumstances" so indicate.[29] It is at least clear that the seller ought not profit by a failure to disclose events which would lead to the passing of risk.[30]

§ 5.5 NON-CARRIER CASES

Articles 67 and 68 (discussed above) both provide gap-filling rules in cases involving carriage of the goods. Article 69 provides the residual, gap-filling rules for non-carriage cases.

Article 69(1) provides the non-carriage rule applicable when the buyer is obligated to take over the goods at the seller's place of business (i.e. when the buyer is not bound to take over the goods at a place other than the seller's place): in this situation the risk generally passes when the buyer actually takes over the goods (just as it does under most domestic sales laws).[31] If the buyer does not take over (available) goods on time, the risk passes at that point in time when the buyer commits this breach.[32] If the contract permits the buyer to collect the goods at the seller's place within a given period, the risk will not pass until the period has passed, even if the goods were held available during that period.[33]

If the buyer is bound to take over the goods at a place other than seller's place of business, e.g., at a warehouse, the risk passes when delivery is due and the buyer is aware of the fact that the goods are placed at his disposal at that place.[34] If the contract permits the buyer to collect the goods within a given period, and the buyer is aware that the goods are available, the risk will pass before the period has passed.[35]

In a German case,[36] the parties entered an agreement for the manufacture and sale of furniture. According to the parties' prior practices,[37] the seller would arrange for the storage of goods, as and when they were manufactured, in a warehouse for the buyer's account; the handing over would then take place in the warehouse. In this instance, however, the goods disappeared following the bankruptcy of the warehouse. Since the buyer had not

---

[29]   *Accord* Hager in Schlechtriem, *Commentary/Kommentar*, Art. 68, Rd.NR. 4. *See also* Berman & Ladd, *Risk* at 430 (distinguishing between "circumstances" and contract terms and noting that the exception, like the rule, applies only where no trade term applies).

[30]   The third sentence of Article 68 applies only to the exception stated in the second sentence. If the goods are non-conforming at the time of contract formation (first sentence), Articles 35–40 apply.

[31]   *Compare* UCC § 2-509(3) where the risk passes to the buyer "on his receipt of the goods."

[32]   *See* Article 69(2). This rule also applies when the seller is to deliver the goods at the buyer's place of business.

[33]   *Accord* paras. 3–4 of the *Secretariat Commentary* on Article 81 of the 1978 Draft Convention (noting that the seller is in the best position to protect the goods).

[34]   Article 69(2).

[35]   In this case, the seller is in no better position than the buyer to protect against the loss. *See* paras. 5–6 of the *Secretariat's Commentary* to Article 81 of the 1978 Draft Convention.

[36]   Oberlandesgericht Hamm (Germany), 23 June 1998, CLOUT Case 338, CISGW3.

[37]   Regarding such practices under Article 9(1) *see supra* § 2.13.

been made aware that the goods had been placed in the warehouse (at the buyer's disposal), the risk had not passed under Article 69(2), and so the buyer did not have to pay for them.

In a dispute settled by ICC arbitration,[38] a Bulgarian buyer purchased goods from a seller in Austria. The contract provided for delivery "DAF"[39] at the Austrian-Hungarian border and for payment of the price by documentary credit. When the credit was not opened on time,[40] the seller deposited the goods in a warehouse and then commenced a legal action, demanding both payment of the price and damages for breach. Although the tribunal held the seller entitled to damages in the form of interest,[41] as well as reimbursement for expenses incurred in depositing the goods,[42] the seller had neither delivered the goods to the buyer nor "placed [them] at his disposal" pursuant to CISG Article 69. For this reason, the risk had not passed, and so the buyer was not liable for injury to the goods due to prolonged deposit in the warehouse.

Like Article 67, Article 69 presupposes identification of the goods.[43] In Article 69, identification is relevant as regards the seller's placement of the goods at the buyer's disposal: such placement will ordinarily effect a transfer of risk. However, if the contract relates to goods not then identified, the goods are first considered to be placed at the disposal of the buyer when such identification takes place: by marking, notice, etc.[44]

§ 5.6 SELLER'S FUNDAMENTAL BREACH: EFFECT ON RISK

Suppose, for example, that a seller in Argentina agrees to ship 10 dozen footballs to a buyer in New York, but that the seller then ships (& thus "delivers")[45] 10 dozen volleyballs instead. If the tanker carrying these volleyballs is then lost during a violent storm at sea, the seller "is liable" for the non-conformity,[46] and the rules which provide the buyer with remedies for breach should take priority over the rules which normally regulate the passing of risk. For this reason, Article 70 provides that the rules in Articles 67, 68 and 69 do not impair the remedies ordinarily available when the seller commits a fundamental breach. These remedies include the right to claim damages, to insist on the delivery of

---

[38] ICC case no. 7197/1992, UNILEX, also noted *supra* § 4.12.

[39] This is the Incoterm acronym: "Delivered at Frontier".

[40] Neither on the date of the contract, nor within the additional period of time granted by the buyer; re. such a "Nachfrist" under the CISG *see infra* § 6.24.

[41] Notwithstanding the fact that the Bulgarian government had ordered the suspension of payment of all foreign debts (re. the buyer's *force majeure* claim *see infra* § 6.32), and further notwithstanding a clause in the contract limiting damages to X% of the contract price (a clause which the arbitrators, applying Austrian rules of validity, held *not* to limit actual damages: *see infra* § 7.4).

[42] *See* Article 85.

[43] *See* Article 69(3) and *supra* § 5.3.

[44] *Compare* Article 67(2). The identification must, of course, accord with seller's rights and obligations under the contract.

[45] Re. the default rule in Article 31(a) *see supra* § 4.3.

[46] Re. the rule in Article 36, which provides that the seller is liable for any non-conformity which exists as of the passing of risk, *see supra* § 4.9.

substitute goods,[47] and even to avoid the contract,[48] since the buyer's inability to make restitution will not bar avoidance in such a case.[49]

The rule as formulated in Article 70 applies only to cases of a fundamental breach. If the breach is non-fundamental, the rule should be applied by analogy,[50] so that an accidental loss will not deprive the buyer of the right to claim damages or a proportionate price reduction.[51] If, however, "the loss or damage is due to [caused by] the act or omission of the seller," the rule in Article 70 is irrelevant, i.e., irrespective of whether the seller's breach is fundamental or not, since in this situation the risk cannot pass by virtue of the rule in Article 66.

---

[47]   Re. Article 46 *see infra* § 6.4 *et seq.*
[48]   Re. Article 49 *see infra* § 6.8.
[49]   Because the impossibility of making restitution of the goods or of making restitution of the goods substantially in the condition in which the buyer received them would not be due to buyer's act or omission, but rather to an Act of God (etc.). *See* Article 82 and *infra* § 6.12.
[50]   *Accord* Hager in Schlechtriem, *Commentary/Kommentar*, Art. 70, Rd.Nr. 3.
[51]   For details re. buyer's remedies *see infra* Chapter 6B.

CHAPTER SIX

REMEDIES FOR BREACH

6A OVERVIEW OF GENERAL PRINCIPLES

§ 6.1 SUPPLEMENTARY REMEDIAL REGIME

If the parties to a CISG contract perform as agreed,[1] they obviously have no use for the remedies in CISG Part III. And even in cases where a CISG party does not live up to his obligations, the remedies set forth in Part III do not apply if the contract itself sets forth different (e.g. more limited) rights for the party injured by the breach.[2] Not uncommonly, however, an international sales contract which sets forth a clear standard for performance does not (fully) address the "consequences" of non-performance or substandard performance. To determine the remedies available for breach, we look to the CISG to fill in the gaps.[3]

§ 6.2 ENFORCEABLE CONTRACTS AND REMEDIES FOR BREACH

For every breach of an enforceable sales contract, there must be some remedy: how else could we speak of "enforcing" the deal?[4]

It is convenient – and, for present purposes, appropriate – to divide the various forms of CISG remedial relief into three basic categories:[5] First comes *specific* relief, designed to compel the breaching promisor to perform his part of the bargain (deliver, pay, etc.). Next comes *substitutionary* relief which requires the breaching party to pay (or return) an amount of money to compensate the loss suffered by the other party.[6] The third major

---

[1]   Re. the obligations of the seller and buyer *see generally supra* Chapter 4.

[2]   An agreement to contract out under Article 6 (*supra* § 2.7) must, however, be valid under the applicable domestic law. Re. Article 4 *see supra* § 2.6; regarding agreed remedies *see* generally Chapter 7 *infra*.

[3]   Assuming, of course, that the CISG applies (because the parties places of business are in CISG Contracting States, etc.). *See generally supra* Chapter 2.

[4]   American and other Common lawyers say that a promise (to deliver goods, to pay) is "enforceable" when the promisor's breach entitles the promisee to a remedy (a money judgment or specific relief), whereas lawyers trained in Civil law systems use terms like "valid" or "binding" to express the concept of a promise or agreement which creates a *legal* (as opposed to a moral) obligation. *See generally* Lookofsky, *Consequential Damages*, Ch. 2.

[5]   *See generally* Lookofsky, *id.*, Ch. 4.1 and 6.2.4. *Accord* (as re. comparative contract theory in general) Treitel, *Remedies I*, § 16.1. *Compare* Gillette & Walt, *Sales Law*, discussing Remedies to Money Damages and Specific Relief in the remedial context (Ch. 9), but discussing Rejection and Avoidance within the context of "Performance" (Ch. 6).

[6]   Although substitutionary/monetary relief under the CISG will usually take the form of damages (*infra* § 6.14 *et seq.*), this is a larger conceptual category which also comprises a "proportionate reduction" (*infra* § 6.13).

remedial heading is *avoidance*, i.e., the right of the promisee to "avoid" the contract and thus terminate (put an end to) the contractual relationship.

Whereas this tripartite method of remedial classification will seem familiar to jurists trained in Civil law systems,[7] American (and other Common) lawyers are used to more complex classifications, especially as regards the remedy which the CISG refers to as "avoidance" (termination, usually by reason of fundamental breach).[8] Since the Convention demands a uniform interpretation, and since blending domestic and international terminology can lead to confusion, American lawyers ought not try to press the CISG system into a domestic mould. It may take some extra time to become familiar with the new international system and its jargon, but the CISG remedial "language" is one which jurists everywhere can learn to understand.

Whether a given breach entitles a CISG buyer or seller to a given category of relief depends both on the particular circumstances and on the applicable CISG rule(s). Of course, the right to demand specific performance is not compatible with the exercise of the right to avoid (terminate),[9] but there is no mutual exclusivity as between the right to demand either specific performance or avoidance (on the one hand) and the right to demand damages (on the other).[10]

At least in terms of placement in the overall CISG superstructural scheme, specific performance is the "primary" Convention remedy. When a party fails to perform a contractual obligation, the Convention seems based on the (Civil law) premise that the most "natural" remedy for breach – at least from a conceptual or superstuctural point of view – is some sort of "direct" enforcement of the obligation incurred by the promisor, (e.g.) to require that the seller deliver as agreed, that she cure defective delivery or (in the case of buyer's breach) that the buyer pay the price agreed.[11]

At first blush, this might seem a far cry from the American (Common) law view which generally regards specific performance as an exceptional remedy.[12] Even so, the Convention rules in this area actually represent a remedial compromise, and we shall see that the right of a CISG obligee to require performance by the obligor is subject to a number of important restrictions.[13]

---

[7]   *See generally* Treitel, *Remedies I*, § 16.1 and Lookofsky, *id.*, Ch. 4.1.

[8]   Though some American lawyers use *recission* to encompass what the UCC defines as "rejection" or "revocation of acceptance," and others use it as a synonym for "cancellation," the term rescission is best confined to cases involving contracts unenforceable by reason of fraud, duress and mistake: *see* White & Summers, *Uniform Commercial Law*, § 8-1; *Restatement Second of Contracts* § 152. *Accord* as re. Common law systems generally Treitel, *Remedies II* at 2. Obviously, this kind of "avoidance" is quite different from "avoidance" under the CISG.

[9]   By definition, a party who terminates a contract puts an end to both parties' right to demand specific relief.

[10]   The same logic applies, of course, under domestic sales laws.

[11]   Re. Article 46 and seller's breach *see infra* § 6.4. Re. Article 62 and buyer's breach *see infra* § 6.20.

[12]   *See* (e.g.) White & Summers, *Uniform Commercial Code*, § 6-6. *See also* Walt & Gillette, *Sales Law*, Ch. 9.III.A.

[13]   In addition to the requirements imposed by Article 46, a court is not bound to enter a judgment for specific performance unless that court would do so under its own law in respect of similar contracts of sale not governed by the CISG: regarding Article 28 *see infra* §§ 6.5 and 6.21.

We should also note an important practical limitation. In today's fast-paced society, most merchants have no time to wait for court-ordered performance of the obligation to deliver (conforming) goods – i.e., even when the letter of the law would otherwise permit – and the CISG case law shows that the buyer's right to obtain damages as monetary compensation (substitutionary relief) is far more important in practice. Specific performance does, however, retain considerable practical significance when it comes to the seller's enforcement of the buyer's obligation to pay.[14]

When it comes to the most important kind of monetry compensation – i.e., damages for breach – American lawyers should feel quite at home as regards the "basis" of CISG liability for (either party's) breach of an international sales contract.[15] Indeed, most observers read the Convention as having adopted the "no-fault" position of the Common law, although the rules regarding liability "exemptions" (situations involving alleged impossibility of performance, force majeure, etc.) do deserve our attention nonetheless.[16]

To the extent a breaching CISG party is held liable on this (no-fault) basis, the other (injured) party's compensation will often be measured on a "foreseeability" scale – yet another CISG feature which is easy for American (and other Common) lawyers to understand.[17] In addition to damages, the Convention also provides buyers with the more limited form of monetary relief which Civilian jurists regularly refer to as the "proportionate reduction in price."[18]

As regards termination, the Convention – as already noted – speaks of "avoidance."[19] Since the effect of avoidance is to release both parties from their obligations under the contract,[20] the default rules in the Convention place limits on this most "drastic" form of remedial relief – not only by restricting avoidance mainly to instances of "fundamental" breach, but also by widening the seller's right to "cure."[21] The CISG rules concerning anticipatory breach are in some respects closely related to the concept of avoidance (for fundamental breach).[22]

6B BUYER'S REMEDIES FOR SELLER'S BREACH

§ 6.3 INTRODUCTION: ARTICLE 45

Article 45(1) summarizes the remedies which the Convention makes available to the buyer for seller's breach. If the seller fails to perform any of his obligations under the contract or the Convention, the buyer may:

(a) exercise the rights provided in Articles 46 to 52;
(b) claim damages as provided in Articles 74 to 77.

---

[14] *See infra* § 6.21.
[15] I.e., the conditions or requirements for the imposition of liability.
[16] Re. Articles 45(1)(b) and 61(1)(b) *see infra* §§ 6.14 and 6.27. Re. Article 79 *see infra* §§ 6.19 and 6.32.
[17] *See infra* §§ 6.15 and 6.16.
[18] Re. Article 50 *see infra* § 6.13.
[19] *See* Articles 49 and 64. *See also supra*, note 8 and accompanying text.
[20] Subject to any damages which may be due: *see* Article 81(1).
[21] *See infra* §§ 6.8 and 6.9, including comparisons made there to the UCC "perfect tender" rule.
[22] Re. seller's stoppage in transit by reason of buyer's insolvency, etc. *see infra* § 6.26.

Subparagraph (a) serves mainly as a convenient "list" of the CISG rules which concern the buyer's right to require (specific) performance and the right to avoid, and the availability of these remedies is defined by Articles 46 to 52 (discussed below).

Subparagraph (b), on the other hand, does more than just refer to the rules (in Articles 74 to 77) which "measure" (mete out) the damages for which a breaching party is liable. Indeed, Article 45(1)(b) is a highly significant Convention provision which lays down the very *basis* of the seller's liability for breach.[23]

§ 6.4 ARTICLE 46: BUYER'S RIGHT TO DEMAND SPECIFIC PERFORMANCE

If a CISG seller fails to perform, the Convention permits the buyer to require (1) that the seller deliver, (2) that the seller deliver substitute goods, or (3) that the seller repair non-conforming goods. We begin with paragraph (1) of Article 46, a rule designed to deal with the situation where the seller's breach consists of a total failure to perform. According to this rule, the buyer may demand performance (delivery) unless she has resorted to an "inconsistent" remedy, i.e., avoidance.[24]

Although actions which seek to compel specific performance by the seller are not all that common in international sales practice,[25] courts and arbitrators should nonetheless be prepared to deal with the potential hardship which can make this an appropriate buyer's remedy. Indeed, a U.S. Federal Court court has indicated its willingness to grant specific performance (and damages) to an American CISG buyer as an appropriate remedial response to a German seller's *anticipatory* breach.[26]

In other cases, however, CISG courts and arbitrators will have reason to show restraint. For one thing, an order which compels specific performance after a market change might permit a CISG buyer to speculate at the seller's expense:

Illustration 6a: S in Toronto contracts to sell 100 silver bars at a fixed price to B in New York, with delivery to be made later that month. On the agreed date of delivery – when the market price of silver exceeds the contract price by 25% – S declares that he will

---

[23] *See infra* § 6.14.
[24] A party who avoids (terminates) a sales contract puts an end to both parties' right to demand specific relief. *See* Article 81(1).
[25] *Accord* Witz, *Premières Applications*, no. 84. The reason, as noted, is that most commercial buyers have little time to wait; for an example of a buyer who gave the seller 11 additional days to deliver and then, following the expiration of this *Nachfrist* period, avoided the contract *see infra* § 6.10 with note 100.
[26] *Magellan International Corporation v. Salzgitter Handel GmbH*, 7 December 1999, U.S. District Court of Illinois, LEXIS 19386, also in CISGW3 and UNLIEX. As re. the seller's threat not to perform its contractual obligations if the letter of credit was not amended, the court held this amounted to an anticipatory breach of contract, because the seller *clearly intended to breach* the contract before the contractual performance date (Art. 72 CISG); in fact, insistence upon amendment of the bill of lading requirement (in the letter) would amount to *a fundamental breach* (Art. 25 CISG). Although the Convention does not expressly authorize specific performance as a remedial response to an anticipitory breach, the holding seems reasonable, since the buyer did not ask for avoidance, and since the requirements for specific performance under Articles 46(1) and 28 seem to have been met (*see* § 6.5 *infra*). As re. the awarding of damages in such a situation *see infra* § 6.11 with note 107.

not perform. Despite repeated refusals by S to deliver the goods, B stands firm and brings an action seeking specific performance in a Toronto court. By the time the case reaches final judgment, the market price of silver bars is twice the price originally agreed.

Although Article 46(1) sets forth no express exception which would let S off the (performance) hook in this situation, many Convention commentators argue that the right to require performance should be interpreted in conjunction with – and as limited by – B's CISG obligation to mitigate damages,[27] and also by the Convention provision (and underlying general principle) concerning good faith;[28] there is, however, considerable support for the contrary view.[29] Then again, even those who discount the mitigation and good faith factors agree that Article 28 (discussed immediately below) might, in a given case, limit the buyer's right to specific performance as set forth in Article 46(1).

§ 6.5   DOMESTIC SALES LAW AS LIMITATION

According to Article 28, a court which holds that the buyer can require performance under the Convention (Article 46) must then consider whether such specific relief would be available pursuant to the domestic sales law of the jurisdiction concerned.[30] And if specific relief would not be available under domestic law, the forum court is "not bound" to require performance under the Convention.

The rule in Article 28 seems originally designed mainly to meet the needs of Common law jurisdictions, including (e.g.) American States, which traditionally grant specific relief only in "exceptional" – or at least "proper" – circumstances.[31] So when a German seller promised (but failed) to deliver hard-to-replace steel to an American buyer, a U.S. District Court declared itself "not bound" to require delivery unless it would do under its "own" sales law.[32]

---

[27] *See* Honnold, *Uniform Law*, § 285; Lookofsky, *United Nations Convention*, No. 214. Re. Article 77 *see infra* § 6.17.

[28] Re. Article 7(1) *see supra* § 2.10.

[29] *See* Gillette & Walt, *Sales Law*, pp. 375–76, opining that the mitigation rule in Article 77 applies (only) as a limitation on the right to recover damages. Re. the legislative history rejecting an amendment to the specific performance rule *see* Walt, *Specific Performance* at 214–16.

[30] The Convention refers to this body of rules as the forum's "*own law* in respect of similar contracts of sales of sale *not governed by this Convention*."

[31] Regarding the main UCC rule on point (§ 2-716) *see* White & Summers, *Uniform Commercial Code*, § 6-6. For a comparison of specific performance in Civil and Common law systems *see* Treitel, *Remedies II*, Chapter III. Re. Article 28 *see also generally* Kastely, *Specific Performance*.

[32] I.e., under the UCC sales statute applicable in the State in which the Federal court sits. *See Magellan International Corporation v. Salzgitter Handel GmbH*, 1999 U.S. Dist. LEXIS 19386, also CISGW3 and UNILEX. In dismissing the seller's request for summary judgment (i.e., a decision in the seller's favor on the basis of the pleadings alone), the court cited Article 28 and stated that "replaceability" was a central issue under the American domestic sales law rule: UCC § 2-716(1). The immediate effect of the ruling was to require a trial to determine whether the steel in question was, in fact, "replaceable" (as the seller claimed); if the court found it to be replaceable, the buyer could not require delivery under the UCC, in which case the court would not be bound to require delivery under the CISG.

But since that court would interpret the UCC as requiring delivery in situations where cover would be "costly" for the buyer, Article 28 would not seem to place significant limits upon a CISG buyer's right to demand performance in an American court.[33] Conversely, Article 28 can serve as a useful safety-valve in other – e.g., Civil law – jurisdictions where specific performance is usually regarded as the domestic remedial "rule."[34]

The 2-step analysis required by Article 28 – where we (first) look to the requirements for specific "performance" under Article 46 and (then) to the corresponding domestic law of the forum – clearly applies in cases falling within paragraph (1) Article 46, i.e., cases where seller has not delivered at all. Presumably, the same Article 28 analysis should be applied to those forms of specific performance described in Article 46, paragraphs (2) and (3).[35]

§ 6.6 BUYER'S RIGHT TO DEMAND RE-DELIVERY

Paragraph (2) of Article 46 deals with the situation where the goods are in fact delivered, but where they do not conform. In this situation, provided certain additional requirements are met, the buyer can demand re-delivery. Typically, the non-conformity referred to in paragraph (2) will relate to a breach of seller's obligations under Article 35, but the right to require re-delivery may also extend to breach of the seller's obligation to deliver unencumbered goods.[36] In either case, since re-delivery of substitute goods by the seller may entail a severe, potentially disproportionate financial burden, and since the buyer who receives non-conforming goods is always entitled to damages, Article 46(2) conditions the buyer's right to re-delivery upon a fundamental breach: in other words, the buyer who seeks resort to this remedy must have suffered a detriment which substantially deprives him of what he is entitled to expect under the contract.[37] In addition, the buyer's request for re-delivery must be made in conjunction with – or shortly after – a timely Article 39 notice which specifies the non-conformity concerned.[38]

In addition to meeting these conditions, the buyer who would require re-delivery must be prepared to return goods already received. Conversely, the buyer (usually) "loses the right to ... require the seller to deliver substitute goods if it is impossible for him to make restitution of the goods substantially in the condition in which he received them."[39]

To require a seller to re-deliver is to require him to perform his obligations as originally agreed. Therefore, it seems clear – at least to jurists trained in Civil law systems – that

---

33   For a fuller expression of this view, *see* Gillette & Walt, *Sales Law*, pp. 376–379.
34   Re. limits on demanding performance which would be unduly burdensome or impossible under Scandinavian law *see* Lookofsky, *Consequential Damages*, pp. 118–119.
35   *See* discussion of these provisions in the text *infra*.
36   *See* Walt, *Specific Performance* at 216–17 (reviewing the inconclusive legislative history).
37   *See* Article 25. In addition, the detriment must be one which a seller ought to foresee. Re. Article 25 (and avoidance under Article 49) *see infra* § 6.8.
38   Re. notice under Article 39 *see supra* § 4.9.
39   *See* Article 82(1) and the exceptions set forth in Article 82(2).

Article 28 should work to limit Article 46(2).[40] In other words, even assuming that the Convention re-delivery requirements (fundamental breach, restitution etc.) are met, a forum court should not consider itself "bound" to require performance if this form of relief would not be available pursuant to the corresponding domestic sales law of the forum State.[41]

§ 6.7   BUYER'S RIGHT TO DEMAND REPAIR

Paragraph (3) of Article 46 deals with the CISG buyer's right to require that the seller "cure" a non-conforming delivery by repair. This provision, which provides the buyer with a remedy for seller's breach, should not be confused with the CISG seller's right to "remedy" (cure) defects under Article 48(1).[42]

Rather than require the buyer to return non-conforming goods (and then require the seller to re-ship replacement goods),[43] it may save both parties time and money to arrange for repair of the non-conformity. Unlike the buyer's right to demand re-delivery, the right to demand repair is not expressly conditioned upon a fundamental breach.[44] In fact, the starting point in Article 46(3) is that any breach of the seller's obligation to deliver conforming goods entitles the buyer to demand repair.[45] On the other hand, since the buyer cannot demand repair if this would be unreasonable, a concrete evaluation of the situation is always required; a seller (or his agents) should not, for example, be required to travel a great distance to cure a minor defect.[46]

Assuming that a repair request is reasonable under the circumstances, the buyer must make that request in conjunction with – or shortly after – the submission of notice under Article 39 which is both timely and which serves to "specify" the non-conformity concerned.[47]

The right to demand repair is best understood as a species of the more general right to demand performance as agreed.[48] For this reason, in situations where the buyer, according to the letter of Article 46(3), would be entitled to demand repair, Article 28 should be read as placing a potential limit upon the operation of Article 46(3).[49]

---

[40]   For a contrary view *see* Honnold, *Uniform Law*, § 285.1 (arguing that Articles 46(2) and (3) should be regarded as *lex specialis* qualifications of Article 28).

[41]   *See supra* § 6.5.

[42]   This right, when available, works to limit the buyer's right to avoid: *see infra* § 6.9.

[43]   *See supra* § 6.6.

[44]   *Compare id.* and (as regards avoidance) *infra* § 6.8.

[45]   *See, e.g.,* Cour d'Appel de Versailles, 29 January 1998, CLOUT Case 225, CISGW3 and UNILEX.

[46]   *Accord* Honnold, *Uniform Law*, § 384. The reasonableness test does not, however, imply that the seller need only repair in circumstances where the defect meets the "fundamental breach" test of Article 46(2).

[47]   Re. notice under Article 39 *see supra* § 4.9.

[48]   *Accord* Walt, *Specific Performance* at 217. *But see* Honnold, *Uniform Law*, § 285.1 and *compare* Schlechtriem, *Uniform Law* at 63.

[49]   *See supra* § 6.5.

§ 6.8 BUYER'S RIGHT TO AVOID FOR SELLER'S FUNDAMENTAL BREACH

Article 49 provides an injured buyer with the right to "declare the contract avoided."[50] A declaration of avoidance, rightfully made and duly communicated to the seller in accordance with the applicable notice rules,[51] serves to terminate the contract, thus putting an end to the performance obligations of both parties.[52]

In international sales, termination (after shipment and delivery) may well result in especially serious consequences and extensive waste. Therefore, unlike the rule in UCC § 2-601 – which, as a starting point, allows the buyer in a domestic sales context to "reject" for any delay or defect (however insignificant)[53] – the general gap-filling rule in Article 49(1)(a) conditions the CISG buyer's right to avoidance upon a "fundamental" breach,[54] and this is true whether the CISG buyer (to borrow UCC parlance) has "accepted" the goods or not.[55]

Article 25 defines fundamental breach in terms of foreseeable and substantial "detriment." In order to avoid, the buyer must show that the breach has caused him to suffer a detriment which substantially deprives him of what he was entitled to expect under the contract; in addition, the detriment must be one which a reasonable seller would have foreseen. Although the "substantial deprivation" test is not easily passed, the delivery of nonconforming goods should certainly qualify as a fundamental breach if the non-conformity is so serious that the buyer can make no use of the goods,[56] (e.g.) a defect which renders the goods unfit for ordinary purposes (and/or for the buyer's particular purpose, if known to the seller).[57] Consider the following situation:

> *Illustration 6b*: Italian seller S enters a contract with Chicago buyer B for the supply of shoes. As S is aware, B intends to re-sell the shoes in his retail stores where only high quality shoes are sold, but the shoes actually delivered by S are of such poor quality that they are unfit for B's intended purpose and therefore essentially useless to B.

The delivery of non-conforming goods in *Illustration 6b* represents a serious breach of the seller's basic obligation to deliver fit-for-purpose goods.[58] So, assuming B provides S with

---

[50]   *See also supra* § 6.2.

[51]   A *declaration of avoidance* under Article 49(1)(a) is effective only if made by *notice* to the seller: *see* Article 26. Re. the "risk of transmission" *see* Article 27.

[52]   Article 81.

[53]   I.e. "if the goods or the tender of delivery fail *in any respect* to conform to the contract." Although this feature is maintained in the (2002) *NCCUSL Draft Revision* of the Code, it should be emphasized that the various exceptions to UCC § 2-601 come close to swallowing the so-called "perfect-tender" rule (*see* White & Summers, *Uniform Commercial Code*, § 8-3) – a fact which obviously narrows the real distance between the UCC and CISG (fundamental breach) rules.

[54]   Regarding the potential for overlap between the Convention and domestic validity rules *see supra* § 2.6.

[55]   Regarding the more complex UCC regime – which makes fundamental distinctions between "rejection" and "revocation of acceptance" – *see* Gilllette & Walt, *Sales Law*, Ch. 6.IV. This complex structure is maintained in the (2002) *NCCUSL Draft Revision*.

[56]   *Accord* OLG Frankfurt, 18 January 1994, UNILEX and CISGW3.

[57]   Re. Article 35 *see supra* §§ 4.7 and 4.8.

[58]   *See supra* § 4.8.

the requisite timely and specific notice under Article 39,[59] the fundamental (and presumably incurable) nature of this particular breach should entitle B to avoid.[60] Had S not been aware of B's intended purpose (resale in high quality stores), the breach might not be fundamental as regards the obligation set forth in Article 35(2)(b); but the fact that S delivers goods far below the "ordinary" standards set by the contract and the Convention under Article 35(2)(a) should still give B the right to avoid, particularly since B is not a middleman (wholesaler) who regularly engages in resale of (low quality) goods of that kind.[61]

In other non-confority cases, the breach may well be characterized as less serious. In one such instance, a Greek seller was required to supply thermoforming line equipment for the manufacture of plastic gardening pots. Although the American buyer "had some legitimate complaints concerning the machinery throughout the delivery and training process," a U.S. Federal Court nonetheless concluded that "these complaints did not constitute a fundamental (or even a substantial) breach of the contract by the seller," especially since the machinery had been successfully operated, and since the buyer (a cash-strapped business) raised performance questions only after the seller had made formal inquiries as to non-payment.[62]

Cases like these show that Article 49(1) sets forth a flexible, gap-filling rule. A CISG buyer who, at the time of contracting, expects she might need more rigorous protection against non-conforming delivery would be well-advised to insist on a contractual term which expressly conditions her duty to accept and pay upon delivery of merchandise which fully conforms to the contractual specifications. Of course, not even a lengthy and detailed contract can provide for every conceivable contingency:

> *Illustration 6c:*[63] Italian seller S enters a contract with Chicago buyer B for the supply of shoes to be produced by S in accordance with the design and specifications provided by B. According to the contract, B maintains the exclusive right to distribute and sell the shoes produced by S. Later, without obtaining B's consent, S displays shoes of B's design at a New York trade fair, thus giving the impression that S has the

---

[59]   Re. this key requirement *see supra* § 4.9. A buyer who avoids for this reason must also provide the seller with a *declaration* of avoidance: *see infra* text with note 79.

[60]   *See, e.g.,* Cour d'Appel de Versailles, 29 January 1998, CLOUT Case 225, (buyer could not use defective machines as expected, entitled to avoid); LG Ellwangen (Germany), 21 August 1995, CISGW3 & UNILEX (paprika containing high concentration of chemical not meeting minimum standards of German food law).

[61]   To require a retailer (B) to go outside his regular market to dispose of (seriously) non-conforming goods would *itself* substantially deprive B of what he entitled to expect, just as S ought to foresee such a result. *Accord* German Supreme Court (Bundesgerichtshof), decision of 3 April 1996, CLOUT Case 171, also in CISGW3 and UNILEX (breach not fundamental since buyer/*wholesaler* failed to show resale of nonconforming chemical would be unreasonably difficult). *See also* Swiss Supreme Court (Bundesgericht), 28 October 1998, CLOUT Case 248 (German S delivered fatty frozen meat, worth 25% less than conforming goods, to Swiss buyer/*wholesaler* (B); considering B's ability to process or re-sell goods at lower price, court held nonconformity *not significant enough* to entitle B to avoid).

[62]   A fact which tended to show that the buyer's complaints about performance were opportunistic and not genuine in character. *See* U.S. District Court, S.D., Michigan, 17 December 2001 (*Shuttle Packaging Systems, L.L.C. v. Jacob Tsonakis, INA S.A., et al.*).

[63]   Inspired by OLG Frankfurt, 17 September 1991, CLOUT Case 6, CISGW3 and UNILEX, commented on by Witz, *Premières Applications*, no. 72.

right to distribute the shoes. Despite a demand by B, S fails to remove the shoes from display.

Even the breach of an ancillary duty – (e.g.) an express obligation not to "compete" or an implied obligation to act in good faith[64] – can amount to a fundamental breach if it so seriously jeopardizes the transaction that the aggrieved party can no longer trust the party in breach. For this reason, the breach committed by S in *Illustration 6c* should give B the right to avoid.[65]

If the contract provides for delivery on a specified date, the buyer is, of course, entitled to expect timely delivery,[66] and a delay should at least entitle the buyer to claim damages. A separate question is whether late delivery – say two days or even two weeks late – constitutes a fundamental breach which should allow the CISG buyer to avoid. Of course, if the agreement expressly states that the buyer's duty to pay is "conditioned" upon timely performance by the seller,[67] we need not look to the CISG gap-filling rule – i.e., assuming that interpretation follows from the application of Article 8.[68]

If, on other hand, the contract is silent on the avoidance issue, we cannot ordinarily presume that "time is of the essence,"[69] and so we need to apply the Article 25 test. If, for example, a Canadian seller promises to deliver Christmas trees to a New Jersey buyer by "mid-November," actual delivery in mid-December might well qualify as "fundamental" breach.[70] Indeed, even a two-day delivery delay which prevents the buyer from performing an existing obligation to re-sell the goods to a third party could be described as a "substantial deprivation," although the buyer's right to avoid would depend on whether his seller (or a reasonable seller) was, at the time of contracting, able to foresee that effect.[71]

In some situations, the issue of just what constitutes "substantial" detriment is a matter on which reasonable minds can and will disagree. In a German case, an Italian seller agreed to deliver fall fashions to a German buyer in 4 installments, specified in the contract as: "July, August, September, +." When the first lot arrived at the end of September, the buyer

---

[64] Re. this CISG (gap-filling) general principle *see supra* text with note §§ 2.10 and 2.11.

[65] *See* the decision by OLG Frankfurt, *supra* note 63.

[66] Article 33 (*supra* § 4.3).

[67] In the Common law world, a "time is of the essence" clause in a sales contract will often be interpreted to mean that the buyer's duty to pay is *conditioned* upon the seller's timely performance. *See* re. English law the Court of Appeal in *Gill v. Duffus S.A. v. Sociètè pour L'exportation des Sucres S.A.* [1986] 1 Lloyd's Rep. 322 (clause requiring seller to specify loading port by November 14 "at latest" interpreted as *express condition* giving buyer right to *terminate* when seller gave notice 5 days late).

[68] *See generally supra* § 2.12.

[69] Unless international trade usage requires strict compliance with time clauses in contracts of that type, such that failure to deliver on time must *ordinarily* be regarded as a fundamental breach in that trade. Regarding Article 9 *see supra* § 2.13.

[70] This example is inspired by a Danish decision involving (not late delivery, but) delivery of non-conforming trees; for a commentary on the case *see* Fogt, *Reklamation*.

[71] *Accord* Corte d'Appello di Milano, 14 January 1998, CISGW3 (taking post contractual "clarifications" into account, the contract turned on availability just before buyer's end-of-year sales; seller's failure to deliver goods on specified date was fundamental breach).

returned the goods, and the seller then sued for damages. Although some might classify the delivery of the first installment of fall fashions in late September as a fundamental breach, the German court found for the seller.[72]

If the seller delivers only part of the goods, or if the goods delivered conform only in part, the starting point is that the buyer may (only) avoid as to such part, provided the breach is fundamental with respect to that part.[73] Only if the (partial) delivery failure amounts to a fundamental breach of the entire contract will the buyer be allowed to declare the entire contract avoided.[74] In one case, a German buyer ordered 11 computer components from a seller in Massachusetts, but the order indicated the price for only 5 of these units. When the seller then delivered only 5 units, the buyer refused to pay. Applying CISG Articles 25 and 51(2), the German court held that the seller was entitled to payment for the units delivered: i.e., even if the contract covered 11 units, the buyer was not entitled to avoid, since he could (and did) obtain 6 substitute units elsewhere.[75]

A seller who delivers early will not, for that reason, ordinarily be guilty of a fundamental breach; although the buyer may refuse early delivery as such, she will later have to accept re-delivery if made at the proper time.[76] If the seller delivers more than that provided for in the contract, the buyer may refuse the excess quantity;[77] but if the buyer takes delivery of all or part of the excess, she must pay for it at the contract rate.[78]

Assuming the breach is fundamental, Article 49(1)(a) entitles the buyer to "declare" the contract avoided. Indeed, a buyer must provide the seller with an avoidance "declaration," thus making it clear that she (the buyer) no longer intends to perform.[79] (As we shall see, the same notice is required when a buyer's right to avoid is based on the seller's failure to comply with a *Nachfrist* notice.)[80] If the buyer faced with a fundamental breach first elects to avoid after the goods have been delivered, she must, as regards late delivery, make her avoidance declaration within a reasonable time after learning that delivery has been

---

[72] Leaving open the possibility that, as the seller had argued, delivery had been made within the period specified (i.e. no breach, let alone a fundamental breach). *See* AG Oldenburg/Holstein, 24 April 1990, CLOUT Case 7, UNILEX. The court also cited the absence of a "*Nachfrist*" notice under Article 49(1)(b), but a delay can be fundamental and justify avoidance, notwithstanding the absence of a "*Nachfrist*" notice: *see infra* § 6.10.

[73] Article 51(1).

[74] Article 51(2).

[75] *See* LG Heidelberg, 3 July 1992, in CISGW3 and UNILEX. *See also* ICC case No. 7660/JK, 23 August 1994, CLOUT Case 302.

[76] Article 52(1). If early delivery does not result in unreasonable inconvenience or expense to the buyer, that buyer's refusal to take delivery may be inconsistent with good faith in international trade, observance of which is mandated by Article 7(1). For a similar restriction of the seller's rights *see* Article 37 and *infra* § 6.9.

[77] In exceptional circumstances the non-conforming tender in the form of quantitative over-performance might constitute a fundamental breach: *see* Honnold, *Uniform Law*, § 320.

[78] Article 52(2).

[79] *Accord* Huber in Schlechtriem, *Commentary/Kommentar*, Art. 49, Rd.Nr. 29. If the avoidance is attributable to a fundamental *non-conformity*, the buyer should usually make her avoidance-declaration at the time when the requisite notice under Article 39 is made: *see* Schwenzer in Schlechtriem, *Commentary* at 313.

[80] *See* Article 49(1)(b). The *Nachfrist* rules are discussed *infra* in § 6.10.

made;[81] in other cases, (e.g.) involving non-conforming delivery, the avoidance notice must be given within a reasonable time after she learns of the breach[82] or after the expiration of an additional performance period fixed in accordance with Article 47(1) or 48(2).[83]

A CISG buyer can rightfully rely on a rightfully dispatched avoidance declaration, even if it does not reach the seller.[84] If a seller receives – but refuses to respect – buyer's (rightful) declaration, the buyer may, in certain circumstances, be entitled to revoke it.[85]

§ 6.9 SELLER'S RIGHT TO CURE

If a CISG seller delivers non-conforming goods before the agreed delivery date,[86] Article 37 permits the seller to "remedy" (repair/cure) the defect, provided the exercise of this right would not cause the buyer unreasonable inconvenience or expense.[87] And if the CISG seller succeeds in "curing" the non-conformity before the delivery date, the buyer cannot avoid on the basis of a fundamental breach,[88] since the non-conformity, once repaired, will not cause the buyer a detriment which substantially deprives her of what she was entitled to expect.[89]

Article 48(1) supplements this early-delivery rule with a right for the CISG seller to remedy a given failure to perform even after the agreed delivery date.[90] As under Article 37, a seller can only exercise this right to cure (and thus "avoid" avoidance) if it will not cause the buyer unreasonable inconvenience or expense. In one German case, a seller's offer to

---

81 *See* Article 49, subparagraphs (2)(a).
82 Or should be aware of it: *see* Article 49(2)(a).
83 *See* Article 49, subparagraph (2)(b). As regards the time for avoidance after a buyer's *Nachfrist* notice in respect of non-conforming goods *see* subparagraph 49(2)(b)(ii) and *infra* § 6.10; re. timely notice of the non-conformity itself *see supra* § 4.9.
84 *See* Articles 26 and 27.
85 Buyer B might elect to pursue this course of action if S refuses to acknowledge the existence of a defect which B has declared to be fundamental; B might then prefer to have the defect cured by a third party and sue S for damages. The question of whether a declaration of avoidance is binding upon the declaring party would seem to be a matter "governed but not settled" by the Convention, and Professor Schlechtriem persuasively uses the general *estoppel* (detrimental reliance) principle to settle it: *see* Schlechtriem, *Commentary/Kommentar*, Art. 27, Rd.Nr. 14; *compare* Huber in Schlechtriem, *id.*, Art. 45, Rd.Nr. 28–28a.
86 Or, in other cases, before the expiration of a reasonable time after the conclusion of the contract: *see* Article 33(c).
87 The currently (2003) applicable version of UCC § 2-501, although differently worded, provides sellers with an essentially similar right (*see generally* Gillette & Walt, *Sales Law* at 224 *et seq.*); the same is true of the (2002) *NCCUSL Draft Revision* of the UCC rule.
88 *See* Honnold, *Uniform Law,* § 246, noting that Article 37 also restricts avoidance under Article 72 for anticipatory breach (*infra* § 6.11).
89 Re. Article 25 *see supra* § 6.8. In the American domestic sales context, the UCC seller's ability to cure "substantially retreats from the effect of the perfect tender rule" (Gillette & Walt, *supra* note 87 at *id.*).
90 The same is true of the current (2003) version of the UCC rule in § 2-508(2). The (2002) *NCCUSL Draft Revision* of § 2-508(2) represents a potential improvement in American domestic sales law and, it would seem, a step in the direction of the corresponding CISG rule: *see* (e.g.) *id.*, Comment 4: "Whether a cure is appropriate and timely should be tested based upon the circumstances and needs of the buyer."

provide substitute goods (blankets) was held to preclude avoidance;[91] in another (involving chemicals), the non-conformity in question required the buyer's customers to stop production, so the inability to promptly return the goods to Italy for treatment meant the seller could not cure the non-conformity without causing the buyer unreasonable inconvenience.[92]

As already indicated the rule in Article 48(1) is significant, because it works in tandem with Article 49(1)(a) and thus limits the CISG buyer's right to avoid on the basis of a fundamental breach. Although the "subject to" reference in this provision is less than clear, most CISG commentators see an interdependence between these provisions, with the result that the buyer who discovers a non-conformity cannot the nullify the seller's right to cure simply by rushing off an avoidance declaration. In other words, provided a given non-conformity can be cured quickly and without great inconvenience to the buyer, that breach should not be regarded as a "fundamental" unless and until the seller, given a reasonable chance, actually fails in his attempt to cure.[93]

§ 6.10   AVOIDANCE FOR NON-COMPLIANCE WITH "NACHFRIST" NOTICE

Unlike some domestic sales law regimes, the CISG does not automatically regard time to be "of the essence," at least not unless the particular sales contract includes a term to that effect.[94] On the contrary: the Convention rules seek to limit resort to the "drastic" avoidance remedy, *inter alia*, in cases of non-delivery.[95] Of course, the seller cannot expect payment in return for nothing, so – at some point or other – non-delivery must entitle the buyer to avoid. But since reasonable minds may differ as to when we actually reach the "critical mass" where a given delay (breach) becomes fundamental, a CISG buyer might find herself in a precarious position, afraid to run the risk of (prematurely) "taking a stand."[96]

---

[91]   OLG Koblenz, 31 January 1997, CLOUT Case 282, CISGW3.

[92]   For this reason, the buyer was entitled to make its own arrangements for cure (treatment of the chemicals) and to deduct the (reasonable) costs incurred from the purchase price. See Amtsgericht München, 23 June 1995, UNILEX.

[93]   *See* Honnold, *Uniform Law*, § 296, Huber in Schlechtriem, *Commentary/Kommentar*, Art. 48, Rd.Nr. 23; *see also* Pretura di Locarno-Campagna (Switzerland), 27 April 1992, UNILEX (Swiss buyer held *not* entitled to avoid, *inter alia*, because he refused to accept offer by Italian seller to cure). *Accord*: Gillette & Walt, *Sales Law* at 235–236. *Contra* Magnus in Staudinger, *Kommentar*, Art. 48, Rd.Nr. 22, 29–30. In any case, the buyer's right to avoid should not be defeated in cases where time is clearly "of the essence" or in cases where the buyer has justifiably lost confidence in a seller due to the latter's fraudulent conduct or incompetence: *see* Huber *id.*, Rd.Nr. 20.

[94]   An established "practice" between the parties would, however, also do the trick: *see supra* § 2.13; regarding the additional possibility of a relevant international usage *see supra* § 6.8, text with note 69.

[95]   I.e., where delivery does not take place at the time fixed by the contract or within a reasonable time. Re. Article 33 *see supra* § 4.3.

[96]   If the buyer, due to the seller's delayed delivery, issues an avoidance declaration and herself refuses to perform, she runs the risk that a court or arbitral tribunal later will hold (a) that the seller's delay (as of the time of the declaration) did *not* constitute a fundamental breach by the seller, and that the *buyer's* own refusal constituted a fundamental breach. Re. this risk (*standpunktrisiko*) under Danish law *see* Andersen & Lookofsky, *Obligationsret*, Ch. 5.1.g.

To help level the playing field in this particular ("buyer-in-waiting") situation – i.e., where the breach involves non-delivery (as opposed to non-conforming delivery) – the Convention provides the buyer with an alternative ground for avoidance of the sales contract. Under Article 47(1) the CISG buyer can fix an additional delivery period of reasonable length (a so-called *Nachfrist*),[97] and if the seller does not then deliver the goods within that additional and reasonable period (or if he declares that he will not comply), Article 49(1)(b) gives the buyer the right to declare the contract avoided for that reason[98] – (i.e.) irrespective of whether the breach, by that time, has reached "fundamental" proportions.[99]

Since these *Nachfrist* rules were designed to provide the buyer with some measure of increased certainty, the buyer's precarious situation (need for delivery without further delay) should be a key consideration when a court or tribunal determines whether the period fixed was reasonable or not.[100] On the other hand, the seller (though in breach) is also entitled to some certainty in a *Nachfrist* situation; for this reason, the buyer may not, during the additional period fixed, resort to any remedy which she might otherwise have by virtue of the breach.[101]

Note that a seller's non-compliance with a *Nachfrist* notice is sanctioned only in the case of non-delivery,[102] (i.e.) so that non-compliance with the notice entitles the buyer to avoid.[103] So, although Article 47 is worded so as to comprise any breach, the CISG (as opposed to the German) version of the *Nachfrist* rule does not provide a separate basis for avoidance when the buyer's notice relates to delivery of non-conforming goods.[104]

---

97   Borrowing a label from German law; *see* the *Secretariat Commentary* at 117, para. 8.

98   By sending a notice (avoidance declaration) pursuant to Article 26.

99   *Accord*: Huber in Schlechtriem, *Commentary/Kommentar*, Article 47, Rd.Nr. 3 (fixing additional time period of "no consequence" re. whether breach fundamental under Article 25).

100   *See* Honnold, *Uniform Law*, § 289; *compare* factors noted by Huber in Schlechtriem, *Commentary/Kommentar*, Art. 47, Rd.Nr. 9 (length of contractual period of delivery, buyer's recognizable interest in rapid delivery, nature of the seller's obligation, nature of 'impediment' to timely delivery). *See also* Oberlandesgericht Celle (Germany), 24 May 1995, CLOUT Case 136, also in CISGW3 and UNILEX (German seller failed to deliver remaining goods within additional 11 day period fixed by Egyptian buyer; *obiter dictum*: such *Nachfrist* notice could be effective even though additional period itself not sufficient to allow seller to arrange transport). If the period fixed is deemed unreasonably short, Huber (*id*. Rd.Nr. 12) would let the notice initiate a reasonable period after which the buyer can avoid under 49(1)(b), but Heuzé (*Vente internationale* no. 402 at 303) rightly disagrees; in any case, the Article 49(1)(a) clock continues to tick, thus allowing the buyer – after the expiration of the additional period (*see* following note) – to claim avoidance if the delay then amounts to a fundamental breach.

101   Article 47(2). In other words, the buyer who has fixed an additional period cannot – during that period – avoid, even if the delay might be considered "fundamental" under Article 49(1)(a).

102   Or a delivery which arrives after the expiration of the additional/reasonable period which the buyer has fixed.

103   Article 49(1)(b).

104   *See* Articles 47(2) and 49(1)(a). If a seller fails to comply with an Article 47(1) notice issued in respect of non-conformity, the notice can only affect the point in *time* at which the buyer can avoid on the basis of seller's *fundamental* breach: *accord* Honnold, *Uniform Law* at 331 with note 6. *Compare* the German domestic version of the *Nachfrist* rule previously applicable under Civil Code § 326 and the new rule in § 323 which both apply to non-delivery and to delivery of non-conforming goods.

§ 6.11   ANTICIPATORY BREACH

In general, the CISG buyer's remedies first become available at the point in time when the seller actually commits a breach, (e.g.) when S actually fails to deliver at the time and place agreed or when he delivers non-conforming goods.

If, however, the buyer has good reason to expect that S will commit a (fundamental) breach, the Convention does not require the buyer to remain committed to performing her part of the deal. In other words, the CISG also provides relief in situations where, prior to the time scheduled for performance, the seller's conduct amounts to an anticipatory breach. In such circumstances, the buyer may be able to suspend her own performance (Article 71) or perhaps even avoid the contract before the seller's performance actually falls due (Article 72).

According to Article 72(1), when the seller – prior to the date of performance[105] – actually repudiates the contract (declares his unwillingness to perform) or when, for other reasons, it becomes "clear" that the seller will commit a fundamental breach, the buyer may declare that contract avoided,[106] thus releasing both parties from their obligations to perform (though the buyer retains her right to claim damages).[107] Although Article 72 does not require a showing of "total certainty," the buyer can only avoid if the circumstances clearly – and with a very high degree of probability – indicate that the seller cannot or will not perform at the time when performance becomes due.[108] Depending on the circumstances, and if time allows, the buyer intending to avoid must give reasonable notice to the seller in order to permit him to provide an "adequate assurance of performance."[109] The UCC provides a similar rule.[110]

Since avoidance is a drastic step, especially within the context of an international sale, the Convention requires a "clear" indication of the seller's intent: (e.g.) a definitive (total) repudiation. If – in somewhat less extreme circumstances – it "becomes apparent" that the seller will not perform a "substantial part" of his obligations,[111] the buyer may suspend

---

[105] *Compare* Bundesgerichtshof (Germany), 15 February 1995, CLOUT Case 124, CISGW3 and UNILEX (once S had delivered, no remedy available under Art. 72, even assuming S could not transfer property in the goods).

[106] *See* (e.g.) OLG Düsseldorf, 14 January 1994, upholding Landgericht Krefeld, 28 April 1993, CLOUT Case 130, CISGW3 and UNILEX (seller had right to avoid second shoe contract when it became "clear" that buyer, who had not yet performed under prior contract, would not furnish security or pay).

[107] CISG damages are based on the failure of a party to perform its *obligations* under the contract or the Convention, but since a CISG promise to perform may be said to include an implied commitment not to deliberately compromise the probability of performance, an action for damages under Articles 74–76 could be grounded upon "breach by anticipatory repudiation": *see* Lookofsky, *United Nations Convention*, No. 284.

[108] *Accord* Leser in Schlechtriem, *Commentary/Kommentar*, Art. 72, Rd.Nr. 12.

[109] The Article 72(2) rule does not apply if the other party has "declared that he will not perform his obligations," i.e., in the case of a seller's express repudiation.

[110] § 2.609. *See generally* Gillette & Walt, *Sales Law*, Ch. 6.II.A.

[111] This should become apparent "[a]s a result of (a) a serious deficiency in [the seller's] ability to perform or in his creditworthiness; or (b) his conduct in preparing to perform or in performing the contract." Article 71(1). *See also infra* § 6.26 with note 293.

performance of her obligations. Although the degree of probability required by this ("becomes apparent") test must be lower than that required for avoidance,[112] the buyer who contemplates suspending performance should still be prepared to later present a court with convincing evidence of seller's impending breach.[113] In addition, the buyer who intends to suspend must give immediate notice so as to provide the seller with an opportunity to lift the restriction by providing an adequate assurance of performance.[114] (Similar considerations apply as regards a buyer's prospective inability to pay.[115])

In the case of an installment sale (a contract for delivery of goods by installments),[116] a seller's fundamental breach with respect to a single installment entitles the buyer to declare the contract avoided with respect to that installment.[117] In addition, the failure with respect to a single installment may give the buyer "good grounds" to conclude that a fundamental breach of contract will occur with respect to future installments;[118] if so, the buyer may (also) declare the contract avoided for the future as well.[119]

§ 6.12 CONSEQUENCES OF AVOIDANCE: RESTITUTION

Under Article 81(1) an effective avoidance releases both parties from their obligations, subject to any damages due. As a consequence, Article 81(2) provides for restitution: an avoiding party who has previously performed in whole or part may claim a return of that performance from the other.[120] Under the Convention restitution is thus available, *inter alia,* for what American lawyers call "total" breach: since the CISG buyer's performance is "impliedly conditioned" on substantial performance by the seller, the buyer who is entitled to avoid by reason of her seller's fundamental breach can claim the return of monies she may have already paid.[121]

---

[112] *See, e.g.,* LG Berlin, 15 September 1994, UNILEX (buyer could suspend performance when it became apparent seller would not deliver conforming goods; nonperformance under Art. 71(1) need not necessarily amount to a fundamental breach).

[113] Absent such evidence, the suspending CISG buyer runs the risk of putting *herself* in breach: *see supra* text with note 96.

[114] *See* Article 71(3). Failure to give prompt notice exposes the suspending party to the risk of committing a breach by withholding performance; this kind of mistake defeated the action in AG Frankfurt, 31 January 1991, CLOUT Case 51, CISGW3 and UNILEX, analyzed by Witz, *Premières Applications*, no. 85.

[115] Re. "stoppage in transit" pursuant to Article 71(2) *see infra* § 6.26.

[116] An installment contract under the CISG is a contract for *delivery of goods* by installments. The concept does not look to the buyer's obligation to pay the price.

[117] Article 73(1).

[118] Also violation of an important ancillary duty may justify this conclusion; *see* (re. a buyer's anticipatory breach) Cour d'Appel Grenoble (France), 22 February 1995, CLOUT Case 154, CISGW3 and UNILEX.

[119] *See* Article 73(2) and (e.g.) Handelsgericht Zürich, 5 February 1997, CLOUT Case 214, CISGW3 and UNILEX (seller's non-delivery of first installment gave buyer good grounds to avoid entire contract). *See also* Schiedsgericht der Börse für Landwirtschaftliche Produkte – Wien, 10 December 1997, UNILEX.

[120] *See* (e.g.) Tribunale di Appello di Lugano (Switzerland), 15 January 1998, CLOUT Case 253, CISGW3 and UNILEX.

[121] Re. American (domestic) law *see* (e.g.) Farnsworth, *Contracts* § 8.15.

Notwithstanding the release of the parties from their primary obligations, Article 81(1) makes it clear that the sales contract relationship has continuing effect with respect to the secondary (i.e. remedial) obligation to pay damages in the event of breach.[122] In addition, an arbitration clause or other forum agreement remains in effect; the same is true as regards a clause fixing liquidated damages and, if valid, a penalty clause.[123]

A related rule in Article 86 requires that a buyer who "intends to reject" take reasonable steps to preserve the goods (e.g. take possession on the seller's behalf); the buyer is then entitled to reimbursement of expenses incurred.[124] Depending on the circumstances, the buyer who is bound to preserve the goods will be entitled – or perhaps even required – to sell the goods for the seller's account (Article 88).

§ 6.13   PROPORTIONATE PRICE REDUCTION

The buyer's right to restitution in the event of seller's total breach involves the return by the seller of all payments received. But the restitutionary concept applies in other situations as well. Where a seller delivers goods which do *not conform*, the CISG entitles the buyer to a certain reduction in price.[125] As an alternative to damages the proportionate price reduction provides the buyer with a restitutionary measure of monetary relief,[126] even where the buyer is not entitled to avoidance or cure.[127] The buyer entitled to a price reduction under Article 50 is thus relieved of the payment obligation in part: this represents a kind of "partial avoidance," corresponding to the degree of breach represented by the non-conformity (defect).

Although price reduction will usually take a back-seat to damages, at least within the larger CISG remedial scheme,[128] U.S. lawyers need to apprehend the nature of this Civilian

---

[122]   *See, e.g.*, LG Landshut (Germany), 5 April 1995, CISGW3 and UNILEX.

[123]   *See* the second sentence of Article 81(1).

[124]   Re. deposit of the goods in a warehouse *see* Article 87.

[125]   *See* Article 50 and (e.g.) OLG Graz (Austria), 9 November 1995, CLOUT Case 175, UNILEX (marble slabs delivered did not conform to model provided by buyer). Note that the seller's delivery of the wrong quantity is a breach covered – not by Article 50, but rather – by Article 51(1). *See* Huber in Schlechtriem, *Commentary*, Art. 50, Rd.nr. 4; see also Flechtner, *More U.S. Decisions*, text with notes 62–69 (discussing *S.V. Braun, Inc. v. Alitalia Linee Aeree Italiane, S.p.A*, No. 91 CIV. 8484 (LBS), 1994 WL 121680 (S.D.N.Y. Apr. 6, 1994), also available at <http://cisgw3.law.pace.edu/cisg/wais/db/cases2/940406u1.html>.

[126]   *See generally* Bergsten & Miller, *Reduction in Price* and Ziegel, *Remedial Provisions* at 9–36. Regarding the essentially "restitutionary" nature of this Civilian remedy *see* Treitel, Remedies II at 107 ff; *see also* Flechtner, *More U.S. Decisions*, note 76 and accompanying text, noting situations in which Article 50 does not yield the same result as would a restitutionary remedy (or an expectation or a reliance remedy) in U.S. domestic law. Re. American sales law under the original version of UCC § 2-508(2) – which (unlike the 2002 *NCCUSL Draft Revision*) speaks of tender "acceptable with or without money allowance" – *see* White & Summers, *Uniform Commercial Code*, § 8-7 (price adjustments most common form of businessmen's cure; UCC buyer should be made to accept price reduction as cure).

[127]   However, under Article 50, if the seller "remedies" [cures] an initially defective delivery (or if buyer refuses to accept such cure), the buyer may not reduce the price.

[128]   *See infra*, note 133 *et seq.* with accompanying text.

remedy, how it departs from the remedial concepts with which Common lawyers are familiar, and how it may be of potential significance in certain CISG scenarios.[129]

According to Article 50, the reduction of the price is proportional to the reduction in value due to the defect and may be derived from the following equation, where "X" designates the price (after reduction) which buyer is to pay:

$$\frac{\text{Price X}}{\text{contract price}} = \frac{\text{value w/defect}}{\text{value w/o defect}}$$

Consider the following example:

Illustration 6d:[130] S (in Iowa) contracts to deliver to B (in Mexico City) 10 tons of No. 2 corn at $400 per ton (the market price for No. 2 corn at that point in time). S delivers 10 tons of No. 3 corn instead. At the time of delivery the market price of No. 3 corn is $300 per ton; that of No. 2 corn is still $400.

S has clearly delivered goods which "do not conform with the contract,"[131] and this fact itself entitles B to reduce the price. So, even if delivery of No. 3 corn does not constitute a fundamental breach (or if it does, but B does not choose to avoid the contract), B can reduce the purchase price from $4,000 to $3,000.[132]

In this way, the proportionate reduction provides quality-gap compensation when the buyer does not or cannot avoid.[133] But the remedy of damages, if (also) available, will often provide the injured buyer with more,[134] and since CISG damages are generally available on a no-fault basis,[135] the proportionate price reduction plays a much more limited remedial role under the Convention than under (e.g.) Civil and Scandinavian sales laws, where damages sometimes require a showing of fault.[136]

§ 6.14 DAMAGES FOR BREACH: A GENERAL INTRODUCTION

The right to obtain damages enjoys a key position within the CISG remedial matrix. In some cases, this kind of monetary compensation supplements the right to demand specific

---

[129] *See* Flechtner, *More U.S. Decisions*, text following note 92.
[130] Similar to Example 46C in the *Secretariat Commentary* to Article 46 of the 1978 Draft.
[131] *See supra* § 4.4.
[132] If no market value exists or none can be determined, courts will usually presume that the contract price constitutes the value of the goods in a conforming (non-defective) condition; *see* (e.g.) Pretura di Locarno-Campagna (Switzerland), 27 April 1992, reported in UNILEX.
[133] *See also* Lookofsky, *Consequential Damages*, pp. 134–36.
[134] If the market price exceeds the contract price, damages under Article 76 will provide compensation for (1) the "non-perfect" part of the goods and (2) the market-price differential corresponding to the said part; in this situation, damages will exceed a price reduction. Note also that a plaintiff entitled only to a price reduction will not get compensation for "consequential" loss. *See generally* Bergsten & Miller, *Reduction in Price* at 259.
[135] *See infra* § 6.14.
[136] If CISG damages are not available because of the exemption rule in Article 79, a price reduction remains an attractive alternative under Article 79(5). It may also be possible to combine a price reduction with

performance or to avoid; in other cases, damages may be the only relief permitted under the CISG scheme.

In some respects, the CISG liability rules represent a compromise between competing Civil and Common law conceptions. There was, to be sure, a significant core of agreement from the outset, but certain choices had to be made, and it seems that the representatives of each of these legal families scored a key point or two. First, as regards what Civil law jurists sometimes refer to as the "basis" of contractual liability for breach, most commentators read the CISG as having adopted the no-fault preference of the Common law. In this connection, there has been much discussion of the "exemption" rule in Article 79,[137] but it is important to emphasize that Article 45(1) does more than simply catalogue the various remedies for seller's breach. Indeed, according to the letter of the law, Article 45(1)(b) is the very source of the buyer's right to claim damages:[138] if the seller "fails to perform any of its obligations under the contract or this Convention, the buyer may . . . claim damages as provided in Articles 74 to 77." In other words, the buyer may claim damages for any breach (failure to perform), in that Articles 74–77 deal only with the extent (measurement) of liability.[139] So, though some would have preferred a more explicitly worded provision,[140] Article 45(1)(b) clearly represents a *no-fault* rule: i.e., the basis of liability is the breach itself.[141]

Illustration 6e:[142] Italian seller S contracts to deliver shoes to American buyer B. Later, while the goods are en route to B, S receives reliable information indicating that B is in serious financial difficulty and may not be able to make timely payment as agreed (upon delivery). For this reason, S orders the carrier to suspend delivery, but S fails to give notice of the suspension to B.

In a situation like this, B's prospective failure to perform presumably gives S the right to suspend his performance, but according to Article 71(3) S "must immediately give notice of the suspension" to B.[143] So, even assuming the suspension is justified, the failure to notify is a failure to perform which – like any CISG breach – makes the breaching party (S) liable in damages under Article 45(1)(b).[144] In this connection, the reason why S

---

      a damages claim, provided the claimant does not thereby receive "double compensation" for the same items of loss: *see* Huber in Schlechtriem, *Commentary/Kommentar*, Art. 50, Rd.Nr. 79.

[137] *See infra* § 6.19.

[138] *See* para. 1 of *Secretariat Commentary* to Article 41 of the 1978 Draft Convention.

[139] In other words, Articles 74–77 answer the question: *how much* compensation should the injured party get?

[140] Professor Krüger's critique from a Nowegian perspective (*Norsk Kjøpsrett*, p. 700) is particularly blunt, but this criticism – like the earlier doubts expressed by Nicholas (*Force Majeure*) – seems to overshoot the mark. The starting point in Art. 45(1)(b) is clearly no-fault, and the CISG waters are hardly "muddied" by the safety-valve in Art. 79 (re. the decision by the *Bundesgerichtshof* in the "Vine Wax" case *see infra* § 6.19).

[141] As opposed to the possibly negligent conduct which might have caused the breach. Of course, the recovery of damages assumes that the party "injured" by the breach has suffered some (at least minimal) loss. Re. the basis of CISG liability *see generally* Lookofsky, *Fault and No-Fault*: *see also* Huber in Schlechtriem, *Commentary/Kommentar*, Art. 45, Rd.Nr. 1 and 10.

[142] This illustration is inspired by the decision of AG Frankfurt am Main, 31 January 1991, UNILEX.

[143] For details *see infra* § 6.26.

[144] The measurement of damages will be determined by Article 74: *see infra* § 6.15.

breached his obligation (failed to give notice) is simply irrelevant,[145] since a CISG buyer's right to recover damages is not dependent upon proof – or even presumption – of seller's culpable breach.[146]

Granted, CISG liability cannot be described as "absolutely strict": just as the domestic no-fault rules in some jurisdictions provide certain "safety valves,"[147] a CISG seller may be exempt from liability in exceptional situations, provided non-performance is attributable to unforeseeable and unavoidable circumstances, i.e., the kind of impediment often associated with what American jurists refer to as impossibility, impracticability or *force majeure*.[148] Still, as more fully explained below (§ 6.19), Article 79 does not "water down" Convention liability to a fault rule based on culpable (negligent or willful) breach,[149] a fact which the Supreme Court of Germany has now made abundantly clear.[150] In other words, the traditional Civilian model, where liability is often based on culpable breach, is quite different.[151]

As already indicated the CISG liability regime represent a compromise, and the Civilian view prevailed as regards the effect of a "legal excuse" (impediment). In Common legal systems, the sweeping effect of impossibility (impracticability, etc.) is total discharge of the obligation concerned;[152] under the CISG, however, the direct effect of an excusing contingency – an "impediment" to performance – is not discharge, but rather a more narrow exemption from liability for damages.[153] There will often be little difference in terms of the ultimate result,[154] but Common lawyers should nonetheless be aware of this "Civilian" aspect of the Convention remedial scheme.

§ 6.15 EXPECTATION PROTECTION FOR FORESEEABLE LOSS

The "Common" provisions concerning damages for breach in Articles 74–77 apply to CISG sellers and buyers alike. So, although our focus here is on buyer's damages for

---

[145] *See also supra* with note 141. In this *Illustration* there are no facts to indicate a liability exemption under Article 79 (*compare infra* § 6.19). Note also that the CISG does not distinguish between "principal" and "ancillary" duties (*see supra* § 6.8).

[146] *See generally* Lookofsky, *Fault and No-Fault* and *compare* Nicholas, *Force Majeure*.

[147] *See generally* Lookofsky, *Consequential Damages*, Ch. 4.4.1.

[148] Re. Article 79 *see infra* § 6.19.

[149] *Accord* Schlechtriem, *Uniform Law* at 101 with note 417. As more fully explained *infra* in § 6.19, the fears previously expressed (e.g.) by Nicholas (*Force Majeure*) with respect to the interpretation of Article 79 in Civil law jurisdictions have proven totally unfounded.

[150] *See* Bundesgerichtshof (Germany), 24 March 1999, CLOUT Case 271. This important decision is discussed *infra* § 6.19.

[151] Though the difference is less dramatic in those situations where the breaching party's culpability is presumed. *See* Treitel, *Remedies II* at 75 and Lookofsky, *Consequential Damages*, Ch. 4.4.1.

[152] This result is tied to the fact that, in these systems, non-performance in the face of impossibility is simply not "breach." *See* (e.g.) the American UCC § 2-615(a) (delay in delivery "not a breach"). *See also* Lookofsky, *Consequential Damages*, Ch. 4.4.1, and *compare* the U.K. Law Reform (Frustrated Contracts) Act 1943.

[153] *See* Article 79.

[154] *Inter alia*, because a CISG obligee cannot require performance of the impossible: *see supra* §§ 6.4 and 6.5 and *infra* § 6.19.

seller's breach, many of the basic principles explained in this Chapter (6B) will apply with equal force when, in Chapter 6C, we shift the focus to the seller's damages for buyer's breach.

Article 74 sets forth the general principle by which the Convention – absent contrary agreement – measures liability for breach.[155] As is also the case under most domestic contract and sales laws, CISG damages are "equal to [and thus designed to compensate] the loss ... suffered as a consequence of the breach." Given a causal connection between breach and loss,[156] the Convention seeks to place the injured party in the position she would have enjoyed "but for" the breach.[157] In this way CISG damages are designed to provide a substitute for the promised performance – a sum of money which protects the injured party's "expectation interest."[158] And since the breach itself is the "basis" of Convention liability,[159] the CISG clearly provides the injured party with expectation interest protection on a no-fault basis,[160] although the broadly formulated rule in Article 74 has been read to include damages measured by the "reliance interest" as well.[161]

Foreseeability is the key Article 74 limitation: damages may not exceed the loss which the breaching party foresaw or ought to have foreseen as a consequence of the breach of contract. This principle – well in tune with what Common lawyers call the *Hadley* rule[162] – is also similar to the corresponding German domestic doctrine.[163] Of course, such similarities ought not lead American or German courts to interpret Article 74 in a parochial way.[164] In accordance with *Hadley*, but in contrast with other domestic systems, the Convention foreseeability standard is to be evaluated solely on the basis of information available to the breaching party at the time of the conclusion (making) of the contract, in the light of the facts and matters which that party then knew or should have known.[165]

---

[155]   The validity (enforceability) of "agreed remedies" such as liquidated damages and penalty clauses in a CISG contract is determined by the applicable domestic law (*lex causa*). *See infra* Chapter 7.

[156]   I.e., that the loss is a "consequence" of the breach.

[157]   I.e. the requirement of a *conditio sine qua non*.

[158]   The remedy of specific performance also protects the buyer's expectation interest: *see supra* § 6.4.

[159]   Re. breach as the basis of CISG liability *see supra* § 6.14.

[160]   So, no-fault expectation protection constitutes the "basic philosophy" of damages under the Convention. *Accord* Stoll in Schlechtriem, *Commentary*, Art. 74, Rd.Nr. 2 with note 4 (in *Kommentar* with note 5) citing the *Secretariat Commentary* p. 132.

[161]   *See* Ziegel, *Remedial Provisions* at 9–37. *See also* the *Delchi* case, cited in the text *infra* with note 176.

[162]   Hadley v. Baxendale, 9 Ex. 341, 156 Eng. Rep. 145 (1854). *See also* the American *Restatement Second of Contracts,* § 351. *See generally* Lookofsky, *Consequential Damages*, Ch. 4.4.4.3.

[163]   *See* Lookofsky at *id.* According to Stoll (in Schlechtriem, *Commentary/Kommentar*, Art. 74, Rd.Nr. 34) Art. 74 seems less expansive than the German *Adäquanz* doctrine which precludes recovery only for the most improbale consequences.

[164]   As a U.S. Federal court did in the *Delchi* case, cited *infra* in note 176. *See also* Cook in 16 *J. Law & Com.* 257 (1997), also available on CISGW3. Re. the goal of uniform CISG interpretation *see supra* § 2.9.

[165]   *See* Article 74 second sentence. The underlying idea is that the parties, at that point in time, should be able to calculate the risks and potential liability they assume by agreement. *See* OLG Köln, 21 May 1996 (seller aware buyer was car dealer at time of conclusion of contract; damages paid by buyer to its customer therefore foreseeable loss under Art. 74). As noted by Stoll in Schlechtriem, *Commentary/Kommentar*, Art. 74, Rd.Nr. 37, the scope of CISG responsibility is not extended if the promisor (e.g. the seller) – after

Article 74 requires only that the loss in question be foreseeable (as opposed to actually foreseen)[166] by the defendant as a "possible consequence" of breach.[167] However, depending on the circumstances, compensation for some kinds of loss may be denied or reduced by reference to the mitigation requirement[168] and/or by evidentiary (procedural) standards applicable in the forum court or arbitral tribunal concerned.[169] In American courts, for example, the standards of proof applicable as regards a lost profits claim lie well beyond the usual burdens of persuasion, but due to a relaxation of the certainty requirement, only "reasonable certainty" is now required.[170] Outside the Common law realm, lost profits may be more difficult to prove, not only because some courts insist on a greater standard of proof, but also becaue Civilian plaintiffs might be more reluctant than their American colleagues to open accounts to the public view.[171]

Article 74 is a general rule which, in principle, protects against all loss caused by the breach, including so-called "direct" loss suffered by a buyer who does not choose to or cannot avoid (whereas avoidance situations are covered by Articles 75–76). For example, Article 74 damages will compensate a buyer for the difference between the value of the goods delivered and the value conforming goods would have had or (alternatively) the cost required to cure the defect.[172] Also "incidental" damages are easily subsumed under the general rule.[173]

Article 74 is also significant as regards more indirect kinds of "consequential" loss, including lost profits (and other "pure economic" loss),[174] as well as physical damage to property.[175] In the *Delchi* case, decided by a U.S. Federal Court,[176] an Italian buyer

---

the conclusion of the contract but before the breach – learns of circumstances which indicate a risk of extraordinary loss; in this respect the extent of liability under Article 74 may differ from domestic systems where liability is based on fault.

[166] *See, e.g.,* Schweizerisches Bundesgericht, 28 October 1998, CLOUT Case 248, also in CISGW3 (buyer's loss of clientele was foreseeable consequence of breach (non-conforming delivery), since buyer was wholesale dealer in sensitive market with no alternative by which to meet its obligations to *its* buyers).

[167] Compare re. American law Farnsworth, *Contracts*, § 12.14 (foreseeable as probable) and re. English law the *Heron II* [1969] 3 All E.R. at 686, 708 (liable to result, serious possibility or real danger).

[168] Re. Article 77 *see* § 6.17 *infra*.

[169] *See* Stoll in Schlechtriem, *Commentary/Kommentar*, Art. 74, Rd.Nr. 24 (general law of *evidence* of the *lex fori* relevant in this regard). *Compare* the *UNIDROIT Principles*, Article 7.4.3.

[170] *See* (e.g.) Farnsworth, *Contracts*, § 12.15.

[171] *See* Hellner, "Consequential Loss and Exemption Clauses," *Oxford Journal of Legal Studies* 13, 24 (1981). *But compare* the sufficient evidence provided by the Italian buyer in the *Delchi* case, discussed *infra* (text with note 176).

[172] *See* para. 6–7 of *Secretariat Commentary* to Article 70 of the 1978 Draft Convention.

[173] E.g., additional costs incurred after the breach in a reasonable attempt to avoid loss: *see* Stoll in Schlechtriem, *Commentary/Kommentar*, Art. 74, Rd.Nr. 19.

[174] *See* Handelsgericht Zürich, 5 February 1997, UNILEX (buyer awarded damages for loss of profit and other consequential damages for losses suffered due to exchange rate fluctuation between US dollars (currency of payment) and German marks).

[175] As regards Article 5 and consequential loss which takes the form of damage to property (other than the goods themselves) *see supra* § 2.6.

[176] *Delchi Carrier, SpA v. Rotorex Corp.*, 9 September 1994, WESTLAW 495787 (N.D.N.Y.), CLOUT Case 85, also in CISGW3 and UNILEX; aff'd in part and rev'd in part, and remanded, 71 F.3d 1024 (2d Cir. 1995).

ordered 10,800 compressors from a seller/manufacturer in Maryland. At the time of contracting the buyer advised that the compressors were intended for use in the production of a particular line of portable air-conditioners to be manufactured by the buyer. When the seller failed to deliver goods which conformed to the contract, the buyer sued to recover damages for various losses incurred as a result of the breach. Noting that CISG Article 74 seeks to provide the injured party with the "benefit of the bargain," including that party's expectation and reliance interests,[177] the court awarded the buyer more than 1 million dollars in compensation, including consequential damages for the following items of foreseeable loss: damages incurred as a result of buyer's (failed, but reasonable) attempts to remedy the non-conformity in seller's compressors,[178] expenses reasonably incurred in mitigation of the loss,[179] costs incurred for handling and storage of the non-conforming compressors, as well as lost profit resulting from a diminished volume of sales.[180]

Another interesting question involves the relationship between Article 74 and the so-called "American rule." Under American rules of procedure (but contrary to the *lex fori* in Europe and elsewhere), the losing party in an American litigation is generally not required to reimburse the winning party for its lawyers' fees.[181] In breach of contract (e.g. sales) cases, this might look like an exception to the principle of full expectation-interest protection,[182] but the general fee-shifting rule, which applies in all kinds of civil cases (not just contract cases) tried in American courts,[183] is best characterized as *procedural*.[184] For this reason, and since the U.S. Supreme Court, when recognizing limited statutory exceptions to the (no-fee-shifing) rule, has required clear evidence of legislative (fee-shifting) intent,[185] the U.S. Court of Appeals in *Zapata* rightly – albeit

---

[177] *See also supra*, note 161 and accompanying text.

[178] Costs that would not have been incurred "but for" the breach.

[179] Re. Article 77 *see infra* § 6.17.

[180] The buyer in *Delchi* was also awarded pre-judgment interest at the US treasury bill rate: re. Article 78 *see infra* § 6.18. A claim for expenses related to the anticipated cost of production was denied, but to this extent the case was reversed and remanded; *see* 71 F.3d 1024, 1030.

[181] As in Europe the losing party in an American litigation is often required to pay the successful party's "costs" (e.g. fees paid to the court), but in the U.S. such costs do *not* generally include lawyers'/attorneys' fees. The principle has been modified in certain instances by "fee shifting" statutes, but no fee-shifting remains the general rule. *See* (e.g.) *Alyeska Pipeline Service Co. v. Wilderness Society*, 421 U.S. 240 (1975) and *Buckhannon Board and Care Home, Inc. v. West Virginia Dept. of Health and Human Resources*, 532 U.S. 598 (2001).

[182] *See* Farnsworth, *Contracts*, § 12.8, and *Bunnett v. Smallwood*, 793 P.2d 157 (Colo. 1990) (party injured by breach not entitled to attorney's fees absent contractual or statutory authorization).

[183] Regarding class actions *see* (e.g.) Rowe, T., "Shift Happens: Pressure on Foreign Attorney-Fee Paradigms from Class Actions," 13 *Duke J. of Int. & Comp. L.* 125 (2003).

[184] As opposed to substantive. Domestic rules which determine whether (or under what circumstances) lawyers' fees are to be "shifted" (born by the losing party) are regarded as *procedural* rules in many CISG jurisdictions: *see* Flechtner, *Attorneys Fees & Foreign Case Law* and Lookofsky, *Zapata. See also* Flechtner & Lookofsky, *Viva Zapata*.

[185] The CISG text and legislative history provide no such evidence of "legislative intent."

controversially – held that CISG Article 74 does not provide authority for a special exception to the American rule.[186]

The application of the foreseeability rule in Article 74 sometimes gives rise to other conundrums. In some sales contract cases, for example, a buyer's loss might swell to a "disproportionate" size, (e.g.) when a given non-conformity causes the buyer to suffer losses amounting to ten or maybe fifty times the price paid for the goods. Depending on the circumstances, some courts and arbitrators might be reluctant to force a CISG seller to shoulder such risks, even if the loss in question was a "foreseeable possibility" at the time of contracting (and although the seller did not then disclaim or limit liability). There would seem to be at least three approaches available to the CISG decision-maker to deal with this kind of situation: (1) use "covert tools" to characterize part of the loss as "unforeseeable" under Article 74,[187] perhaps emphasizing *lex fori* evidenciary rules which require very "certain" proof of disproportionate loss;[188] (2) characterize the (sub)issue of "liability for disproportionate loss" as a matter "governed but not settled" by the Convention,[189] and then attempt to locate a CISG "general principle" to deal with it;[190] (3) supplement Article 74 by purely domestic – (e.g.) American – rules designed specifically to deal with the problem of disproportionate compensation.[191] Although this third route might be said to "disrupt" the CISG uniformity goal,[192] some courts and arbitrators will find it hard to ignore the law otherwise applicable in domestic contexts, especially if the disproportionate loss problem is tied to fundamental notions of justice in the jurisdiction concerned.[193]

---

[186] *Zapata Hermanos Sucesores, S.A. v. Hearthside Baking Co., Inc., etc.*, U.S. Court of Appeals (7th Cir.), 19 November 2002, available at <http://cisgw3.law.pace.edu/cisg/wais/db/cases2/021119u1.html>, reversing 2001 U.S. Dist. LEXIS 15191 and 2001 WL 1000927 (N.D. III), also in CISGW3. *See generally* Flechtner & Lookofsky, *Viva Zapata*. For a contrary view *see* Felemegas, *Counsel's Fees*. On December 1, 2003 the U.S. Supreme Court denied Zapata's petition for certiorari. *See* 124 S.C. 803 (Mem.).

[187] Re. the use of this covert technique in American domestic law *see* Farnsworth, *Contracts* § 12.17.

[188] *Compare* the corresponding *UNIDROIT Principle* in Article 7.4.3.

[189] Re. Article 7(2) *see supra* § 2.11.

[190] According to Judge Richard Posner (generally recognized as the "father" of the Law & Economics discipline), the "animating principle" behind the American version of the *Hadley* rule (text *supra* with note 162) is that the consequences of breach should be avoided by the party who can do so at the least cost: *see Evra v. Swiss Bank Corp.*, 673 F.2d 951 (7th Cir. 1982). It would hardly seem (more) far-fetched if Judge Posner, confronted with a large lost profits claim in a CISG context, were to read "least-cost-avoidance" in between the lines of the Convention rules on damages, i.e., as a "general [animating] principle" underlying Articles 74 and 77 (*infra* § 6.17).

[191] In this context, the principle codified in § 351(3) of the American *Restatement (Second) of Contracts* is clearly significant: *see* Farnsworth, *Contracts*, § 12.17; a similar principle is codified in the (essentially uniform) Scandinavian Liability Acts. For a comparison of the American and Scandinavian rules *see* Lookofsky, *Consequential Damages*, Ch. 4.4.5.1.

[192] I.e., even more than the other solutions just mentioned. For a discussion of the uniform interpretation problem *see supra* §§ 2.8 and 2.9.

[193] E.g., in Scandinavian jurisdictions, where the Liability Acts contain a rule which expressly authorizes courts to deny compensation for "disproportionate" loss (*see supra* note 191); in Denmark and Sweden, where the limitation applies to both tort and contract liability, the disproportionate loss limitation is closely akin to Article 36 of the Scandinavian Contracts Acts, a validity rule used to police unreasonable contract terms. Re. Art. 4 *see supra* § 2.6.

§ 6.16 CONTRACT/COVER AND CONTRACT/MARKET DIFFERENTIAL

The Convention contains two specific rules which measure damages for direct loss in situations where an injured buyer or seller exercises the right to avoid the sales contract.[194] The first of these practical provisions is Article 75. If a seller's delayed or non-conforming delivery constitutes a fundamental breach, the buyer may first avoid the contract, then "cover" – i.e., arrange for a reasonable substitute transaction[195] – and then claim damages measured by the difference in price, as well as any further losses recoverable under Article 74.[196] Technically speaking, the injured party is under no duty to "cover," but an avoiding buyer who fails to make a reasonable effort to procure substitute goods should be denied compensation for loss which she, by inaction, failed to mitigate.[197]

Article 76 provides a more abstract alternative to the contract/cover differential.[198] If there is a current (i.e., market) price for the goods concerned,[199] the avoiding party may, if she has not covered by purchase or resale under Article 75, recover the difference between the price fixed by the contract and such current price at the time of avoidance.[200] Unlike the UCC, the Convention does not make a formal distinction between rejected and accepted goods;[201] but if the party claiming damages has avoided the contract after "taking over" the goods, the current price at the time of such taking over shall be applied instead of the price at the time of avoidance.[202]

If neither the contract/market nor the contract/cover differentials are adequate to compensate a given loss, the general Article 74 rule can be used (as a supplement or alternative) to provide the expectation protection deserved.[203]

§ 6.17 MITIGATION: NO RECOVERY FOR AVOIDABLE LOSS

A party to a CISG contract who is (or may be) injured by breach is not under a "duty" to mitigate his loss.[204] However, under Article 77, a party who fails to take reasonable

---

[194] *See supra* § 6.8.

[195] *See* ICC Court of Arbitration (Paris), no. 8128/1995, UNILEX (cover transaction reasonable if buyer acted as prudent and careful businessman; short period which buyer had to cover to make timely delivery to third party justified cover price higher than market price).

[196] *Supra* § 6.15.

[197] *Infra* § 6.17.

[198] According to Article 76(1) the market-price formula is available only if the avoiding party "has not made a purchase or resale under article 75." The domestic rule in UCC § 2-713 leads to the same result; *see* White & Summers, *Uniform Commercial Code* § 6-4 and Comment 7 to the (2002) *NCCUSL Revised Draft* of the rule.

[199] As defined in Article 76(2).

[200] Article 76(1), first sentence.

[201] Re. UCC § 2-606 *compare* White & Summers, *Uniform Commercial Code*, § 8-2.

[202] Article 76(1), second sentence. This rule is designed to discourage delayed avoidance by the buyer motivated by speculation after receiving the goods.

[203] *See* Articles 75 and 76(1).

[204] If there were a real duty to mitigate, the Convention would have to provide a remedy for breach of that duty.

measures to mitigate cannot recover damages for the loss which could have been mitigated.

Illustration 6f: A CISG contract obligates S to deliver goods to B for $100,000, with delivery to take place on May 1. At the time of contracting, the market price for similar goods is $125,000. When delivery becomes due, S informs B that he no longer intends to deliver. B (rightfully) declares avoidance of the contract but does not make a cover purchase before July 1, at which time the market price for similar goods has reached $150,000.[205]

In these circumstances, B cannot recover $ 50,000 as damages under Article 75 or Article 76. Rather, his recovery is limited to $ 25,000 (plus "incidental" damages, if any). In this way, the avoidability/mitigation principle determines the point in time at which we calculate the contract-cover and contract-market price differentials,[206] i.e. buyer's "direct" loss.

But Article 77 also limits compensation for "indirect" losses otherwise recoverable under Article 74.[207] If, for example, the seller fails to deliver goods intended to serve as a key ingredient or tool in buyer's production, and the buyer makes no reasonable efforts to secure a substitute, any profits subsequently lost by the buyer will not have been suffered (solely) "in consequence" of seller's breach.[208] Of course, the extent to which a given loss is avoidable (and therefore non-compensable) may depend in part on the buyer's ingenuity, experience, and financial resources (ability to obtain credit quickly, etc.), so the question of what constitutes "reasonable" mitigation will depend on the court's evaluation of the situation in the concrete case.[209]

Article 77 applies directly when a party relies on an actual breach. Presumably, the same rule, or a similar general principle,[210] applies as regards a prospective breach: once the buyer has reason to know that the seller's performance will not be forthcoming, he is expected to take such affirmative steps as are appropriate in the circumstances to avoid loss.[211]

---

[205] *Compare* the somewhat more complicated example (73A) in the *Secretariat Commentary* to Article 73 of the 1978 Draft.

[206] *See supra* § 6.16. *See also* OLG Hamburg, 28 February 1997, CLOUT Case 277, CISGW3 and UNILEX (buyer's substitute purchase at higher price consistent with obligation to mitigate under Art. 77).

[207] *See* (e.g.) International Court of Commercial Arbitration, Chamber of Commerce & Industry of the Russian Federation, 24 January 2000, CISGW3.

[208] So, to this extent, such losses will not be compensable, even if they were "foreseeable" by the seller at the time of contracting.

[209] *See* Amtsgericht München, 23 June 1995, UNILEX (chemical for production of pharmaceuticals; German buyer's customers complained of non-conformity, Italian seller agreed to cure in Italy; cure delayed, buyer secured more costly cure in Germany; buyer's failure to inform seller of customers' urgent needs was not breach of "duty to mitigate"). *Compare* German Supreme Court (BGH), 25 June 1997, CLOUT Case 235, UNILEX (denying CISG buyer right to recover expenses incurred in adapting its equipment to process defective metal, since such expenses unreasonable in relation to purchase price).

[210] Re. Article 7(2) *see supra* § 2.11.

[211] *See* Comment 4 of *Secretariat Commentary* to Article 73 of 1978 Draft and *supra* 6–11 (re. anticipatory breach). *Compare* re. American law *Restatement (Second) of Contracts*, Comment b to § 350.

Although Article 77 seems geared mainly to post-breach mitigation, the Convention only provides compensation for loss "suffered . . . as a consequence of the breach."[212] So if a given buyer suffers a loss which seems partly "caused by" (attributable to) her own pre-breach, negligent act or omission – (e.g.) where the harm caused by seller's delayed delivery of a simple standard part is aggravated by the fact that buyer keeps no such spares on hand – Article 77 might be read to prevent the recovery of compensation to the extent such a loss was reasonably avoidable;[213] put another way, one could describe an easily preventable (extensive) loss as not "caused" by the breach in the Article 74 sense.[214]

§ 6.18 INTEREST

CISG Article 78 makes interest available to injured buyers and sellers alike. In this section, we consider some general aspects of the interest issue, as well as interest as a remedy for seller's breach.[215]

Some national systems take the view that interest is a component of damages; others do not.[216] In most countries, it is permissible for a court or tribunal to award interest; in others, for religious reasons, it is not.[217] Article 78 may resolve some, but surely not all of these conflicting views.

It is at least clear that the Convention authorizes an award of interest in those fora where such an award would otherwise be valid under national law. Since Article 78 sets forth a general obligation for the breaching party to pay interest, it has been argued persuasively that an award of interest ought not be declared invalid under the applicable domestic law,[218] although such an award would probably be unenforceable in those fora where domestic law prohibits interest payments.

To the extent that interest is recoverable, the injured party will often be left with a choice between Articles 74 and 78. Sometimes, however, only Article 78 will provide suitable authority, since interest may be awarded even where there is no evidence of actual damage

---

[212] Article 74: *see supra* § 6.15.

[213] If I do not keep such a spare on hand, I cannot take reasonable measures to mitigate. Ought I not then bear the resulting risk?

[214] *Accord* (re. American domestic law) Farnsworth, *Breach of Contract*, p. 1184: "Where [avoidable loss] takes the form of other [indirect] loss, the considerations are much like those encountered in connection with contributory negligence in the law of torts."

[215] As regards the seller's right to interest in respect of buyer's breach *see infra* § 6.31.

[216] Viewed as a component of damages, interest represents compensation for the lost use of capital: *see* Farnsworth, *Contracts*, §12.10. *Compare UNIDROIT Principles*, Comment 1 to Art. 7.4.9 (harm resulting payment delay subject to "special regime").

[217] In some countries, the mere *mention* of interest will render a contract invalid: *see* Hunter & Treibel, "Awarding Interest in International Arbitration," 6 *Journal of International Arbitration* at 8 with note 4 (1989). But there are significant exceptions to the Islamic rule prohibiting interest; *see* Klein, 23 *Denv. J. L. & Pol'y* 535 (1995).

[218] *See* Schlechtriem, *Uniform Law* at 100 with note 414; Ferrari, *Interest Rates* at 478. Re. Article 4 *see supra* § 2.6. In two Austrian arbitrations (nos. SCH-4318 and SCH-4366, 15 June 1994, UNILEX) the arbitrator suggested, as *dictum*, that CISG interest might be awarded even if contrary to domestic law.

suffered.[219] A claim under Article 78 will be preferred where a party cannot claim damages by virtue of an Article 79 exemption.[220]

The Convention does not itself determine the rate of interest. In the opinion of most courts and commentators, this is a CISG gap which – if not filled by the contract – must be resolved by the otherwise applicable domestic law;[221] there are other possible solutions, however, to be discussed below in the context of buyer's breach.[222]

Article 78 authorizes an award of interest for any "sum that is in arrears."[223] This should be read to mean that interest accrues as of the date payment of the "sum" in question is due.[224] A U.S. Federal Court has cited CISG Article 78 as authority for awarding a buyer prejudgment interest, calculated as of the date the seller's performance (conforming delivery) became due[225] – a result which accords with American domestic law.[226] In other domestic systems, where interest does not begin to accrue until the sum in arrears has been "liquidated," or until the passage of a certain additional (e.g. 30 day period), courts might be tempted to read Article 78 more narrowly, but neither the Convention text nor policy reasons would support such a view.[227]

§ 6.19 LIABILITY EXEMPTIONS FOR FAILURE TO PERFORM

The CISG exemption provisions deal with the kinds of problems often discussed in domestic sales law under such labels as impossibility, impracticability, and *force majeure*. Article 79(1) contains the main general rule which applies to either party's failure to perform. As regards seller's breach,[228] the rule provides a limited exception to the no-fault starting point set forth in Article 45(1).[229] Taken together, these two provisions constitute the CISG gap-filling liability base: they answer the question of whether the injured party is entitled to damages (at all).[230]

---

[219] *See* (e.g.) LG Frankfurt, 16 September 1991, UNILEX.

[220] *See infra* § 6.19.

[221] As determined by the private international law rules of the forum (§ 2.11 *supra*).

[222] § 6.31 *infra*.

[223] This would, among other things, cover the situation where seller delays refunding the price upon buyer's justified exercise of the right to avoid, but Article 84(1) contains a special rule on point: *see* Honnold, *Uniform Law*, § 421 with note 3 (explaining the apparent overlap).

[224] *Accord* Eberstein/Bacher in Schlechtriem, *Commentary*, Art. 78, Rd.Nr. 12, 15, and Bacher in Schlechtriem, *Kommentar*, Art. 78, Rd.Nr. 6, 10–12. *Compare* Article 7.4.10 *UNIDROIT Principles* ("only natural" that aggrieved party be compensated as of date of the harm).

[225] *See* the *Delchi* case, cited *supra* note 176.

[226] *Restatement (Second) of Contracts* § 354, Comment c to para. 1 (interest recoverable for failure to render performance with fixed or ascertainable monetary value). *See also* Honnold, *Uniform Law*, § 422 with note 4.

[227] *Accord* (as re. the relationship between the Convention and Danish domestic law) Gomard & Rechnagel, *International købelov*, p. 218.

[228] Re. buyer's breach and possible exemptions *see infra* § 6.32.

[229] *See supra* § 6.14.

[230] *If* we find a "basis" of liability, we then use Articles 74–77 to *measure* compensation due.

Liability for non-performance is sometimes regulated by the parties' agreement,[231] and the express terms of the contract may provide either for absolute liability (without exemption) or (e.g.) set forth a milder standard of liability based only on the breaching party's fault. Not uncommonly, an express *force majeure* clause in the contract will be interpreted as a limit or supplement to the Article 79 default rule.

According to Article 79(1), the seller who seeks a liability exemption bears the burden of proof: the non-performing seller remains liable unless he proves that four conditions are fulfilled.[232] First, the seller must demonstrate the existence of an "impediment": something which gets "in the [performing party's] way." The kind of impediments alleged as exempting contingencies will most often relate to the seller's obligation to make timely delivery, but it is also possible to conceive of "impediments" which might impact upon the seller's obligation to deliver conforming goods;[233] the decision rendered by the Supreme Court of Germany in 1999 in the "Vine Wax" case lends clear and convincing support to this more expansive reading of Article 79.[234]

At the same time, the *Bundesgerichtshof* explained how the second Article 79 condition – that the party seeking an exemption prove the impediment lies beyond his control – itself reduces the possibility of a non-conformity exemption to something near nil. Since a party should always be deemed "in control" of his/her own business and financial condition in general, internal "excuses" connected with business operations (poor quality control, etc.) or financial management will never be "beyond" that party's control.[235] In other words, Article 79 does not alter the basic CISG allocation of risk: just as the seller will generally bear the risk of possible delay or non-delivery,[236] the seller must also assure that his supplier provides him with defect-free goods. For this reason, we need not distinguish between cases where the seller is the manufacturer and cases where the seller obtains the goods from others; nor should the risk of non-conformity depend on whether the defect is "discoverable" by inspection or not.[237]

To this we add the third condition: the non-performing party must demonstrate that, at the time of the conclusion of the contract, the impediment could not reasonably have been foreseen (taken into account). Because nearly all potential impediments to performance – even wars, fires, embargoes and terrorism (let alone late trains and defective goods) – are

---

[231]   *See* Article 6, discussed *supra* § 2.7.

[232]   *See generally* Lookofsky, *Fault and No-Fault.* Some group the "impediment" and "control" factors together, thus reducing the list of conditions to three.

[233]   *Accord* Lookofsky, *Fault and No-Fault,* 2.4 and 3.3; Stoll in Schlechtriem, *Commentary/Kommentar,* Art. 79, Rd.Nr. 12, 45–47. *But see* Honnold, *Uniform Law* § 427.

[234]   *See* Bundesgerichtshof, 24 March 1999, CLOUT Case 271. *See also* Schlechtriem, *Bundesgerichtshof* (in English at <http://cisgw3.law.pace.edu/cases/990324g1.html>).

[235]   *Accord* Schlechtriem, *Int. UN-Kaufrecht,* Rd.Nr. 289.

[236]   *See* – as regards delayed delivery – the arbitral award rendered by Schiedsgericht der Handelskammer – Hamburg (Germany), 21 March 1996, UNILEX.

[237]   *See* the BGH decision and Schlechtriem's case commentary (both cited *supra,* note 234). *But see* Stoll in Schlechtriem, *Commentary/Kommentar,* Art. 79, Rd.Nr. 47 (seller not responsible if defect not reasonably discoverable by inspection).

increasingly foreseeable in the modern commercial environment, this may well be the most difficult Article 79 element to prove.[238] And this seems fair enough: Article 79 is, after all, a gap-filling rule, and the party damaged by the fruition of a foreseeable contingency might have protected himself by a more lenient (express) *force majeure* clause in the CISG contract concerned.

One of the most persistent impracticability problems under domestic sales law has involved relief-claims by sellers faced with radically increased costs, and the same problem will surface under Article 79 of the CISG. Although increased cost might "impede" performance from the obligor's point of view, a contractor's inability to make a profit on a particular contract will not, in and of itself, serve as a liability exemption under the CISG. This is because price increases – even dramatic ones – are generally foreseeable.[239] Put another way, sellers who regularly sell long-term are "in the business" of assuming this kind of risk. At some point, we might reach the "sacrifice threshold"[240] – or perhaps even "economic *force majeure*" – but if such an exemption/exception is ever granted, it will serve mainly to confirm that the overwhelming general rule of the Convention is strict liability for breach.[241]

Last – but not least – Article 79(1) requires that the non-performing party make reasonable efforts to "avoid or overcome" the impediment in question or its consequences. Since this requirement must be met even in cases where the impediment could not reasonably be foreseen, it represents a formidable barrier to a would-be exemptee, particularly in the common case of generically defined obligations. Suppose, for example, that the seller's obligation is to deliver coal or wood, and that his obligation is not limited (by the terms of the contract) to any particular source of supply. The fact that the seller (at the time of contracting) intends to obtain the goods from a particular source of supply which later "dries up" will not exempt him from liability under Article 79(1), in that he can avoid or overcome the impediment simply by securing an alternative source. So, assuming performance is still practicable, the seller remains liable for breach.[242]

Conversely, if specific goods (for example, a valuable work of art) are destroyed by an unforeseeable and unavoidable contingency beyond the seller's control – a violent

---

[238] *See* para. 5 of *Secretariat Commentary* to Article 65 of the 1978 Draft Convention.

[239] *See* Rechtbank van Koophandel, Hasselt (Belgium), 2 May 1995, UNILEX (significant drop in market price of goods/strawberries after conclusion of contract did not constitute "force majeure" exempting buyer under Art. 79; price fluctuations foreseeable events in international trade, do not render performance impossible but result in loss within normal risk of commercial activities). *See also* Tribunal of Int'l Commercial Arbitration at Russian Federation Chamber of Commerce, 17 October 1995, CLOUT Case 142.

[240] *See* Stoll in Schlechtriem, *Commentary/Kommentar*, Art. 79, Rd.Nr. 8, 39–40, 57.

[241] *Accord* as re. "impracticability" by reason of increased costs in domestic American law, White & Summers, *Uniform Commercial Code*, § 3-9. For a comparison of American and Scandinavian domestic law, *see* Lookofsky, *Consequential Damages*, Part 3.2.3.

[242] *Accord* para. 5 of *Secretariat Commentary* to Article 65 of the 1978 Draft Convention (party required to provide commercially reasonable substitute). *See also* Example 65B at *id.* (delivery of replacement machine tools) and OLG Hamburg, 28 February 1997, CLOUT Case 227, also in CISGW3 and UNILEX (seller not exempt under Art. 79 or under standard force majeure clause, since "seller's risk" covers non-delivery caused by its supplier; seller only exempt if impossible to find goods of similar quality on market).

earthquake tips a valuable statue before S ships it to B – S would not be held liable for failing to "do the impossible" (deliver the goods as originally agreed).[243]

A much-discussed – but rarely exempting – contingency is a party's financial inability to
perform, i.e., insolvency and the like. Even if classified as an "unavoidable impediment," a
party's inability to finance his performance should not lead to an exemption under Article
79(1), since such a contingency – like an "unexpected" price increase – is one which a
(commercial) seller or buyer should reasonably foresee; put another way, a party who vol-
untarily makes a promise to sell or buy goods must generally assume the risk of not being
able to finance his performance.[244] On the other hand, an unforeseeable imposition of
exchange controls by public authorities might lead to a liability exemption for the buyer,[245]
but only if the particular impediment could not reasonably be overcome (e.g.) by arranging
for alternative payment means.[246]

Paragraph (2) of Article 79 deals with the situation where a party's failure to perform is
"due to the failure by a third person whom he has engaged to perform the whole or a part
of the contract." In this case the party claiming the exemption is exempt from liability only
if: (a) he is exempt under Article 79(1) *and* (b) the person whom he has so engaged would
be so exempt if the provisions of that paragraph were applied to him.

Although Article 79(2) has provoked a good deal of discussion,[247] this CISG rule
should be interpreted as one having a limited range of application.[248] In particular, the
"third persons" to which it refers should not be read to include general suppliers of the
goods or of raw materials to the seller;[249] simply because such suppliers are not "engaged
to perform the whole or a part of the contract."[250] So if a seller's general supplier fails to

---

[243] Of course, since the risk of loss in this case remains with S, B would not be required to pay. *Compare*
Example 65A in the *Secretariat Commentary* (*id.*). *See also supra* § 5.1.

[244] *See* the arbitral award by Schiedsgericht der Handelskammer, Hamburg, 21 March 1996, UNILEX (difficul-
ties due to financial problems of seller or seller's supplier, even when connected to act of public authority,
not impediment beyond seller's control, but rather part of seller's area of risk).

[245] *See* award rendered by ICC Court of Arbitration (Paris), no. 7197/1992, UNILEX (suspension of payment of
foreign debts ordered by Bulgarian Government not "force majeure" contingency which "prevented" buyer
from opening documentary credit: buyer did not prove that failure to open the credit was "due to" the suspension; suspension had been declared at time of contracting was "impediment" which buyer could reasonably have foreseen).

[246] Para. 10 of the *Secretariat Commentary* to Article 65 of the 1978 Draft Convention is in *accord*.
"Avoidability" presumes the availability of alternative measures consistent with the contractual obligation
assumed; if the contract requires payment from a particular source, the impediment would not be avoidable
by alternative means.

[247] Both at the time of the Vienna conference where the provision was originally drafted and afterwards.

[248] *Accord*: Gillette & Walt, *Sales Law* at 258.

[249] *Id. See also* para. 12 of *Secretariat Commentary* to Article 65 of the 1978 Draft Convention, Honnold,
Uniform Law § 434, and Tallon, *Commentary* at 585 (requiring an "organic link" between the main contract
and the subcontract). *But compare* Schlechtriem, *Uniform Law* at 104 and Stoll in Schlechtriem,
Commentary/Kommentar, Art. 79, Rd.Nr. 38 (making exceptions in cases where supplier has a natural
monopoly or where all suppliers are affected (embargo etc.); *compare also* Schlechtriem at <http://cisgw3.
law.pace.edu/cases/990324gl.html>.

[250] *Accord* Audit, *Vente internationale*, no. 183 at 176.

deliver, and the seller's buyer claims damages for the seller's subsequent failure to perform, the seller's possible liability exemption should be determined under the main rule Article 79(1).[251]

If, on the other hand, a seller actually delegates all or part of his performance to a third party ("sub-contractor"),[252] and assuming such delegation is not itself a breach of the seller's obligations vis-a-vis the buyer, the seller might then be exempt from liability under Article 79(2) for a failure to perform "due to" the failure of the third party.[253] To qualify for an exemption in this "double force majeure" situation, however, the seller faces the heavy burden of proving (a) that he could not himself foresee or avoid the "impediment" to performance beyond his control and (b) that the impediment was unforeseeable and not avoidable by – and beyond the control of – the third party as well.[254]

The exemption provided by Article 79 has effect only for the period during which the impediment exists.[255] Therefore, when a temporary impediment to performance abates, the non-performing seller becomes liable once again. On the other hand, since Article 79 does not prevent the buyer from exercising any right other than to claim damages,[256] a serious delay (e.g.) by the seller will entitle the buyer to avoid, thus ending the contract by reason of fundamental breach.[257]

The seller who fails to perform must give notice of the impediment and its effects on his ability to perform. If the notice is not received by the buyer within a reasonable time after the seller knew or ought to have known of the impediment, the seller is liable for damages resulting from such non-receipt.[258]

An Article 79 exemption from damages does not preclude a claim to interest,[259] just as a buyer who receives non-conforming goods remains entitled to a proportionate reduction in price.[260] But what about the buyer's right to specific performance? Suppose, for example, that the delivery of conforming goods, for instance chemicals, has become illegal in the

---

[251] As indicated by the OLG Hamburg decision cited *supra* (note 242), such liability is not easily escaped. Indeed, given the strict standard of Article 79(1), the practical effect of the distinction between the two rules will usually be insignificant; *accord* Stoll in Schlechtriem, *Commentary/Kommentar*, Art. 79, Rd.Nr. 38.

[252] This term was dropped from earlier Convention drafts because corresponding terms are either unknown in non-English speaking systems or only applied in the field of construction contracts; *see* Stoll in Schlechtriem, *Commentary/Kommentar*, Art. 79, Rd.Nr. 3, 35.

[253] As noted by Gillette & Walt, *Sales Law*, 258–59, the line between Articles 79(1) and (2) may be difficult to draw, since raw materials suppliers can themselves be viewed as subcontractors (citing the award by the ICC Court of Arbitration (Paris), no. 8128/1995).

[254] In effect, the cumulative requirements of Article 79(2) tend to result in even stricter liability than Article 79(1); *accord* Stoll in Schlechtriem, *Commentary/Kommentar*, Art. 79, Rd.Nr. 35. On strikes as "impediments" *see* Stoll, *id.*, Art. 79, Rd.Nr. 42, 43.

[255] Article 79(3).

[256] Article 79(5).

[257] *See supra* § 6.8.

[258] Article 79(4) thus provides an exception to the risk principle stated in Article 27. The notifying party's liability extends also to cases where a party intends to perform by furnishing a commercially reasonable substitute: *see* para. 16 of the *Secretariat Commentary* to Article 65 of the 1978 Draft Convention.

[259] Article 79(5); *see also supra* § 6.18.

[260] Article 50 (*supra* § 6.13).

territory specified in the contract as the place of delivery. Assuming this impediment to performance was not reasonably foreseeable at the time of contracting, the seller should not only be exempt from a damages claim under Article 79; he should also be insulated from a demand that he perform the now illegal act.[261]

Article 80 states that a party may not rely on a failure of the other party to perform, to the extent that such failure was caused by the first party's act or omission. The legislative history of this provision is not clear,[262] but judging by its placement, the rule might well be read as an adjunct to Article 79, including the rule in Article 79(5). Under this interpretation, a buyer whose own act or omission renders the seller's performance impossible can neither demand interest nor avoid.[263] If, for example, the buyer fails to supply the seller with plans necessary for the manufacture of the goods,[264] the buyer cannot exercise any rights against the seller, and this is true even if the buyer's failure is itself due to an exempting contingency (the destruction of the plans in a fire).[265]

6C SELLER'S REMEDIES FOR BUYER'S BREACH

§ 6.20 INTRODUCTION

Article 61(1) summarizes the remedies which the Convention makes available to the seller in the event of buyer's breach. If the buyer fails to perform any of his obligations under the contract or the Convention, the seller may:

(a) exercise the rights provided in Articles 62 to 65;
(b) claim damages as provided in Articles 74 to 77.

Articles 62 to 65 (referred to in subparagraph a) concern the right to require specific performance and the right to avoid. The right to demand specific performance (i.e., require that the buyer accept delivery and pay the price agreed) is not compatible with the exercise of the right to avoid (i.e., demand an end to the obligations of both parties), but there is no mutual exclusivity as between the right to demand either specific performance or termination (on the one hand) and the right to demand damages (on the other).[266]

Subparagraph (b) of Article 61(1) does more than merely refer to the rules which detail the extent and measurement of damages for breach (Articles 74–77); indeed, subparagraph (b) lays down the very "basis of liability" in the event of buyer's breach.[267]

---

[261] This clearly reasonable result can be premised on a teleological interpretation of Article 46(1) and is further supported by the rule in Article 28. For similar illustrations *see* Stoll in Schlechtriem, *Commentary/ Kommentar*, Art. 79, Rd.Nr. 55.

[262] *See* Stoll, *id.*, Art. 80, Rd.Nr. 2.

[263] I.e., Article 79(5) notwithstanding. *See* Schlechtriem, *Uniform Law* at 105–06 and Honnold, *Uniform Law*, § 436.

[264] *See also* Article 65.

[265] *Accord* Magnus in Staudinger, *Kommentar*, Art. 80, Rd.Nr. 7.

[266] Article 61(2). *See also supra* § 6.2.

[267] *See infra* § 6.27.

§ 6.21 SELLER'S RIGHT TO REQUIRE (SPECIFIC) PERFORMANCE

If the buyer fails to perform her promise to pay the price, take delivery, or perform her other obligations,[268] the Convention permits the seller to require that the buyer keep her word. According to the letter of Article 62, the seller may demand performance unless he has resorted to an inconsistent remedy (i.e., avoidance).

> *Illustration 6g:*[269] American seller S agrees to manufacture goods for a Bulgarian buyer B, and B agrees to make payment by a letter of credit on a certain date. When no such credit is opened, the seller demands that the buyer open the letter of credit. In addition, the seller seeks to hold B liable for damages.

Since B has not performed her obligation to make payment as promised, S is as a starting point entitled to a judgment or award ordering the buyer to open the letter and pay as agreed.[270] In addition, damages can be claimed under Article 74.

In certain circumstances, however, other Convention provisions may affect the seller's right to compel buyer's performance under Article 62. For one thing, a CISG seller must sometimes take reasonable measures to sell goods which the buyer has purchased but not paid for.[271] Some say that the mitigation principle expressed in Article 77 also limits the application of Article 62, but there is also considerable support for the contrary view.[272] Time – and CISG case law – will tell.

§ 6.22 SPECIFIC PERFORMANCE LIMITED BY FORUM LAW

A court or arbitral tribunal asked to require that buyer perform must look beyond the limitations indicated above. Even if a court holds that the seller can require that buyer perform under Article 62, it must also take the rule in Article 28 into account and consider whether such specific relief would be available pursuant to the otherwise applicable domestic sales law of the forum concerned.[273] If specific relief would not be so available,[274] the forum court is "not bound" to require performance under the CISG. In the United States, Article 28 might

---

[268] Re. the CISG buyer's obligations *see supra* Chapter 4C.

[269] Inspired by the essentially similar facts in ICC case no. 7197/1992, CLOUT Case 104, also in CISGW3 and UNILEX.

[270] As to the possible application of Article 28 *see infra* § 6.22.

[271] I.e., as opposed to merely preserving the goods for the buyer's account while demanding and awaiting payment of the price. *See* Articles 85 and 88(2).

[272] *See* sources cited *supra* in § 6.4. *See also* para. 3 of *Secretariat Commentary* to Article 73 of the 1978 Draft Convention and *compare* Schlechtriem, *Uniform Law* at 99 and Walt, *Specific Performance* at 215–16.

[273] Re. specific performance in Civil and Common law systems, *see* Treitel, *Remedies II*, Chapter III. Some commentators argue that the buyer's obligation to pay the price (unlike the obligation to take delivery) has nothing to do with specific performance issues in the sense of Article 28, because it has never been understood to raise such issues in the Common law world: *see* Huber in Schlechtriem, *Commentary/Kommentar*, Art. 28, Rd.Nr. 13–15.

[274] *Compare* UCC § 2-709 with the English SGA sec. 49, 50, which limit the seller's price action to cases where the "property has passed" to the buyer, whether or not delivery has occurred.

assume significance (e.g.) in cases where the seller demands payment for goods sold, notwithstanding the seller's ability to resell them at a reasonable price.[275]

§ 6.23   SELLER'S RIGHT TO AVOID FOR BUYER'S BREACH

Article 64 provides an injured seller with the right to avoid the contract, thus putting an end to the performance obligations of both parties.[276] The default rule in Article 64(1)(a) permits the seller to "declare the contract avoided"[277] (only) in the case of buyer's "fundamental" breach.[278] This provision applies to any of buyer's obligations under the contract and the Convention – not just the obligation to pay,[279] but also (e.g.) where buyer is obligated to apply for a letter of credit or a bank guarantee to facilitate the payment of the price.[280] As indicated previously,[281] the failure to perform even an "ancillary" obligation may sometimes amount to a fundamental breach.[282]

The seller is, of course, entitled to expect payment on time.[283] If, however, the buyer tenders payment (e.g.) two days later than agreed, the difficult question is whether the seller has thereby suffered a substantial deprivation under Article 25. If the court or arbitral tribunal answers yes, the seller will be entitled to avoid, provided that the buyer (or a reasonable buyer) had reason to know that such a breach would have this substantial effect.[284]

The right to avoid is also limited by other Convention requirements. If the seller first elects to avoid after the buyer has paid the price, he must do so (as regards late performance) before he learns that performance has been rendered or (in other cases) within a reasonable time after learning of the breach.[285]

---

[275] *See* UCC § 2-709(1)(b). As previously indicated, however, the possible applicability of the mitigation principle in Article 77 in such a (specific performance) context might affect the more basic CISG issue of whether such a seller has the right to demand performance under Article 62; *see supra* § 6.21.

[276] *See* Article 81.

[277] Such a declaration of avoidance is effective only if made by notice to the buyer: *see* Article 26. Re. the risk of transmission *see* Article 27.

[278] If a CISG contract expressly provides that "any delay gives the right to avoid," that term should of course be interpreted as displacing the gap-filling (fundamental breach) rule.

[279] *See, e.g.* U.S. District Court, S.D., Michigan, 17 December 2001 (*Shuttle Packaging Systems, L.L.C. v. Jacob Tsonakis, INA S.A., et al.*), where the Court accepted seller's contention that the buyer's non-payment of (substantial) progress payments on the machinery constituted a "fundamental breach of contract."

[280] *See* Article 54 and *Illustration 6g supra. See also* Supreme Court of Queensland (Australia), 17 November 2000, CISGW3 and UNILEX (refusal to establish a timely letter of credit clearly fundamental breach).

[281] § 6.8 *supra.*

[282] *See* Court of Appeal (Grenoble), 22 February 1995, CLOUT Case 154, CISGW3 and UNILEX (French seller sold jeans to American buyer with contract stipulating that jeans would be re-sold in South America; buyer's re-sale of goods in Spain and refusal to reveal true destination was fundamental breach giving seller right to avoid).

[283] *See* Articles 53 and 58–59.

[284] Re. this Article 25 requirement *see supra* § 6.8.

[285] *See* Article 64, subparagraphs (2)(a) and (2)(b)(i).

§ 6.24 AVOIDANCE FOR BUYER'S NON-COMPLIANCE WITH "NACHFRIST" NOTICE

Depending on the circumstances, the seller may have reason to doubt whether a court would characterize a given delay in the buyer's performance as a "fundamental" breach under Article 64(1)(a). For this reason CISG Article 63(1) gives the seller the right to fix an additional period of time of reasonable length (*Nachfrist*) for performance by the buyer of "his obligations," after which the seller need not speculate as to whether the (total) performance delay has reached fundamental proportions.[286] If, after the giving of such notice, the buyer does not make payment or take delivery within the additional (reasonable) period of time so fixed (or if buyer declares that he will not comply),[287] Article 64(1)(b) gives the seller the right to avoid.[288]

§ 6.25 RESTITUTION OF GOODS DELIVERED

According to Article 81(2), a seller who delivers the goods and then rightfully avoids under the CISG may claim their restitution from the buyer. This general – and seemingly generous – right to restitution must be read together with the relevant non-CISG rules of the applicable law. An avoiding seller who seeks restitution of goods delivered (as an alternative or supplement to damages for buyer's breach) is not likely to be buyer's only unpaid creditor. Therefore, the avoiding seller's claim to restitution *in specie* under Article 81(2) is likely to conflict with the claims of other (unsecured) creditors, even though the Convention rules which make restitution generally available to either party as an "effect of avoidance" seem to condition the seller's right to restitution only upon his own refund of any price received.[289]

Significantly, the CISG is simply "not concerned" with the entire subject of the "property" in the goods sold, so issues relating to the rights of third parties must be resolved by reference to the applicable (domestic property) law.[290] Under these rules, the rights of an unpaid (and unsecured) seller as against the rights of other creditors of a buyer in possession are quite likely to be severely limited.[291] Where, however, an unpaid seller enjoys a broader retention-of-title right, as for instance under German law, her chances to compete successfully with other creditors are improved.

---

[286] *See generally supra* § 6.10. re seller's breach.

[287] Re. anticipatory breach *see infra* § 6.26.

[288] Although the seller may fix an additional performance period for any of the buyer's obligations (Article 63(1)), non-compliance with a *Nachfrist* notice only entitles the seller to avoid under Article 64(1)(b) in the case of failure to pay or take delivery. *Accord* Hager in Schlechtriem, *Commentary/Kommentar*, Art. 63(2), Rd.Nr. 2. Note also that a seller who has received payment will rarely face irreparable loss from buyer's delay in taking delivery: *see* Honnold, *Uniform Law* § 354.

[289] *See* Article 81(2) and Article 84(1), which provides: "If the seller is bound to refund the price, he must also pay interest on it, from the date on which the price was paid."

[290] *See supra* § 2.6. *See also* Honnold, *Uniform Law*, § 444.

[291] Regarding the interplay between the right to restitution and the rights of creditors of the buyer *see* Flechtner, *Remedies*, pp. 60–61. Re. the currently (2003) applicable version of UCC § 2-702 *see* Gillette & Walt, *Sales Law*, Ch. 10.I; *compare* the (2002) NCCUSL *Draft Revision* which omits the 10-day limitation as well as the 3-month exception to the 10-day limitation (though if the buyer is in bankruptcy at the time of reclamation,

§ 6.26   ANTICIPATORY BREACH

The general rule in Article 71(1) regarding anticipatory breach (by either party) applies, *inte, alia*, to the seller's remedial rights. The seller can suspend performance if it becomes "apparent" that the buyer will not perform a "substantial part" of his obligations. In addition, Article 71(1) requires that the prospect of nonperformance be the result of (a) a serious deficiency in the obligor's ability to perform or creditworthiness,[292] or (b) his conduct in preparing to perform or in performing the contract. A buyer's late payments in respect of other contracts might provide the seller with sufficient evidence as regards the first criterion; a seller's use of defective raw materials in other contracts might provide buyer with evidence of the second.[293]

A seller who elects to suspend must give immediate notice or face a claim for damages by the buyer under Article 71(3). If the buyer provides an "adequate assurance" of performance, the seller must then resume delivery.

The Convention also provides additional anticipatory breach protection more carefully tailored to the seller's special needs. Under Article 71(2), if the seller has already dispatched the goods before the grounds described in Article 71(1) become "evident," the seller may prevent the handing over of the goods to the buyer even though the buyer holds a document which entitles him to obtain them. The duty to notify applies in this situation as well, and a German court has awarded damages to the buyer where the seller failed to comply with Article 71(3).[294]

Finally, the seller can avoid the agreement entirely if the prospect of buyer's fundamental breach "becomes clear."[295]

§ 6.27   SELLER'S DAMAGES FOR BUYER'S BREACH: THE BASIS OF LIABILITY

The seller's right to claim damages is, in principle, an independent remedial right: so, by exercising his right to demand performance or avoid the sale, the seller is not deprived of a monetary claim.[296] And though an injured seller will often make use of the right to claim interest on "sums in arrears,"[297] the buyer is also strictly liable in damages under the CISG: the buyer's failure to perform any obligation – i.e. the breach itself – entitles the seller to damages. As already indicated, Article 61(1)(b) is properly described as the "basis" of the

---

the seller will have to comply with the Bankruptcy Code which includes a 10-day limit). Note also in this connection that the rights of even an unsecured seller prior to physical delivery are protected by the CISG rules regarding anticipatory breach: *see infra* § 6.26.

[292] *See* Article 71(1)(a)–(b). *Compare* Oberster Gerichtshof (Austria), 12 February 1998, CLOUT Case 238, CISGW3 (seller failed to establish sufficient probability of buyer's prospective inability to pay).

[293] *See* Rechtbank van Koophandel, Hasselt (Belgium), 1 March 1995, UNILEX (seller could suspend delivery of second order by reason of buyer's serious (7-month) delay in payment of first order). Re. seller's breach *see supra* § 6.11 with note 111.

[294] *See* AG Frankfurt, 31 January 1991, reported in UNILEX.

[295] *See* OLG Düsseldorf (Germany), 14 January 1994, CLOUT Case 130, also reported in CISGW3 and UNILEX, upholding Landgericht Krefeld, 28 April 1993 (seller could avoid second shoe contract since it had become "clear" that buyer, who had not yet performed under prior contract, would not pay). *See supra* § 6.11 re. Article 72 and buyer's corresponding right to avoid.

[296] *See* Article 61(2).

[297] *See infra* § 6.31.

buyer's liability,[298] whereas the rules used to calculate the amount of damages payable are discussed in the sections below.

§ 6.28 EXPECTATION PROTECTION FOR FORESEEABLE LOSS

Articles 74–77 are important "common" provisions which apply to CISG sellers and buyers alike.[299] Therefore, the principles discussed previously with respect to buyer's damages for seller's breach apply with equal force in the present context, (i.e.) seller's damages for buyer's breach.[300] Article 74 sets forth the general principle by which the Convention measures the buyer's liability for breach. Assuming a causal connection between breach and loss,[301] the Convention seeks to place the injured seller in the position he would have enjoyed "but for" buyer's breach.[302] Reading Article 74 together with Article 61(1)(b), we see once again that the Convention provides the seller with expectation-interest protection on a no-fault basis.[303]

The seller's damages may not exceed the loss which the buyer foresaw or ought to have foreseen as a consequence of the breach of contract concerned. Although a buyer will normally be able foresee that his breach might possibly end up causing the seller to suffer all kinds of losses, including the costs of (expensive) litigation, a U.S. Court of Appeals has held that the special question of whether a successful CISG plaintiff (e.g. the seller) is entitled to recover his own attorneys' fees is as a procedural question to be settled in accordance with the otherwise applicable domestic (procedural) law (*lex fori*).[304]

Although nearly all kinds of loss are recoverable by the seller under Article 74, the Convention supplements this general rule with a more specific rule (discussed below)[305] which can be used to measure the "direct loss" suffered by a seller (S) who avoids his contract with the breaching buyer (B1) and then enters a "cover" transaction, (i.e.) a "substitute" sale of the same goods to a second buyer (B2).[306] In some cases, however, the second (S-B2) contract cannot rightly be regarded as a substitute for the first.

Illustration 6h: Dealer S in Detroit accepts an order for 5 new GM trucks (FOB Detroit) from buyer B in Toronto. S happens to have 5 such vehicles in stock, but before he can complete the shipping arrangements, B sends a fax advising that the

---

[298] *See supra* § 6.20. *Compare* the corresponding rule applicable to seller's breach: *supra* § 6.14.

[299] *See* the "heading" to Chapter V of CISG Part III.

[300] *See generally supra* §§ 6.15, 6.16 & 6.17.

[301] I.e., that the loss is a "consequence" of the breach.

[302] As in the case of a seller's breach, this includes so-called "incidental" losses, e.g. reasonable expenses incurred in an attempt to collect the price with the assistance of a lawyer; *see* Witz, *Premières Applications*, no. 78. *But see* LG Frankfurt, 16 September 1991, CLOUT Case 6 (denying collection agency costs).

[303] *See supra* § 6.15.

[304] *See* the U.S: Court of Appeals decision in the *Zapata* case, discussed *supra* § 6.15, notes 176 *et seq.* and accompanying text.

[305] § 6.29 *infra*.

[306] Indeed, such a "cover" transaction may be obligatory in the sense that a CISG seller cannot demand compensation for any loss which could reasonably have been *prevented* by resale: regarding the mitigation principle underlying Article 77 *see infra* § 6.17.

deal is off. Later, S resells the same 5 trucks to a third party (B2) and brings a suit for damages (profits lost under the first sale) against B.[307]

In a situation like this, where we can assume that the seller's own supply exceeds his own market demand, the seller cannot enter a substitute transaction to "cover" buyer's breach, simply because a subsequent sale of the 5 trucks in stock to another buyer is not a "substitute" for the first transaction. Since we assume that S can obtain from the manufacturer as many such trucks as his various buyers demand, there is no causal relationship between this particular buyer's breach and the seller's subsequent sale. In this scenario, the loss suffered as a consequence of B's breach is *unavoidable*, which means that the Article 75 contract/market differential would be "inadequate to put the seller in as good a position as performance would have done."[308] So in this kind of case, the profit lost by reason of buyer's breach is a "direct" loss which can only be recovered by damages pursuant to the general Article 74 rule.[309] Domestic (e.g., American) sales law recognizes this same kind of expectation protection,[310] and an Austrian court has acknowledged that the argument for permitting recovery by a CISG "lost-volume-seller" is equally strong.[311]

Delayed payment of the price sometimes causes sellers to suffer a loss as a consequence of interim currency fluctuation. Such developments are frequently foreseeable at the time of contracting from an informed buyer's perspective.[312]

§ 6.29   CONTRACT/COVER AND CONTRACT/MARKET DIFFERENTIAL

The Convention contains two rules, previously introduced,[313] which measure damages for direct loss, *inter alia*, in situations where an injured seller exercises the right to avoid the sales contract (for fundamental breach, etc.).[314]

---

[307] Since the same (CISG) law applies in the United States and Canada, the outcome of such a lawsuit should be the same irrespective of whether the action is brought in a U.S. or a Canadian court.

[308] *Compare* re. the American UCC § 2-708(2) White & Summers, *Uniform Commercial Code*, § 7-9.

[309] Although the CISG does not distinguish between various forms of loss as such, it may be noted that the loss suffered here relates – not to so-called "collateral transactions" – but rather to the value of the breached transaction itself. *Accord* (re. American law) Farnsworth, *Contracts*, § 12.9.

[310] *See* note 308 *supra*.

[311] *See* Oberster Gerichtshof, 28 April 2000, CISG and UNILEX (seller's failure to enter cover transaction was not breach of obligation to mitigate under Art. 77; seller, who would have lost profit even if goods "resold" to third person, entitled to claim difference between contract price and costs of manufacturing under Art. 74). Article 75 authorizes the recovery of additional damages pursuant to Article 74 which, in turn, authorizes damages for foreseeable "lost profits." *Accord* Ziegel, *Remedial Provisions* at 9–41, Fletchner, *Remedies* at 101–102, and Lookofsky, *United Nations Convention*, No. 292 (all opposing the contrary position by Hellner); *see also* Stoll in Schlechtriem, *Commentary/Kommentar*, Art. 75, Rd.Nr. 10–11.

[312] The seller may suffer such losses (e.g.) if the exchange rate between the contractually agreed currency and the seller's currency has shifted (loss in external value); in other cases the seller's currency (assuming this to be the contractually agreed currency) may suffer from inflation (loss in internal value). *See generally*, Magnus in Staudinger, *Kommentar*, Art. 74, Rd.Nr. 48–49 (seller should at least be entitled to compensation for loss in external value).

[313] *See supra* § 6.16.

[314] *See supra* §§ 6.23, 24.

The first of these practical provisions is Article 75. If the seller elects to avoid, (e.g.) because of the buyer's failure to pay, and if the seller resells the goods in a reasonable manner, she may recover the contract-cover price differential, as well as any further damages recoverable under Article 74.[315] Assuming the second transaction is a substitute for the first,[316] there will be little or no loss if the cover price obtained equals or exceeds the price which the first buyer fails to pay.[317]

As an alternative to the contract/cover differential, a more abstract measure of damages available to an avoiding seller is defined in Article 76. If there is a current (i.e., market) price for the goods concerned,[318] the seller may, if she has not covered by resale under Article 75, recover the difference between the price fixed by the contract and such current price at the time of avoidance.

If neither the contract/market nor the contract/cover differentials are adequate to compensate a given loss, the general Article 74 rule can be used to provide the expectation protection deserved.[319]

§ 6.30 MITIGATION: NO RECOVERY FOR AVOIDABLE LOSS

A seller cannot recover damages for loss which he could have avoided by reasonable action. This follows not only from the argument that the CISG seller is under a general duty of good faith,[320] but also (more specifically) because losses otherwise recoverable under the more general Article 74 rule are limited by the mitigation principle in Article 77. Once a seller has reason to know that performance by the other party will not be forthcoming, he is expected to take appropriate affirmative steps to avoid loss.[321]

§ 6.31 INTEREST

If the buyer fails to pay the price, the seller is entitled to interest on it under Article 78, and the same general considerations previously discussed (with respect to interest as a CISG remedy for sums as to which the seller is in arrears)[322] apply in the more common situation where the seller seeks interest as a remedy for buyer's breach: the failure to pay or to

---

[315] "Incidental" damages, such as the administrative costs of cover, are surely recoverable under this rule.

[316] If not, the situation may call for the application of Article 74: *see supra* § 6.28.

[317] Technically speaking, there is no "duty" to cover, but a seller who, after avoiding a sale, hesitates to enter a substitute transaction may later be barred from compensation for loss which she, by her delay, failed to mitigate.

[318] As defined in Article 76(2).

[319] *See supra* § 6.28.

[320] Which includes a duty to take reasonable steps to protect the other party's interests. *See generally supra* § 2.10.

[321] *See supra* § 6.17. *Accord* Internationales Schiedsgericht der Bundeskammer der gewerblichen Wirtschaft – Wien (Vienna), Austria, arbitral award of 15 June 1994, reported in UNILEX (CISG seller had right – and presumably also duty – to cover under Art. 77).

[322] *See supra* § 6.18.

make timely payment of the price. Thus, in a case involving buyer's breach, interest begins to accrue as of the date that payment was due.[323]

To repeat one particularly important point: the Convention does not determine the rate of interest. So, assuming the contract is silent as to the rate, the matter will usually have to be determined by resort to the "applicable law."[324] Determining the otherwise applicable law in cases of delayed payment, German courts have awarded interest at the average lending rate in the country where the seller should have received payment;[325] if the contract does not specify the place of payment, Article 57 may be used to fill in this gap.[326]

In two international commercial arbitrations held in Austria,[327] it was held that the rate of interest is a matter governed but not expressly settled by the CISG. Referring to the "general principle" of full compensation underlying Articles 74 and 78,[328] the Tribunal used the Article 7(2) technique to help determine an appropriate rate. By contrast, a German case expressly rejected the Article 7(2) solution on the convincing ground that the CISG drafters tried, but failed to solve the interest-rate problem;[329] for this reason, the German court applied the applicable domestic rule.

§ 6.32 Liability Exemption under Article 79

Article 79 was designed as a *force majeure*-type safety valve, applicable, *inter alia*, in respect of buyer's failure to perform.[330] The CISG buyer is liable irrespective of fault,[331] but in certain exceptional circumstances, a (truly "innocent") buyer may qualify for an "exemption" from the general Article 61 strict liability rule.

Because Article 79 is a CISG common provision which applies to both parties with equal force, the general requirements discussed previously in respect of a seller's exemption apply here as well.[332] The buyer who seeks an exemption must establish that the failure to perform was due to an impediment beyond his control and that the impediment was not reasonably foreseeable at the time of contracting or avoidable once its existence became known.[333]

---

[323] *See* Article 59 and *supra* § 6.18 with note 224; *see also* AG Oldenburg/Holstein, 24 April 1990, UNILEX. Where the seller fixes an additional period for buyer's performance, interest begins to accrue after the expiration of the period: *see* LG Heidelberg, 3 July 1992, UNILEX.

[324] The CISG case law also provides examples where "general [CISG] principles" have been used to fill the interest gap. *See supra* § 2.11 and text *infra*.

[325] *See* LG Stuttgart, 31 August 1989, LG Hamburg, 26 September 1990, and OLG Frankfurt, 13 June 1991, all reported in UNILEX.

[326] *See* ICC arbitration award no. 7153/1992, 14 *J. L. & Com.* 217 (1995), UNILEX.

[327] Internationales Schiedsgericht der Bundeskammer der gewerblichen Wirtschaft – Wien, Arbitral awards no. SCH-4318 and SCH-4366, 15 June 1994, UNILEX.

[328] At least Article 74 is clear in this regard: *see supra* §§ 6.15 and 6.28.

[329] *See* LG Aachen, 20 July 1995, UNILEX.

[330] *Supra* § 6.19.

[331] *Supra* § 6.27.

[332] *See supra* § 6.19.

[333] *Id.*

As regards the buyer's main obligation to pay, insolvency – even if classified as an "impediment"[334] – would not lead to an exemption under Article 79(1), in that such a contingency is surely among those which a buyer should reasonably "take into account" and thus foresee. In other words, as regards financial inability, "a party generally assumes the risk of his own inability to perform his duty."[335] For similar reasons, even a significant drop in market prices after the conclusion of the contract is not likely to provide the buyer with grounds for a liability exemption.[336]

The unanticipated imposition of exchange controls might lead to a damages exemption, but only if the particular impediment was one which could not reasonably have been foreseen or overcome, (e.g.) by arranging for alternative payment means. If the contract concerned requires that payment be made from a particular source, such an impediment might not be avoidable by alternative means.[337]

The buyer's general obligation to pay the price includes an implied obligation to take such steps as may be required – by contract or by law – to enable payment to be made.[338] In a case arbitrated under the auspices of the ICC,[339] a sales contract provided for payment of the price by a documentary credit to be opened in Bulgaria by a certain date. When the credit was not opened on time, the seller claimed damages under Article 61(1)(b). The buyer alleged an impediment to performance, in that the Bulgarian government had ordered the suspension of payment of foreign debts, but the tribunal held that the buyer did not qualify for a liability exemption under Article 79: not only was the buyer unable to prove that the failure to open the credit was due to (caused by) the payment suspension; the suspension had, in any case, already been declared at the time of the conclusion of the contract, so the alleged impediment was one which the buyer could easily have foreseen.

The exemption provided by Article 79 has effect only for the period during which the impediment exists.[340] Therefore, when a temporary impediment to payment abates, the buyer becomes liable once again. On the other hand, since Article 79 does not prevent the injured party from exercising any right other than to claim damages,[341] a serious delay by the buyer will entitle the seller to avoid, and thus end, the contract by reason of fundamental breach.[342] As regards specific performance, the same approach as previously

---

[334] *Compare* para. 10 of the *Secretariat Commentary* to Article 65 of the 1978 Draft Convention (probably not an impediment).

[335] *See* Lookofsky, *Consequential Damages* at 90–91 (comparing American and Scandinavian law).

[336] *See* Rechtbank van Koophandel, Hasselt (Belgium), 2 May 1995, UNILEX (significant drop in market price of the goods/strawberries after the conclusion of the contract did not constitute "force majeure" exempting the buyer for non-performance under Art. 79, in that price fluctuations are foreseeable events in international trade which do not render performance impossible but result in economic loss well within the normal risk of commercial activities).

[337] *See supra* § 6.19 with notes 245–46.

[338] Article 54, *supra* § 4.12.

[339] ICC case no. 7197/1992, UNILEX, previously discussed in § 4.12.

[340] Article 79(3).

[341] Article 79(5).

[342] *See supra* § 6.23.

discussed in connection with the seller's exemption should yield sensible results,[343] just as an Article 79 exemption for buyer's non-performance would not preclude a claim to interest.[344]

The buyer who fails to perform must give notice to the seller of the impediment and its effects on his (the buyer's) ability to perform. If the notice is not received by the seller within a reasonable time after the buyer knew or ought to have known of the impediment, he is liable for damages.[345]

---

[343] *See supra* § 6.19 with note 261.

[344] *Supra* § 6.31.

[345] Article 79(4). Such liability extends also to cases where a party intends to perform by furnishing a commercially reasonable substitute: *see* para. 16 of the *Secretariat Commentary* to Article 65 of the 1978 Draft Convention.

CHAPTER SEVEN

AGREED REMEDIES

§ 7.1 INTRODUCTION TO DISCLAIMERS, LIMITATIONS AND OTHER AGREED REMEDIES

Since the CISG is a default set of rules, the provisions of the Convention apply only to the extent that the parties have not agreed to put something else in their place.[1] And the remedial rules of the CISG (discussed in the preceding Chapter) are among the provisions which contracting merchants most often seek to amend or displace.[2]

The heading agreed remedies is used here to encompass a mixed bag of contract terms, including (e.g.) what American lawyers call a "liquidated damages" clause designed to measure compensation in advance or a clause designed to impose "penalty" on the party in breach.[3] It might also be understood to include a sales contract provision which declares "time [to be] of the essence," if these words are meant to imply that one party is entitled to avoid (terminate) the contract, irrespective of whether the breaching party's delay would be characterized as "fundamental" under the gap-filling test in Article 25.[4]

The actual content of the contract will, among other things, depend on the relative positions of the parties in the concrete case. Buyers who enjoy superior bargaining power might, for example, seek advance agreement on a high liquidated damages figure which a defaulting seller would be liable to pay irrespective of buyer's actual loss. Another kind of pro-buyer clause might expressly provide for the right to reject goods which fail to conform to the contract "in any respect."

Well-positioned sellers, on the other hand, often seek protection in standard terms which contain a combination of so-called "disclaimer clauses" which limit both the seller's obligations and the buyer's remedies for breach.[5] Depending on the circumstances, such terms

---

[1]   Re. Article 6 *see supra* § 2.7.

[2]   Consider, for example, the currently applicable version of the Nordic General Conditions, NL 01 (in English at <http://www.vi.se/files/uploadfiles/nl01eb.pdf>) which contain an applicable law clause often leading to CISG application, i.e., as regards issues not expressly covered by the NL terms. Although the NL sets forth an extremely detailed set of rules governing the *remedies* available to the parties in the event of non-conforming delivery ("defects"), the NL says virtually *nothing* as to when goods are "defective" (do not conform). For this reason, CISG Article 35 will usually be left to govern the non-conformity issue in NL contracts "by default."

[3]   If the provision, evaluated under American domestic law, is deemed a "penalty" (*see* Farnsworth, *Contracts* § 12.18), it would fail the "validity" test described *infra*, § 7.4.

[4]   I.e., even in the case of an arguably "minor" breach. This was the interpretation given by the English Court of Appeal in a case decided under the SGA: *Gill & Duffus S.A. v. Société pour L'Exportation des Sucres S.A.* [1986] 1 Lloyd's Rep. 322 (C.A.); *see supra* § 6.8 note 67.

[5]   A "disclaimer clause" may relate either to the obligation and/or to the remedy for breach. A disclaimer of *warranty* purports to modify the seller's obligations to deliver conforming goods (one example is an "as is" clause); if the obligation in question has been effectively disclaimed (*caveat emptor*), there can be no breach.

might purport to limit or disclaim the seller's "warranty" obligations (the Article 35 obligation to deliver conforming goods) and/or disclaim the seller's liability for "indirect or consequential loss." In the event the goods delivered prove defective, the standard terms concerned obligate the seller only to "repair or replace";[6] alternatively, in the case of a serious (fundamental and incurable) defect which would entitle the buyer to avoid, the seller's liability would be limited to the selling price (perhaps a bit more).[7]

The starting point seems clear enough: the CISG parties are free to make their own deal,[8] not only with respect to substantive duties, but also as regards their remedial rights; this is often part of the bargain, the allocation of risk. On the other hand, the parties' power to displace certain rights and duties under the CISG supplementary regime may be limited by various factors (within and without the Convention), so not every onerous clause included (to the "strong" party's advantage) will ultimately achieve its intended effect. To be sure, the law still seeks to hold merchants to their promises and to protect their expectations, but a court or arbitrator is not likely to hold a promise binding if to do so would lead to an unfair result.[9] In other words, the traditional laissez-faire (freedom-of-contract) view is today sometimes, at least in some places and contexts, tempered by a paternalistic (protection-of-the-weak) view of fairness, so that – even in a commercial environment – an unreasonable or unconscionable "expectation" does not always equate with an "expectation interest" worthy of (full) protection.

To take one practical example, disclaimers and related agreed-remedy clauses are often placed amidst the "boilerplate," i.e., the fine-print language, of one party's standard terms of agreement. The need to police the agreement in this regard arises not so much because a given clause is a standard term, but because and to the extent that it is non-negotiated and therefore (perhaps) unusual and/or unfair.

American lawyers are, of course, familiar with the restriction against "unconscionable" contract terms set forth in the UCC and *Restatement* rules.[10] But since the relevant (domestic) "validity" standard to be applied in an international sales transaction will often depend on the outcome of a conflict-of-laws determination by the forum court (or arbitral tribunal),[11] it should be noted that the laws of many foreign jurisdictions extend considerably further.

    Accord as re. American domestic/UCC law: White & Summers, *Uniform Commercial Code* § 12-11. A disclaimer or limitation of *liability*, on the other hand, purports to exclude or limit the measure of monetary relief which would otherwise inure to the party injured by breach. In this sense, a liability limitation or disclaimer is one kind of remedy limitation or exclusion; a clause which obligates the seller only to "repair-or-replace" purports to limit the whole range of remedies otherwise available: *see* text *infra* and § 7.3.

6   This is, for example, the Nordic General Conditions standard scheme: *see* note 2 *supra*.

7   *Id.*

8   Article 6, discussed *supra* § 2.7.

9   *See* as regards American and Scandinavian law, Lookofsky, *Consequential Damages* pp. 36–37. *Accord*: Burrows, *Obligations* at 4, speaking of developments in English law and noting the affinity of such notions as mistake and "frustration" due to changed circumstances; *compare* re. "exemptions" under CISG Article 79 *supra* §§ 6.19 and 6.32; *see also* Lookofsky, *id.*, Part 3.4.

10   UCC § 2-302; *Restatement Second* § 208.

11   *See supra* § 2.6.

For example, the laws applicable in some European Union States,[12] such as France and England, include special statutes enacted to deal with unfair standard terms,[13] just as the relevant German statutory rules – applicable, *inter alia*, to international transactions – must also be considered in connection with the CISG;[14] the same is true of the very broadly drafted Scandinavian "General Clause."[15]

When dealing with seemingly onerous clauses (e.g., in contracts between merchants of disparate bargaining power) which purport to displace gap-filling rules, courts and arbitrators are likely to proceed cautiously, employing a series of "tests." The first of these asks whether the clause in question has been incorporated into the overall contract between the parties. If this hurdle is passed, courts and arbitrators often employ an interpretation test to determine whether the term applies to the dispute at hand.[16] Finally, as regards incorporated terms held applicable, courts sometimes proceed to examine the validity of such terms, and – depending on the circumstances and the applicable domestic law – refuse to give effect to an "unconscionable" or otherwise "unreasonable" clause.[17]

§ 7.2   Incorporation: the First of Three Tests

The first task for a judge or arbitrator asked to enforce a disclaimer or liability limitation is to determine whether the clause should be read as part of the deal. One practically important subset of this problem of incorporation relates to the standard (non-negotiated) terms just discussed, especially if they depart substantially from the otherwise applicable supplementary (CISG) rules. The mere fact that the parties have entered (and perhaps even subsequently performed) a sales agreement does not necessarily lead to the conclusion that a given set of standard terms proffered by one party has become part of the overall CISG deal.[18]

---

[12]   So far, (uniform) European Union law in this area is of only marginal interest since the relevant efforts of the Union have been limited mainly to the harmonization of rules applicable to unfair terms in consumer contracts, and since CISG Article 2 effectively excludes sales to consumers from its scope of application: *see supra* § 2.5.

[13]   In France a 1978 statute protecting consumers and "non-professionals" from unfair contract terms was consolidated into the *Code de la consommation*; it applies to individually negotiated terms as well as to those in standard forms, provided the clause results in a significant disproportion between the parties' rights and obligations. The English Unfair Contract Terms Act of 1977 (UCTA) applies in principle to sales between merchants, though (many) international sales are exempt from its scope.

[14]   In principle, §§ 305 ff. of the BGB (formerly AGBG) apply not only in favour of consumers, but also as regards merchants and others involved in non-consumer transactions.

[15]   According to § 36 of the (essentially uniform) Contracts Acts, a purported liability disclaimer will only be effective, even as between merchants, if it passes a reasonableness test. *See* Lookofsky, *Consequential Damages* at 36; *see also* Lookofsky, *Limits*.

[16]   *See infra* § 7.3.

[17]   *See infra* § 7.4.

[18]   Some standard terms, if considered fair, might – by virtue of their recognition and widespread use within a given national context – be more readily held incorporated by national courts. However, the same courts should be reluctant to hold foreign parties bound by provisions unfamiliar within the international trade concerned: *see* Article 9 (*supra* § 2.13).

The CISG provides at least a few tools to help resolve the incorporation issue, although the general declaration confirming contractual freedom (in Article 6) itself provides no guidance in this regard.[19] As a starting point, the question of whether an offeror's standard form conditions have become part of the offer should be resolved by application of the rules in Article 14 and Article 8. Absent a prior course of dealings between the parties (Article 9), only standard terms referred to in the offer and made available to the offeree (in a language accessible to him) are candidates for incorporation into the CISG contract.[20]

In one of the German CISG cases where a standard form clause was invoked, the court was quick to find that incorporation did occur. The seller in this case had included in the text of its invoice a clause requiring notices of non-conformity to be given within 8 days after arrival of the goods.[21] The result is hardly surprising, especially since other German courts have required equally prompt notice even absent express agreement between the parties.[22]

In other situations, perhaps involving a "battle of forms," the rule in Article 19 may be relevant, (e.g.) when considering whether a seller's standard liability disclaimer should knock out a contrary term in the buyer's standard form.[23] Then again, Article 19 would seem of little use in the (not uncommon) situation where the liability question arises long after the parties have exchanged diverging forms, without objection.[24] In this situation, the CISG rules can provide support for a mechanical (i.e. "last-shot") approach; but when fairness so dictates, the Convention will also permit courts and arbitrators to apply the gap-filling solution set forth in the Convention's remedial regime.[25]

When asked to determine what the contract includes (and what it does not), we are often left mainly with notions of fairness and good common sense – notions which sometimes find expression in the traditional, flexible maxims of commercial law.[26] As American

---

[19]   *Accord* Honnold, *Uniform Law* (2d ed. 1990) p. 239, text at note 17.

[20]   Re. the application of Articles 14 and 8 to resolve the issue of incorporation of standard terms *see* Bundesgerichtshof (Germany), 31 October 2001, CISGW3. *Accord* Schlechtriem in Schlechtriem, *Commentary/Kommentar*, Art. 14, Rd.Nr. 16–17. For an application of the "accessible-language" doctrine *see* OLG Koblenz, 16 January 1992, UNILEX (sale of "boat" treated as CISG sale notwithstanding Article 2(e)); *see also* OLG Hamm, 8 February 1995, UNILEX. Re. "contracting out" of the CISG by means of standard forms *see supra* § 2.7.

[21]   *See* LG Giessen, 5 July 1994, UNILEX. Re. Article 19(2) in this connection *see also* LG Baden-Baden, 14 August 1991, 12 *J. L. & Com.* 277 (1993), UNILEX; Art. 19 is discussed *supra* § 3.8.

[22]   Re. the generally "tough" interpretation of CISG Articles 38 and 39 by German courts *see supra* § 4.9.

[23]   "A reply to an offer which purports to be an acceptance but contains [material] additions, limitations or other modifications [e.g., a limitation of liability] is a rejection of the offer and constitutes a counter-offer." *See generally supra* § 3.8.

[24]   *See* Honnold, *Uniform Law*, pp. 188 ff.

[25]   *Id.* Heuzé, *Vente internationale*; no. 187 and Audit, *Vente internationale*, no. 71 are in *accord. See also supra* § 3.8.

[26]   Article 19 notwithstanding, it seems doubtful that the incorporation matter is *governed* (solely) by the CISG; nor could such a matter likely be settled solely by CISG general principles: regarding Article 7(2) *see supra* § 2.11 and *compare* Hyland, *Conforming Goods* at 331–33 re. the *discussion principle* (CISG party cannot rely on an ambiguous statement or act without first attempting to clarify it). Re. incorporation and related (disclaimer) issues under American and Scandinavian law *see* Lookofsky, *Consequential Damages*, pp. 203–216.

commentators have noted, the need to police the "boilerplate" arises not so much because a given clause is standard,[27] but because it is non-negotiated and therefore (perhaps) unusual and/or unfair.[28] Standard ("non-dickered") terms which depart substantially from the supplementary (CISG) rules are less likely to be deemed incorporated into the "bargain in fact,"[29] for as to these terms, there is arguably "no assent at all."[30]

In the international commercial context, arbitrators might find the UNIDROIT provision on "surprising" terms applicable as a supplementary standard in a CISG case. This "formation" provision – which also should qualify as a "validity-related" rule[31] – states that "[n]o term contained in standard terms which is of such a character that the other party could not reasonably have expected it, is effective unless it has been expressly accepted by that party."[32] German domestic law contains a similar provision,[33] and since German courts regularly apply this rule to all kinds of contracts, it would likely be held applicable in CISG cases,[34] (e.g.) on the ground that it too "functions as a validity rule."[35] Alternatively, rules such as these might at least provide courts and arbitrators with guidance when applying the CISG rules which directly "govern" the incorporation "matter," i.e., Articles 8, 14, 18 and 19.[36]

§ 7.3 INTERPRETATION

In the event that a court holds that a given disclaimer or limitation clause has been incorporated in the parties' agreement, the next step is to consider how that particular clause should be construed (interpreted): e.g., whether a repair-or-replace clause remains the buyer's exclusive remedy if the seller fails to repair or replace, whether a clause which in general terms purports to disclaim or limit liability for breach effectively operates to disclaim liability for negligence, etc.[37]

---

[27] Courts and arbitrators may be particularly reluctant to consider burdensome clauses as incorporated (e.g.) if the terms appear in fine print or (worse yet) if the standard terms are merely referred to among the individual (negotiated) terms, but not actually appended thereto. *See* (e.g.) Farnsworth, *Contracts*, § 4.26.

[28] The distinction between standard terms and "dickered" terms should be made on the basis of substance, not form – especially when computers facilitate the merger of all contract provisions into a single, seamless word-processed document.

[29] *See* note 18 *supra*.

[30] *See* Farnsworth, *Contracts*, § 4.26, and Llewellyn, *The Common Law Tradition* 370 (1960).

[31] *See* Lookofsky, *Limits*, at 496 with note 88.

[32] *UNIDROIT Principles*, Article 2.20, which also provides: "In determining whether a term is of such a character, regard shall be had to its content, language and presentation."

[33] BGB § 305 c (1), formerly AGBG § 3, provides that a standard clause which is so "unusual" that the other party could not have expected its inclusion does not become an enforceable part of the contract.

[34] If, in such a case, the relevant PIL rules point to German domestic law. *See supra* § 2.6.

[35] *See* Schlechtriem in Schlechtriem, *Commentary/Kommentar*, Vor Artt. (Intro to Arts) 14–24, Rd.Nr. 9. Re. UNIDROIT § 2.20 *see* Lookofsky, *Limits* at 496 with note 88 (noting that this rule *denies effect* to an "unexpected" and thus likely unreasonable standard term).

[36] Re. Article 7(2) *see supra* § 2.11.

[37] For a German case involving a French seller's standard business terms (providing for notices by registered letter) *see* LG Stuttgart, 13 August 1991, UNILEX.

In this connection, CISG Article 8 provides us with a tool to help deal with the common situation where the parties attach different meanings to the same contractual language, and the Convention version of the reasonable person standard hardly signals a shift in the patterns previously established under domestic laws.[38] On the other hand, Article 8 hardly provides all the tools needed to interpret one party's standard terms, especially if the language supplied by one party is susceptible to two "reasonable" interpretations, one of which favours each party. In this case, it may be most reasonable to construe a standard warranty exclusion and/or liability limitation clause (purporting to displace the otherwise applicable CISG rules) "narrowly," i.e., against the drafter (*contra proferentem/stipulatorem*),[39] especially if the standard terms do not, as a whole, represent a "balanced" result.[40] The *contra proferentem* idea, though perhaps not discernable as a CISG "general principle,"[41] is at least consistent with the letter and spirit of Article 8;[42] it is also an internationally accepted rule.[43]

Illustration 7a: Seller S in America sells manufacturing equipment to buyer B in Denmark. According to the technical specifications set forth in the contract, the equipment can operate at a certain speed; according to the "warranty" clause in S's standard form (attached to the end of the contract), however, S "warrants the machine against defects in material or workmanship, but makes no other warranties, express or implied, unless the word 'guarantee' is used." As it turns out, the equipment delivered cannot operate at the stated speed.[44]

Any apparent conflict between the description (technical specifications) of the goods and the "disclaimer clause" in this contract should be resolved in accordance with a *contra proferentem* approach. Since the disclaiming language (drafted by S in the interest of that party only) seems inherently inconsistent with the express obligation created by the

---

38   Re. Article 8 *see supra* § 2.12.
39   *Accord* (re. American law) Farnsworth, *Contracts*, § 7.11, noting the principle also applies as between parties who *bargained as equals*. Re. English law *see* Treitel, *Law of Contract*, Ch. 7, Sec. 1(2). In German law this approach is codified in BGB § 305 c (2), formerly AGBG § 5.
40   I.e. the result which could be expected to follow from negotiations between equally "strong" organizations, representing the interests of sellers and buyers alike. *Accord* Junge in Schlechtriem, *Commentary/ Kommentar*, Art.8, Rd.Nr. 8. *Compare* (e.g.) *George Mitchell v. Finney Lock Seeds*, 1 All England Law Reports 111 [1983], distinguishing *R.W. Green Ltd. v. Cade Bros. Farm*, 1 Lloyd's Rep. 602 [1978]. Although Scandinavian sellers often claim that the Nordic Standard Terms of Agreement (NL 01: *supra* note 2) fall within the "agreed document" category, the NL terms serve best to protect the interests of sellers, at least when measured against the more balanced CISG solution.
41   Re. *contra proferentem* and Article 7(2) *see supra* § 2.11.
42   *See* Magnus in Staudinger, *Kommentar*, Art.8, Rd.Nr.18.
43   *See* (e.g.) Article 4.6 of the *UNIDROIT Principles*. The UNIDROIT formulation, which speaks only of "interpretation" of "unclear" terms, ignores the "construction" aspect of the *contra proferentem* principle. Re. this latter, *covert* means of dealing with *unfair* contract terms, *see* Farnsworth, *Contracts*, § 7.11.
44   Re. the possible availability of a non-contractual claim *compare supra* § 4.6, *Illustration 4b*. This alternative is of particular interest to the buyer where contractual liability has been effectively limited or excluded.

technical description,[45] the warranty disclaimer should not be interpreted so as to relieve S of his obligation to deliver conforming goods to B.[46]

Taking a similar approach in a contract for the sale of a furnace, a U.S. District Court rejected a Canadian seller's argument that its "repair-or-replace" clause should be interpreted as a disclaimer of any express or implied warranty for the conformity of the goods. By including that provision, the parties did not agree that the furnace would not have to perform as other similar furnaces would or as the seller expressly or implied made known it would (Art. 35 (2) CISG); they only aimed at limiting the buyer's remedies for non-conformity.[47]

Although oral and written contracts usually bind with equal force under the CISG,[48] a special problem arises when an oral statement made during the negotiations is said to serve as a promissory supplement to the contract which the parties later signed.

Illustration 7b: Same facts as in *Illustration 4a*,[49] except that the written contract provides: "Any oral statements made by S concerning the product or otherwise shall not be relied upon by B and are not part of this contract of sale. This writing constitutes the entire contract."

Even if the oral statement by S is not deemed excluded from the contract by virtue of the (American) parol evidence rule, an express clause in the contract which purports to deny effect to oral statements (even if made)[50] might be held to achieve what the parol rule does not. Then again, courts should scrutinize carefully any attempt to disclaim the effect of significant statements actually made, (e.g.) when the seller seeks to hide behind such a non-negotiated "merger clause" in his own standard terms.[51]

A CISG seller who, in its own standard form, undertakes to "repair or replace" non-conforming goods will typically do so with a view to limiting the buyer's options under the supplementary CISG rules (avoidance in case of a fundamental breach and/or compensation for losses which flow from a breach).[52] However, courts and arbitrators are likely to restrict

---

[45] According to CISG Article 35(1) the seller must deliver goods which are of the quantity, quality and description required by the contract: *see supra* § 4.4. Re. fitness for purpose *see supra* § 4.8.

[46] *Accord* Huber in Schlechtriem, *Kommentar*, Art. 49, Rd.Nr. 72. *See also* (re. English law) Treitel, *Law of Contract*, Ch. 7, Sec. 1(1). Regarding the corresponding UCC principle, *see* White & Summers, *Uniform Commercial Code* §§ 12-2 and 12-3. Even if the letter of UCC § 2-316(1) has been pre-empted by the CISG and thus displaced in the international context, the spirit of the UCC rule might well be said to reside within CISG Article 8, thus leading to similar results.

[47] This notwithstanding the fact that the clause concerned bore the label: "WARRANTY." *See* U.S. District Court, Northern District of Illinois, Eastern Division, 29 January 2003, UNILEX (*Ajax Tool Works, Inc. v. Can-Eng Manifacturing Ltd.*), also available at CISGW3.

[48] *See supra* § 2.14.

[49] *See supra* § 4.5.

[50] And which expressly renders the written contract to be the entire, final and exclusive agreement.

[51] The general acceptance of such clauses in Article 2.17 of the *UNIDROIT Principles* seems to ignore the distinction between dickered and unreasonable standard terms: no party should "expect" that an honest merchant who makes a significant oral representation will later hide behind a standard merger clause. *Compare* Art. 2.20, *id.*

[52] Even without the repair-and replace clause, the buyer will often have the right to demand this kind of specific performance; *see supra* §§ 6.6 and 6.7.

the applicability of this kind of standard term – again, by means of narrow interpretation – to cases where the supplier *can and will* cure defects within a reasonable time,[53] just as the doctrines of waiver and estoppel may provide additional barriers for sellers who seek the protection of clauses like this.[54]

Another application of the interpretation test is to determine whether a contractual disclaimer or limitation clause should be construed to exclude or limit liability for one party's negligence.[55] As a starting point, liability disclaimers are likely to be construed narrowly (and therefore) as not applying to negligent conduct – at least in the absence of clear and express language to this effect.[56] More generally, courts and arbitrators interpret disclaimers so as to give the party injured the benefit of the doubt, especially in cases where the allegedly "agreed" remedy would leave the injured party with no meaningful (minimum adequate) remedy in actual fact.[57]

§ 7.4 VALIDITY

Even assuming that a given clause passes the incorporation and interpretation hurdles just described, the validity issue remains. The validity (enforceability)[58] of a standard term which (e.g.) purports to disclaim the obligations set forth in Article 35(2) and/or limit liability in the event of breach is a question outside the CISG: the Convention is simply "not concerned with" the validity of clauses like these.[59]

---

53 Regarding the application of UCC § 2-719(2) in American domestic law *see* White & Summers, *Uniform Commercial Code*, § 12-10; Gillette & Walt, *Sales Law*, Ch. 9.IV.B.

54 *See* (e.g.) the decision of the U.S. District Court in the *Ajax Tool* case, *supra* note 47, which turned to domestic law on the waiver/estoppel issue, perhaps unaware of CISG doctrine and foreign precedent holding estoppel to be a *general Convention principle* (*see supra*, § 2.10 with note 170 and § 2.11with note 177).

55 Both in the sense of a negligent breach of a contractual obligation and as regards the tort of "negligence" as such.

56 *Accord*, as re. English law, Treitel, *Law of Contract*, Ch. 7, Sec. 1(2)(2). Some contract disclaimers distinguish between simple and "gross" negligence; indeed, under the applicable domestic validity rules, it may not be possible to effectively disclaim a seller/supplier's liability for gross negligence, irrespective of the language used. Of course, a clause which does not mention negligence (in any form) can not, in and of itself, serve to disclaim liability for "gross" negligence.

57 *Accord* as regards American domestic law *Milgard Tempering, Inc. v. Selas Corp.*, 902 F.2d 703 (9th Cir. 1990)(loss not part of "bargained-for allocation of risk"). *See also* (e.g) *Parsons & Whittemore Overseas Co. Inc. v. RAKTA*, 508 F.2d 969 (2d Cir. 1974)(lost profits compensated by arbitrators in an international context despite contract limitation; award enforced by Court of Appeals). The "minimum adequate remedy" idea presumably explains the decision of the South Carolina Supreme Court to award consequential damages to the plaintiff in *Hill v. BASF Wyandotte Corp.*, 311 S.E. 2d 734, 38 UCC Rep. 1254 (1984), this in apparent disregard of the "guidance" provided by the U.S. Court of Appeals in 696 F.2d 287, 292 (1982). *Accord* as re. German law Huber in Schlechtriem, *Kommentar*, Art. 49, Rd.Nr. 72 (note, however, that the German approach is to treat this as a validity question).

58 Obviously, a party can only seek enforcement of contract terms which are valid (not subject to viable defenses and thus enforceable).

59 Re. Article 4(a) *see supra* § 4.2. The seller's duty to supply conforming goods under Article 35(2) applies unless the parties have "agreed otherwise," but this clause does *not* give seller a "licence" to impose unreasonable standard terms upon the buyer, nor does the "expressly provided" exception in Article 4 lead to that result. *Accord*: Schwenzer in Schlechtriem, *Commentary/Kommentar*, Art. 35, Rd.Nr. 42. Addressing the

So, as regards validity problems, we must continue to apply non-CISG rules, such as the rule in UCC § 2.302,[60] i.e., the applicable domestic contract law, as determined by the forum's rules of private international law. In the absence of a choice-of-law clause in the contract, the seller's law will frequently be the *lex contractus*.[61] This law will then decide the validity issue.

The implied obligations set forth in Article 35(2) apply "[e]xcept where the parties have agreed otherwise."[62] A seller who (e.g.) "accepts no responsibility whatsoever that the goods are fit for ordinary purposes or any particular purpose, whether or not such purpose has been made known to him" purports to disclaim the implied fitness-for-purpose obligations under Article 35(2)(a)–(b). Whether such a disclaimer of warranty will be given effect depends – not only on the outcome of the incorporation and interpretation tests (discussed above), but also – on the letter and spirit of the applicable validity rule. These days, a purported disclaimer might be more likely to survive censorship if judged by American ("unconscionability"), as opposed to European ("reasonableness) standards,[63] but even hard-nosed American courts and arbitrators are likely to take a restrictive stance as regards the seller's "freedom" to enforce terms which purport to deny buyers the fundamental protection provided by Article 35(2).[64]

---

issue of whether a CISG disclaimer might be invalidated pursuant to UCC 2-316, Gillette and Walt (*Sales Law*, rev. ed. at 325) go so far as to suggest the possibility that "the effectiveness of a disclaimer *simply involves interpretation of the contract terms* concerning quality" (emphasis added). Viewed from an international perspective, however, this argument does seem "too much of a stretch" (*compare id.*), even from the strictly American/UCC perspective set forth in Comment 6 to the original version of § 2-313 and the corresponding comment to the (2002) *NCCUSL Draft Revision*: "A clause generally disclaiming 'all warranties, express or implied' cannot reduce the [UCC]seller's obligation for the description and therefore cannot be given literal effect under Section 2-316(1). This is not intended to mean that the parties, if they consciously desire, cannot make their own bargain as they wish. But in determining what they have agreed upon good faith is a factor and consideration should be given to the fact that the probability is small that a real price is intended to be exchanged for a pseudo-obligation." Re. the currently (2003) applicable version of UCC § 2-316(2)-(3) and its relation to CISG Article 4: *see* Lookofsky, *United Nations Convention*, No. 177.

[60] Under some domestic systems, a clause excluding or limiting liability must meet certain *formal* requirements; *see* e.g. the Italian Civil Code Articles 1341 (2), 1342 (2). If such requirements affect the validity of the sale under the *lex contractus*, they should be regarded as validity rules under Article 4: *accord* Stoll in Schlechtriem, *Commentary/Kommentar*, Art. 79, Rd.Nr. 63; *contra* Schlechtriem in Schlechtriem, *Commentary/Kommentar*, Art. 11, Rd.Nr. 14.

[61] *See* Article 4(2) of the 1980 Rome Convention on the Applicable Law to Contractual Obligations and Article 3 of the 1955 Hague Convention on the Law Applicable to the International Sale of Goods (Corporeal Movables). Re. American law *see supra* § 1.2.

[62] This specific proviso repeats the more general Article 6 freedom-of-contract rule: the parties may "derogate from or vary the effect of *any* [Convention] provisions."

[63] For a pesimistic, yet fascinating evaluation of "post-modern" trends in this and related areas of American domestic contract law *see generally* Knapp, C., "Taking Contracts Private: The Quiet Revolution in Contract Law," 71 *Fordham L.R.* 761 (2002); *see also id.* at 771re. unconscionability under UCC § 2.302. Re. the "reasonableness" test under § 36 of the (essentially uniform) Scandinavian Contracts Acts *see* Lookofsky, *Limits*.

[64] Part V of the U.S. District's decision in the *Ajax* case (*supra* n. 47), purporting to "interpret" the parties' CISG agreement (without mention of Article 8, let alone domestic validity standards) seems nonetheless to *accord* with this (minimum adequate remedies) view: "Contrary to [seller]'s assertion, the parties' agreement does not contain an express disclaimer of any implied warranties. The parties have not agreed expressly that the furnace did not have to perform in a similar fashion as other like furnaces would perform or as [seller] expressly or impliedly made known that the furnace would. The parties' agreement simply limited [buyer]'s remedies."

In a CISG dispute resolved by means of ICC arbitration,[65] a "penalty clause" purported to limit damages – in the case of non-performance by either party – to X% of contract price. Applying Austrian domestic law to determine the validity of the purported agreed remedy, the tribunal held that the clause was *not* effective to limit the seller's actual damages in the case of buyer's breach.[66] The application of American domestic law in such a situation might well have led to a similar result.[67]

As regards American law in this area, UCC § 2-302 is applied sparingly – perhaps increasingly so – by U.S. courts.[68] Still, the reported decisions provide at least some examples of application as between merchants, in a few cases even between merchants of equal bargaining power, thus "censoring" the content of contracts containing "unconscionable" – i.e., highly unreasonable – disclaimers and limitation clauses.[69] And even in (the majority of) instances where courts and arbitrators would be very reluctant to overtly confront and limit the principle of contractual freedom codified in CISG Article 6 – (e.g.) by direct application of UCC § 2-302 – the same decision makers can achieve essentially similar (and equally reasonable) results indirectly, by the application of "covert tools."[70]

Although the CISG is "not [generally] concerned" with sales contract validity, the Convention is not just a gap-filler, but a yardstick as well.[71] Its supplementary remedial system, considered to be a fair solution in the average case, "aims at justice between the parties";[72] it is therefore at least indirectly relevant as regards the application of rules of validity which strive to maintain a reasonable balance between contractual obligations and remedial relief. This is not to say that the Convention provides the only fair remedial regime, but the alternative regime set forth in a given contract (including its standard terms) must at least provide each party with the potential for minimum adequate remedial relief.

If, for example, the contract in question provides, not for minimum adequate remedies, but (e.g.) for damages "unconscionably low," the reasonableness-tests of domestic law, working in tandem with the CISG good-faith principle (*supra* § 2.10), should serve to (re)activate the supplementary CISG remedial rule.[73] The same principle clearly underpins the award rendered by the Arbitration Institute of the Stockholm Chamber of Commerce in 1998,[74] where an American seller (S) and Chinese buyer (B) had concluded s contract for the sale of a large press for the production of frame rails for trucks. The tribunal held S – who had "consciously disregarded" facts regarding the non-conformity in

---

[65]   ICC Case no. 7197/1992, UNILEX.
[66]   This case is noted *supra* (§ 4.12) in connection with the obligations of the CISG.
[67]   *See generally* Gillette & Walt, *Sales Law*, Ch. 9.IV.D.
[68]   *See* Knapp, C., *supra* note 63, at 771 re. UCC § 2-302.
[69]   *See generally* White & Summers, *Uniform Commercial Code*, § 4-9.
[70]   *See, e.g.,* note 43 *supra. See also* Lookofsky, *Limits* at 501.
[71]   *See* Schlechtriem, *Seller's Obligations* at 6.6 (re. clauses imposed through the use of standard terms, etc.).
[72]   Hellner, *Vienna Convention* at 351.
[73]   *Accord* (re. American domestic sales law): *Phillips Petroleum Co. v. Bucyrus-Erie Co.*, 131 Wis.2d 21, 388 N.W.2d 584, 1 UCC Rep. 2d 667, reconsideration denied by 132 Wis.2d 393, 394 N.W.2d 313 (1986).
[74]   *See* the award of 5 June 1998, CLOUT Case 237, CISGW3 and UNILEX.

question – liable in damages, notwithstanding the fact that B first gave notice of defects some 3 years after delivery.[75] Indeed, if a standard term contradicts CISG "fundamental principles" (*Grundwertungen*), a court might deny the contract effect for that reason alone, (i.e.) even if the term in question would be valid under the otherwise applicable domestic law.[76]

Since unreasonably onerous clauses in standard form contracts are likely to be treated as invalid,[77] and since the invalidation of any contractual remedy is likely to re-activate the supplementary Convention rule,[78] CISG merchants with superior bargaining power are ill-advised to impose excessively one-sided standard terms; in other words, he who tries to get it "all" may end up with nothing.[79]

---

[75]   The contract also contained a clause excluding consequential or incidental damages, but the published award (*id.*) does not reveal the nature or extent of the damages awarded.

[76]   *See* Oberster Gerichtshof (Austria), 7 September 2000, CISGW3 and UNILEX, where German seller's terms provided that S could *cure* defects, *replace* the goods (gravestones) or *refund* the price, whereas B could *not withhold payment*. Held: term restricting B's right to withhold payment (valid under German domestic law) did not contravene CISG fundamental principles: term would not be interpreted/applied to deprive B of fundamental right to avoid or claim compensation if goods remained useless despite S's attempts to cure.

[77]   As opposed to "moderated." Suppose, for example, that a CISG contract for the sale of machinery to be used in buyer's ongoing production provides for liquidated damages of $1,000 per day if seller defaults. If the court considers this amount excessive, whereas $500 per day seems a reasonable estimate of buyer's lost profits, the court's options under the applicable domestic law might be: (a) invalidation of the unreasonable clause or (b) "moderation" of the clause (to $500 per day), so as to make it reasonable and thus enforceable.

[78]   Including, for example, the full expectation measurement of damages under Article 74. *Accord* (re. American domestic law): *Phillips Petroleum Co. v. Bucyrus-Erie Co.*, *supra* note 73. *See also* Lookofsky, *Loose Ends* at 410–12.

[79]   American business people have, for example, been warned that such attempts can backfire in countries like Germany; *see* Nemmers & Bartsch, "Boilerplate" U.S. Contracts Often Miss the Mark: Contract Drafters Should Keep in Mind that German Commercial Law Protects the Weaker Party, *The National Law Journal*, 4 September 1995, p. C9. *Compare* White & Summers, *Uniform Commercial Code*, § 4-9.

CHAPTER EIGHT

CISG RESERVATOINS
(AND OTHER FINAL PROVISIONS)

§ 8.1 INTRODUCTION

Part IV of the Convention entitled "Final Provisions" contains, *inter alia*, the rules which define when the CISG enters into force in those States which ratify it.[1] (As noted previously, the Convention applies only to contracts concluded on or after its entry into force in the Contracting States referred to in Article 1.)[2]

The Final Provisions also contain rules which define the relationship between the CISG and other treaties (most importantly, the 1955 and 1964 Hague Conventions),[3] and rules which define the rights of Contracting States to make certain declarations (reservations) with respect to specified articles and/or parts of the CISG.

The most important reservation from an American perspective is Article 95 – a rule which entitles Contracting States, such as the United States, to declare that they will not be bound by the private-international-law rule in subparagraph (1)(b) of Article 1.[4] Another significant provision permits States to declare that only will be bound by the rules in Part II of the Convention (Contract Formation) or the rules in Part III (Sale of Goods); the four Scandinavian States have all made such declarations with respect to CISG Part II.[5] Another rule of practical significance permits Contracting States to recognize only sales contracts and modifications if in writing.[6]

§ 8.2 RELATIONSHIP TO THE 1955 AND 1964 HAGUE CONVENTIONS

According to Article 90, the CISG does not prevail over any international agreement which has already been or may be entered into and which contains provisions concerning the

---

[1] In the case of each new State, the Convention enters into force approximately one year after the deposit of its instrument of adherence: *see* Article 99(2).

[2] *See* Article 100 and *supra* §§ 1.1 and 2.1 ff.

[3] *See infra* § 8.2.

[4] *See infra* § 8.7.

[5] Re. Article 92 *see infra* § 8.4. Although the Article 92 reservation does not necessarily render the Part II rules insignificant in CISG contracts with Scandinavian parties, the combined effect of the U.S. declaration pursuant to Article 95 and the Scandinavian Article 92 declarations will always require the application of *domestic* contract formation rules in contracts between American and Scandinavian-based merchants (*id.*).

[6] Re. Article 96 *see infra* § 8.8.

matters governed by the CISG.[7] In limited circumstances, this may be significant for those States which, prior to ratifying the CISG, had already ratified the 1955 Hague Convention on the Law Applicable to the International Sale of Goods (Corporeal Moveables).[8]

As noted with respect to the provisions which regulate the CISG sphere of application, those States which have ratified both the 1955 Convention and the CISG will utilize the 1955 treaty when applying CISG Article 1(1)(b),[9] i.e., to determine when the rules of private international law lead to the application of the law of a CISG Contracting State.[10] In this respect, the two treaties work in tandem.

As regards the application of CISG Article 1(1)(a), the relationship between the CISG and the 1955 Convention seems less clear,[11] and the possibility of a certain (limited) degree of conflict remains.[12] A primary goal of the 1986 revision of the 1955 Convention is to eliminate potential conflicts with the CISG.[13]

The 1955 Hague Convention (just discussed) deals not with substance, but with choice of law. CISG Part IV also defines the relationship between the CISG and its predecessor in the field of substantive sales law: the not-so-successful ULF and ULIS (Hague) Conventions of 1964.[14] To put it simply: as the CISG is phased in, these 1964 Hague Conventions are phased out.[15]

§ 8.3 RESERVATIONS: GENERALLY

The only reservations (declarations) which Contracting States are permitted to make are those expressly authorized in CISG Part IV.[16] The more significant reservations are discussed below, including the Article 95 declaration made by the United States.

---

[7] Provided that the parties have their relevant places of business in States parties to such agreement.

[8] This group of States includes Belgium, Denmark, Finland, France, Italy, Norway, Sweden and Switzerland. Niger has not (as of mid- 2003) adopted the CISG.

[9] Assuming, at least, that the State concerned has not made a declaration pursuant to Article 95 which limits the applicability of Article 1(1)(b). *See infra* § 8.7.

[10] *Supra* § 2.4.

[11] Although Article 1(1)(a) makes the CISG generally applicable without recourse to the rules of private inter-national law, the 1980 CISG does not, according to Article 90, prevail over the 1955 Convention to the extent that the older treaty contains provisions concerning the matters governed by the CISG. *See generally* Winship, *Private International Law.*

[12] The potential for conflict is limited because when the CISG would apply by virtue of Article 1(1)(a), the "seller's law" rule in Article 3 the 1955 Convention would usually lead to the application of the CISG as well. In a few limited situations, however – e.g., where a sales contract calls for delivery in a non-CISG State and a problem arises as to the rules re. inspection and notification in that State – the two conventions might lead to different results; presumably, in such a case the 1955 Convention would prevail. Under Article 4 of the 1955 Convention, the law applicable to inspection and notification is determined by the place of delivery.

[13] The 1986 Convention (not yet in force) "shall not prejudice" the application of the CISG. *See generally* Winship, *Scope* at 1-43 and Honnold, *Uniform Law* § 464.

[14] *See generally supra* § 1.2.

[15] *See generally* Article 99, paragraphs (3)–(6).

[16] Re. the unofficial German "declaration" with respect to Article 95 *see infra* § 8.7.

§ 8.4 Article 92 Declarations

Surely the most far-reaching reservation permitted by the Convention is that contained in Article 92, whereby a CISG Contracting State may declare at the time of adherence that it will "not be bound" by Part II of this Convention (Contract Formation) or that it will not be bound by Part III (Sale of Goods).

The Scandinavian delegates to the Vienna Conference made it clear that certain rules in CISG Part II regarding sales contract formation would be unacceptable from a Scandinavian point of view. It is therefore not surprising that the Scandinavian States[17] (and only these)[18] have all made Article 92 reservations, whereby these States are "not bound" by CISG Part II. (Thus far, no Contracting State has made an Article 92 reservation with respect to Part III.)

The actual *effect* of these Part II reservations is that Denmark, Finland, Norway and Sweden are not to be considered "Contracting States" within paragraph (1) of Article 1 in respect of matters governed by that (Contract Formation) Part.[19] For this reason, as regards contracts entered between a party residing in a Scandinavian State and a party residing in a non-Scandinavian State (which has ratified the whole CISG), the Convention Part II rules can not apply by virtue of Article 1(1)(a).[20]

On the other hand, according to Article 1(1)(b), the CISG applies "where the rules of private international law lead to the application of the law of a Contracting State."[21] Depending on the circumstances, this rule can serve to activate the Convention's Part II in CISG contracts involving a party residing a Scandinavian State.[22] On the hand, the Article 95 declaration made by the United States should effectively preclude the application of CISG Part II in contracts involving one American and one Scandinavian party.[23]

§ 8.5 Contracting States with Territorial Units

In most States operating under a federal system, the central government is endowed with the treaty-making power to bind the entire federation to the CISG. The effect of the United States ratification, for example, is to bind all 50 "territorial units" (the individual states) within the U.S.

---

[17] Denmark, Finland, Norway and Sweden.

[18] Iceland (a State which is usually counted within the "Nordic," but not the "Scandinavian" group) has *not* made a similar declaration.

[19] Article 92(2).

[20] *See also supra* § 2.3 with Illustration 2b. In its decision of 4 March 1994 (UNILEX and CISGW3) OLG Frankfurt seems to have overlooked the Swedish Article 92 reservation. However, since the decision (denying contract formation) was based both on Part II of the CISG and on the German Civil Code (the seller's law), the result can be seen as supported by Article 1(1)(b).

[21] *See supra* § 2.4.

[22] For further details *see* Lookofsky, *CISG/Scandinavia*, § 8.4.

[23] *Compare infra* § 8.7 re. the effect of the unoffical "German" declaration as to the interaction of Article 1(1)(b) and declarations pursuant to Article 95.

In some nation-States, such as Australia and Canada, the federal government does not possess a this power.[24] For this reason, Article 93 permits a State, upon its ratification of the CISG, to declare that the CISG is to extend to only some, but not all of its territorial units. In such event, even if the place of business of a party is located in that State, this place of business is considered not to be in a Contracting State unless it is in a territorial unit to which the Convention extends.[25]

Originally, the Canadian CISG ratification did not extend to Quebec and Saskatchewan, but that Article 93 reservation was subsequently withdrawn. Upon its ratification of the CISG, Denmark declared that, pursuant to paragraph 1 of Article 93, that "the Convention shall not apply to the Faroe Islands and Greenland;" as of 2003, that reservation is still in effect.

§ 8.6 STATES HAVING CLOSELY RELATED LEGAL RULES

Article 94(1) of the Convention provides as follows: "Two or more Contracting States which have the same or closely related legal rules on matters governed by this Convention may at any time declare that the Convention is not to apply to contracts of sale or to their formation where the parties have their places of business in those States." When Denmark, Finland, Norway and Sweden ratified the CISG, they all made declarations pursuant to this provision.

The "matters governed by this Convention" – i.e. the matters to which Article 94(1) refers – relate both to the formation of the contract of sale (CISG Part II) and to the rights and obligations of the seller and the buyer arising from such a contract (CISG Part III). Because the reservations made by the Scandinavian States pursuant to Article 92 may be said to render the Article 94 reservations irrelevant with respect to CISG Part II,[26] the effect of the Article 94 reservations made by Scandinavia States relates mainly to CISG Part III. However, since it no longer seems appropriate to describe the Scandinavian States as a homogeneous group of jurisdictions which share "closely related" domestic sales law rules (i.e., as required by CISG Article 94), it has been suggested that the Scandinavian Article 94 declarations be withdrawn.[27]

§ 8.7 PRIVATE INTERNATIONAL LAW AND ARTICLE 1(1)(b)

The CISG applies to contracts for the sale of goods between parties having their relevant places of business in different States. More specifically, according to the two main rules of applicability in Article 1(1), the Convention applies (a) when these States are both CISG "Contracting States" and (b) when the rules of private international law lead to the application

---

[24] *See* Winship, *Scope* at 1–45, Honnold. *Uniform Law*, § 468, and Ziegel in 12 *Canadian Business Law Journal* 366 (1986–87).

[25] Article 93(3).

[26] The effect of the declarations made by the Scandinavian States pursuant to *Article 92* is that no Scandinavian court would apply CISG Part II vis-a-vis another Scandinavian court, and this would be true even if the Scandinavian States had not also made declarations pursuant to Article 94. Re. the Article 92 reservations *see also* § 8.4 *supra*.

[27] For additional details *see* Lookofsky, *CISG/Scandinavia*, § 8.6.

of the law of a (single) Contracting State.[28] This latter rule proved controversial and led to the declaration set forth in Article 95 whereby a State may declare upon ratification that it will not be bound by subparagraph (1)(b) of Article 1. The United States and China are prominent among those States which ratified the CISG subject to this reservation. In Europe the reservation is in force for the Czech Republic and Slovakia.

If, for example, a seller in the New York sells to a buyer in Portugal, which (as of May 2002) is a *non*-Contracting State, Article 95 means that a (state or Federal) court in New York (or elsewhere in the U.S.) is not bound to apply the Convention rules to that transaction, even if the relevant (forum) rules of private international law lead to the application of New York State law,[29] and notwithstanding the undeniable fact that the Convention, as a treaty, is part of the (U.S.) "law of the land."

Upon ratifying the Convention the government of Germany declared that it would not apply Article 1(1)(b) in respect of any State that had made an Article 95 declaration to the effect that it would not apply Article 1(1)(b). This German "declaration," while not expressly authorized by CISG Part IV, can be viewed as a statement which contains a reasonable inter-pretation of the CISG concept of "Contracting States" in Article 1(1)(b), the effect of which is to exclude from that concept States which have made Article 95 declarations.[30]

Given the number of variables (parties' places of business, situs of forum court, appli-cable private international law), the number of possible permutations involving Article 1(1)(b) and the Article 95 reservation is large.[31]

§ 8.8   PRESERVATION OF FORMAL REQUIREMENTS

Article 11 dispenses with the formal requirement, posed by some domestic laws, that sales contracts be in writing; the Convention also dispenses with the writing requirements as regards contract formation and contract modification.[32] But because some States still attach importance to formal requirements, Article 12 of the CISG provides that Article 11 and related rules do "not apply" where any party has his place of business in a Contracting State which has made a declaration under Article 96.[33] Argentina, Belarus, Chile, China, Estonia, Hungary, Latvia, Lithuania, Russia, and Ukraine are among the Contracting States which have made this – the most popular – CISG reservation.

---

[28] *See generally supra* §§ 2.1 ff.

[29] In the United States private international law is almost always a question of state (not Federal) law. *See* (e.g.) Lookofsky & Hertz, *Transnational Litigation,* Ch. 3.3.

[30] *Accord*: F. Ferrari, "Cross References and Editorial Analysis" of Article 1, notes 22–24 and accompanying text, available at <http://cisgw3.law.pace.edu/cisg/text/cross/cross-1.html>. *See also* § 2.4 *supra.* For criti-cism *see* Herber in von Caemmerer & Schlechtriem, *Kommentar,* Article 1, Rd.Nr. 43–45 (also in Schlechtriem, *Commentary* at *id.*); *see also* Ferrari in Schlechtriem, *Kommentar,* Art. 1, Rd.Nr. 79. Strangely, the German declaration was ignored by OLG Düsseldorf, 2 July 1993, UNILEX. According to Schlechtriem, *Int. UN-Kaufrecht,* Rd.Nr. 18, the German declaration merely restates the legal situation as it exists *ipso iure.*

[31] *See generally* Winship, *Scope* (page 1–26 ff. and the Appendix to same: p. 1–53).

[32] *See* CISG Part II and Article 29 which allows modification or termination by mere agreement.

[33] *See supra* § 2.14.

What happens when CISG State makes an Article 96 declaration, so that (e.g.) the "no writing required" rule in Article 11 does not apply? The surprising answer to this question has been explained by Professor Flechtner,[34] using the example of an oral sales contract concluded between one party doing CISG business in the United States, the other in Argentina. The fact that Argentina has made the Article 96 reservation does *not* (itself) mean that the transaction is subject to a writing requirement. Rather, the resolution of that issue will depend on a choice of law analysis. If, on the one hand, the private international law principles applied by the forum court (or an arbitral tribunal) lead to the application of Argentinian law, then the writing requirements of Argentinian domestic sales law will apply. If, however, the relevant private international law rules lead to the application of American law, then the writing requirements of U.S. domestic sales law will apply:[35] in other words, because one party is in Argentina (a Contracting State which has made an Article 96 reservation), the transaction becomes subject to the American Statute of Frauds (UCC § 2.201, which requires certain sales transactions to be in writing), even though the United States, by not making an Article 96 declaration, in effect declared its willingness to forego the writing requirement in CISG international sales!

To take another (more simple) illustration, a Hungarian court has held that a Hungarian buyer who accepted an oral offer was bound nonetheless under the CISG, notwithstanding the fact that Hungary made a declaration under Article 96. The court found that German law (the law of the seller's place of business) was generally applicable as regards the question of formal requirements. And since German law does not pose a writing requirement in connection with the sale of goods, the oral contract entered was binding under the CISG, and the Hungarian Article 96 reservation was irrelevant to the disposition of the case.[36]

---

[34] *See* Flechtner, *Several Texts*, note 36 and accompanying text. *Compare* the different (and less convincing) analysis set forth in § 8.8 of the first edition of *Understanding the CISG*.

[35] *Accord* Herber in Schlechtriem, *Commentary*, Art. 96, Rd.Nr. 3; Ferrari in Schlechtriem, *Kommentar*, Art. 96, Rd.Nr. 3.

[36] *See* Metropolitan Court of Budapest, 24 March 1992, UNILEX. *See also supra* § 3.2.

CHAPTER NINE

THE LIMITATION PERIOD IN INTERNATIONAL SALES

§ 9.1 INTRODUCTION AND OVERVIEW

The United Nations Convention on the Limitation Period in the International Sale of Goods (the "Limitation Convention" or the "LPISG") provides a uniform (4-year) statute of limitations for international sales. The LPISG determines the period during which one party can assert a sales-related claim against the other.

The original version of the Limitation Convention, adopted in 1974, met with limited success.[1] In 1980 the original version of the Limitation Convention was amended by a Protocol which was designed to harmonize it (the LPISG) with the CISG. Riding on the coattails of the CISG (which entered into force January 1, 1988), both the original and the amended versions of the Limitation Convention entered into force on August 1, 1988.[2]

So far, the list of States which have ratified the amended LPISG is much shorter that the list of CISG Contracting States, but it may prove significant for the ratification process that the United States joined the LPISG group in 1994.[3] Unless otherwise indicated, the discussion in the present chapter refers to the LPISG as amended by the 1980 Protocol.

Both in function and duration, the LPISG regime resembles § 2-725 of the American UCC.[4] In cases where the LPISG applies, the corresponding domestic statute of limitation is displaced.

The LPISG establishes and defines a limitation period – usually 4 years – within which a party to a contract for the international sale of goods must commence legal proceedings in order to assert a claim arising from that contract or relating to its breach, termination or

---

[1]   See <www.uncitral.org>. The former German Democratic Republic [East Germany] was among the States which ratified the original (unamended) LPISG, and although there is some controversy as to its continuing effect in Germany's Eastern territory, the prevailing opinion denies it: see Schlechtriem in Schlechtriem, *Kommentar*, VertragsG Art. 3, Rd.Nr. 1.

[2]   For an extensive and authoritative commentary on the 1974 LPISG, including additional editorial notes on the 1980 Protocol, see generally Sono, *Commentary on LPISG* at <http://cisgw3.law.pace.edu/cisg/biblio/sono1.html>. See also Sono, *Limitation Convention*.

[3]   As of June 2003 the *LPISG Convention as amended by the Protocol* had entered into force in the following States: Argentina, Belarus, Cuba, Czech Republic, Egypt, Guinea, Hungary, Mexico, Poland, Republic of Moldova, Romania, Slovakia, Slovenia, Uganda, USA, Uruguay and Zambia. For updated information see <www.uncitral.org>. See also id. for the somewhat longer list of States which have ratified the (original) unamended Convention; see also supra with notes 1 and 2.

[4]   UCC § 2-725(1) provides that "[a]n action for breach of any contract for sale must be commenced within four years after the cause of action has accrued." Under subsection (2) a cause of action for breach of warranty ordinarily accrues upon "tender of delivery," but suits for damages for failure to pay or tender accrue when payment or tender is due. See generally White & Summers, *Uniform Commercial Code*, § 11-9.

invalidity. No claim shall be recognized or enforced in any legal proceedings commenced after the expiration of the limitation period.

The LPISG does not affect a rule such as that set forth in CISG Article 39: the rule whereby a buyer who fails to give notice of non-conformity to the seller within a given (reasonable or 2-year) period of time loses the right to rely on (demand a remedy for) a breach.[5] In other words, a buyer who fails to comply with Article 39 will lose his right to rely (including the right to sue) long before the 4-year LPISG period has run.

Like the CISG, the LPISG treaty sets forth a gap-filling regime. Although the 4-year limitation period set forth in the LPISG cannot be modified by the agreement of the parties, the parties do have the freedom to contract out of the LPISG altogether.[6]

§ 9.2 FIELD OF APPLICATION

The scope and applicability of the LPISG coincides in large measure with that of the CISG. To determine whether the Limitation Convention applies in a given situation – i.e., whether we are within or without the LPISG – we can ask the following questions (similar to those asked previously in relation to the CISG):[7]

– Does the Limitation Convention apply by virtue of the *internationality* criterion?
– Is this an LPISG *sale of goods*?
– Is the particular issue or matter in question *governed by* the LPISG?
– Have the parties exercised their freedom to *contract out* of the LPISG?

First, as regards internationality, the LPISG (as amended) establishes a two-pronged test in Article 3(1): the LPISG applies (a) when both parties in an international sale of goods have their places of business in different Contracting LPISG States, or (b) when the rules of private international law point to the law of a (single) LPISG Contracting State. This dual LPISG criterion coincides with the similar test in the CISG.[8]

As is the case under the similar CISG rule, the LPISG permits Contracting States to opt out of the rule in subparagraph (b).[9] The United States ratified the LPISG subject to a declaration (reservation) whereby the U.S. is not bound by the private international law rule in subparagraph (b). So if an American court is asked to rule (e.g.) on the timeliness of a claim made by an American seller against a buyer in Sweden, which has not ratified the LPISG, the court would be obliged to choose the relevant national statute of limitation (presumably the UCC).[10] On the other hand, courts in a State like Sweden, which has not

---

5   *See* LPISG Article 1(1) and *supra* § 4.9 and § 4.10.
6   *Accord* Spanogle & Winship, *International Sales Law* at 309.
7   *See supra* § 2.1.
8   *See supra* §§ 2.2 ff.
9   Article 3(1)(b) of the LPISG is a new rule added by virtue of the 1980 Protocol. States which have only ratified the original LPISG can only apply the rule in Article 3(1)(a).
10   But for the declaration, the relevant American rule of private international law might, in the example given here, have led to the application of the law of an LPISG Contracting State (USA), with the result that the LPISG (and not UCC § 2-725) would apply.

ratified the Limitation Convention, may still end up applying the Convention rules in cases where the relevant private international law rules point to the application of the law of a LPISG Contracting State.[11]

Having passed this hurdle, we ask whether the transaction in question is a sale of goods under the LPISG. Following the CISG technique, the LPISG does not provide a positive definition of this phrase;[12] instead, the Limitation Convention tells us what a LPISG sale of goods is *not*.

As under the CISG, a consumer sale will usually fall outside the LPISG. Also excluded are sales by auction, forced sales, sales of negotiable instruments, ships (aircraft, etc.) and electricity, contracts of manufacture where the buyer supplies a substantial part of the raw materials, and mixed (goods and services) transactions where the sale of goods is but a minor element.[13]

The next question is whether the particular issue or matter is governed by the LPISG. The starting point here is Article 1, with coverage extending to inter-partes claims "arising from" an international sales contract or "relating to its breach, termination or invalidity." Unlike the CISG, validity-claims are thus clearly within the LPISG scope.[14] As with the CISG, however, the LPISG does not apply to death and personal injury claims.[15] Nor does the Limitation Convention apply to claims based on nuclear damage caused by the goods sold, security interests in property, judgments or awards, documents which support direct execution, or promissory notes.[16]

Last but not least, we must ask whether the parties have exercised their (somewhat limited) freedom to contract out of the LPISG. The Limitation Convention requires that this be done by an *express* provision in the contract:[17] it seems that the safest (and perhaps the only sure) way to contract out is to mention the LPISG by name.[18]

While it is thus possible to expressly contract out of the (entire) LPISG, it is *not* possible to remain within the regime and at the same time effectively vary the 4-year LPISG limitation period (e.g.) by a clause which purports to bar litigation not commenced within 1 year after a creditor's claim accrues; similar clauses relating to arbitration, however, provide an exception to the rule.[19]

---

[11] Though not if the rules point to a State like the U.S. which has made a reservation in respect of Article 3(1)(b). *Compare supra* § 2.4 with note 26 and Illustration 2d.

[12] As regards the CISG delimitation of "sale of goods" *see supra* § 2.5

[13] Articles 4 and 6. Re. the corresponding CISG rules *see supra* § 2.5.

[14] *Compare* Article 4(a) of the CISG, *supra* § 4.2.

[15] Article 5(a). Re. Article 5 of the CISG *see supra* § 2.6.

[16] *See* Article 5 (b)–(f). Some, but not all of the claims excluded here would also fall outside the CISG scope. Security interests, for example, are property rights under CISG Article 4(b).

[17] Article 3(2).

[18] A more general clause choosing (e.g.) California law would not do the job, since the LPISG *is* the law of that State as regards the statute of limitations for international sales.

[19] By virtue of Article 22(3) the general Article 22(1) rule does "not affect the validity of a clause in the contract of sale which stipulates that arbitral proceedings shall be commenced within a period shorter than 4 years, provided that such a clause is valid under the law applicable to the contract of sale." Presumably, such a

§ 9.3 THE LIMITATION PERIOD: DURATION, CESSATION, GENERAL LIMIT, CONSEQUENCES

The (binding) 4-year limitation period under the LPISG is set forth in Article 8. The limitation period begins to run on the date the claim in question accrues.[20] A breach of contract claim generally accrues on the date of breach; however, claims which arise from defective or non-conforming goods accrue cn the date the goods are actually handed over to the buyer.[21] A fraud claim accrues upon discovery.[22] In certain situations, the LPISG provides a special rule which defines the commencement of the 4-year limitation period. This is true in cases where the seller guarantees the goods for a certain period of time;[23] where a party, in accordance with applicable substantive (e.g. CISG) law, declares the contract terminated prior to the time for performance;[24] and in the case of contracts which provide for delivery or payment by installments.[25]

Article 23 sets forth an ultimate limitation period, in that the period shall in any event expire not later than ten (10) years from the date on which it commenced to run under Articles 9–12.

The LPISG limitation period ceases to run when the creditor performs an act which serves to institute judicial proceedings. To determine what act serves this purpose, the LPISG refers to the national law of the forum court.[26] Where the parties have agreed to arbitration, the period ceases to run when arbitral proceedings are begun.[27] The Limitation Convention also sets forth special cessation rules in respect of the debtor's death or bankruptcy, in respect of counterclaims, and in a variety of other special circumstances.[28]

---

clause would also have to pass muster under the applicable *lex arbitri*, which would not necessarily correspond to law of the contract: *see, e.g.,* Lookofsky & Hertz, *Transnational Litigation*, Ch. 6.2.3.

[20] Article 9.

[21] Or the date tender is refused. *See* Article 10(1)–(2).

[22] Or when the fraud reasonably could have been discovered: *see* Article 10(3).

[23] The limitation period in such cases commences on the date on which the buyer notifies the seller of the fact on which the claim is based, but not later than on the date of the expiration of the period of the undertaking: Article 11.

[24] Under Article 12(1) the period in respect of such a claim commences on the date on which the declaration is made to the other party, or if the contract is not declared terminated before performance becomes due, on the date on which performance is due. As regards (e.g.) buyer's avoidance upon seller's breach under CISG Article 49 *see supra* § 6.8.

[25] Article 12(2).

[26] Article 13.

[27] In the manner provided in the contract or by the applicable law (*lex arbitri*): Article 14(1). A default rule is provided in Article 14(2).

[28] *See generally* Article 15 (death, bankruptcy, etc.), Article 16 (counterclaims), Article 17 (no binding decision on merits), Article 18 (joint and several liability, proceedings by subpurchaser), Article 19 (act serving to recommence limitation period), Article 20 (debtor's acknowledgement), Article 21 (commencement prevented by "force majeure").

Although the limitation period cannot be modified by any declaration or agreement between the parties, the debtor may, during the running of the period, extend the period by a written declaration to the creditor.[29]

The consequence of the expiration of the limitation period is that "no claim shall be recognized or enforced in any legal proceedings commenced thereafter."[30] One party may, however, rely on his claim as a defense or, in certain circumstances, for the purpose of a set-off against a claim asserted by the other.[31] And it is in any event up to the parties to invoke the limitation period; the court shall not do so of its own accord.[32]

---

[29]   *See* Article 22(1)–(2). Re. arbitration clauses providing for a shorter commencement period *see* Article 22(3) and text *supra* with note 20.

[30]   Article 25(1). The obligation to pay interest on a debt expires with the debt itself (Article 27). A debtor who performs after the expiration of the limitation period is not entitled to restitution: Article 24.

[31]   Under Article 25(2) a party may rely on a claim for set-off purposes, if both claims relate to the "same contract or to several contracts concluded in the course of the same transaction," or if the claims could have been set-off at any time before the expiration of the limitation period.

[32]   Article 24.

NATIONS ADHERING TO THE CISG

Table of nations adhering to the CISG and the dates when the Convention came, or will come into force in respect of them on or before 1 November 2003 .
For additional information, including reservations, see "Status of Texts" at <http://www. uncitral.org>

State	Accession/Ratification	Entry into Force
Argentina	19 July 1983	1 January 1988
Australia	17 March 1988	1 April 1989
Austria	29 December 1987	1 January 1989
Belarus	9 October 1989	1 November 1990
Belgium	31 October 1996	1 November 1997
Bosnia and Herzegovina	12 January 1994	6 March 1992
Bulgaria	9 July 1990	1 August 1991
Burundi	4 September 1998	1 October 1999
Canada	23 April 1991	1 May 1992
Chile	7 February 1990	1 March 1991
China	11 December 1986	1 January 1988
Columbia	10 July 2001	1 August 2002
Croatia	8 June 1998	8 October 1991
Cuba	2 November 1994	1 December 1995
Czech Republic	30 September 1993	1 January 1993
Denmark	14 February 1989	1 March 1990
Ecuador	27 January 1992	1 February 1993
Egypt	6 December 1982	1 January 1988
Estonia	20 September 1993	1 October 1994
Finland	15 December 1987	1 January 1989
France	6 August 1982	1 January 1988
Georgia	16 August 1994	1 September 1995
Germany	21 December 1989	1 January 1991
Greece	12 January 1998	1 February 1999
Guinea	23 January 1991	1 February 1992
Honduras	10 October 2002	1 November 2003
Hungary	16 June 1983	1 January 1988
Iceland	10 May 2001	1 June 2002
Iraq	5 March 1990	1 April 1991
Israel	22 January 2002	1 February 2003

Italy	11 December 1986	1 January 1988
Kyrgyzstan	11 May 1999	1 June 2000
Latvia	31 July 1997	1 August 1998
Lesotho	18 June 1981	1 January 1988
Lithuania	18 January 1995	1 February 1996
Luxembourg	30 January 1997	1 February 1998
Mauritania	20 August 1999	1 Septermber 2000
Mexico	29 December 1987	1 January 1989
Mongolia	31 December 1997	1 January 1999
Netherlands	13 December 1990	1 January 1992
New Zealand	22 September 1994	1 October 1995
Norway	20 July 1988	1 August 1989
Peru	25 March 1999	1 April 2000
Poland	19 May 1995	1 June 1996
Republic of Moldova	13 October 1994	1 November 1995
Romania	22 May 1991	1 June 1992
Russian Federation	16 August 1990	1 September 1991
Saint Vincent & the Grenadines	12 September 2000	1 October 2001
Singapore	16 February 1995	1 March 1996
Slovakia	28 May 1993	1 January 1993
Slovenia	7 January 1994	25 June 1991
Spain	24 July 1990	1 August 1991
Sweden	15 December 1987	1 January 1989
Switzerland	21 February 1990	1 March 1991
Syrian Arab Republic	19 October 1982	1 January 1988
Uganda	12 February 1992	1 March 1993
Ukraine	3 January 1990	1 February 1991
United States of America	11 December 1986	1 January 1988
Uruguay	25 January 1999	1 February 2000
Uzbekistan	27 November 1996	1 December 1997
Yugoslavia	12 March 2001	27 April 1992
Zambia	6 June 1986	1 January 1988

UNITED NATIONS CONVENTION ON CONTRACTS FOR THE INTERNATIONAL SALE OF GOODS (1980)

Official (English) Convention Text

THE STATES PARTIES TO THIS CONVENTION,

BEARING IN MIND the broad objectives in the resolutions adopted by the sixth special session of the General Assembly of the United Nations on the establishment of a new International Economic Order,

CONSIDERING that the development of international trade on the basis of equality and mutual benefit is an important element in promoting friendly relations among States,

BEING OF THE OPINION that the adoption of uniform rules which govern contracts for the international sale of goods and take into account the different social, economic and legal systems would contribute to the removal of legal barriers in international trade and promote the development of international trade,

HAVE AGREED as follows:

PART I
Sphere of Application and General Provisions

Chapter I
SPHERE OF APPLICATION

Article 1

(1) This Convention applies to contracts of sale of goods between parties whose places of business are in different States:
   (a) when the States are Contracting States; or
   (b) when the rules of private international law lead to the application of the law of a Contracting State.
(2) The fact that the parties have their places of business in different States is to be disregarded whenever this fact does not appear either from the contract or from any dealings between, or from information disclosed by, the parties at any time before or at the conclusion of the contract.

(3) Neither the nationality of the parties nor the civil or commercial character of the parties or of the contract is to be taken into consideration in determining the application of this Convention.

Article 2

This Convention does not apply to sales:

(a) of goods bought for personal, family or household use, unless the seller, at any time before or at the conclusion of the contract, neither knew nor ought to have known that the goods were bought for any such use;
(b) by auction;
(c) on execution or otherwise by authority of law;
(d) of stocks, shares, investment securities, negotiable instruments or money;
(e) of ships, vessels, hovercraft or aircraft;
(f) of electricity.

Article 3

(1) Contracts for the supply of goods to be manufactured or produced are to be considered sales unless the party who orders the goods undertakes to supply a substantial part of the materials necessary for such manufacture or production.
(2) This Convention does not apply to contracts in which the preponderant part of the obligations of the party who furnishes the goods consists in the supply of labour or other services.

Article 4

This Convention governs only the formation of the contract of sale and the rights and obligations of the seller and the buyer arising from such a contract. In particular, except as otherwise expressly provided in this Convention, it is not concerned with:

(a) the validity of the contract or of any of its provisions or of any usage;
(b) the effect which the contract may have on the property in the goods sold.

Article 5

This Convention does not apply to the liability of the seller for death or personal injury caused by the goods to any person.   NO TORTS

Article 6

The parties may exclude the application of this Convention or, subject to article 12, derogate from or vary the effect of any of its provisions.

Chapter II
GENERAL PROVISIONS

Article 7

(1) In the interpretation of this Convention, regard is to be had to its international character and to the need to promote uniformity in its application and the observance of good faith in international trade.

(2) Questions concerning matters governed by this Convention which are not expressly settled in it are to be settled in conformity with the general principles on which it is based or, in the absence of such principles, in conformity with the law applicable by virtue of the rules of private international law.

Article 8

(1) For the purposes of this Convention statements made by and other conduct of a party are to be interpreted according to his intent where the other party knew or could not have been unaware what that intent was.

(2) If the preceding paragraph is not applicable, statements made by and other conduct of a party are to be interpreted according to the understanding that a reasonable person of the same kind as the other party would have had in the same circumstances.

(3) In determining the intent of a party or the understanding a reasonable person would have had, due consideration is to be given to all relevant circumstances of the case including the negotiations, any practices which the parties have established between themselves, usages and any subsequent conduct of the parties.

Article 9

(1) The parties are bound by any usage to which they have agreed and by any practices which they have established between themselves.

(2) The parties are considered, unless otherwise agreed, to have impliedly made applicable to their contract or its formation a usage of which the parties knew or ought to have known and which in international trade is widely known to, and regularly observed by, parties to contracts of the type involved in the particular trade concerned.

Article 10

For the purposes of this Convention:

(a) if a party has more than one place of business, the place of the business is that which has the closest relationship to the contract and its performance, having regard to the circumstances known to or contemplated by the parties at any time before or at the conclusion of the contract;

(b) if a party does not have a place of business, reference is to be made to his habitual residence.

Article 11

A contract of sale need not be concluded in or evidenced by writing and is not subject to any other requirement as to form. It may be proved by any means, including witnesses.

Article 12

Any provision of article 11, article 29 or Part II of this Convention that allows a contract of sale or its modification or termination by agreement or any offer, acceptance or other indication of intention to be made in any form other than in writing does not apply where any party has his place of business in a Contracting State which has made a declaration under article 96 of this Convention. The parties may not derogate from or vary the effect of this article.

Article 13

For the purposes of this Convention "writing" includes telegram and telex.

PART II
Formation of the Contract

Article 14

(1) A proposal for concluding a contract addressed to one or more specific persons constitutes an offer if it is sufficiently definite and indicates the intention of the offeror to be bound in case of acceptance. A proposal is sufficiently definite if it indicates the goods and expressly or implicitly fixes or makes provision for determining the quantity and the price.
(2) A proposal other than one addressed to one or more specific persons is to be considered merely as an invitation to make offers, unless the contrary is clearly indicated by the person making the proposal.

Article 15

(1) An offer becomes effective when it reaches the offeree.
(2) An offer, even if it is irrevocable, may be withdrawn if the withdrawal reaches the offeree before or at the same time as the offer.

Article 16

(1) Until a contract is concluded an offer may be revoked if the revocation reaches the offeree before he has dispatched an acceptance.
(2) However, an offer cannot be revoked:
   (a) if it indicates, whether by stating a fixed time for acceptance or otherwise, that it is irrevocable; or
   (b) if it was reasonable for the offeree to rely on the offer as being irrevocable and the offeree has acted in reliance on the offer.

Article 17

An offer, even if it is irrevocable, is terminated when a rejection reaches the offeror.

Article 18

(1) A statement made by or other conduct of the offeree indicating assent to an offer is an acceptance. Silence or inactivity does not in itself amount to acceptance.
(2) An acceptance of an offer becomes effective at the moment the indication of assent reaches the offeror. An acceptance is not effective if the indication of assent does not reach the offeror within the time he has fixed or, if no time is fixed, within a reasonable

time, due account being taken of the circumstances of the transaction, including the rapidity of the means of communication employed by the offeror. An oral offer must be accepted immediately unless the circumstances indicate otherwise.

(3) However, if, by virtue of the offer or as a result of practices which the parties have established between themselves or of usage, the offeree may indicate assent by performing an act, such as one relating to the dispatch of the goods or payment of the price, without notice to the offeror, the acceptance is effective at the moment the act is performed, provided that the act is performed within the period of time laid down in the preceding paragraph.

Article 19

(1) A reply to an offer which purports to be an acceptance but contains additions, limitations or other modifications is a rejection of the offer and constitutes a counter-offer.

(2) However, a reply to an offer which purports to be an acceptance but contains additional or different terms which do not materially alter the terms of the offer constitutes an acceptance, unless the offeror, without undue delay, objects orally to the discrepancy or dispatches a notice to that effect. If he does not so object, the terms of the contract are the terms of the offer with the modifications contained in the acceptance.

(3) Additional or different terms relating, among other things, to the price, payment, quality and quantity of the goods, place and time of delivery, extent of one party's liability to the other or the settlement of disputes are considered to alter the terms of the offer materially.

Article 20

(1) A period of time for acceptance fixed by the offeror in a telegram or a letter begins to run from the moment the telegram is handed in for dispatch or from the date shown on the letter or, if no such date is shown, from the date shown on the envelope. A period of time for acceptance fixed by the offeror by telephone, telex or other means of instantaneous communication, begins to run from the moment that the offer reaches the offeree.

(2) Official holidays or non-business days occurring during the period for acceptance are included in calculating the period. However, if a notice of acceptance cannot be delivered at the address of the offeror on the last day of the period because that day falls on an official holiday or a non-business day at the place of business of the offeror, the period is extended until the first business day which follows.

Article 21

(1) A late acceptance is nevertheless effective as an acceptance if without delay the offeror orally so informs the offeree or dispatches a notice to that effect.

(2) If a letter or other writing containing a late acceptance shows that it has been sent in such circumstances that if its transmission had been normal it would have reached the offeror in due time, the late acceptance is effective as an acceptance unless, without delay, the offeror orally informs the offeree that he considers his offer as having lapsed or dispatches a notice to that effect.

Article 22

An acceptance may be withdrawn if the withdrawal reaches the offeror before or at the same time as the acceptance would have become effective.

Article 23

A contract is concluded at the moment when an acceptance of an offer becomes effective in accordance with the provisions of this Convention.

Article 24

For the purposes of this part of the Convention, an offer, declaration of acceptance or any other indication of intention "reaches" the addressee when it is made orally to him or delivered by any other means to him personally, to his place of business or mailing address or, if he does not have a place of business or mailing address, to his habitual residence.

PART III
Sale of Goods

Chapter I
GENERAL PROVISIONS

Article 25

A breach of contract committed by one of the parties is fundamental if it results in such detriment to the other party as substantially to deprive him of what he is entitled to expect under the contract, unless the party in breach did not foresee and a reasonable person of the same kind in the same circumstances would not have foreseen such a result.

Article 26

A declaration of avoidance of the contract is effective only if made by notice to the other party.

Article 27

Unless otherwise expressly provided in this Part of the Convention, if any notice, request or other communication is given or made by a party in accordance with this Part and by means appropriate in the circumstances, a delay or error in the transmission of the communication or its failure to arrive does not deprive that party of the right to rely on the communication.

Article 28

If, in accordance with the provisions of this Convention, one party is entitled to require performance of any obligation by the other party, a court is not bound to enter a judgement for specific performance unless the court would do so under its own law in respect of similar contracts of sale not governed by this Convention.

Article 29

(1) A contract may be modified or terminated by the mere agreement of the parties.
(2) A contract in writing which contains a provision requiring any modification or termination by agreement to be in writing may not be otherwise modified or terminated by
agreement. However, a party may be precluded by his conduct from asserting such a
provision to the extent that the other party has relied on that conduct.

Chapter II
OBLIGATIONS OF THE SELLER

Article 30

The seller must deliver the goods, hand over any documents relating to them and transfer
the property in the goods, as required by the contract and this Convention.

Section I. Delivery of the goods and handing over of documents

Article 31

If the seller is not bound to deliver the goods at any other particular place, his obligation
to deliver consists:

(a) if the contract of sale involves carriage of the goods – in handing the goods over to the
first carrier for transmission to the buyer;
(b) if, in cases not within the preceding subparagraph, the contract relates to specific
goods, or unidentified goods to be drawn from a specific stock or to be manufactured
or produced, and at the time of the conclusion of the contract the parties knew that the
goods were at, or were to be manufactured or produced at a particular place – in
placing the goods at the buyer's disposal at that place;
(c) in other cases – in placing the goods at the buyer's disposal at the place where the seller
had his place of business at the time of the conclusion of the contract.

Article 32

(1) If the seller, in accordance with the contract or this Convention, hands the goods over
to a carrier and if the goods are not clearly identified to the contract by markings on
the goods, by shipping documents or otherwise, the seller must give the buyer notice
of the consignment specifying the goods.
(2) If the seller is bound to arrange for carriage of the goods, he must make such contracts
as are necessary for carriage to the place fixed by means of transportation appropriate
in the circumstances and according to the usual terms for such transportation.
(3) If the seller is not bound to effect insurance in respect of the carriage of goods, he
must, at the buyer's request, provide him with all available information necessary to
enable him to effect such insurance.

Article 33

The seller must deliver the goods:

(a) if a date is fixed by or determinable from the contract, on that date;

(b) if a period of time is fixed by or determinable from the contract, at any time within that period unless circumstances indicate that the buyer is to choose a date; or

(c) in any other case, within a reasonable time after the conclusion of the contract.

Article 34

If the seller is bound to hand over documents relating to the goods, he must hand them over at the time and place and in the form required by the contract. If the seller has handed over documents before that time, he may, up to that time, cure any lack of conformity in the documents, if the exercise of this right does not cause the buyer unreasonable inconvenience or unreasonable expense. However, the buyer retains any right to claim damages as provided for in this Convention.

Section II. Conformity of the goods and third party claims

Article 35

(1) The seller must deliver goods which are of the quantity, quality and description required by the contract and which are contained or packaged in the manner required by the contract.

(2) Except where the parties have agreed otherwise, the goods do not conform with the contract unless they:

    (a) are fit for the purposes for which goods of the same description would ordinarily be used;

    (b) are fit for any particular purpose expressly or impliedly made known to the seller at the time of the conclusion of the contract, except where the circumstances show that the buyer did not rely, or that it was unreasonable for him to rely, on the seller's skill and judgement;

    (c) possess the qualities of goods which the seller has held out to the buyer as a sample or model;

    (d) are contained or packaged in the manner usual for such goods or, where there is no such manner, in a manner adequate to preserve and protect the goods.

(3) The seller is not liable under subparagraphs (a) to (d) of the preceding paragraph for any lack of conformity of the goods if at the time of the conclusion of the contract the buyer knew or could not have been unaware of such lack of conformity.

Article 36

(1) The seller is liable in accordance with the contract and this Convention for any lack of conformity which exists at the time when the risk passes to the buyer, even though the lack of conformity becomes apparent only after that time.

(2) The seller is also liable for any lack of conformity which occurs after the time indicated in the preceding paragraph and which is due to a breach of any of his obligations, including a breach of any guarantee that for a period of time the goods will remain fit for their ordinary purpose or for some particular purpose or will retain specified qualities or characteristics.

Article 37

If the seller has delivered goods before the date for delivery, he may, up to that date, deliver any missing part or make up any deficiency in the quantity of the goods delivered, or deliver goods in replacement of any non-conforming goods delivered or remedy any lack of conformity in the goods delivered, provided that the exercise of this right does not cause the buyer unreasonable inconvenience or unreasonable expense. However, the buyer retains any right to claim damages as provided for in this Convention.

Article 38

(1) The buyer must examine the goods, or cause them to be examined, within as short a period as is practicable in the circumstances.

(2) If the contract involves carriage of the goods, examination may be deferred until after the goods have arrived at their destination.

(3) If the goods are redirected in transit or redispatched by the buyer without a reasonable opportunity for examination by him and at the time of the conclusion of the contract the seller knew or ought to have known of the possibility of such redirection or redispatch, examination may be deferred until after the goods have arrived at the new destination.

Article 39

(1) The buyer loses the right to rely on a lack of conformity of the goods if he does not give notice to the seller specifying the nature of the lack of conformity within a reasonable time after he has discovered it or ought to have discovered it.

(2) In any event, the buyer loses the right to rely on a lack of conformity of the goods if he does not give the seller notice thereof at the latest within a period of two years from the date on which the goods were actually handed over to the buyer, unless this time-limit is inconsistent with a contractual period of guarantee.

Article 40

The seller is not entitled to rely on the provisions of articles 38 and 39 if the lack of conformity relates to facts of which he knew or could not have been unaware and which he did not disclose to the buyer.

Article 41

The seller must deliver goods which are free from any right or claim of a third party, unless the buyer agreed to take the goods subject to that right or claim. However, if such right or claim is based on industrial property or other intellectual property, the seller's obligation is governed by article 42.

Article 42

(1) The seller must deliver goods which are free from any right or claim of a third party based on industrial property or other intellectual property, of which at the time of the conclusion of the contract the seller knew or could not have been unaware, provided that the right or claim is based on industrial property or other intellectual property:

(a) under the law of the State where the goods will be resold or otherwise used, if it was contemplated by the parties at the time of the conclusion of the contract that the goods would be resold or otherwise used in that State; or

(b) in any other case, under the law of the State where the buyer has his place of business.

(2) The obligation of the seller under the preceding paragraph does not extend to cases where:

(a) at the time of the conclusion of the contract the buyer knew or could not have been unaware of the right or claim; or

(b) the right or claim results from the seller's compliance with technical drawings, designs, formulae or other such specifications furnished by the buyer.

Article 43

(1) The buyer loses the right to rely on the provisions of article 41 or article 42 if he does not give notice to the seller specifying the nature of the right or claim of the third party within a reasonable time after he has become aware or ought to have become aware of the right or claim.

(2) The seller is not entitled to rely on the provisions of the preceding paragraph if he knew of the right or claim of the third party and the nature of it.

Article 44

Notwithstanding the provisions of paragraph (1) of article 39 and paragraph (1) of article 43, the buyer may reduce the price in accordance with article 50 or claim damages, except for loss of profit, if he has a reasonable excuse for his failure to give the required notice.

Section III. Remedies for Breach of Contract by the Seller

Article 45

(1) If the seller fails to perform any of his obligations under the contract or this Convention, the buyer may:

(a) exercise the rights provided in articles 46 to 52;

(b) claim damages as provided in articles 74 to 77.

(2) The buyer is not deprived of any right he may have to claim damages by exercising his right to other remedies.

(3) No period of grace may be granted to the seller by a court or arbitral tribunal when the buyer resorts to a remedy for breach of contract.

Article 46

(1) The buyer may require performance by the seller of his obligations unless the buyer has resorted to a remedy which is inconsistent with this requirement.

(2) If the goods do not conform with the contract, the buyer may require delivery of substitute goods only if the lack of conformity constitutes a fundamental breach of contract and a request for substitute goods is made either in conjunction with notice given under article 39 or within a reasonable time thereafter.

(3) If the goods do not conform with the contract, the buyer may require the seller to remedy the lack of conformity by repair, unless this is unreasonable having regard to all the circumstances. A request for repair must be made either in conjunction with notice given under article 39 or within a reasonable time thereafter.

Article 47

(1) The buyer may fix an additional period of time of reasonable length for performance by the seller of his obligations.
(2) Unless the buyer has received notice from the seller that he will not perform within the period so fixed, the buyer may not, during that period, resort to any remedy for breach of contract. However, the buyer is not deprived thereby of any right he may have to claim damages for delay in performance.

Article 48

(1) Subject to article 49, the seller may, even after the date for delivery, remedy at his own expense any failure to perform his obligations, if he can do so without unreasonable delay and without causing the buyer unreasonable inconvenience or uncertainty of reimbursement by the seller of expenses advanced by the buyer. However, the buyer retains any right to claim damages as provided for in this Convention.
(2) If the seller requests the buyer to make known whether he will accept performance and the buyer does not comply with the request within a reasonable time, the seller may perform within the time indicated in his request. The buyer may not, during that period of time, resort to any remedy which is inconsistent with performance by the seller.
(3) A notice by the seller that he will perform within a specified period of time is assumed to include a request, under the preceding paragraph, that the buyer make known his decision.
(4) A request or notice by the seller under paragraph (2) or (3) of this article is not effective unless received by the buyer.

Article 49

(1) The buyer may declare the contract avoided:
    (a) if the failure by the seller to perform any of his obligations under the contract or this Convention amounts to a fundamental breach of contract; or
    (b) in case of non-delivery, if the seller does not deliver the goods within the additional period of time fixed by the buyer in accordance with paragraph (1) of article 47 or declares that he will not deliver within the period so fixed.
(2) However, in cases where the seller has delivered the goods, the buyer loses the right to declare the contract avoided unless he does so:
    (a) in respect of late delivery, within a reasonable time after he has become aware that delivery has been made;
    (b) in respect of any breach other than late delivery, within a reasonable time:
        (i) after he knew or ought to have known of the breach;

    (ii) after the expiration of any additional period of time fixed by the buyer in accordance with paragraph (1) of article 47, or after the seller has declared that he will not perform his obligations within such an additional period; or

    (iii) after the expiration of any additional period of time indicated by the seller in accordance with paragraph (2) of article 48, or after the buyer has declared that he will not accept performance.

Article 50

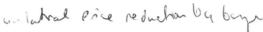

If the goods do not conform with the contract and whether or not the price has already been paid, the buyer may reduce the price in the same proportion as the value that the goods actually delivered had at the time of the delivery bears to the value that conforming goods would have had at that time. However, if the seller remedies any failure to perform his obligations in accordance with article 37 or article 48 or if the buyer refuses to accept performance by the seller in accordance with those articles, the buyer may not reduce the price.

Article 51

(1) If the seller delivers only a part of the goods or if only a part of the goods delivered is in conformity with the contract, articles 46 to 50 apply in respect of the part which is missing or which does not conform.

(2) The buyer may declare the contract avoided in its entirety only if the failure to make delivery completely or in conformity with the contract amounts to a fundamental breach of the contract.

Article 52

(1) If the seller delivers the goods before the date fixed, the buyer may take delivery or refuse to take delivery.

(2) If the seller delivers a quantity of goods greater than that provided for in the contract, the buyer may take delivery or refuse to take delivery of the excess quantity. If the buyer takes delivery of all or part of the excess quantity, he must pay for it at the contract rate.

Chapter III
OBLIGATIONS OF THE BUYER

Article 53

The buyer must pay the price for the goods and take delivery of them as required by the contract and this Convention.

Section I. Payment of the price

Article 54

The buyer's obligation to pay the price includes taking such steps and complying with such formalities as may be required under the contract or any laws and regulations to enable payment to be made.

Article 55

Where a contract has been validly concluded but does not expressly or implicitly fix or make provision for determining the price, the parties are considered, in the absence of any indication to the contrary, to have impliedly made reference to the price generally charged at the time of the conclusion of the contract for such goods sold under comparable circumstances in the trade concerned.

Article 56

If the price is fixed according to the weight of the goods, in case of doubt it is to be determined by the net weight.

Article 57

(1) If the buyer is not bound to pay the price at any other particular place, he must pay it to the seller:
(a) at the seller's place of business; or
(b) if the payment is to be made against the handing over of the goods or of documents, at the place where the handing over takes place.
(2) The seller must bear any increase in the expenses incidental to payment which is caused by a change in his place of business subsequent to the conclusion of the contract.

Article 58

(1) If the buyer is not bound to pay the price at any other specific time, he must pay it when the seller places either the goods or documents controlling their disposition at the buyer's disposal in accordance with the contract and this Convention. The seller may make such payment a condition for handing over the goods or documents.
(2) If the contract involves carriage of the goods, the seller may dispatch the goods on terms whereby the goods, or documents controlling their disposition, will not be handed over to the buyer except against payment of the price.
(3) The buyer is not bound to pay the price until he has had an opportunity to examine the goods, unless the procedures for delivery or payment agreed upon by the parties are inconsistent with his having such an opportunity.

Article 59

The buyer must pay the price on the date fixed by or determinable from the contract and this Convention without the need for any request or compliance with any formality on the part of the seller.

Section II. Taking delivery

Article 60

The buyer's obligation to take delivery consists:

(a) in doing all the acts which could reasonably be expected of him in order to enable the seller to make delivery; and
(b) in taking over the goods.

Section III. Remedies for breach of contract by the buyer

Article 61

(1) If the buyer fails to perform any of his obligations under the contract or this Convention, the seller may:
   (a) exercise the rights provided in articles 62 to 65;
   (b) claim damages as provided in articles 74 to 77.
(2) The seller is not deprived of any right he may have to claim damages by exercising his right to other remedies.
(3) No period of grace may be granted to the buyer by a court or arbitral tribunal when the seller resorts to a remedy for breach of contract.

Article 62

The seller may require the buyer to pay the price, take delivery or perform his other obligations, unless the seller has resorted to a remedy which is inconsistent with this requirement.

Article 63

(1) The seller may fix an additional period of time of reasonable length for performance by the buyer of his obligations.
(2) Unless the seller has received notice from the buyer that he will not perform within the period so fixed, the seller may not, during that period, resort to any remedy for breach of contract. However, the seller is not deprived thereby of any right he may have to claim damages for delay in performance.

Article 64

(1) The seller may declare the contract avoided:
   (a) if the failure by the buyer to perform any of his obligations under the contract or this Convention amounts to a fundamental breach of contract; or
   (b) if the buyer does not, within the additional period of time fixed by the seller in accordance with paragraph (1) of article 63, perform his obligation to pay the price or take delivery of the goods, or if he declares that he will not do to within the period so fixed.
(2) However, in cases where the buyer has paid the price, the seller loses the right to declare the contract avoided unless he does so:
   (a) in respect of late performance by the buyer, before the seller has become aware that performance has been rendered; or
   (b) in respect of any breach other than late performance by the buyer, within a reasonable time:
       (i) after the seller knew or ought to have known of the breach; or
       (ii) after the expiration of any additional period of time fixed by the seller in accordance with paragraph (1) of article 63, or after the buyer has declared that he will not perform his obligations within such an additional period.

Article 65

(1) If under the contract the buyer is to specify the form, measurement or other features of the goods and he fails to make such specification either on the date agreed upon or within a reasonable time after receipt of a request from the seller, the seller may, without prejudice to any other rights he may have, make the specification himself in accordance with the requirements of the buyer that may be known to him.

(2) If the seller makes the specification himself, he must inform the buyer of the details thereof and must fix a reasonable time within which the buyer may make a different specification. If, after receipt of such a communication, the buyer fails to do so within the time so fixed, the specification made by the seller is binding.

Chapter IV
PASSING OF RISK

Article 66

Loss of or damage to the goods after the risk has passed to the buyer does not discharge him from his obligation to pay the price, unless the loss or damage is due to an act or omission of the seller.

Article 67

(1) If the contract of sale involves carriage of the goods and the seller is not bound to hand them over at a particular place, the risk passes to the buyer when the goods are handed over to the first carrier for transmission to the buyer in accordance with the contract of sale. If the seller is bound to hand the goods over to a carrier at a particular place, the risk does not pass to the buyer until the goods are handed over to the carrier at that place. The fact that the seller is authorized to retain documents controlling the disposition of the goods does not affect the passage of the risk.

(2) Nevertheless, the risk does not pass to the buyer until the goods are clearly identified to the contract, whether by markings on the goods, by shipping documents, by notice given to the buyer or otherwise.

Article 68

The risk in respect of goods sold in transit passes to the buyer from the time of the conclusion of the contract. However, if the circumstances so indicate, the risk is assumed by the buyer from the time the goods were handed over to the carrier who issued the documents embodying the contract of carriage. Nevertheless, if at the time of the conclusion of the contract of sale the seller knew or ought to have known that the goods had been lost or damaged and did not disclose this to the buyer, the loss or damage is at the risk of the seller.

Article 69

(1) In cases not within articles 67 and 68, the risk passes to the buyer when he takes over the goods or, if he does not do so in due time, from the time when the goods are placed at his disposal and he commits a breach of contract by failing to take delivery.

(2) However, if the buyer is bound to take over the goods at a place other than a place of business of the seller, the risk passes when delivery is due and the buyer is aware of the fact that the goods are placed at his disposal at that place.

(3) If the contract relates to goods not then identified, the goods are considered not to be placed at the disposal of the buyer until they are clearly identified to the contract.

Article 70

If the seller had committed a fundamental breach of contract, articles 67, 68 and 69 do not impair the remedies available to the buyer on account of the breach.

Chapter V
PROVISIONS COMMON TO THE OBLIGATIONS OF THE SELLER AND OF THE BUYER

Section I. Anticipatory breach and instalment contracts

Article 71

(1) A party may suspend the performance of his obligations if, after the conclusion of the contract, it becomes apparent that the other party will not perform a substantial part of his obligations as a result of:
  (a) a serious deficiency in his ability to perform or in his creditworthiness; or
  (b) his conduct in preparing to perform or in performing the contract.

(2) If the seller has already dispatched the goods before the grounds described in the preceding paragraph become evident, he may prevent the handing over of the goods to the buyer even though the buyer holds a document which entitles him to obtain them. The present paragraph relates only to the rights in the goods as between the buyer and the seller.

(3) A party suspending performance, whether before or after dispatch of the goods, must immediately give notice of the suspension to the other party and must continue with performance if the other party provides adequate assurance of his performance.

Article 72

(1) If prior to the date for performance of the contract it is clear that one of the parties will commit a fundamental breach of contract, the other party may declare the contract avoided.

(2) If time allows, the party intending to declare the contract avoided must give reasonable notice to the other party in order to permit him to provide adequate assurance of his performance.

(3) The requirements of the preceding paragraph do not apply if the other party has declared that he will not perform his obligations.

Article 73

(1) In the case of a contract for delivery of goods by instalments, if the failure of one party to perform any of his obligations in respect of any instalment constitutes a fundamental

breach of contract with respect to that instalment, the other party may declare the contract avoided with respect to that instalment.

(2) If one party's failure to perform any of his obligations in respect of any instalment gives the other party good grounds to conclude that a fundamental breach of contract will occur with respect to future instalments, he may declare the contract avoided for the future, provided that he does so within a reasonable time.

(3) A buyer who declares the contract avoided in respect of any delivery may, at the same time, declare it avoided in respect of deliveries already made or of future deliveries if, by reason of their interdependence, those deliveries could not be used for the purpose contemplated by the parties at the time of the conclusion of the contract.

Section II. Damages

Article 74

Damages for breach of contract by one party consist of a sum equal to the loss, including loss of profit, suffered by the other party as a consequence of the breach. Such damages may not exceed the loss which the party in breach foresaw or ought to have foreseen at the time of the conclusion of the contract, in the light of the facts and matters of which he then knew or ought to have known, as a possible consequence of the breach of contract.

Article 75

If the contract is avoided and if, in a reasonable manner and within a reasonable time after avoidance, the buyer has bought goods in replacement or the seller has resold the goods, the party claiming damages may recover the difference between the contract price and the price in the substitute transaction as well as any further damages recoverable under article 74.

Article 76

(1) If the contract is avoided and there is a current price for the goods, the party claiming damages may, if he has not made a purchase or resale under article 75, recover the difference between the price fixed by the contract and the current price at the time of avoidance as well as any further damages recoverable under article 74. If, however, the party claiming damages has avoided the contract after taking over the goods, the current price at the time of such taking over shall be applied instead of the current price at the time of avoidance.

(2) For the purposes of the preceding paragraph, the current price is the price prevailing at the place where delivery of the goods should have been made or, if there is no current price at that place, the price at such other place as serves as a reasonable substitute, making due allowance for differences in the cost of transporting the goods.

Article 77

A party who relies on a breach of contract must take such measures as are reasonable in the circumstances to mitigate the loss, including loss of profit, resulting from the breach. If he fails to take such measures, the party in breach may claim a reduction in the damages in the amount by which the loss should have been mitigated.

Section III. Interest

Article 78

If a party fails to pay the price or any other sum that is in arrears, the other party is entitled to interest on it, without prejudice to any claim for damages recoverable under article 74.

Section IV. Exemptions

Article 79

(1) A party is not liable for a failure to perform any of his obligations if he proves that the failure was due to an impediment beyond his control and that he could not reasonably be expected to have taken the impediment into account at the time of the conclusion of the contract or to have avoided or overcome it or its consequences.

(2) If the party's failure is due to the failure by a third person whom he has engaged to perform the whole or a part of the contract, that party is exempt from liability only if:
   (a) he is exempt under the preceding paragraph; and
   (b) the person whom he has so engaged would be so exempt if the provisions of that paragraph were applied to him.

(3) The exemption provided by this article has effect for the period during which the impediment exists.

(4) The party who fails to perform must give notice to the other party of the impediment and its effects on his ability to perform. If the notice is not received by the other party within a reasonable time after the party who fails to perform knew or ought to have known of the impediment, he is liable for damages resulting from such non-receipt.

(5) Nothing in this article prevents either party from exercising any right other than to claim damages under this Convention.

Article 80

A party may not rely on a failure of the other party to perform, to the extent that such failure was caused by the first party's act or omission.

Section V. Effects of avoidance

Article 81

(1) Avoidance of the contract releases both parties from their obligations under it, subject to any damages which may be due. Avoidance does not affect any provision of the contract for the settlement of disputes or any other provision of the contract governing the rights and obligations of the parties consequent upon the avoidance of the contract.

(2) A party who has performed the contract either wholly or in part may claim restitution from the other party of whatever the first party has supplied or paid under the contract. If both parties are bound to make restitution, they must do so concurrently.

Article 82

(1) The buyer loses the right to declare the contract avoided or to require the seller to deliver substitute goods if it is impossible for him to make restitution of the goods substantially in the condition in which he received them.

(2) The preceding paragraph does not apply:

(a) if the impossibility of making restitution of the goods or of making restitution of the goods substantially in the condition in which the buyer received them is not due to his act or omission;

(b) if the goods or part of the goods have perished or deteriorated as a result of the examination provided for in article 38; or

(c) if the goods or part of the goods have been sold in the normal course of business or have been consumed or transformed by the buyer in the course of normal use before he discovered or ought to have discovered the lack of conformity.

Article 83

A buyer who has lost the right to declare the contract avoided or to require the seller to deliver substitute goods in accordance with article 82 retains all other remedies under the contract and this Convention.

Article 84

(1) If the seller is bound to refund the price, he must also pay interest on it, from the date on which the price was paid.

(2) The buyer must account to the seller for all benefits which he has derived from the goods or part of them:

(a) if he must make restitution of the goods or part of them; or

(b) if it is impossible for him to make restitution of all or part of the goods or to make restitution of all or part of the goods substantially in the condition in which he received them, but he has nevertheless declared the contract avoided or required the seller to deliver substitute goods.

Section VI. Preservation of the goods

Article 85

If the buyer is in delay in taking delivery of the goods or, where payment of the price and delivery of the goods are to be made concurrently, if he fails to pay the price, and the seller is either in possession of the goods or otherwise able to control their disposition, the seller must take such steps as are reasonable in the circumstances to preserve them. He is entitled to retain them until he has been reimbursed his reasonable expenses by the buyer.

Article 86

(1) If the buyer has received the goods and intends to exercise any right under the contract or this Convention to reject them, he must take such steps to preserve them as are

reasonable in the circumstances. He is entitled to retain them until he has been reimbursed his reasonable expenses by the seller.

(2) If goods dispatched to the buyer have been placed at his disposal at their destination and he exercises the right to reject them, he must take possession of them on behalf of the seller, provided that this can be done without payment of the price and without unreasonable inconvenience or unreasonable expense. This provision does not apply if the seller or a person authorized to take charge of the goods on his behalf is present at the destination. If the buyer takes possession of the goods under this paragraph, his rights and obligations are governed by the preceding paragraph.

Article 87

A party who is bound to take steps to preserve the goods may deposit them in a warehouse of a third person at the expense of the other party provided that the expense incurred is not unreasonable.

Article 88

(1) A party who is bound to preserve the goods in accordance with article 85 or 86 may sell them by any appropriate means if there has been an unreasonable delay by the other party in taking possession of the goods or in taking them back or in paying the price or the cost of preservation, provided that reasonable notice of the intention to sell has been given to the other party.

(2) If the goods are subject to rapid deterioration or their preservation would involve unreasonable expense, a party who is bound to preserve the goods in accordance with article 85 or 86 must take reasonable measures to sell them. To the extent possible he must give notice to the other party of his intention to sell.

(3) A party selling the goods has the right to retain out of the proceeds of sale an amount equal to the reasonable expenses of preserving the goods and of selling them. He must account to the other party for the balance.

PART IV
Final Provisions

Article 89

The Secretary-General of the United Nations is hereby designated as the depositary for this Convention.

Article 90

This Convention does not prevail over any international agreement which has already been or may be entered into and which contains provisions concerning the matters governed by this Convention, provided that the parties have their places of business in States parties to such agreement.

Article 91

(1) This Convention is open for signature at the concluding meeting of the United Nations Conference on Contracts for the International Sale of Goods and will remain open for signature by all the States at the Headquarters of the United nations, New York until 30 September 1981.
(2) This Convention is subject to ratification, acceptance or approval by the signatory States.
(3) This Convention is open for accession by all States which are not signatory States as from the date it is open for signature.
(4) Instruments of ratification, acceptance, approval and accession are to be deposited with the Secretary-General of the United Nations.

Article 92

(1) A Contracting State may declare at the time of signature, ratification, acceptance, approval or accession that it will not be bound by Part II of this Convention or that it will not be bound by Part III of this Convention.
(2) A Contracting State which makes a declaration in accordance with the preceding paragraph in respect of Part II or Part III of this Convention is not to be considered a Contracting State within paragraph (1) of article 1 of this Convention in respect of matters governed by the Part to which the declaration applies.

Article 93

(1) If a Contracting State has two or more territorial units in which, according to its constitution, different systems of law are applicable in relation to the matters dealt with in this Convention, it may, at the time of signature, ratification, acceptance, approval or accession, declare that this Convention is to extend to all its territorial units or only to one or more of them, and may amend its declaration by submitting another declaration at any time.
(2) These declarations are to be notified to the depositary and are to state expressly the territorial units to which the Convention extends.
(3) If, by virtue of a declaration under this article, this Convention extends to one or more but not all of the territorial units of a Contracting State, and if the place of business of a party is located in that State, this place of business, for the purposes of this Convention, is considered not to be in a Contracting State, unless it is in a territorial unit to which the Convention extends.
(4) If a Contracting State makes no declaration under paragraph (1) of this article, the Convention is to extend to all territorial units of that State.

Article 94

(1) Two or more Contracting States which have the same or closely related legal rules on matters governed by this Convention may at any time declare that the Convention is not to apply to contracts of sale or to their formation where the parties have their places of business in those States. Such declarations may be made jointly or by reciprocal unilateral declarations.

(2) A Contracting State which has the same or closely related legal rules on matters governed by this Convention as one or more non-Contracting States may at any time declare that the Convention is not to apply to contracts of sale or to their formation where the parties have their places of business in those States.

(3) If a State which is the object of a declaration under the preceding paragraph subsequently becomes a Contracting State, the declaration made will, as from the date on which the Convention enters into force in respect of the new Contracting State, have the effect of a declaration made under paragraph (1), provided that the new Contracting State joins in such declaration or makes a reciprocal unilateral declaration.

Article 95

Any State may declare at the time of the deposit of its instrument of ratification, acceptance, approval or accession that it will not be bound by subparagraph (1) (b) of article 1 of this Convention.

Article 96

A Contracting State whose legislation requires contracts of sale to be concluded in or evidenced by writing may at any time make a declaration in accordance with article 12 that any provision of article 11, article 29, or Part II of this Convention that allows a contract of sale or its modification or termination by agreement or any offer, acceptance, or other indication of intention to be made in any form other than in writing, does not apply where any party has his place of business in that State.

Article 97

(1) Declarations made under this Convention at the time of signature are subject to confirmation upon ratification, acceptance or approval.

(2) Declarations and confirmations of declarations are to be in writing and be formally notified to the depositary.

(3) A declaration takes effect simultaneously with the entry into force of this Convention in respect of the State concerned. However, a declaration of which the depositary receives formal notification after such entry into force takes effect on the first of the month following the expiration of six months after the date of its receipt by the depositary. Reciprocal unilateral declarations under article 94 take effect on the first day of the month following the expiration of six months after the date of the receipt of the notification by the depositary.

(4) Any State which makes a declaration under this Convention may withdraw it at any time by a formal notification in writing addressed to the depositary. Such withdrawal is to take effect on the first day of the month following the expiration of six months after the date of the receipt of the notification by the depositary.

(5) A withdrawal of a declaration made under article 94 renders inoperative, as from the date on which the withdrawal takes effect, any reciprocal declaration made by another State under that article.

Article 98

No reservations are permitted except those expressly authorized in this Convention.

Article 99

(1) This Convention enters into force, subject to the revisions of paragraph (6) of this article, on the first day of the month following the expiration of twelve months after the date of deposit of the tenth instrument of ratification, acceptance, approval or accession, including an instrument which contains a declaration made under article 92.

(2) When a State ratifies, accepts, approves or accedes to this Convention after the deposit of the tenth instrument of ratification, acceptance, approval or accession, this Convention, with the exception of the Part excluded, enters into force in respect of that State, subject to the provisions of paragraph (6) of this article, on the first day of the month following the expiration of twelve months after the date of the deposit of its instrument of ratification, acceptance, approval or accession.

(3) A State which ratifies, accepts, approves or accedes to this Convention and is a party to either or both the Convention relating to a Uniform Law on the Formation of Contracts for the International Sale of Goods done at The Hague on 1 July 1964 (1964 Hague Formation Convention) and the Convention relating to a Uniform Law on the International Sale of Goods done at The Hague on 1 July 1964 (1964 Hague Sales Convention) shall at the same time denounce, as the case may be, either or both the 1964 Hague Sales Convention and the 1964 Hague Formation Convention by notifying the Government of the Netherlands to that effect.

(4) A State party to the 1964 Hague Sales Convention which ratifies, accepts, approves or accedes to the present Convention and declares or has declared under article 92 that it will not be bound by Part II of this Convention shall at the time of ratification, acceptance, approval or accession denounce the 1964 Hague Sales Convention by notifying the Government of the Netherlands to that effect.

(5) A State party to the 1964 Hague Formation Convention which ratifies, accepts, approves or accedes to the present Convention and declares or has declared under article 92 that it will not be bound by Part III of this Convention shall at the time of ratification, acceptance, approval or accession denounce the 1964 Hague Formation Convention by notifying the Government of the Netherlands to that effect.

(6) For the purpose of this article, ratifications, acceptances, approvals and accessions in respect of this Convention by States parties to the 1964 Hague Formation Convention or to the 1964 Hague Sales Convention shall not be effective until such denunciations as may be required on the part of those States in respect of the latter two Conventions have themselves become effective. The depositary of this Convention shall consult with the Government of the Netherlands, as the depositary of the 1964 Conventions, so as to ensure necessary co-ordination in this respect.

Article 100

(1) This Convention applies to the formation of a contract only when the proposal for concluding the contract is made on or after the date when the Convention enters into

force in respect of the Contracting States referred to in subparagraph (1) (a) or the Contracting State referred to in subparagraph (1) (b) or article 1.

(2) This Convention applies only to contracts concluded on or after the date when the Convention enters into force in respect of the Contracting States referred to in subparagraph (1) (a) or the Contracting State referred to in subparagraph (1) (b) of article 1.

Article 101

(1) A Contracting State may denounce this Convention, or Part II or Part III of the Convention, by a formal notification in writing addressed to the depositary.

(2) The denunciation takes effect on the first day of the month following the expiration of twelve months after the notification is received by the depositary. Where a longer period for the denunciation to take effect is specified in the notification, the denunciation takes effect upon the expiration of such longer period after the notification is received by the depositary.

DONE at Vienna, this day of eleventh day of April, one thousand nine hundred and eighty, in a single original, of which the Arabic, Chinese, English, French, Russian and Spanish texts are equally authentic.

IN WITNESS WHEREOF the undersigned plenipotentiaries, being duly authorized by their respective Governments, have signed this Convention.

TABLE OF CASES AND ARBITRAL AWARDS

Argentina

Camara Nacional de Apelaciones en lo Comercial de Buenos Aires, decision of 24 April 2000, § 2.11 n. 182.

Australia

Australian Federal Court, South District of Adelaide, decision of 28 April 1995, § 2.6 n.92.
Supreme Court of Queensland, decision of 17 November 2000, § 6.23 n. 280.

Austria

Oberster Gerichtshof, decision of 10 November 1994, § 3.2 n.19; § 3.3 n.31.
Oberster Gerichtshof, decision of 6 February 1996, § 4.11 n.166.
Oberster Gerichtshof, decision of 11 February 1997, § 2.5 n.42.
Oberster Gerichtshof, decision of 8 September 1997, § 2.5 n.204.
Oberster Gerichtshof, decision of 12 February 1998, § 6.26 n.292.
Oberster Gerichtshof, decision of 15 October 1998, § 4.9 n.120 and n.129.
Oberster Gerichtshof, decision of 29 June 1999, § 2.11 n.188.
Oberster Gerichtshof, decision of 28 August 1999, § 4.9 n.129 & n.137.
Oberster Gerichtshof, decision of 21 March 2000, § 4.9 n.120.
Oberster Gerichtshof, decison of 13 April 2000, § 4.7 n.87.
Oberster Gerichtshof, decision of 28 April 2000, § 6.28 n.311.
Oberster Gerichtshof, decision of 7 September 2000, § 7.4 n.76.
OLG Graz, decision of 9 November 1995, § 4.4 n.45; § 6.13 n.125.
Internationales Schiedsgericht der Bundeskammer der gewerblichen Wirtschaft – Wien, awards no. SCH-4318 and SCH-4366 of 15 June 1994, § 2.10 n.170; § 2.11 n.194; § 4.9 n.138; § 6.18 n.218; § 6.31 n.321 & n.327.
Schiedsgericht der Börse für Landwirtschaftliche Produkte – Wien, decision of 10 December 1997, § 6.11 n.119.

Belgium

Tribunal Commercial de Nivelles, decision of 19 September 1995, § 3.8 n.87.
Rechtbank van Koophandel, Hasselt, 1 March 1995, § 6.26 n.293.
Rechtbank van Koophandel, Hasselt, 2 May 1995, § 6.19 n.239; § 6.32 n.336.

Canada

La San Giuseppe v. Forti Moulding Ltd., § 4.9 n.115.

Denmark

Eastern High Court, decision of 23 April 1998, § 3.7 n.58.
Eastern High Court, decision of 7 March 2002, § 2.5 n.74.

Western High Court, decision of 10 November 1999, § 4.9 n.122.
Maritime & Commercial Court, decision of 31 January 2002, § 3.1 n.9; § 4.4 n.37.
Supreme Court (HØjesteret), decision of 15 February 2001, § 4.2 n.14; § 4.3 n.30.

England
Brinkebon Ltd. v. Stahag Stahl, § 3.9 n.100.
George Mitchell v. Finney Lock Seeds, § 7.3 n.40.
Gill v. Duffus S.A. v. Société pour L'exportation des Sucres S.A., § 6.8 n.67; § 7.1 n.4.
Hadley v. Baxendale, § 6.15 n.162 & n.190.
R.W. Green Ltd. v. Cade Bros. Farm, § 7.3 n.40.

European Court of Justice
Custom Made Commercial v. Stawa Metallbau, decision of 29 June 1994, § 2.11 n.204.
Handelskwekerij Bier v. Mines de Potasse d'Alsace, 1976, § 2.9 n.141.

Finland
Helsinki Court of Appeals, decision of 30 June 1998, § 4.9 n.142.

France
Arbitral Awards by ICC Court of Arbitration (Paris): see "ICC Awards" (below)
Cour de Cassation, decision of 4 January 1995, § 3.3 n.36; § 3.8 n.80.
Cour de Cassation, decision of 17 December 1996, § 2.4 n.27; § 4.4 n.44.
Cour de Cassation, decision of 27 January 1998, § 3.7 n.58.
Cour de Cassation, decision of 16 July 1998, § 1.4 n.45; § 3.8 n.79 & n.88.
Cour de Cassation, decision of 26 May 1999, § 4.9 n.123.
Cour d'Appel de Colmar, 24 October 2000, § 4.9 n.123.
Cour d'Appel de Chambéry, decision of 25 May 1993, § 2.5 n.54.
Cour d'Appel de Grenoble, Chambre Commerciale, decision of 26 April 1995, § 2.5 n.51.
Cour d'Appel de Grenoble, Chambre Commerciale, decision of 13 September 1995, § 4.8 n.95.
Cour d'Appel de Grenoble, decision of 16 June 1993, § 1.4 n.46.
Cour d'Appel de Grenoble, decision of 22 February 1995, § 6.11 n.118, § 6.23 n.282.
Cour d'Appel de Grenoble, decision of 29 March 1995, § 1.4 n.46.
Cour d'Appel de Paris, decision of 10 November 1993, § 1.4 n.46.
Cour d'Appel de Versailles, 29 January 1998, § 4.9 n.123; § 6.7 n.45; § 6.8 n.60.

Germany
Bundesgerichtshof, decision of 15 February 1995, § 2.6 n.92; § 6.11 n.105.
Bundesgerichtshof, decision of 8 March 1995, § 2.8 n.135; § 4.7 n.86.
Bundesgerichtshof, decision of 3 April 1996, § 6.8 n.61.
Bundesgerichtshof, decision of 25 June 1997, § 4.9 n.139; 6.17 n.209.
Bundesgerichtshof, decision of 23 July 1997, § 2.5 n.50.
Bundesgerichtshof, decision of 25 November 1998, § 4.9 n.141.
Bundesgerichtshof, decision of 24 March 1999, § 6.14 n.140; § 6.19 n.234.
Bundesgerichtshof, decision of 3 November 1999, § 4.9 n.127 & n.145.

Bundesgerichtshof, decision of 31 October 2001, § 7.2 n.20.

Amtsgericht Duisberg, decision of 13 April 2000, § 5.2 n.17.

Amtsgericht Frankfurt, decision of 31 January 1991, § 6.11 n.114; § 6.14 n.142; § 6.26 n.294.

Amtsgericht Kiel, decision of 6 October 1995, § 3.8 n.88.

Amtsgericht München, decision of 23 June 1995, § 6.9 n.92; § 6.17 n.209.

Amtsgericht Oldenburg/Holstein, decision of 24 April 1990, § 6.8 n.72; § 6.31 n.323.

Landgericht Aachen, decision of 14 May 1993, § 2.6 n.81, n.103; § 4.6 n.65.

Landgericht Aachen, decision of 20 July 1995, § 2.11 n.199 & 206; § 6.31 n.329.

Landgericht Baden-Baden, decision of 14 August 1991, § 3.8 n.81; § 4.9 n.148; § 7.2 n.21.

Landgericht Berlin, decision of 15 September 1994, § 6.11 n.112.

Landgericht Düsseldorf, decision of 23 June 1994, § 4.9 n.149.

Landgericht Düsseldorf, decision of 11 October 1995; § 2.7 n.121.

Landgericht Ellwangen, 21 August 1995, § 4.7 n.87; § 6.8 n.60.

Landgericht Frankfurt, decision of 16 September 1991, § 6.18 n.219; § 6.28 n.302.

Landgericht Giessen, decision of 5 July 1994, § 7.2 n.21.

Landgericht Hamburg, decision of 26 September 1990, § 2.12 n.211; § 2.13 n.228; § 6.31 n.325.

Landgericht Heidelberg, decision of 3 July 1992, § 6.8 n.75; § 6.31 n.323.

Landgericht Krefeld, decision of 24 November 1992, § 3.7 n.56.

Landgericht Landshut, decision of 5 April 1995, § 6.12 n.122.

Landgericht Memmingen, decision of 1 December 1993, § 2.12 n.221.

Landgericht München, decision of 3 July 1989, § 4.9 n.144.

Landgericht München, decision of 8 February 1995, § 2.5, n.72; § 3.2 n.18; § 4.8 n.94; § 4.14 n.197.

Landgericht Paderborn , decision of 26 June 1996, § 4.9 n.139.

Landgericht Stuttgart, decision of 31 August 1989, § 4.9 n.135 & n.147; § 6.31 n.325.

Landgericht Stuttgart, decision of 13 August 1991, § 7.3 n.37.

Oberlandesgericht Celle, 24 May 1995, § 6.10 n.100.

Oberlandesgericht Düsseldorf, decision of 12 November 1982, § 2.13 n.223.

Oberlandesgericht Düsseldorf, decision of 8 January 1993, § 2.4 n.29; § 2.7 n.124; § 4.4 n.34.

Oberlandesgericht Düsseldorf, decision of 2 July 1993, § 2.6 n.93; § 2.11 n.201; § 8.7 n.30.

Oberlandesgericht Düsseldorf, 14 January 1994, § 6.11 n.106; § 6.26 n.295.

Oberlandesgericht Frankfurt, decision of 13 June 1991, § 6.31 n.325.

Oberlandesgericht Frankfurt, decision of 17 September 1991, § 2.5 n.54; § 6.8 n.63.

Oberlandesgericht Frankfurt, decision of 18 January 1994, § 6.8 n.56.

Oberlandesgericht Frankfurt, decision of 20 April 1994, § 2.8 n.135; § 4.7 n.86.

Oberlandesgericht Frankfurt, decision of 4 March 1994, § 8.4 n.20.

Oberlandesgericht Frankfurt, decision of 23 May 1995; § 3.8 n.68.

Oberlandesgericht Frankfurt, decision of 30 August 2000, § 2.7 n.118.

Oberlandesgericht Hamm, decision of 22 September 1992, § 3.8 n.68; § 4.5 n.46.

Oberlandesgericht Hamm, decision of 8 February 1995, § 7.2 n.20.

Oberlandesgericht Hamm, decision of 23 June 1998, § 5.5 n.36.
Oberlandesgericht Hamburg, decision of 28 February 1997, § 6.17 n.206; § 6.19 n.242 & 251.
Oberlandesgericht Karlsruhe, decision of 20 November 1992, § 5.2 n.11.
Oberlandesgericht Karlsruhe, decision of 25 June 1997, § 4.9 n.141 & 148.
Oberlandesgericht Koblenz, decision of 23 February 1990, § 1.4 n.46; § 2.11 n.204.
Oberlandesgericht Koblenz, decision of 16 January 1992, § 2.5 n.44; § 7.2 n.20.
Oberlandesgericht Koblenz, 17 September 1993, § 2.5 n.50, n.59 & 65; § 2.7 n.121.
Oberlandesgericht Koblenz, 31 January 1997, § 6.9 n.91.
Oberlandesgericht Köln, decision of 22 February 1994, § 2.7 n.124; § 3.7 n.58.
Oberlandesgericht Köln, decision of 26 August 1994, § 2.5 n.58 & n.65.
Oberlandesgericht Köln, decision of 21 May 1996 , § 4.8 n.99; § 6.15 n.165.
Oberlandesgericht Oldenburg, decision of 5 December 2000, § 4.9 n.127.
Oberlandesgericht Saarbrücken, decision of 3 June 1998, § 4.9 n.121.
Schiedsgericht der Handelskammer – Hamburg, 21 March 1996, § 6.19 n.236 & n.244.

Hungary
Metropolitan Court of Budapest, decision of 24 March 1992, § 3.2 n.22; § 4.13 n.191; § 8.8 n.36.
Supreme Court of Hungary, decision of 25 Sept.1992, § 2.5 n.45; § 3.3 n.29.

ICC Arbitral awards
ICC Case no. 7153/1992 , § 6.31 n.326.
ICC Case no. 7197/1992, § 4.12 n.189; § 5.5 n.38; § 6.19 n.245; § 6.21 n.269; § 7.4 n.65.
ICC Case no. 6653/1993, § 1.4 n.52; § 2.7 n.117; § 4.4 n.39; § 4.9 n.108.
ICC Case no. 7565/1994, § 2.7 n.118.
ICC Case no. 7660/JK 1994, § 1.4 n.52; § 2.7 n.117; § 6.8 n.75.
ICC Case no. 8128/1995, § 6.16 n.195; § 6.19 n.253.
ICC Case no. 8611/HV/JK 1997, § 2.5 n.50.
ICC Case no. 9887/1999, § 2.11 n.208.

Italy
Corte d'Appello di Milano, decision of 14 January 1998, § 6.8 n.71.
Corte d'Appello di Milano, decision of 11 December 1998, § 2.6 n.102.

Mexico
COMPRIMEX, award of 29 April 1996, § 4.8 n.95; § 4.9 n.102.

Netherlands
Hoge Raad, 20 February 1998, § 4.9 n.149.
Arrondissementsrechtbank Roermond, decision of 19 December 1991, § 4.9 n.113, n.135.
Gerechtshof Arnhem, decision of 24 August 1995, § 2.6 n.85.
Gerechtshof Hertogenbosch, decision of 24 April 1996, § 2.13 n.228.
Gerechtshof Hertogenbosch, decision of 15 December 1997, § 4.9 n.153.

Russian Federation
Tribunal of International Commercial Arbitration at the Russian Federation Chamber of Commerce, 17 October 1995, § 6.19 n.239.

International Court of Commercial Arbitration, Chamber of Commerce & Industry of the Russian Federation, decision of 24 January 2000, § 2.7 n.120; § 4.9 n.119; § 6.17 n.207.

Sweden

Arbitration Institute, Stockholm Chamber of Commerce, award of 5 June 1998, § 4.9 n.152; § 7.4 n.74.

Switzerland

Bundesgericht, 28 October 1998, § 6.8 n.61; § 6.15 n.166.

Bezirksgericht der Saane, decision of 20 February 1997, § 2.3 n.22.

Cour de Justice Genève, decision of 10 October 1997, § 4.10 n.163.

Handelsgericht Zürich, decision of 26 April 1995, § 2.5, n.51; § 2.6 n.93.

Handelsgericht Zürich, decision of 5 February 1997, § 6.11 n.119; § 6.15 n.174.

Handelsgericht St. Gallen, decision of 24 August 1995, § 2.6 n.84.

Pretura di Locarno-Campagna, decision of 27 April 1992, § 4.7 n.85; § 6.9 n.93; § 6.13 n.132.

Tribunal Cantonal Valais, decision of 28 October 1997, § 4.8 n.97.

Tribunale di Appelo di Lugano, decision of 15 January 1998, § 4.9 n.109; § 5.2 n.13; § 6.12 n.120.

Obergericht Kanton Luzern, 8 January 1997, § 4.9 n.127.

USA

Advent Systems Ltd. v. Unisys Corp., § 2.5 n.64.

Ajax Tool Works, Inc. v. Can-Eng Manufacturing Ltd, § 2.7 n. 119, § 7.3 n.47, n.54.

Alyeska Pipeline Service Co. v. Wilderness Society, § 6.15 n.181.

Asante Technologies, Inc. v. PMC-Sierra, Inc., § 2.3 n.11; § 2.7 n.121; § 2.12 n.216.

Beijing Metals v. American Business Center, § 4.5 n.49 & n.55.

BP Oil International v. Empresa Estatal Petroleos de Ecuador, § 2.3 n.12; § 5.2 n.14.

Buckhannon Board and Care Home, Inc. v. W. Virginia Dept. of Health, § 6.15 n.181.

Bunett v. Smallwood, § 6.15 n.182.

Burger King Corp. v. Rudzewicz, § 4.12 n.179.

Calzaturificio Claudia s.n.c. v. Olivieri Footwear Ltd., § 2.13 n.224.

Chateau des Charmes Wines Ltd. v. Sabate USA, Sabate S.A., § 2.6 n. 81; § 3.8 n.93.

Chicago Prime Packers, Inc. v. Northam Food Trading Co., § 4.9 n.125.

Delchi Carrier, SpA v. Rotorex Corp., § 2.3 n. 7; § 6.15 n.176, n.180; § 6.18 n.225.

Evra v. Swiss Bank Corp., § 6.15 n.190.

Filanto S.p.a. v. Chilewich Internat'l Corp., § 3.8 n.79.

Frigaliment Importing Co. v. B.N.S. International Sales Corp., § 2.12 n.220.

Geneva Pharmaceuticals Technology Corp. v. Barr Laboratories, Inc., § 2.6 n.82, n.97, n.107; § 3.2 n.20; § 3.6 n 49; § 3.7 n. 64; § 3.10 n.115.

Lloyd F. Smith Co. v. Den-Tal-Ez, § 2.6 n.94.

GPL Treatment, Ltd. v. Louisiana-Pacific Corp., § 2.9 n.144.

Hill v. BASF Wyandotte Corp., § 7.3 n.57.

Magellan International Corporation v. Salzgitter Handel GmbH, § 6.4 n.26; § 6.5 n.32.

MCC-Marble Ceramic Center Inc. v. Ceramica Nuova D'Agostino S.p.A., § 4.5 n.55.

TABLE OF AUTHORITIES

cited previously in abbreviated form

Amato, *Open Price Term*	Amato, P., "U.N.Convention – The Open Price Term and Uniform Application: An Early Interpretation by the Hungarian Courts", 13 *J. L. & Com. L.* 1 (1993).
Andersen, *Reasonable Time*	Andersen, C., "Reasonable Time in Article 39(1) of the CISG . . .", *1998 Review of the CISG* (1999), also available at: <http://www.cisgw3.law.pace.edu/cisg/biblio/ andersen.html>.
Andersen, *IT-retten*	Andersen, M.B., *IT-retten* (Copenhagen 2001), also available at: <http://www.it-retten.dk>.
Andersen & Lookofsky, *Obligationsret*	Andersen, M.B., & Lookofsky, J., *Lærebog i Obligationsret* (Copenhagen 2000).
Atiyah & Adams, *Sale of Goods*	Atiyah, P.S., and Adams, J.N., *The Sale of Goods* (9th ed., London 1995).
Audit, *Vente internationale*	Audit, B., *La vente internationale de marchandises* (Paris 1990).
Baily, *Facing the Truth*	Bailey, J., "Facing the Truth: Seeing the Convention . . . as an Obstacle to a Uniform Law . . .", 32 *Cornell Int'l L.J.* 273 (1999).
Bergem & Rognlien, *Kjøpsloven*	Bergem, J., and Rognlien, R., *Kjøpsloven 1988 og FN-Konvensjonen 1980 om internasjonale løsørekjøp* (2d ed. Oslo 1995).
Bergsten & Miller, *Reduction in Price*	Bergsten E. and Miller A., "The Remedy of Reduction in Price," 27 *Am. J. Comp. L.* 255 (1979).
Berman & Ladd, *Risk*	Berman, I., and Ladd, M., "Risk of Loss or Damage in Documentary Transactions . . .," 21 *Cornell Int. L. J.* 423 (1988).
Bernstein & Lookofsky, *CISG/Europe*	Bernstein, H. & Lookofsky, J., *Understanding the CISG in Europe* (2d ed. Hague/London/Boston 2002)
Bianca & Bonell, *Commentary*	Bianca, C., and Bonell, M., *Commentary on the International Sales Law: The 1980 Vienna Sales Convention* (Milan 1987).
Bonell, *Restatement*	Bonell, M., *An International Restatement of Contract Law* (2d ed. New York 1997)
Bonell, *UNIDROIT Principles*	Bonell, M., "The UNIDROIT Principles . . . and the CISG – Alternatives or Complementary Instruments?", 1 *Unif. L. Rev.* 26 (1996).

Burrows, *Obligations*	Burrows, A., *Understanding the Law of Obligations* (Oxford 1998).
Cox, *Chaos*	Cox, T., "Chaos v. uniformity: divergent views of software . . .", 4 *Vindobona J. of Int. Comm. Law & Arb.* 3 (2000) and <http://cisgw3.law.pace.edu/ cisg/biblio/cox.html>.
von Caemmerer & Schlechtriem, *Kommentar*	von Caemmerer, E., and Schlechtriem, P., *Kommentar zum Einheitlichen UN-Kaufrecht – CISG*, (2d ed. Munich 1995).
CISGW3	CISG (Internet) Database <http://cisgw3.law. pace.edu> produced and maintained by the Pace Law School Institute of Internatinal Commercial Law and the Pace Law Library (New York).
CLOUT	Case Law on UNCITRAL Texts (UNCITRAL Secretariat) <http://www.uncitral.org>.
Diedrich, *Maintaining Uniformity*	Diedrich, F., "Maintaining Uniformity . . . Via Autonomous Interpretation: Software Contracts and the CISG", VIII *Pace U. International L. Rev.* 303 (1996).
Eiselen, *Electronic Commerce*	Eiselen, S., "Electronic Commerce and the UN Convention . . .", 6 *EDI Law Review* (1999) 21–46. Also available at: <http://cisgw3.law.pace.edu/ cisg/biblio/eiselen1.html>.
Eörsi, *General Provisions*	Eörsi, G., "General Provisions" in *International Sales* (Galston and Smit eds., New York 1984).
Erauw & Flechtner, *Remedies*	Erauw, J. and Flechtner, H., "Remedies under the CISG and Limits to their Uniform Character", in *International Sale of Goods Revisited* (Sarcevic & Volken eds. Hague 2001).
EwiR	Entscheidungen im Wirtschaftsrecht.
Farnsworth, *Breach of Contract*	Farnsworth, E.A., "Legal Remedies for Breach of Contract", 70 *Colum. L. Rev.* 1145 (1970).
Farnsworth, *Contracts*	Farnsworth, E.A., *Contracts* (3rd ed., 1999).
Farnsworth, *Formation*	Farnsworth, E.A., "Formation of Contract", in *International Sales* (Galston & Smit eds. New York 1984).
Felemegas, *Counsel's Fees*	Felemegas, J., "The Award of Counsel's Fees under Article 74 CISG", 6 *Vindobona J. of Int. Comm. L. & Arbitration* 30 (2002), also available at <http://cisgw3.law.pace.edu/cisg/ biblio/felemegas1.html>.
Ferrari, *Interest Rates*	Ferrari, F., "Uniform Application and Interest Rates Under the . . . Convention", 24 *Ga. J. Int. & Comp. L.* 467 (1995).
Ferrari, *Specific Topics*	Ferrari, F., "Specific Topics of the CISG in the Light of Judicial Application and Scholarly Writing", 15 *J. Law & Commerce* 1 (1995), also available at <http://cisgw3.law.pace. edu/cisg/biblio/2ferrari.html>.
Ferrari, *Uniform Interpretation*	Ferrari, F., "Uniform Interpretation of the 1980 Uniform Sales Law", 24 *Ga. J. Int. & Comp. L.* 183 (1994), also available at <http://cisgw3.law.pace.edu/cisg/biblio/franco.html>.

Flechtner, *Attorneys Fees & Foreign Case Law*

Flechtner, H., "Recovering Attorneys Fees as Damages under the U.N.Sales Convention: A Case Study on the New International Commercial Practice and the Role of Case Law in CISG Jurisprudence, with Comments on *Zapata Hermanos Sucesores, S.A. v. Hearthside Baking Co.*", 22 *Northwestern J.Bus. L. & Policy* 121 (2002), also available at <http://cisgw3.law.pace.edu/cisg/bib.lio/flechtner4.html>.

Flechtner, *Buyer's Obligation*

Flechtner, Harry, M., "The Buyer's Obligation to Give Notice of Lack of Conformity (CISG Articles 38, 39, 40 and 44)," in *Beyond the Draft Uncitral Digest: Cases, Analysis and Unresolved Issues in the U.N. Sales Convention* (R. Brand, F. Ferrari & H. Flechtner eds., 2003).

Flechtner, *More U.S. Decisions*

Flechtner, H., "More U.S. Decisions on the U.N. Sales Convention: Scope, Parol Evidence, 'Validity,' and Reduction of Price under Article 50," 14 *J.L. & Com.* 153, 166–69 (1995), also available at <http://cisgw3.law.pace.edu/cisg/biblio/flechtner.html>.

Flechtner, *Pitfalls*

Flechtner, H., "Another CISG Case in the U.S. Courts: Pitfalls for the Practitioner and the Potential for Regionalized Interpretations," 15 *J.L. & Comm.* 127 (1995), also available at: <http://www.cisgw3.law. pace.edu/cisg/biblio/jvcvol14.html>.

Flechtner, *Remedies*

Flechtner, H., "Remedies Under the New International Sales Convention: The Perspective from Article 2 of the UCC", 8 *J. L. & Com.* 53 (1988).

Flechtner, *Several Texts*

Flechtner, H., "The Several Texts of the CISG in a Decentralized System: . . . Challenges to the Uniformity Principle in Article 7(1)", 17 *J.L. & Com.* (1998) 187–217. Also available at: <http:// www.cisgw3.law.pace.edu/cisg/biblio/ flecht1.html>.

Flechtner & Lookofsky, *Viva Zapata!*

Flecthner, H. and Lookofsky, J., "Viva Zapata! American Procedure and CISG Substance in a U.S. Circuit Court of Appeal", 7 *Vindobona Journal of International Commercial Law and Arbitration* (2003) 93, also available at <http://cisgw 3.law.pace.edu/cisg/biblio/flechtner5.html>.

Fogt, *Reklamation*

Fogt, M., "Rettidig reklamation og ophævelse . . .", *Ugeskrift for Retsvæsen*, 2002 B 129–135.

Frost, *Informationsydelsen*

Frost, K., *Informationsydelsen* (Copenhagen 2002).

Gillette & Walt, *Sales Law*

Gillette, P. and Walt, S., *Sales Law. Domestic and International* (Rev. ed. New York 2002).

Gomard & Rechnagel, *International købelov*

Gomard, B. & Rechnagel, H., *International købelov* (Copenhagen 1990).

Hagstrøm, *Kjøpsrettskonvenjon*

Hagstrøm, V., "Kjøpsrettskonvenjon, Norsk Kjøpslov og Internasjonal Rettsenhet", *Tidssrift for Rettsvitenskap* 561 (1995).

Hartnell, *Rousing the Sleeping Dog*	Hartnell, H., "Rousing the Sleeping Dog: The Validity Exception to the Convention on Contracts for the International Sale of Goods," 18 *Yale J. Int. L.* (1993), also available at <http://cisgw3.law.pace.edu/cisg/biblio/hartnell.html>.
Hellner, *Vienna Convention*	Hellner, J., "The Vienna Convention and Standard Form Contracts" in *International Sale of Goods*: *Dubrovnik Lectures* (Šarčević & Volken eds. New York 1986).
Heuzé, *Vente internationale*	Heuzé, V., *La vente interntionale de marchandises* (Paris 1990).
Honnold, *Documentary History*	Honnold, J., *Documentary History of the 1980 Uniform Law for International Sales* (Deventer 1989).
Honnold, *Uniform Law*	Honnold, J., *Uniform Law for International Sales Under the 1980 United Nations Convention* (3rd ed. Deventer 1999).
Hov, *Aftalebrudd*	Hov, J., *Aftalebrudd og partsskifte* (Oslo 1997).
Hunter & Treibel, *Awarding Interest*	Hunter, M. and Treibel, V., "Awarding Interest in International Arbitration", 6 *J. Int. Arbitr.* 8 (1989).
Hyland, *Conformity of Goods*	Hyland, R.,"Conformity of Goods to the Contract Under the . . . Convention and the Uniform Commercial Code", in *Einheitliches Kaufrecht und nationales Obligationenrecht* (Schlechtriem ed. Baden-Baden 1987).
J. L. & Com.	Journal of Law and Commerce.
Kastely, *Performance*	Kastely, A., "The Right to Require Performance in International Sales: Towards an International Interpretation . . .", 63 *Wash. L. Rev.* 607 (1988).
KBL	*Købeloven* (Danish Sales Act of 1906).
Klein, *Usury*	Klein, D., The Islamic and Jewish Law of Usury, 23 *Denv. J. L. & Pol'y* 535 (1995).
Kritzer,*Guide/Manual*	Kritzer, A., *Guide to the Practical Application of the UN Convention on Contracts for the International Sale of Goods,* Vol.2. (Boston 1994).
Krüger, *Kjøpsrett*	Krüger, K*., Norsk kjøpsrett* (4th ed., Oslo 1999).
Kuoppala, *Examination*	Kuoppala, S., "Examination of the Goods . . ." (2000) at: <http://cisgw3.law.pace.edu/cisg/biblio/kuoppala.html>
Lookofsky, *Alive & Well*	Lookofsky, J., "Alive and Well in Scandinavia: CISG Part II", 18 *Journal of Law & Commerce* 289–299 (1999), also available at <http://cisgw3.law.pace.edu/cisg/biblio/lookofsky1.html>.
Lookofsky, *CISG Foreign Case Law*	Lookofsky, J., "CISG Foreign Case Law: How Much Regard Should We Have? A Commentary on the UNCITRAL Draft Digest of CISG Part I", in *Beyond the Draft Uncitral Digest: Cases, Analysis and Unresolved Issues in the U.N. Sales Convention* (R. Brand, F.Ferrari & H. Flechtner eds., 2003).

Lookofsky,*CISG/Scandinavia*

Lookofsky, J., *Understanding the CISG in Scandinavi*, (2d ed. Copenhagen 2002).

Lookofsky, *Consequential Damages*

Lookofsky, J., *Consequential Damages in Comparativ Context* (Copenhagen 1989).

Lookofsky, *Fault and No-Fault*

Lookofsky, J., "Fault and No-Fault in Danish, American and International Sales Law . . .", 27 *Scandinavian Studies in Law* 109 (1983). Also available at: <www.cisgw3.law pace.edu/cisg/biblio/lookofsky4.html>

Lookofsky *In Dubio Pro Conventione*

Lookofsky, J., "In Dubio Pro Conventione? Some Thoughts about Opt-Outs, Computer Software and Preëmption Under the CISG," 13 *Duke J. Int. & Comp. L.* 258, also available at <http://www.law.duke.edu/journals/djcil/>.

Lookofsky, *International Sales Contracts*

Lookofsky, J., "International Sales Contracts: A Scandinavian View", in *Suum Cuique* (Copenhagen 1993).

Lookofsky, *Køb*

Lookofsky, J., *Køb. Dansk indenlandsk købsret* (Danish Domestic Sales Law) (2d ed. Copenhagen 2002).

Lookofsky, *Limits*

Lookofsky, J., "The Limits of Commercial Contract Freedom . . .", 46 *Am. J. Comp. Law* (1998) pp. 485–508, also available at <http://cisgw3.law.pace.edu/cisg/biblio/ lookofsky6.html>.

Lookofsky, *Loose Ends*

Lookofsky, J., "Loose Ends and Contorts in International Sales: Problems in the Harmonization of Private Law Rules," 39 *Am. J. Comp. L.* 403 (1991), also available at <http://cisgw3.law.pace.edu/cisg/biblio/lookofsky6.html>.

Lookofsky, *United Nations Convention*

Lookofsky, J., *The 1980 United Nations Convention on the International Sale of Goods*, in *International Encyclopedia of Laws, Contracts* (Supp. 29: Deventer 2000).

Lookofsky, *Zapata*

Lookofsky, J., Case Note, *Zapata Hermanos v. Hearthside Baking*, 6 Vindobona Journal of International Commercial Arbitration (2002) 27, also available at <http://cisgw3.law. pace.edu/cisg/biblio/lookofsky5.html>.

Lookofsky & Hertz, *Transnational Litigation*

Lookofsky, J. and Hertz, K., *Transnational Litigation and Commercial Arbitration* (2d. ed. New York & Copenhagen 2003).

Lynge Andersen & Nørgaard, *Aftaleloven*

Lynge Andersen, L. and Nørgaard, J., *Aftaleloven* (3rd ed. Copenhagen 1999).

Magnus in Staudinger, *Kommentar*

von Staudinger, J., *Kommentar zum Bürgerlichen Gesetzbuch mit Einführungsgesetz und Nebengesetzen: Wiener UN-Kaufrecht (CISG)* (Neubearbeitung 1999 von Magnus, Berlin 2000).

Murray, *Formation*

Murray, L., "An Essay on the Formation of Contracts and Related Matters Under the United Nations Convention . . .", 8 *J. L. & Com.* 11 (1988).

NCCUSL Draft Revision	National Conference of Commissioners on Uniform State Laws, *Proposed Amendments to Uniform Commercial Code*, 2002 Annual Meeting Draft, available (as of September 2003) at <http://www.law.upenn.edu/bll/ulc/ulc_frame.htm>.
Nicholas, *Force Majeure*	Nicholas, B., "Force Majeure and Frustration", 27 *Am. J. Comp. L.* 231 (1979), also available at <http://cisgw3.law.pace.edu/cisg/biblio/nicholas.html>.
Nicholas, *Vienna Convention*	Nicholas, B., "The Vienna Convention on the International Sales Law", 105 *L. Qu. Rev.* 201 (1989).
NJA	*Nytt juridisk Arkiv* (Swedish law reports)
NRt	*Norsk Rettstidende* (Norwegian law reports)
Nørager & Theilgaard, *Købeloven*	Nørager-Nielsen, J. and Theilgaard, S. *Købeloven med kommentarer* (2d ed. 1993).
Piltz, *Internationales Kaufrecht*	Piltz, B., *Internationales Kaufrecht* (Munich 1993).
Ramberg, *Köplagen*	Ramberg, J., *Köplagen* (Stockholm 1995).
Ramberg & Herre, *Internationella köplagen*	Ramberg, J., og Herre, J., *Internationella köplagen(CISG)* (Stockholm 2001).
Schlechtriem, *Attorneys' Fees*	Schlechtriem, P., "Attorneys' Fees as Part of Damages", *Pace International Law Review* (Forthcoming 2002).
Schlechtriem, *Borderland*	Schlechtriem, P., " The Borderland of Tort and Contract – Opening a New Frontier?", 21 *Cornell Int. L. J.* 469 (1988).
Schlechtriem, *Bundesgerichtshof*	Schlechtriem, P., "Uniform Sales Law in the Decisions of the *Bundesgerichtshof*", reproduced (in English) in <http://cisg. law.pace.edu/cisg/biblio/schlechtriem3.html>.
Schlechtriem, *Commentary*	Schlechtriem, P., *Commentary on the UN Convention on the International Sale of Goods (CISG)* (Oxford 1998).
Schlechtriem, *Experience*	Schlechtriem, P., "Uniform Sales Law – The Experience with Uniform Sales Laws in the Federal Republic of Germany", *Juridisk Tidsskrift vid Stockholms Universitet* (1992), also available at <http://cisgw3.law.pace.edu/cisg/biblio/schlech2.html>.
Schlechtriem, *Int. UN-Kaufrecht*	Schlechtriem, P., *Internationales UN-Kaufrecht* (Tübingen 1996).
Schlechtriem, *Kommentar*	Schlechtriem, P., *Kommentar zum Einheitlichen UN-Kaufrecht – CISG* (3d ed. Munich 2000).
Schlechtriem, *Seller's Obligations*	Schlechtriem, P., "The Seller's Obligations under the United Nations Convention . . .", in *International Sales* (Galston and Smit eds. New York 1984).
Schlechtriem, *Uniform Law*	Schlechtriem, P., *Uniform Sales Law* (Vienna 1986).
Schlesinger, *Formation*	Schlesinger, R., *Formation of Contracts: A Study of the Common Core of Legal Systems* (London 1968).

Schneider, *Consequential Damages*	Schneider, E., "Consequential Damages in the International Sale of Goods . . .", 16 *J. Int. Bus. L.* (1996).
Secretariat Commentary	*Secretariat Commentary* to the 1978 UNCITRAL Draft Convention, A/CONF. 97/5.
Sevón, *Obligations of Buyer*	Sevón, L., "Obligations of the Buyer under the UN Convention . . .", in *International Sale of Goods*: *Dubrovnik Lectures* (Šarčevic and Volken eds. New York 1986)., also at <http://cisgw3.law.pace.edu/cisg/biblio/sevon.html>.
Sevón, Wilhelmsson & Koskelo, *Huvudpunkter*	Sevón, L., Wilhelmsson, T., and Koskelo, P., *Huvudpunkter i Köplagen* (2d ed. Helsinki 1999).
Sono, *Commentary on LPISG*	Sono, K., *Commentary on the Convention on the Limitation Period in the International Sale of Goods, done at New York, 14 June 1974* (A/CONF.63/17) 145–173. Also at <http://cisgw3.law.pace.edu/cisg/biblio/sono1.html>.
Sono, *Limitation Convention*	Sono, K., "The Limitation Convention: The Forerunner to Establish UNCITRAL Credibility," available at <http://cisgw3.law.pace.edu/cisg/biblio/sono3.html>.
Spanogle & Winship, *International Sales Law*	Spanogle, J. and Winship, P., *International Sales Law* (St. Paul 2000).
TfR	*Tidsskrift for Rettsvitenskap* (Norwegian law journal).
Treitel, *Law of Contract*	Treitel, G., *The Law of Contracts* (11th ed., London 2003).
Treitel, *Remedies I*	Treitel, G., "Remedies for Breach of Contract", in *International Encyclopedia of Comparative Law* Ch. 16 (Tübingen 1979).
Treitel, *Remedies II*	Treitel, G., *Remedies for Breach of Contract* (Oxford 1988).
UCC	(American) Uniform Commercial Code.
UfR	*Ugeskrift for Retsvæsen* (Danish Law Reports).
UNIDROIT Principles	UNIDROIT, *Principles of International Commercial Contracts* (Rome 1994).
UNILEX	The UNILEX Database of International Case Law and Bibliography on the United Nations Convention on Contracts for the International Sale of Goods (CISG) and the UNIDROIT Principles of International Commercial Contracts, Transnational Publishers (Irvington, New York), available on-line at <http://www.unilex.info/>.
Walt, *Specific Performance*	Walt, S., "For Specific Performance Under the United Nations Sales Convention", 26 *Texas Int. L. J.* 211 (1981).
White & Summers, *Uniform Commercial Code*	White, J. & Summers, R., *Handbook of the Law Under the Uniform Commercial Code* (5th ed. St. Paul 2000).
Winship, *Private International Law*	Winship, P., "Private International Law and the U.N.Sales Convention", 21 *Cornell Int. L. J.* 487 (1988).
Winship, *Scope*	Winship, P., "The Scope of the Vienna Convention . . .", in *International Sales* (Galston and Smit eds. New York 1984).

Witz, *Premières Applications*   Witz, C., *Les premières applications jurisprudentielles du droit uniforme de la vente internationale* (Paris 1995).

Witz, *Premier arrêt*   Witz, C., Le premier arrêt de la Cour de Cassation confronté à la Convention de Vienne, *Dalloz Sirey, JR,* 1995, 290.

Ziegel, *Canada*   Ziegel, J., "Canada and the Vienna Convention", 12 *Can.Bus. L. J.* 366 (1986 – 87).

Ziegel, *Remedial Provisions*   Ziegel, J., "The Remedial Provisions in the Vienna Sales Convention . . ." in *International Sales* (Galston & Smit eds. New York 1984).

Zweigert & Kötz, *Comparative Law*   Zweigert, K. and Kötz, H., *Introduction to Comparative Law* (3rd ed., Oxford 1998).

TABLE OF CISG PROVISIONS

Article 33:   § 4.2; § 4.3.
Article 34:   § 4.3.
Article 35(1):   § 4.4; § 7.3.
Article 35(2):   § 4.7; § 4.8; § 7.4.
Article 35(3):   § 4.7.
Article 36:   § 4.4.
Article 37:   § 6.9.
Article 38:   § 4.4; § 4.9; § 4.10; § 4.10; § 4.12.
Article 40:   § 4.9.
Article 41:   § 4.11.
Article 42:   § 4.11.
Article 43:   § 4.11.
Article 44:   § 4.9; § 4.11; § 6.15.
Article 45:   § 4.2; § 6.2; § 6.3; § 6.14; § 6.19.
Article 46:   § 4.11; § 6.2; § 6.4; § 6.5; § 6.6; § 6.7; § 6.19.
Article 47:   § 6.10.
Article 48:   § 6.8; § 6.9.
Article 49:   § 6.2; § 6.6; § 6.8; § 6.9; § 6.10.
Article 50:   § 4.9; § 6.8; § 6.13.
Article 52:   § 6.8.
Article 53:   § 4.2; § 4.12.
Article 54:   § 4.12; § 6.23.
Article 55:   § 3.3; § 4.13.
Article 57:   § 1.4; § 4.12.
Article 58:   § 4.12; § 6.23.
Article 59:   § 4.12; § 6.23.
Article 60:   § 4.14.
Article 61:   § 4.2; § 6.2; 6.20; § 6.27; § 6.28; § 6.32.
Article 62:   § 6.2; § 6.21; § 6.22.
Article 63   § 6.24.
Article 64:   § 6.2; § 6.23; § 6.24.
Article 65:   § 6.19.
Article 66:   § 5.1.
Article 67:   § 5.2; § 5.3; § 5.5; § 5.6.
Article 68:   § 2.6; § 5.1; § 5.4; § 5.5; § 5.6.
Article 69:   § 4.14; § 5.5; § 5.6.
Article 70:   § 5.6.
Article 71:   § 6.11; § 6.14; § 6.26.
Article 72:   § 6.11; § 6.26.
Article 73:   § 6.11.
Article 74:   § 4.6; § 6.14; § 6.15; § 6.16; § 6.17; § 6.18; § 6.21; § 6.29; § 6.30; § 6.31.
Article 75:   § 6.15; § 6.16; § 6.17; § 6.28; § 6.29.
Article 76:   § 6.15; § 6.16; § 6.17; § 6.28; § 6.29.

Article 77:   § 6.17; § 6.28; § 6.30.
Article 78:   § 2.11; § 6.18; § 6.31.
Article 79:   § 6.14; § 6.18; § 6.19; § 6.32.
Article 80:   § 6.19.
Article 81:   § 6.4; § 6.6; § 6.8; § 6.12; § 6.23; § 6.25.
Article 82:   § 6.6.
Article 84:   § 6.18; § 6.25.
Article 85:   § 4.14; § 5.5.
Article 86:   § 6.12.
Article 87:   § 6.12.
Article 88:   § 6.12.
Article 90:   § 8.2.
Article 92:   § 3.1; § 8.1; § 8.3; § 8.4; § 8.6.
Article 93:   § 8.3; § 8.5.
Article 94:   § 8.3; § 8.6.
Article 95:   § 2.4; § 8.3; § 8.7.
Article 96:   § 2.14; § 8.8.
Article 97(4):   § 8.4.
Article 99:   § 1.2; § 2.3; § 8.1; § 8.2.
Article 100:   § 1.1; § 1.4; § 2.7; § 8.1.
Article 101:   § 2.7.

INDEX